6½″

Each clear area gives the outline for one frame of a single-frame filmstrip made with a standard 35mm camera. The toned area surrounding the clear areas indicates the position and spacing of the two frames

4″

2¾″

9½″

5/8″

2¾″

4″

1 11/16″

PLANNING
AND
PRODUCING
AUDIOVISUAL
MATERIALS

PLANNING AND PRODUCING AUDIOVISUAL MATERIALS

THIRD EDITION

By JERROLD E. KEMP

San José State University

With the assistance of

RON CARRAHER (Art)
University of Washington

RICHARD F. SZUMSKI (Photography, Second & Third Editions)
San José State University

WILLARD R. CARD (Photography, First Edition)
Brigham Young University

Thomas Y. Crowell, New York, Established 1834

Library of Congress Cataloging in Publication Data

Kemp, Jerrold E.
    Planning and producing audiovisual materials.

    Bibliography: p.
    Includes index.
    1. Audiovisual materials. 2. Audio-visual
equipment. I. Title
LB1043.K4 1975   371.33   75-16470
ISBN 0-690-00805-8

Thomas Y. Crowell Company
666 Fifth Avenue
New York, New York 10019

Typography design by A Good Thing, Inc.

Manufactured in the United States of America

CONTENTS

Part Three
FUNDAMENTAL SKILLS

Part Four
PRODUCING YOUR AUDIOVISUAL
MATERIALS

PREFACE

Because the reader often skips the preface to a book, this one is purposely printed in large type in the hope that it will catch your attention. I would like you to read it before you turn to any particular section of the book. There are things about the content, its organization, and correlated materials you should know.

This book is designed to provide information and experiences that will enable the reader to gain competencies relative to:

☐ Recognizing changing and broadening roles of audiovisual materials in instructional programs.

☐ Recognizing contributions of locally produced materials in systematically planned programs.

☐ Using information about perception, communications, and learning theory when planning audiovisual materials.

☐ Using evidence from media research when designing and preparing audio-visual materials.

☐ Selecting the most appropriate medium to serve instructional needs for group teaching or individualized learning.

☐ Applying necessary planning steps prior to production.

☐ Using fundamental skills in photography, graphics, and sound recording for preparing materials.

☐ Applying techniques for producing photographic print series, slide series, filmstrips, overhead transparencies, tape recordings, motion pictures, visual materials for television, and multi-image/multimedia materials.

While your initial interest in using this book may be solely with those sections devoted to techniques of photography or graphic skills like picture mounting, bulletin-board lettering, and transparency preparation, it is hoped you will also explore the information in the chapters relating to the more advanced objectives. Cross references throughout the book will help you to make use of the fundamental skills in your specific area of interest.

In addition to the descriptive and explanatory material comprising the words and pictures of the 25 chapters in this book, other features which are designed to make your learning effective include:

☐ Availability of *Still/Motion Super 8-mm films* correlated with specific topics to provide further visualizations and demonstrations of concepts and techniques. You will find reference to particular Still/Motion films at appropriate places in the text. Further explanation, a list of films available, and their sources are included in Appendix A.

☐ Review questions and suggested activities. These are designed not only for you to test your recall of information, but also for you to apply concepts and principles as you study them. These self-check exercises are found at the ends of chapters and of many sections within the longer chapters. Check your answers at the end of each chapter.

Make use of all the instructional elements described here. Each one extends and reinforces the others, and thus will help you to become more knowledgeable and proficient in the competencies that can be derived from using this book.

Now read on . . .

ACKNOWLEDGMENTS

In preparing this third edition, I again express my sincere thanks to colleagues for their suggestions and direct efforts. In particular, to David Curl, Western Michigan University, and Malcolm Fleming, Indiana University, who both reviewed and commented on the revised manuscript.

The actual preparation of a book like this requires the ideas and cooperative work of a capable production team. I am fortunate in having available the creative, artistic talents of Ron Carraher, the broad photographic experience and practical approach to communication of Dick Szumski, and the patience and skills of Lydia Lopez, who assisted with the lay-out and page paste-up. To each my appreciation. Also, special thanks to Daryle Webb, a graphic artist par excellence, for solving some of the last-minute problems.

I thank my wife, Dorothy, for her continuing understanding and patience during the many hours of planning, writing, visualizing, and organizing the topics and content of this book.

PLANNING
AND
PRODUCING
AUDIOVISUAL
MATERIALS

PART 1

BACKGROUND IN AUDIOVISUAL COMMUNICATIONS

1

AUDIOVISUAL MATERIALS IN INSTRUCTION

The purpose of this opening chapter is to place audiovisual materials in perspective with regard to changes and new developments in education. Attention will be given to seven topics:

1. Factors facilitating learning
2. Patterns for teaching and learning
3. Contributions of audiovisual materials to improvement in learning
4. Procedures for designing instruction
5. Audiovisual materials within the instructional design plan
6. Levels of audiovisual production
7. Student activity in audiovisual production

Although you may be using this book principally as a reference for one or more production techniques, the information in this chapter provides a background and awareness so that your selecting and designing of materials will better serve your purposes.

Factors Facilitating Learning

In conventional educational programs, audiovisual materials are typically used as supplements to instruction or for enrichment purposes. As such, they make only limited contributions to improvement in learning. Under these traditional conditions, audiovisual materials are costly additions to the usual instructional materials the teacher may select for use.

The customary teacher-centered methods of instruction have been questioned on the bases of uniformity of quality and efficiency of learning. Furthermore, the schools are expected to respond creatively to the fundamental transformations that are taking place in our society during this last quarter of the Twentieth Century. Educational programs on all levels must meet a broader range of objectives than formerly, and must do this effectively with diverse student groups.

The implications of these concerns and the attempts to find solutions require new ways of approaching and organizing for learning. Among the new procedures receiving attention are the following:

1. *A shift from teaching by the teacher to learning by the student as the key outcome of instruction.* Until the early 1960s, good teaching was considered the key to good learning. It is more clearly recognized now that learning is the goal of education, and learning is an activity that must be performed *by the student*, not something the teacher can do *for* or *to* the student. The teacher's job is to structure experiences so that learning can take place most conveniently and be successful for the student.

2. *A shift from a static to a dynamic structure in instructional programs.* It is necessary to provide alternatives to the lockstep methods of conventional instruction. Adaptations can be made through the application of such techniques as nongraded groupings, peer teaching, **3**

involving students in determining what they will study, providing alternatives to the conventional school program, and using the community, with its physical environments and resources, as the center for much learning activity.

3. *A shift from seeing the student as a part of a group to recognizing him as an individual by providing alternatives for an individualized approach to learning.* Most learning experiences prior to 1960 were group based—under direct control of the teacher. But with the introduction of programmed instruction and better identification of how people learn, attention has become more focused on the student as an individual, recognizing his capabilities, needs, and interests. Essentially the emphasis is on *what the learner does,* rather than on *what is done to the learner.* The student is able to select his own method of learning; to work at his own pace, engaging in preferred activities with appropriate resources; and most often having successful learning results.

4. *A shift from the use of audiovisual materials primarily for group instruction to expanded uses in new formats for individualized learning.* What students *do* determines what they learn, and they learn by working with ideas and with resources of many kinds. The need for a variety of instructional materials is supported by two contentions. First, because there are different modes of learning and some students find certain methods and materials more appealing or more effective than others, alternative resources are necessary. Second, certain types of audiovisual and other resources may be more appropriate than others in support of a given topic. The materials suitable for student use in new-type programs may differ markedly from traditional materials controlled by, or used by, the teacher. Now such factors as *specificity* in serving objectives, *adaptability* for certain individuals or groups, *flexibility* in method of use, and *integration* with other experiences become of major importance.

5. *A more probable guarantee of success in learning when instructional planning follows a systematic procedure.* In the changing framework of education, traditional curriculum and casual lesson planning methods are limited in their effectiveness. A new total-program-planning structure in which a number of interrelated components are all considered is being recognized as essential to facilitate learning. The process of learning now is carried out and evaluated in terms of specific objectives to be accomplished by the student.

Patterns for Teaching and Learning

There are three broad methods within which most learning takes place: (1) presentation of information to groups of students, (2) independent study, or individualized learning, with each student working on his own, and (3) small-group interaction between teacher and students or among students. When changes take place within instructional programs as indicated above, students spend much more time studying independently than they do attending classroom presentations.

In terms of their contributions to learning, audiovisual and other resources provide many necessary learning experiences within each of these patterns. By recognizing the features of these three methods, you should be better able to decide on appropriate audiovisual materials for use in any of them, and then to design the materials to fit the requirements of the pattern.

INSTRUCTOR PRESENTATION

This method is typified by one-way communications from teacher to students, as in a lecture.

Information is presented at the instructor's rate of delivery. Students are physically passive, although listening, taking notes, or completing related worksheets. In this pattern, the flexibility of individual pacing and choice of study methods and materials by students is lacking. With the current trend to reduce the amount of time spent in the conventional presentation of subject content by the teacher in preference for independent study of content by students, the purposes served by this pattern are changing. Often, for efficiency, essential information may be transmitted to numbers of students, in regular classes or in large groups, to serve these needs:

☐ Introduce new topics and provide orientation to activities in a unit of study.
☐ Provide motivation for studying a subject or topic, possibly through a motion picture, a

television program, or a multi-image presentation.

☐ Illustrate relations or integration of one topic with another.
☐ Point out special applications or new developments in a topic that may be too recent for inclusion in the independent study materials.
☐ Provide special enrichment materials and experiences, like a film, or a guest speaker who cannot be available to small groups or individual students.

To complement or even replace an instructor's usual verbal presentation, audiovisual materials, such as overhead transparencies, slides, motion pictures, television, or multi-image presentations, may be selected to serve one or more of these instructional needs relative to a topic. The usual film or other media formats, consisting of 10–30 minute presentations, can be modified to more succinct structures in terms of specific objectives to be treated. Also, the value of learner participation during a presentation can be increased by providing activities for students, like responding periodically to questions on an exercise sheet or selecting items for follow-up work.

INDIVIDUALIZED LEARNING

The individualization of learning may take many forms and is given numerous labels. See the references on page 291. Its main attributes include the student's assuming responsibility for his own learning, proceeding with activities and materials at his own level, and studying at his own pace. In a basic program all students may follow the same track, using the same materials, with only their individualized pace of study being different. In more advanced programs, alternative methods for accomplishing the objectives are provided along with a correlated variety of materials. Choice of learning experiences is made by the student.

The principles derived from the programmed

instruction concept contribute to many individualized learning approaches. These elements are often included:

☐ Learning objectives and required levels of student knowledge or performance are clearly stated.
☐ Pretesting permits the student to skip study of one or more objectives if competency is demonstrated.
☐ Alternative procedures for accomplishing the objectives are specified.
☐ Participation activities and required responses for the learner are included.
☐ Confirmation or correction of performance or response is immediately available to the learner.
☐ Opportunities are provided for the learner to self-check his understanding, progress, and performance against the objectives.
☐ The learner decides when he is ready to have his knowledge or performance evaluated by the teacher.

The treatment of topics in minicourses, study modules, or other self-learning packages is on specific *concept* levels rather than as broad, general subjects are handled in conventional courses, units, or textbook chapters. The supporting resources, such as photographs, slides, filmstrips, cassette recordings, or 8-mm motion pictures, are developed on the concept level also. This means that media selected must be in a form suitable for independent study, should be brief in serving one or a few objectives, and should be carefully integrated with other activities.

TEACHER-STUDENT INTERACTION

The third pattern for teaching and learning provides opportunities for teachers and students to work together in small groups to discuss, to question, to report, to be evaluated, or to engage in other forms of personalized interchange. In light of the shift toward individualized learning, with the student spending more time working on his own, it is necessary to provide opportunities for direct contact with instructors and with other students. This pattern provides such experiences.

Some of the same resources used in presentations and for individualized learning may be available for reference during small-group discussion. Also, special materials can be prepared for the purposes of motivating discussion, illustrating concepts, presenting problem situations for group consideration, and evaluating learning. A real need exists for imaginatively designed media materials for use in group activities.

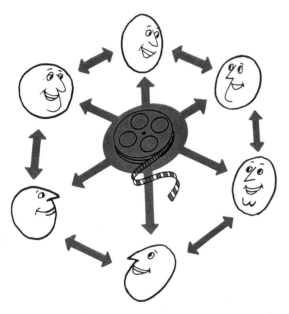

A prime advantage of small-group interaction is the encouragement of student participation for socialization, leadership development, and peer recognition purposes. One of the best methods of providing experiences that lead to accomplishing one or more of these important purposes is to encourage and assist students to plan and produce their own audiovisual materials, then present the results to their group. The last section of this chapter gives further attention to student activities with audiovisual materials.

Contributions of Audiovisual Materials to Learning

There are recognized contributions that audiovisual materials can make as they are moved from a peripheral to an integral element within the newer formats of the instructional process. Anyone engaging in the planning, production, and use of audiovisual materials should not only recognize the following broad contributions to learning, but actively employ them for the benefits they can offer in his program:[1]

☐ *Make education more productive* through increasing the rate of learning by providing worthwhile experiences for learners that teachers need not, or cannot, furnish. By providing materials for student use, a teacher can often make better use of his instructional time in other activities with students.

---

1. Adapted from *To Improve Learning, A Report to the President and the Congress of the United States by the Commission on Instructional Technology* (New York: R. R. Bowker, 1970).

☐ *Make education more individual* through providing many alternative paths with a variety of resources so that learning can take place according to the learner's study preference, at his own pace, and convenience.

☐ *Make learning more immediate* through bridging the gap between the worlds inside and outside the classroom by means of the experiences these resources can provide.

☐ *Make access to education more equal for learners* wherever they are, through the portability of various materials (audio and video cassettes, filmstrips, films, self-study packages) and through the use of effective delivery systems (air transmission, cables, satellites) for transmitting information.

☐ *Give instruction a more scientific base* through providing a framework for systematic instructional planning. While audiovisual materials can be more broadly referred to as *educational media,* they are only one component in the field of *instructional technology.* Another aspect of technology is its *process function,* which is related to the planning, design, implementation, and evaluation of instructional programs, and within which the necessary equipment and media are selected for use. Based on learning theory and communications research, the technology of instruction provides the means whereby learning can be effective and efficient.

Designing for Instruction

In conventional curriculum planning, decisions are most often made in intuitive fashion and may be based on ambiguous purposes. Subject content is the basis for planning, and only casual attention is given to other details. It is now recognized that the instructional process is complex and that attention must be given to many factors if outcomes are to be successful.

The term *instructional development* applies to the broad process of designing an instructional program—whether a single module, a complete unit, or a total course—using an objective, systematic procedure. This method starts with answers to three questions:

1. What must students learn? (the objectives)
2. What procedures and resources are required to accomplish the learning? (the teaching and learning strategies)
3. How will you know when the required learning has taken place? (the evaluation)

These three elements—objectives, strategies,

and evaluation—form the framework of instructional development procedures. In addition, there are other factors that either support or relate to these three elements. Taking all these pieces together, we can develop an *instructional-design plan,* which consists of these interrelated components:[2]

☐ Choose *topics* to be treated.
☐ State *general purposes* to be served by the topic.
☐ Enumerate the important characteristics of the *student group* for which the instruction will be designed.
☐ Indicate the *subject content* that will lead to the objectives.
☐ Specify the *learning objectives* to be achieved as related to the content and purposes.
☐ Develop *pretests* to determine each student's background and present level of competence with the topic.
☐ Select *teaching/learning activities* and *instructional resources* that will treat the subject content to accomplish the objectives.
☐ Coordinate necessary *support services,* such as budget, personnel, facilities, equipment, and schedules to carry out the instructional plan.
☐ *Evaluate student learning* in terms of the accomplishment of objectives, with a view to revising and reevaluating any phases of the plan that need improvement.

This is an example of one systematic approach to instructional planning. There are others, but they all include essentially the same items. More extensive plans may be termed *instructional systems,* although the sequence presented here comprises a reasonable and practical method for developing a new instructional program. For anyone interested in the production of audiovisual materials, whether for group-based or individualized learning programs, an examination of systematic planning procedures provides a framework within which the selection of your materials should take place. Also, you will discover in Part 2 of this book that a development procedure similar to that listed above is applied when planning takes place for the production of the audiovisual material itself.

Professional film production, instructional television, and programmed instruction have all contributed to the instructional-design approach. Film production, when properly carried out, is a

systematic way to plan, to involve personnel, to consider content, and to select visual experiences that will serve a particular objective. Television includes all that film production does and in addition considers the interrelationships of all media and how they can best be brought together to serve a specific purpose. This purposeful combination is a key attribute of the instructional-design approach.

Media personnel and others filling the role of instructional designers can assist teachers or teaching teams to develop effective instructional-design plans. Success with an instructional design demands careful planning and a realistic approach to the numerous problems that must be solved. This is not a casual activity. It is a rigorous method in which the designer and instructors must face up to decisions and then take action. This process requires a high degree of creative intellectual activity, but the results can be mentally satisfying to those who participate and materially successful to those who learn from the product.

Media in the Instructional-Design Plan

Audiovisual materials of any type can be planned and produced, whether they will be part of an application of an instructional-design plan or individual entities of their own. The techniques described in subsequent chapters apply to materials being prepared for any purpose.

Media to be used within the instructional design are determined by the requirements of objectives, content, and instructional methods. Media are *not* supplementary to, or in support of, instruction, but *are* the instructional input itself. In this light, the old concept of audiovisual *aids* as supplements to teaching can no longer be accepted. Determination must be made of which media, in what form, and at what time, will most effectively and efficiently provide the most relevant experiences for learners.

Just as various instructional objectives require different kinds of learning, appropriate instructional resources require matching to required tasks. Each separate concept to be taught should require a separate consideration of resources. Certain media can best serve certain purposes (sound or print, motion or still pictures). In other cases, available equipment, convenience, costs, and such factors may be the determiners of choice. See page 47 for further discussion of media-selection methods.

This approach to teaching and learning is developed around specificity—specificity in terms of behavior objectives to serve the needs of par-

2. Jerrold E. Kemp, *Instructional Design: A Plan for Unit and Course Development* (Belmont, Calif.: Fearon Publishers, 1971), pp. 6–10.

ticular students. Commercial materials will usually not be suitable, since in the main they are too generalized and too broad in treatment of subjects. On the other hand, dependence on local production for all necessary materials is unduly costly in time and money. Perhaps forward-looking producers will treat the most commonly taught subject topics and concepts by providing carefully designed and interrelated materials that may be of use in a variety of locally developed instructional systems. But openings will remain for the addition of materials having local applications or particular local emphases. For example, a unit on community health includes the

An Example of Elements within an Instructional Design

```
Subject:
     Community health
Topics:
     Water pollution and purification
     Sewage treatment
     Air pollution
     Food processing and preservation
     [Other pertinent topics]
General Purposes:
     1. To understand the causes and effects of water pollution
     2. To learn about methods of water purification
        [Other pertinent purposes]
[The following treats only the topic "Water pollution and
purification."]
Objectives:
     1. To identify the major causes of water pollution
     2. To describe the effects that water pollution can have
        on a community
     3. To list the steps in general water treatment
     4. To examine local methods of water treatment
        [Other pertinent objectives]
Teaching/Learning Activities:              Media Resources:
A. Presentation: Teacher to Student
   group
     1. General sources of water supply   Overhead transparencies
     2. Causes of water pollution         16-mm commercial film
                                          clips
     3. General methods of water          Printed sheets
        treatment
   [Other pertinent presentations]
B. Independent study:
     1. Local method of treating water    Slides—tape recording;
                                          worksheet review;
                                          laboratory exercises
     2. New, emerging methods of water    Library research
        purification (desalting, for
        example)
   [Other pertinent independent study]
C. Discussion group: Teacher with
   students
     1. Review of independent-study
        activities
     2. Student reports on emerging       Overhead transparencies;
        methods                           slides; chalkboard
     3. Discussion of anticipated prob-   Tape recording of
        lems in water shortage, overuse, comments by water
        and so forth                      conservationist
   [Other pertinent discussion
    activities]
   (Note: The slides and tape recording for B-1 above are
planned in detail in the chapters of Part 2.)
```

the study of water-purification methods. Commercial materials may describe the principles of water treatment with examples taken from various general processes, but the particular method of local water treatment will need to be learned with locally prepared materials.

Levels of Audiovisual Production

Audiovisual materials can be obtained from commercial sources or produced locally. It may be expedient to use commercial products if they fit the needs of your objectives, are suitable for the individuals or student group, are of acceptable technical quality, and are of reasonable cost. But if commercial materials are unavailable, too costly, or unsuitable for the needs of your students, local production may be the answer. On the other hand, you may wish to plan and produce materials of your own with no regard to commercial forms.

The local production of audiovisual materials can take place on any of three levels.

MECHANICAL LEVEL: PREPARATION

First, there is the *mechanical* level; here the concern is solely with the techniques of preparation. Mounting pictures on cardboard or cloth, copying pictures on film for slides, and running a printed page or clipping through a copy machine to make a transparency are examples of the mechanical preparation of materials. Even though the individual has a purposeful use in mind, little planning is required and the actual preparation follows a routine procedure. Many persons start at this level in audiovisual production and go on to other levels of activity.

CREATIVE LEVEL: PRODUCTION

A step above the mechanical level is the *creative* level. Here, materials being considered for production require decisions; planning accordingly becomes an important forerunner of production. *Production* implies an order of activity beyond *preparation,* with its more routine connotations. The design and production of an instructional bulletin board, of a slide series with a recording, of a filmstrip for self-instruction, of a set of thoughtfully designed transparencies to teach a concept, or of an 8-mm film that illustrates a process—all are examples of materials produced on the creative level. The skills developed on the mechanical level become tools for use on this level.

DESIGN LEVEL: CONCEPTION

As previously explained, the production of audiovisual materials that can be carefully integrated into learning activities to serve specific instructional objectives and to meet the needs of individuals or a specific group of students, may be part of a *design for instruction.* This is a third level to be served by locally planned and produced materials. Now audiovisual materials are conceived within a carefully designed instructional framework for group or individual uses. The skills developed on both the mechanical and creative levels serve important functions here.

While your interest in using this book may start with the mechanical level, it is hoped that you will find potentials for developing materials on either the creative or design levels.

On each level of audiovisual production you can prepare appropriate materials to serve personal or instructional purposes of your own. Or, you might be developing materials for other persons to use in satisfying their training, instructional, or informational communication needs.

But another group is showing increasing interest in activities involving audiovisual materials. They are *students* on all levels of education —preschool to graduate school. Many teachers plan specific activities that will involve students in the preparation of photographs, slides, motion pictures, or television programs. Others find that students, on their own, are ready to engage in such enterprises. Whatever the base, this increasing interest and enthusiasm on the part of students for planning and producing audiovisual materials should be recognized and encouraged. There are definite educational benefits for students who engage in media activities. Most of the techniques described in this book are suitable for study and application by mature students on many levels.

Students and Audiovisual Production

The recognition of the need to involve students with audiovisual materials in an active and productive way is a recent thrust in education. Its purpose is to make students more visually literate. Developing the skills to understand and use visual communication techniques is especially important in our society since so much information is transmitted in nonverbal modes—graphic design, still photography, motion pictures, and television. Learners need opportunities to become perceptive and analytical of the visual world in which they live so as to make their own judgments and choices of what may be appropriate and aesthetically pleasing in a situation. To do this, students must develop the skills needed for interpreting the messages they receive in visual form and must also become fluent in expressing their own ideas visually.

This visual awareness, comprehension, and expression can be obtained first by developing an intimate familiarity with design principles and visual tools (page 113) and elements of composition (page 97), and then by manipulating these items through involvement with a variety of graphic, pictorial, and other nonverbal communications media.

The skills an individual develops in interpreting, judging, responding to, and using visual representations of reality (i.e., his visual intelligence) are known as *visual literacy*. For students on all levels, the process of becoming visually literate requires experiences which allow them to:

☐ Recognize and "read" graphic and photographic illustrations that represent objects, events, places, and people
☐ Sort and organize such visual representations into patterns and relationships that apply a *vocabulary* of nonverbal visual expression
☐ Produce their own visual materials as interpretations of actual objects, events, places, and people

Visual literacy can be developed in many ways. See the references on page 292, including the variety of materials available from the Association for Educational Communications and Technology (AECT) to provide experiences for students in one or more of the aspects of visual expression listed above.

One of the best ways for students to become literate in this visual sense is by actively selecting an idea, developing it by planning as described in Part 2 of this book, and then translating the written words and sketches into an audiovisual form. This can be done by students individually or in groups.

When students work together to successfully plan and produce a photographic picture display, a slide series, a motion picture, or a videotape recording of a school or community activity, they take part in a mentally vigorous process. The planning phase includes the assumption of responsibilities by individuals in the group, doing research work, expressing and organizing ideas, and structuring the visual presentation to communicate the intended ideas. Then follows the hard work and excitement of production, which brings the verbal thoughts to visual life in a logical sequence.

For students of any age, such an activity can be a stimulus to growth and toward visual intelligence, which means toward better interpretation and understanding of meanings and expressions that take visual forms and require visual decisions in their lives.

Now, Review What You Have Read About the Place of Audiovisual Materials with Regard to Changes and New Developments in Education.

1. What four newer procedures are influencing shifts in instructional programs?
2. What three patterns for teaching and learning are emerging in educational programs?
3. What are three major attributes of individualized learning?
4. What are five recognized contributions of audiovisual media to learning?
5. What three elements form the basis of instructional development?
6. What is meant by the expression *instructional design*? What are its sequential steps?
7. What are the particular contributions of film production and television to the concept of instructional design?
8. Differentiate between the concept of audiovisual "aids" and audiovisual "media" within an instructional design plan.
9. By example, differentiate among the three levels of audiovisual production activity.
10. What are some of the benefits to students who engage in audiovisual production activities?
11. Define visual literacy.

Answers to Review Questions

1. Shift from teaching to student learning.
   Shift from static to dynamic structure in instruction.
   Shift from group to individualized approach in learning.
   Shift from audiovisual materials for group use only to expanded uses in new formats.
   Shift from traditional curriculum planning to systematic instructional planning.
2. Presentation to groups, independent or individualized study, teacher-student and small-group interaction.
3. Student assumes responsibilities for own learning, has access to materials on own level, studies at own pace and convenience.
4. Make education: more productive, more individual, more immediate, more accessible, more equal, more scientifically based.
5. Objectives of instruction; teaching/learning strategies; evaluation of learning.
6. A systematic procedure for planning instruction that includes nine essential elements (page 7).
7. Systematic planning, selection of visuals to serve specific objectives, interrelationships of media, involving a number of people in planning and production.
8. Audiovisual aids are supplements or enrichments to regular instruction; in an instructional design plan they are direct instruc-

tional inputs and essential to the teaching/learning process.
9. Mechanical—creative—design (add your own examples).
10. Take responsibility, share within a group, become perceptive and analytical of visual world, become fluent in expressing ideas verbally and visually.
11. Skills in interpreting, judging, responding to, and using visual representations of reality.

2

PERCEPTION, COMMUNICATION, AND LEARNING THEORY

Slides, filmstrips, motion pictures, and other audiovisual materials have been produced for many years. Some of these materials do excellent jobs of imparting knowledge, of teaching skills, of motivating, or of influencing attitudes. Other materials are less effective, and some are of poor quality or may even be detrimental to accomplishing the purposes for which they were made to serve.

Too often the production of a film or the planning for multimedia instruction is based on intuition, subjective judgment, personal preferences for one's own way of doing things, or even on a committee decision. These, unfortunately, are relatively ineffective ways for insuring satisfactory results.

How can you be somewhat more sure that the materials you plan and produce will be effective for the purposes you intend? Is there evidence from research and some general principles to guide you?

Three areas should be of particular concern. One is the logical steps of developing objectives, of planning, and of getting ready to take or draw pictures and to make recordings. These procedures will insure some degree of success for your audiovisual materials. Part 2 of this book presents the planning steps you should consider using.

The second area from which you can obtain help in designing effective audiovisual materials includes reports on experimental studies measuring the effectiveness of such materials. In such studies specific elements that affect production have been controlled, thus providing evidence for handling such elements in audiovisual productions. Summaries of these research findings are reported in the next chapter.

Third, and fundamental to both audiovisual research and careful planning for media production, is the need to know how people perceive things around them, how people communicate with each other, and how people learn. Therefore, our immediate concern is to examine evidence from the fields of psychology and communication.

The discussions that follow have one purpose —to make the reader aware of (or to review for him) some generalizations from the areas of perception, communication, and learning theory. Admittedly the treatment of each topic is greatly simplified, and only the minimum essentials are presented. But even these can be useful to you as you plan your materials and consider the place of your materials in an instructional sequence.

Perception

Perception is the process whereby an individual becomes aware of the world around him. In perception we use our senses to apprehend objects and events. The eyes, ears, and nerve endings in the skin are primary means through which we maintain contact with our environment. These, and other senses, are the tools of perception; they **13** collect data for the nervous system. Within the nervous system the impressions so received are changed into electrical impulses, which then trigger a chain of further electrical and chemical events in the brain. The result is an internal awareness of the object or event. Thus, perception precedes communication. Communication, hopefully, leads to learning.

Two things are of major importance about perception. First, any perceptual event consists of many sensory messages that do not occur in isolation, but are related and combined into complex patterns. These become the basis of a person's knowledge of the world around him. Second, an individual reacts to only a small part of all that is taking place around him at any one instance. He "selects" the part of an event he wants to experience, or that attracts his attention, at any one time. Hence, one needs first to design materials that will attract the attention and hold the interest of the learner; and then to make certain that in this sampling procedure he gets the "right" sample, relevant to the learning task. The experience of perception is individual and unique. It is not exactly alike for any two people. A person perceives an event in terms of his past experiences, present motivation, and present circumstances.

The most pertinent review of the research literature on perception was done by Fleming.[1] As a result of this detailed study he translated the findings and generalizations into a number of "perceptual principles for the design of instructional materials." A total of 61 principles were stated, many with corollaries. They are grouped under these categories:

1. Attention and preattention
2. Perceptual elements and processing
3. Perception of objects, pictures, words
4. Perceptual capacity
5. Perceptual distinguishing, grouping, organizing
6. Perception of size, depth, space, time, motion
7. Perception and cognition

Space does not permit an enumeration of the principles derived by Fleming under each heading. The serious designer of audiovisual materials is referred to the publication for detailed study. It includes not only statements of the 61 principles, but explanations, examples, and some illustrations.

In another summary of research on perception, Toch and McLean concluded the following:[2]

☐ There is no purposive behavior without perception.
☐ Behavior is an outcome of past perceptions and a starting point for future perceptions.
☐ The perceiver and his world do not exist independently.
☐ Meanings are given to things by the perceiver in terms of all the prior experiences he has accumulated.
☐ Perceptual experiences are personal and individual.
☐ A percept is a link between the past, which gives it its meaning, and the future, which it helps to interpret.
☐ Those things that have been tied in most closely and most often with past personal experiences predominate perceptually over the unusual or the unfamiliar.
☐ Since two persons cannot be in the same place at the same time, they must see at least slightly different environments.
☐ Though no two persons can have exactly the same meanings for things observed, common experiences tend to produce shared meanings which make communication possible.

From these statements we can conclude that while any one perceptual experience is uniquely individual, a series of perceptions by different persons can be related to become nearly identical. If you walk around a statue, its shape will constantly change as you change the angles at which you look at it. If someone else then walks around the same statue and looks at it from the same angles, he will have different individual experiences, but the series for him will be much the same as it was for you. Thus a succession of individual experiences enables us to agree upon what we have experienced, even though the individual experiences are somewhat different.

The audiovisual field rests on the assumptions that people learn primarily from what they perceive and that carefully designed visual experiences can be common experiences and thus influence behavior in a positive way.

Therefore, as you design audiovisual materials, keep in mind the importance of providing carefully for desirable perceptual experiences in terms of the learner's experience background and of the present situation. Such production ele-

1. Malcolm L. Fleming, "Perceptual Principles for the Design of Instructional Materials," *Viewpoints* 46, no. 4 (July 1970): 69–200.

2. Selected from Hans Toch and Malcolm S. MacLean, Jr., "Perception, Communication and Educational Research: A Transactional View," *AV Communication Review* 10, no. 5 (September–October, 1962): 66–68.

ments as methods of treating the topic (expository, dramatic, inquiry, or other), vocabulary level, kinds and number of examples, pacing of narration and visuals, and graphic techniques can each contribute to successful perception. In this way communication will be more effective and learning should be positive.

Communication

Perception leads to communication. In all communication, however simple or complex, a sequence similar to this occurs:

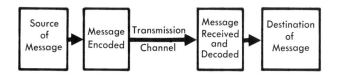

This model illustrates that a *message* (at the mental level), generally in the form of information, originated by a *source* or *sender* (the brain of an individual), is *encoded*—converted into transmittable form (a thought verbalized by being turned into sound waves, words of script). The message then passes through a *transmitter* (print, film, television) via a suitable *channel* (air, wire, paper, light) to the *receiver* (a person's senses—eyes, ears, nerve endings), where the message is *decoded* (within the nervous system, conversion into mental symbols) at the *destination* (brain of the receiver).

Effective communication depends upon the receiver being active. He reacts by answering, questioning, or performing, mentally or physically. There is then a return, or response, loop of this cycle, from receiver to sender. It is termed *feedback*. Feedback enables the originator to correct omissions and errors in the transmitted message, or to improve the encoding and transmission process, or even to assist the recipient in decoding the message.

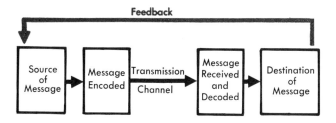

One additional element must be added to this communication model:

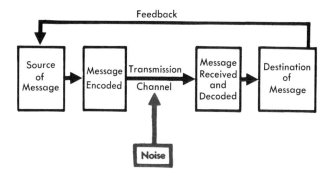

Noise is *any* disturbance that interferes with or distorts transmission of the message. The factor of *noise* can have serious impact on the success or failure of communication. Static on a radio broadcast is a simple example of noise. A flashing light can be a distracting "noise" when a person is reading a book. Ambiguous or misleading material in a film can be deemed noise. Noise can be created internally, within the receiver, to upset satisfactory communication—for example, a lack of attention. Even conflicting past experience can be an inhibiting noise source. Recall the importance of an individual's background experience in affecting perception. Noise clouds and masks information transmission to varying degrees and must be recognized as an obstacle to be overcome.

At times noise cannot be avoided, and in planning materials the factor of *redundancy* is often used to overcome the effect of evident or anticipated noise. Redundancy refers to the repeated transmission of a message, possibly in different channels, to overcome or bypass distracting noise. Some examples of redundancy are: showing and also explaining an activity, projecting a visual and distributing paper copies of the same material for study, and providing multiple applications of a principle in different contexts.

In working with audiovisual materials you should understand where the materials, as channels of communication, fit within the framework and process of message movement between senders and receivers, and how the various elements, along with factors of noise and redundancy, function to affect the success of your efforts to communicate effectively.

Learning Theory

The process of learning is an individual experience for each person. Learning takes place whenever an individual's behavior is modified—when he thinks or acts differently, when he has acquired new knowledge or a new skill, and so forth.

Since a major purpose for preparing audiovisual materials is to effect behaviors that serve objectives, it is appropriate to turn to the psychology of learning for some help in locating principles that would guide the planning of effective audiovisual materials. Unfortunately, learning theory, as a body of knowledge, as yet has contributed little directly to the design of such materials. All we can do is offer some interpretations of generalizations.

Learning theories fall into two major families. One is the so-called *behaviorist*, or *connectionist*, group, which interprets man's behavior as connections between stimuli and responses. This is the *stimulus-response (S-R)* pattern of learning. Each specific reaction is an exact *response* to a specific sensation, or *stimulus*. Spoken and written words, simple pictures, and all audiovisual materials are examples of stimuli. Some stimuli are more effective than others for certain purposes.

Much instruction is of this stimulus-response type. This concept is implicit in the "programmed-instruction" approach introduced by B. F. Skinner. The emphasis here, as in most newer approaches to instruction, is on the learner and his response. In programmed instruction, each sequence of learning is broken into small steps, requiring an appropriate response to each item followed by immediate knowledge of results. If the response is correct, the knowledge is a *reinforcement*, a rewarding recognition of each correct response. Much of the attention being given to individualized learning follows this pattern.

The second group of theories is referred to variously as the *organismic, gestalt, field*, or *cognitive* theories. The common feature of these theories is that they assume that cognitive processes—insight, intelligence, and organizational abilities—are the fundamental characteristics of human behavior. Concern is more for the *how* of learning rather than for the *what*. Human action is seen as marked by a quality of intelligence and the ability to create relationships.

Various psychologists have pointed out areas of emphasis and agreement among all learning theories. Two writers in the media field have offered practical interpretations of selected psychological concepts. C. R. Carpenter, a psychologist, and Edgar Dale, an educator, focus on audiovisual materials in terms of learning. Ten of their principles follow, the first seven from Carpenter[3] and the other three from Dale[4]:

3. C. R. Carpenter, "Psychological Concepts and Audio-Visual Instruction," *AV Communication Review* 5, no. 1 (Winter, 1957), 361–369.

4. Edgar Dale, "Principles of Learning," *The News Letter* 29, no. 4 (January, 1964), Bureau of Educational Research and Service, Ohio State University, Columbus.

1. *Importance of motivation to the learner.* The most important and persistently basic tasks of teaching are to release, instigate, and increase such motivational processes and forces as interest and the need, desire, and wish to learn.

2. *The personal relevance concept.* Teaching materials are effective in an ordered manner depending on the degree of their *personal relevance* (meaningfulness) to individual students. The production and use of teaching materials require judgments of their relevance to the individuals to be taught—abilities, levels of achievement, activated and latent interests, and accepted objectives of academic achievement.

3. *Selected processes and audiovisual instruction.* What is presented to students and what is accepted and learned by them are very different. Chains of communication, which include teaching, can be conceived as a sequence of events with selective filters operating between each major contiguous link in the chain. The "output" or response can be expected to differ greatly from the "input" or stimulus. The individual interposes his entire *relevant* life history between the stimulus material and his own response.

4. *The need for organization.* More information can be learned more enduringly when materials are meaningfully and systematically organized than when they are unorganized or poorly organized.

5. *The need for participation and practice.* Learning is activity. A widespread criticism of audiovisual materials and methods is the lack of participation and overt practice. Seeing and hearing are activities. Perception is an activity. Thinking is action. Using symbols, abstracting, deducing, generalizing, inferring, and concluding are all activities intimately involved in learning.

6. *Repetition and variation of stimuli.* Generally it can be said that nothing absolutely new is ever learned effectively with one exposure. Repetition functions to reinforce and extend learning and to make the learned information more enduring. Variations operate to sustain attention, to instigate interest, and to broaden the pattern of learning. Variations of stimuli in all probability aid students to generalize and apply more widely and surely what they have learned. Repetition with variation provides *time* for learning and time for learning is absolutely essential.

7. *The rate of presentation of material to be learned.* The rate of presentation of information in relation to the comprehension rates of

students is a fundamental consideration in learning. Rate is determined in part by the number, complexity, and subjective difficulty of the materials to be learned.

8. *Clarity, relevance, and effectiveness.* The clearer, the nearer, the more realistic and relevant the statement of desired outcomes, the more effective the learning. If a learner can't see the target clearly, the chances of his hitting it are not good. Be sure he knows from the first what is expected of him.

9. *Teaching for transfer.* Old learning doesn't automatically transfer to new learning. You must teach for transfer. Students need guided practice in learning to transform or reconstruct habitual ways of doing things. Teachers and planners can increase transfer by providing for new learning in varied contexts, by generalizing experiences, and by building attitudes favorable to learning.

10. *Reporting results promptly.* Learning is increased by knowledge of results. Information about the nature of a good performance, knowledge of mistakes, and knowledge of successful results aid learning.

KINDS OF LEARNING

Starting in 1948 an attempt was made to develop a system for classifying the goals of the educational process. Its purpose was to standardize the terminology used to appraise learning. Such goals, stated in behavioral terms, could represent most kinds of human behavior. The result has been the development of *taxonomies*, or classification systems, in three areas:

☐ *Cognitive domain*—knowledge, information, other intellectual skills
☐ *Affective domain*—attitudes, values, appreciations
☐ *Psychomotor domain*—skeletal-muscle use and coordination

For both the cognitive and affective domains, progressive levels of higher-order behavior have been identified. The cognitive domain includes six levels of intellectual activity:[5]

1. *Knowledge*—recalling information
2. *Comprehension*—interpreting information
3. *Application*—applying information
4. *Analysis*—breaking information into parts

5. *Synthesis*—bringing together elements of information to form a new whole
6. *Evaluation*—making judgments against agreed criteria

The affective domain consists of five levels of attitudes, interests, and/or personal involvement:[6]

1. *Receiving*—attracting the learner's attention
2. *Responding*—learner willing to reply or take action
3. *Valuing*—commiting oneself to take an attitudinal position
4. *Organization*—making adjustments or decisions from among several alternatives
5. *Characterization of a value complex*—integrating one's beliefs, ideas, and attitudes into a total philosophy

Although no widely accepted taxonomy in the psychomotor domain has as yet been developed, various individuals have suggested scales of their own. One recognized grouping is:[7]

1. *Gross bodily movements*—arms, shoulders, feet and legs
2. *Finely coordinated movements*—hand and fingers; hand and eye; hand and ear; hand, eye, and foot
3. *Nonverbal communication*—facial expression, gestures, bodily movements
4. *Speech behaviors*—sound production and projection, sound-gesture coordination

These three taxonomies can be appropriate references as audiovisual materials are planned and developed. The objectives to be served by any media form represent the organizing point for your planning. Since a majority of audiovisual materials serve objectives in the cognitive domain, by recognizing the higher intellectual levels that are identified here, you could develop materials that serve other than the usual simple explanations and information presentations representative of lower cognitive levels.

Robert Gagné, another psychologist, classified observations about learning and decided that various educational objectives require different *conditions of learning*. He developed a hierarchy (a classification sequence similar to a taxonomy) that includes eight kinds of learning, cutting across all learning theories, ranging from simple

5. Benjamin S. Bloom et al., *A Taxonomy of Educational Objectives: Handbook I, the Cognitive Domain* (New York: Longmans, Green, 1956).

6. David Krathwohl et al., *A Taxonomy of Educational Objectives: Handbook II, The Affective Domain* (New York: David McKay, 1964).

7. Robert J. Kibler et al., *Behavioral Objectives and Instruction* (Boston: Allyn & Bacon, 1970), pp. 66–75.

fact learning to more complex and abstract levels. Gagné recognized that his treatment of these conditions of learning is restricted to knowledge (cognitive tasks) and skill types (psychomotor tasks) of educational objectives and does not treat objectives of motivation and the establishment of attitudes and values (the affective domain of learning):[8]

1. *Signal learning.* Learning to respond to a signal. This is the involuntary *conditioned* response typified by the Pavlovian experiments with dogs.
2. *Stimulus-Response (S-R) learning.* Voluntary learning that involves making a specific response to a specified stimulus, such as a child saying "doll" when mother says "doll."
3. *Chaining.* Learning to connect together, in a sequence, two or more previously learned stimulus-response situations, as when a child learns to call an object by its name.
4. *Verbal association.* Learning on the verbal level, related to chaining, such as learning to translate an English word into a foreign language.
5. *Multiple discrimination.* Learning an extensive series of simple chains, as when distinguishing the names of a variety of plants and calling each one by its correct name.
6. *Concept learning.* Learning to make a common response to a number of stimuli that may differ from each other in appearance, as recognizing that various objects are all "plants."
7. *Principle learning.* Learning a chain consisting of two or more previously and separately learned concepts, such as geometric propositions based on axioms, or the names of chemical compounds related to the names of individual chemical elements.
8. *Problem-solving.* Learning, based on two or more previously acquired principles, that requires internal thinking toward the result of a new, higher-level principle; an example is the housewife's making decisions for the selection of items in a market on the basis of price or contents.

Of these eight categories of behavior, the first four are simple forms that Gagné considers primarily as objectives in connection with learning by young children as they acquire knowledge of their surroundings. Most learning experiences provided in school situations fit the higher four levels. These abilities are hierarchical in nature,

so that successful experience in problem-solving requires the prelearning of *principles,* which requires the prelearning of *concepts,* which requires the prelearning of *discriminations,* and so on.

Applications of Gagné's conditions for the design of instruction have been made in a research project and are described as part of a publication.[9] In this report, after statements of behavioral objectives are made, types of learning involved (from Gagné's list) are identified, then media and experiences are selected to serve the indicated conditions of learning. The report provides further details of how Gagné's learning principles are related to media selection, a topic considered in Chapter 7.

In another paper Gagné summarized what to him are the most important events of instruction:[10]

☐ Gaining and maintaing attention
☐ Insuring recall of previously acquired knowledge
☐ Guiding learning by verbal and pictorial materials that provide "cues" or hints to new principles
☐ Providing feedback of his accomplishments to the learner in terms of stated objectives
☐ Establishing conditions for recall and transfer of learning through the use of carefully designed problems and situations to which application of the newly learned principle is made
☐ Assessing outcomes through test and other evaluations

Some investigators from the engineering sciences explain thought and behavior in terms of models derived from the study of control mechanisms (known as *cybernetics*). Such mechanisms operate by *negative feedback.* This involves adjustments in a system to keep it in a steady state by compensating for any deflections from that state (like a thermostat, which, reacting to a drop in temperature, turns on the furnace to make the temperature rise). There are many such mechanisms, and cybernetics attempts to apply their principles to problems in psychology and related fields. The feedback model has the advantage of combining S-R analysis with a recognition that

---

8. Robert M. Gagné, *The Conditions of Learning* (New York: Holt, Rinehart & Winston, 1970).

9. Leslie J. Briggs et al., *Instructional Media: A Procedure for the Design of Multiple-Media Instruction* (Pittsburgh: American Institute for Research, 1967), chap. 2.

10. Robert M. Gagné, "Learning Theory, Educational Media, and Individualized Instruction" (Paper presented at the Faculty Seminar on Educational Media, Bucknell University, Lewisburg, Pa., November 16, 1967).

behavior is not merely a collection of S-R units but a continuously on-going process.[11]

The instructional design procedure for systematic unit or course planning, presented in Chapter 1, makes use of two factors that are part of this cybernetic feedback model. First, all elements of the plan are interrelated, meaning that students' needs affect the selection of objectives, objectives in turn influence activities and evaluation, or vice versa, and so forth. Second, if the outcomes are not satisfactorily accomplished, recycling permits revision of any elements, leading to program improvement.

Finally, recognition must be given to one other thought bearing on learning. Where formerly it was generally accepted that only the *content* of the stimulus material (book, film, television, radio, or whatever) was important to the learner, there is now some concern, notably by the Canadian philosopher and communications theorist Marshall McLuhan, that the *medium* itself (film, radio, television) is more than a transmission belt.[12] Media have certain characteristics of their own, which influence the reception of the message. Furthermore, the exposure to each medium is a direct experience itself, according to McLuhan. His expression, "the medium is the message," may hold important implications for

the design and effectiveness of audiovisual materials.

It should be clear from the information in this section that there are no concise principles of learning that can be directly transferred to the practical design of audiovisual materials. But the generalizations relating to motivation, careful organization, participation and practice, repetition, rate of presentation, and so forth, summarized by Carpenter and Dale, and the conditions of learning described by Gagné, do have definite bearing both on the selection of media to serve instructional objectives and on the planning of specific materials. Keep these generalizations in mind. In effect, many of the findings related to production elements reported in the next chapter are examples of the applications of these broad principles.

But lacking more direct guidance from psychology, educators must proceed with planning for instruction starting with objectives, then to designing of materials largely on an *empirical* basis, using experience, reactions of others, and "best-guesses." These must then be tried with the potential student group, refined or changed as necessary, and tested again until ready for operational use. This approach applies both to materials for group use and to materials for independent student use.

Now, Review What You Have Read About Perception, Communication, and Learning Theory.

1. In your own words, what is "human perception"? How does perception relate to the design of audiovisual materials?
2. If you wished to make an in-depth study of perception as background for designing audiovisual materials, to what articles and books would you refer?
3. Recall the seven elements of the communication process in the communications model presented in this chapter. Where do audiovisual materials fit into the model?
4. Which learning theories support the shift in instruction from teacher-centered to individualized learning?
5. How do you relate each of the ten principles of learning enumerated by Carpenter and Dale and the "important events of instruction" summarized by Gagné on page 17 to their importance in planning audiovisual materials?
6. What are the three domains into which most instructional objectives can be grouped? Which domain is it most difficult for audiovisual materials to serve?
7. Which of Gagné's conditions of learning relate to experiences that audiovisual materials could provide in a school instructional program?

11. Karl U. Smith and Margaret F. Smith, *Cybernetic Principles of Learning and Educational Design* (New York: Holt, Rinehart & Winston, 1966).

12. Marshall McLuhan, *Understanding Media: The Extension of Man* (New York: McGraw-Hill, 1964).

Answers to Review Questions

1. Perception—the internal awareness a person develops for recognizing an event or object in his environment. Gaining a person's attention, holding his or her interest, and making sure the correct message is received are important considerations in designing audiovisual materials relating to perception.
2. Fleming.
3. See diagram, page 15. Audiovisual materials relate to the transmission-channel step.
4. Behaviorism.
5. Reader makes own choices and explanations.
6. Cognitive, affective, psychomotor. Affective domain most difficult to serve.
7. Discriminations, concept learning, principle learning, problem-solving.

3

RESEARCH IN THE DESIGN OF AUDIOVISUAL MATERIALS

Much research has been conducted about audiovisual materials. A large portion of the studies concerns utilization practices and proof of the instructional value of specific materials as compared with traditional teaching methods. In a smaller number of experiments, a particular aspect of an audiovisual presentation was varied in order to determine the effect on learning of that particular variable. Results of the latter group have relevancy for the planning and subsequent production of audiovisual materials.

Summaries of research findings, including production elements, have been prepared by a number of writers. From these summaries the findings relating to production aspects of audiovisual materials are abstracted and presented in this chapter. Readers who have access to the original reports should refer to them for full information.

These findings are fairly numerous and probably cannot be remembered or applied easily. At the end of the chapter, to assist in your understanding and recall of these findings, applications are offered for appraisal in a review exercise. The number of each finding is referred to in the review exercise.

Hoban and Van Ormer (1950)

In 1950, Hoban and Van Ormer surveyed a large number of experiments and other studies that had been made in the previous 30 years concerning the instructional values of motion pictures.[1] Among their findings were some directly relating to variables in film production. Most of these points are also of value in the production of other materials, such as slides and filmstrips. Only the briefest summary statements of the detailed explanations are included here.

1. *Camera angle.* Show a performance on the screen the way the learner would see it if he were doing the job himself (subjective camera position).
2. *Rate of development.* The rate of development or pacing of a film should be slow enough to permit the learners to grasp the material as it is shown.
3. *Succinct treatment.* Presenting only the bare essentials or too rapid coverage of subject matter may be very ineffective.
4. *Errors.* The learning of performance skills from films will be increased if you show common errors and how to avoid them.
5. *Repetition.* Organize a film so that important sequences or concepts are repeated. Repetition of films, or parts within a film, is one of the most effective means for increasing learning.
6. *Organizational outline.* Films that treat discrete factual material appear to be improved

---

1. See Charles F. Hoban and Edward B. Van Ormer, *Instructional Film Research, 1918–1950* (Port Washington, N. Y.: U.S. Naval Special Devices Center, 1950).

by the use of an organizational outline in titles and commentary.

7. *Introduction.* Present the relevant information in an introduction and tell the viewer what he is expected to learn from the film.

8. *Summary.* Summarize the important points in the film in a clear, concise manner. Summaries probably do not significantly improve learning unless they are complete enough to serve as repetition and review.

9. *Visual potentialities.* Take advantage of the ability of the motion-picture medium to show motion, to speed motion up and slow it down, to telescope and otherwise control timing of events and processes, to bridge space, and to organize events and action.

10. *Picture-commentary relationship.* The commentary of a typical informational film appears to teach more than the pictures of that same film when learning is measured by verbal tests. This observation does not necessarily mean that the commentary has greater inherent effectiveness than the pictures; it may mean that producers rely more heavily on commentary than on pictures or on the optimum integration of the two. With films designed to teach performance skills, where learning is measured by nonverbal tests, the pictures appear to carry the main teaching burden.

11. *Concentration of ideas.* Ideas or concepts should be presented at a rate appropriate to the ability of the audience to comprehend them.

12. *Commentary.* The number of words (per minute of film) in the commentary has a definite effect on learning. Care should be taken not to "pack" the sound track. Application of readability formulas to improve a commentary may not do so.

13. *Use of personal pronouns.* Use direct forms of address (imperative or second person) in film commentaries. Avoid the passive voice.

14. *Nomenclature.* Introduction of new names or technical terms in a film imposes an additional burden on learners, and may impede the learning of a performance skill.

15. *Special effects.* Special effects used as attention-getting devices have no positive influence on learning.

16. *Optical effects.* A film in which straight cuts have replaced optical effects (such as fades, wipes, and dissolves) teaches just as effectively as a film that uses these effects.

17. *Color.* Experimentation has not yet demonstrated any general overall increased learning as a result of using color in instructional films.

18. *Music.* Preliminary experimentation suggests that music does not add to the instructional effectiveness of an informational film.

19. *Pretesting.* Scripts, workprints, demonstrations, and final prints can be evaluated quickly using the learning-profile method of film evaluation, which requires a group of trainees to estimate their own learning.

20. *Film loops.* Short film loops, which can be repeated continuously as many times as desired, appear to be good materials for teaching difficult skills.

21. *Participation.* Learning will increase if the viewer practices a skill while it is presented on the screen, provided the film develops slowly enough, or provided periods of time are allowed in which the learner is permitted to practice without missing new material shown on the screen.

22. *Dramatic sequences.* Incorporation of dramatic sequences, such as comedy, singing commercials, or realistic settings, in films to teach factual information have not been shown to improve the film.

23. *Filmograph.* Filmographs, which incorporate still shots rather than motion, may be equally effective and less expensive.

24. *Visual recordings.* Films can be produced to make a visual recording of a task that may be difficult to describe with words alone.

25. *Inexpensive films.* Because color, optical effects, and dramatic effects have little to do with increasing learning from films, it is possible to eliminate them. Films prepared in this manner can be made inexpensively and can be produced quickly.

Saul (1954)

Another review of literature, relating this time to graphic training aids, was done in 1954 under the direction of Ezra V. Saul.[2] The objective of this report was "to prepare annotated reviews of the literature in specific areas pertinent to the problem of developing standards and criteria on the design, preparation, and utilization of effective graphic training aids."

Materials for the report were derived from the literature on psychophysiology of vision, visual perception, experimental aesthetics and art, advertising, visual education, psychology of learning, engineering drawing, and instructor

2. Ezra V. Saul et al., *A Review of the Literature Pertinent to the Design and Use of Effective Graphic Training Aids* (Port Washington, N.Y.: U.S. Naval Special Devices Center, 1954).

utilization of graphic materials. Many of the reports are valuable for their findings related to design principles, uses of color, and graphic depiction of relationships, to mention just a few. Evaluations of findings are provided at the end of each section, but no generalized factual summaries are made from which specific principles can be drawn.

May and Lumsdaine (1958)

Between 1946 and 1954 a series of experimental studies concerning problems in production and utilization of teaching films were conducted under the Yale Motion Picture Research Project.[3] Some findings correlated closely with the results reported by Hoban and Van Ormer in these categories: *concentration of ideas, color, music, participation,* and *dramatic sequences.* In addition, other findings were:

26. *Pictorial quality.* A crude presentation (pencil sketches of visuals) may be at least equal in effectiveness to a polished color film.
27. *Live dialogue and off-stage narration.* Except where the use of live dialogue can have marked superiority for meeting particular objectives, the narrated film has great advantages.
28. *Printed titles and questions.* Liberal use of titles, questions, and other printed words can improve teaching effectiveness.

May (1965–1966)

A different approach to reporting research results was taken in May's series of papers for the United States Office of Education.[4] He examined selected areas of instructional variables as related to the production of audiovisual materials. These were treated from the standpoint of the functions they perform for *motivating, reinforcing, cueing,* and *simplifying* the responses that are required for learning.

29. *Motivators* are devices, effects, and procedures to cause the learner to pay close attention, to look or listen for relevant and crucial clues, to have a "set" or put forth effort to learn, and to respond or practice. Positive motivators may include the use of color (to gain and hold attention); dramatic presentations; humor and comic effects; and inserted printed questions.
30. *Reinforcers* are techniques to increase the probability that the learner will remember and can reproduce what was presented. There are no clear indicators of ways to accomplish this increase, but there is evidence that stimuli in materials that are pleasing, interesting, and satisfying are positive reinforcers.
31. *Cue identifiers* are devices and effects that help the learner identify and recognize the relevant cues. These include color, arrows and pointers, animation, "implosion" techniques (having assembled parts fall into place without being handled by the demonstrator), subjective camera angles, and directed narration.
32. *Simplifiers* are procedures for making presentations more effective. They include improving the readability of narration, eliminating irrelevant pictorial materials, repeating illustrations or adding additional illustrations, or using filmstrips or filmographs (still pictures or diagrams on motion-picture film) in place of live film action for some purposes.

In this review May, as did other writers, indicated that some techniques did little or nothing to improve learning in audiovisual materials. These included musical backgrounds, introductory and review sections, and optical effects for transitions (fades, dissolves, and wipes).

Travers (1967)

In 1964 Travers, a psychologist, made available an interim report on his project, sponsored by the United States Office of Education. The preliminary report, with additions, was the basis for Travers's *Research and Theory Related to Audiovisual Information transmission.*[5] His purpose was to search the literature relating to the transmission of information through the senses and to point out implications for the design of audiovisual teaching materials. This report differs from that of Hoban and Van Ormer in two ways. First, Travers examined reports of psychology-oriented studies and of studies involving other media as well as motion pictures. Second, the majority of

3. Mark A. May and A. A. Lumsdaine, *Learning from Films* (New Haven, Conn.: Yale University Press, 1958).

4. "Enhancements and Simplifications of Motivational and Stimulus Variables in Audiovisual Instructional Materials" (1965), "The Role of Student Response in Learning from the New Educational Media" (1966), "Word-Picture Relationships in Audio-Visual Presentations" (1965). U.S. Office of Education Contral No. OE 5-16-006.

5. Washington, D.C., U.S. Office of Education contract no. OES-16-006.

the studies described by Travers were performed after 1950, whereas the Hoban and Van Ormer report included studies from 1918 to 1950.

Here are the major findings reported by Travers. Compare them with the summary list from Hoban and Van Ormer.

Embellishments and simplifications

33. The fact that color adds to the attractiveness of a training device does not necessarily mean that it improves learning. Black-and-white is as effective as color for instructional purposes except when the learning involves an actual color discrimination. Learners prefer color versions despite the fact that the addition of color does not generally contribute to learning.
34. A demonstration should include only the basic elements of what is to be demonstrated, but oversimplification can have a deleterious effect.
35. The special effects (fades, dissolves, and the like that are used to represent lapses of time and other events were not effective in conveying the intended meanings. Print titles seem to be more effective. Special sound effects appear to provide much more challenge to the film producer than aid to the learner. The same can be said of humor and of other special means intended to retain the interest of the learner.

Audio readability, density of information, and rate of presentation

36. Verbal simplification in film commentaries increases teaching effectiveness. Comprehension of audio inputs can be predicted by readability formulas to measure their difficulty.
37. Some verbalization is better than none, but there is no optimum amount. Slow speeds for transmitting verbal information are favored, but they can be too slow.
38. If time is not a factor, listening comprehension is likely to be most effective at speeds of around 160 words per minute. This generalization is probably true only for relatively simple material, and the intellectual level of the audience must also be taken into account. When narration is accompanied by video, the optimum rate of the narration appears to be slower.

Audience participation and practice

39. Overt (visible) response, practiced by the learner during the film, results in increased learning.

40. Furnishing knowledge of results as part of the participation process also has positive effects upon learning.
41. Activities related to the presentation of a film indicate that learners experience difficulty in following a continuous demonstration and, at the same time, undertaking the task themselves. But when the film or other continuous flow of information is stopped and the learner then participates, learning is more effective. Participation does not have to be overt. Mental practice is as effective.

In 1966 Travers completed his project, including a series of experiments designed to investigate the validity of certain accepted elements in the design of audiovisual materials. On the basis of the results of his experiments, he builds a useful case for presentations via a single sense with this conclusion:[6]

42. "The simultaneous use of two senses (visual and audio) are likely to be of value only when the rate of input of information is very slow. The silent film with the alternation of picture and print would appear to find much theoretical support as a teaching device."

HARTMAN (1961)

This matter of single- versus multiple-channel presentation is of particular importance with attention being given to 8-mm silent- and sound-film production. Hartman had reviewed the literature to that date on single- and multiple-channel communication and concluded with these two points:[7]

43. The meaning of a visual message is often ambiguous and subject to personal interpretation. The use of words to direct attention is essential.
44. The audio channel is much more capable of obtaining attention if it is used as an interjection on the pictorial channel rather than being continuously parallel with the pictorial.

---

6. Conway [Jerome Conway, "Multiple Sensory Modality Communications and the Problems of Sign Types," *AV Communication Review* (Winston, 1967): 371–383] questioned the assumptions underlying the Travers studies, indicating that a disparity does exist between experimental settings, in which the studies were conducted, and relevant real-life situations and applications.

7. Frank R. Hartman "Single and Multiple Channel Communication: A Review of Research and a Proposed Model," *AV Communications Review* (Nov.-Dec., 1961): 235–262.

GROPPER (1966)

The relation of visuals and words for developing *programmed* audiovisual materials has been studied by Gropper.[8] He found that:

45. While concepts and principles can be acquired on the basis solely of visual presentations, to rely *only* on visual lessons is inefficient. Gropper concluded that words serve an important cueing role and should be incorporated, for this secondary purpose, into a visual presentation.

Allen (1973)

More recent research efforts, which have considered elements of programmed instruction and television as well as motion pictures, support and extend much of the former research results and findings relative to learning theory. Among the generalizations Allen[9] presents are the following, not previously included:

46. *Active student response and participation.* When a student participates frequently by responding actively to some stimulus, his learning of the materials will be increased.
47. *Establishing and directing attention.* It is useful to direct the learner's attention to particular elements of instructional messages through visual cueing or other attention-attracting devices.
48. *Repetition of stimuli.* Instructional content may be more completely learned if it is presented to the learner two or more times, in identical or varied forms.
49. *Sequencing and organizing instruction.* Learning may be enhanced by organizing instruction sequentially to permit establishing subordinate skills before teaching those of higher order.

Levie and Dickie (1973)

The purpose of the literature review by Levie and Dickie[10] was to consider the effectiveness of various instructional media in learning contexts prior to 1971. Among their generalizations is this one, which can have bearing on the design of audiovisual materials:

50. *Learning is facilitated by increasing the number of relative cues and reducing the number of irrelevant ones in terms of the concept to be learned.* When a presentation involving a media form can be reduced in complexity so that only the factors that directly contribute to accomplishing the task (like realism, color, motion, picture detail, and so on) are included, learning will be more predictable and replicable.

Allen (1974)

Allen searched the literature to determine what recommendations could be made between the intellectual abilities of learners and the ways instructional media can be designed. After exploring a number of relationships, he presented generalized statements that can assist a producer to design audiovisual materials that will better serve the intellectual abilities of each of three groups of learners—low, middle, and high mental abilities.[11]

The study concludes with specific applications for instructional-media design factors in terms of each one of the three mental-ability groups. Although this summary relates closely to many findings previously indicated in this chapter, the relation to intellectual abilities is of special importance because of the increasing attention being given to individualized learning programs.

A need exists for instructional materials that can provide successful learning opportunities for students of all intellectual abilities. If this is a concern of yours, you are referred to the report for specific statements, detailed analyses, and lists of generalizations.

A person interested in planning and producing audiovisual materials should review and weigh all the evidence from the research findings and theory reported in this and the preceding chapter. These findings, rather than intuition, should be considered as you design your own materials for instruction. Start with these results and recommendations, realizing that some may have been derived from situations far afield of

---

8. George L. Gropper, "Learning from Visuals: Some Behavioral Considerations," *AV Communications Review* (Spring, 1966): 37–70.

9. William H. Allen, "Research in Educational Media" in *Educational Media Yearbook* 1973, James W. Brown, editor (New York: R. R. Bowker, 1973).

10. Howard W. Levie and Kenneth E. Dickie, "The Analysis and Application of Media" in *Second Handbook of Research on Teaching* (Chicago: Rand McNally, 1973).

11. William H. Allen ,*Intellectual Abilities and Instructional Media Design* (Stanford, Calif.: ERIC Clearing House on Information Resources, 1974).

the applications you plan to make. (Yet they are starting points with positive evidence for improved learning at lower costs in terms of time, materials, and services.) Then adapt and change as you gain experience and test the results of your efforts.

Now, Review What You Have Read About Research Findings for the Design of Audiovisual Materials.

Following are statements concerning audiovisual materials that apply one or more of the findings described in this chapter. Some make recommended applications, while others apply elements in nonrecommended fashion. For each example indicate your *agreement* or *disagreement* with the proposed plan. Then check your answer, using the reference numbers at the right to locate the relevant numbered finding(s) used as a basis for each example.

	AGREE OR DISAGREE / EVIDENCE
1. When demonstrating the proper method to use in casting with a fishing rod, show errors commonly made and ways to avoid them.	—— 4
2. In demonstrating a skill, like fingering a musical instrument, color will add to the instructional value of the medium used.	—— 17, 25, 33
3. In explaining the operation of a machine, use arrows to indicate each part as it is referred to.	—— 31, 47
4. Slides (still pictures) can be as effective as a motion picture for presenting a school's program orientation to students.	—— 23, 32
5. To demonstrate how a woman sews an intricate stitch by hand, film the action from over her shoulder.	—— 1, 31
6. In teaching a how-to-do-it skill like welding, limit the amount of narration and depend on the visuals for the major instructional effect. In narration, use words in the present tense to direct attention ("hold the tool . . . "; "notice the color . . . ")	—— 10, 13, 31, 42–44
7. A film that shows action in many locations is more effective if an optical effect like a dissolve (page 244) is used between scenes to bridge distance rather than abrupt cuts from one scene to the next. Also, background music will enhance the presentation.	—— 16, 18, 25, 35
8. To explain for teachers a new method of teaching algebra, present only the essential facts without repetition of any of the concepts. A brief, general summary should be included.	—— 5, 8, 11, 34, 48
9. In describing an industrial process, quickly present only the essential information. The commentary should describe, at length, what cannot easily be visualized. If it is a	

lengthy subject, plan that the commentary moves along rapidly.

—— 2, 3, 11, 12, 36

10. Picture sketches from storyboard cards (page 54), converted to film, may be as effective as a high-quality polished treatment for illustrating a farming procedure.

—— 26, 32

11. In treating the subject of animal life at the seashore, color should be used and important concepts presented through multiple examples.

—— 5, 17, 25, 33, 50

12. Introduce the demonstration of a laboratory procedure with an explanation of the purpose of the demonstration and what the student is expected to learn from it. Include titles that indicate the sequence of steps in the procedure. Describe carefully and visualize new technical terms.

—— 6, 7, 14, 28, 35

13. For learning to operate a piece of equipment, like a laboratory chemical balance, a continuous loop film that can be viewed any number of times may have advantages. Directions for the learner to stop the film, answer questions, and practice steps in the skill should be included. Correct answers to questions should be provided immediately after the questions are answered.

—— 21, 28, 39–41, 46

14. A self-learning package treating a topic for a science lab course includes a cassette recording on which the instructor outlines the facts basic to the topic and leads the student to laboratory applications.

—— 49

Answers to Review Questions

1. Agree
2. Disagree
3. Agree
4. Agree
5. Agree
6. Agree
7. Disagree
8. Disagree
9. Disagree
10. Agree
11. Agree
12. Agree
13. Agree
14. Agree

PART 2

PLANNING YOUR AUDIOVISUAL MATERIALS

4

GETTING STARTED

Start with an idea, and from it develop your objectives in terms of the specific audience with which you plan to use your audiovisual materials.

All too often someone says, "Let's make a movie about our school," or, "How about shooting some slides to train salesmen?" or, "We should have some transparencies for use in our instructional design."

Unfortunately, such thoughts are frequently the signal to start taking pictures prematurely and produce audiovisual materials that are unorganized and ineffective. These proposals are no more than bare ideas; they require further consideration, such as decisions about the specific content and its organization into planned sequences of pictures.

Occasionally, it is necessary to make pictures without any prior planning (there are "one-chance-to-get-the-picture" situations), but desirable audiovisual materials are usually attained through careful plans.

Start with an Idea

An idea, a problem situation, or a need identified within an instructional-design plan for a unit or a course should be the starting point for your audiovisual materials. An idea may indicate an area of interest you have, but the more useful ideas are those conceived in terms of a need relating to a specific group—an audience's need for certain information or for a skill, or the need to establish a desired attitude.

So here is the first step: Express your idea concisely. For example:

In my science classes we study about community health services. As part of our study we consider methods of water purification. I need some pictures (possibly slides) that would help my students to understand better the methods used in treating our local water supply. (Note: This example of the water-purification process will serve as an illustration of the planning steps that follow.)

In the instructional-design approach described in Chapter 1, the first step was to *recognize broad general purposes.* Essentially, these are the beginning *ideas* referred to here. They also need amplification before objectives are developed. Stated purposes (as, for a social-studies course, "to understand the structure of national, state, and local governments"; or, for a mathematics unit, "to learn the advantages of displaying data in tabular or graphic form") are fine as a start, but they do not lead directly and easily to definitive learning experiences.

Develop the Objectives

Build upon the idea or generalized statement of purposes. Doing this means translating the general idea into a clear-cut and specific statement of one or more objectives for the planned learning.

Today much attention is given in the literature (references on page 294) to the topic of *learning objectives;* these have a key role in instructional design as well as in separate learning activities. This focus is an aspect of the shift from teacher- and subject-centered instruction to the emphasis on the student and his needs.

To plan successful audiovisual materials and other learning experiences, it is necessary to know specifically what must be learned. The purpose of formulating objectives is to provide clear guidance that permits an orderly presentation of content.

When learning takes place, a person behaves differently than he did before the learning experience. The evidence for learning is that he has become able to do something that he formerly could not do. Or he may have acquired new knowledge—another measure of learning. Again, through learning a person may respond differently in terms of an attitude or an appreciation. Learning encompasses any one or two or all of these kinds of change.

So the objectives of learning can be grouped into three major categories as described in Chapter 2—the *psychomotor* area, represented by performance skills involving the use of skeletal muscles; the *cognitive* area, which includes knowledge, information, and intellectual skills; and the *affective* area of attitudes, appreciations, and values.

The difficult problem is to spell out the objectives so that (1) learning experiences can be developed to satisfy each objective, and (2) tests or performance measurements can be designed to find out whether the learning has taken place.

Military and industry-business training programs have been dealing with objectives for some time. Their emphasis has been on specific *task-analysis* objectives for operational skills. Just as applying an instructional system in education is more complex than developing weapons or communication systems in the military or industry, so likewise educational objectives, with their greater emphasis on the affective area, are more difficult to define and put into effect.

The general nonspecific words that are often used to describe instructional purposes—to *know,* to *understand,* to *become familiar with,* to *appreciate,* to *believe,* to *gain insight into,* to *accept,* to *enjoy,* and so forth—are unsatisfactory guide words for objectives. They do not permit verification through specific observable behavior and they are open to many interpretations of how their accomplishment may be measured.

Useful statements of objectives are made up of two grammatical parts. First: a specific ACTION VERB like one of these—to *identify,* to *name,* to *demonstrate,* to *show,* to *make* or *build,* to *order* or *arrange,* to *distinguish between,* to *compare,* to *apply,* and so forth. Second, CONTENT REFERENCE that follows the verb, like—to name the *five steps in the process,* to kick a *football* at least 30 yards, to write a 500-word *theme,* to apply a *rule,* to solve four of five *problems,* and so forth.

Notice that in addition to the action verb and the content reference, we may add a STANDARD OF COMPETENCY (at least *30 yards, 500 words, four of five problems*). The standard further provides for setting an attainment level that can be measured.

With this awareness of measurable learning objectives, how can we specifically indicate the objectives for the general idea example on methods of water purification indicated previously?

It is *not* sufficiently specific to say:

☐ To know how our local water supply is treated.

It *is* specific to say:

1. To name the five steps in the purification of our local water supply.
2. To compare the local methods of water treatment to techniques of purification used elsewhere.
3. To practice the conservation of water.

Statements 1 and 2 above specify cognitive (informational) objectives (1 on a low level; 2 much higher intellectually). Statement 3 specifies an attitudinal behavior. It is much more difficult to indicate behaviors and measurements for attitudes and appreciations than to do so for either knowledge/intellectual skills or performance skills. Admittedly some objectives must lead to unpredictable outcomes, as opposed to learnings that build up immediate connections between specific stimuli and specific responses. The attainment of other objectives may not be fully measurable until the individual is on the job or faced with a particular situation. But attempts should be made, even indirectly, to devise the best measurable ways of stating objectives. To repeat, only when the objectives are stated in terms of an individual's performance is there much guidance for the design of instruction.

Remember that each topic for instruction (like the water-purification topic) requires a number of objectives, each to be considered individually in designing learning experiences. Therefore, it takes time and careful thought to develop and state objectives. Also, as was indicated during the discussion of instructional design in Chapter 1, it is natural to move gradually from general to specific objectives. Finally, realize that some objectives may become clearly evident only when content is being selected or even when specific audiovisual materials are in the planning stage. In such a case, return to this beginning point, the statement of objective, and check how well the content and learning experiences fit the stated objective; you may want to revise the statement.

You might prepare audiovisual materials for many purposes. Here are some major general purposes with specific examples. They are stated as objectives in terms of audience changes, from the audience viewpoint.

☐ *To learn about a subject;* for example, "to recognize the location and the significance of 10 landmarks important in the early history of our community."
☐ *To apply the steps in a process;* for example, "to locate and use the major reference books in the school library."
☐ *To exercise a skill;* for example, "to make slides of interior and exterior subjects with a 35-mm camera."
☐ *To practice a certain attitude;* for example, "to form the habit of using safe procedures in operating shop equipment."
☐ *To respond to a social need;* for example, "to offer your services in a youth recreation program."

In planning materials, limit yourself to no more than one or two concisely stated achievable objectives. However much you feel it necessary *to cover the whole topic,* you will realize eventually that limitations should be set. If you do not set limits, your materials may become too complex and unmanageable. You can maintain limits by aiming at a series of related audiovisual materials, each of which includes a single phase of a large topic.

In developing an independent study *module,* or learning package, a number of short materials (cassette recording, filmstrip, 8-mm film, and so on) might be developed, with each one treating an objective for the concept relating to the module topic.

It is also important to make the learner aware of the objectives of his learning. Inform him what he is to learn from a film, a self-instructional activity, or a multimedia program. There is much evidence to show that better results are obtained

when students clearly know what they are expected to learn. Often students are informed of their objectives in connection with the activities that accompany the use of the materials. See the instructor and student study guides on pages 71 and 72.

Finally, objectives do not stand alone. It is obvious that they are dependent on the subject content that will be treated and are influenced by the needs and dispositions of the learner or intended audience.

Consider the Audience (the Learner)

The characteristics of the learner or audience—those who will be using and learning from your materials—cannot be separated from your statement of objectives. One influences the other. Such audience characteristics as age and educational level, knowledge of the subject and attitude toward it, and individual differences within the group, all have bearing on your objectives and treatment of the topic. The audience is the determinant when you consider the complexity of ideas to be presented, the rate at which the topic is developed, the vocabulary level for captions and narration, the number of examples to use, the kinds of involvement and degree of participation of the learner, and similar matters that influence the complexity of the objectives and your handling of the topic.

At times more than one audience may fit your plans, but generally it is advisable to plan for *one major audience group.* Then consider other *secondary* ones which also might use your materials. Describe the major audience, explicitly.

For the example, *Our Water Supply:*

The major audience will be ninth-grade general-science classes. The students have sufficient science background to understand the applications of filtration and chlorination in the treatment of water, but other concepts, such as aeration and coagulation, may be new and will require careful development.

A word of caution: If you plan audiovisual materials for use with younger groups, make sure that the subject and the activities selected are appropriate to their interests and their abilities. Your own enthusiasm for a topic may take you far beyond the limited amount of interest in it that others have. Also, give careful consideration to the complexity of the subject so that your group does not become burdened with too many details and lose interest as a result.

Some Examples

The planning steps thus far examined are: (1) start with an idea, (2) from the idea develop your objectives, with due regard for the intended audience and its characteristics.

Examine the examples in Table 4-1. Are the steps clearly stated and easy to follow? Are the objectives stated in behavioral terms? Which of them may not be so stated? The review questions that follow help you to correct any improperly stated objectives.

TABLE 4-1 Examples of Initial Planning Steps

IDEA	OBJECTIVE	AUDIENCE
Plant life common to our community	To recognize and name the 25 most common species of seed-bearing plants in our county	(1) High-school biology classes (2) Nature clubs
Our school library	(1) To use the resources of our elementary-school library (2) To check books out properly and return them when due	Upper elementary grades of the school
Operation of our insurance company	To understand my role in the successful operation of our company	Employees of the ABC Insurance Company
Lettering aids for making displays	To use a variety of lettering resources for preparing classroom displays	All teachers in the district
Support the school-bond drive at the next election	To vote Yes for new school construction at the election	General community voting public
Our church's youth program	(1) To take part in youth-group activities (2) To know how youth activities help to develop sound character and religious understanding among our young people	(1) Children and teen-agers of church members (2) Church sponsors and adult members

Now Apply What You Have Read

1. The examples in Table 4-1 relate to the five major purposes listed on page 33. Identify each example according to the appropriate category.
2. Again with the examples in Table 4-1, are any objectives in the middle column not properly stated and how might they be reworded?
3. It has been indicated that the preparation of audiovisual materials may be based upon the feeling that something is needed to do a

better job, or the belief that something is needed where presently *nothing exists*. Select one topic that you would like to see developed into an audiovisual material and *express it as an idea.*

4. Now write the specific objectives you want such an audiovisual material to serve.
5. With what audience would you use such materials?
6. What are some of the audience characteristics you should consider?

Answers to Review Questions

1. Cognitive
   Affective/Cognitive
   Cognitive
   Psychomotor
   Affective
   Affective/Cognitive
2. To *understand* my role . . .
   (reword) To *explain* to another employee my role . . .
   To *know* how youth activities help . . .
   (reword) To *cite* four instances of how youth activities help . . .
3–6. Reader's activity

5

GETTING SOME HELP

Consider individuals who may assist you with your planning and production. Examine already-made audiovisual materials relating to your topic.

A Team Approach

You may be capable of planning and preparing your audiovisual materials without the assistance of others. If you are, you have skills in three areas. First, you have a good knowledge of the subject. Second, you know how to plan audiovisual materials and how to interpret the subject visually. Third, you have the necessary technical skills in photography, graphic arts, and sound recording.

But if you feel inadequate in any of these areas, you should obtain assistance or carefully use this book (in the second and third areas). Even so, there is value in getting reactions and suggestions from other people, so plan to involve others during some phases of the planning and preparation processes. In a class or group, specific jobs may be assigned to individuals, but at various stages group interaction is desirable.

In keeping with this team approach, one former leader in the field of visual communications has offered a pattern of personnel involvement.[1] Three individuals or three groups might make up the *production team.* The *subject specialist* is the person or persons having broad knowledge and familiarity with the potential audience. The *communications specialist* is the individual who

knows how to handle the content (treatment, scriptwriting, camera angles, and the like) and knows the advantages, limitations, and uses of the various audiovisual media so that the resulting materials will achieve the anticipated purposes. This person may also serve as the *instructional designer* during the planning described in Chapter 1. Finally, the *technical staff* comprises those responsible for the photography, the art work, the lighting, and the sound recording.

These separately described areas naturally overlap: the communications person may also take the pictures; or, as was mentioned, you may fill all three jobs. The important thing to recognize is that all three jobs exist. Keep them in mind as you consider the stages of planning and preparation that follow. For example:

While planning audiovisual materials on Our Water Supply, *I will consult with the supervisor of the city water department. The supervisor and I in combination will fill the role of subject specialist. I will request assistance also from the school's audiovisual coordinator, who will thus function as communications specialist. Since I have a good skill in photography, I will prepare the visual materials, but I will be assisted by a technical staff of three students who have abilities in photography and art.*

1. Adrian TerLouw, formerly Educational Consultant, Eastman Kodak Company, Rochester, New York.

Within an instructional design you are concerned with more than just the planning and physical production of audiovisual materials. Since the materials are to arise out of planned instruction, evaluation for effectiveness is important. Therefore, the instructional staff and those in charge of evaluation must also play roles during the planning of instructional materials.

Related Materials

Before carrying the planning of your audiovisual materials to an advanced stage, locate and examine any materials already prepared on your general topic or on topics closely related to it. They may offer you some useful ideas, or you may find that all or part of such materials may fit one or more of your objectives. This is especially true of the single-concept 8-mm films that have, in part, been derived from 16-mm commercial films.

Communicate with audiovisual specialists in school systems, universities, colleges, or business and industry for suggestions of other possible materials and also for their reactions to your plans. Check your library for these references:[2]

☐ Educators Progress Service, Randolph, Wisc., 53956
Educators Guide to Free Films

Educators Guide to Free Filmstrips
Educators Guide to Free Tapes, Scripts, and Transcriptions
☐ National Information Center for Educational Media (NICEM), University of Southern California, Los Angeles, Calif., 90007
Index to Educational Audio Tapes
Index to Educational Overhead Transparencies
Index to Educational Records
Index to Educational Slide Sets
Index to Educational Video Tapes
Index to 8-mm Motion Picture Cartridges
Index to 16-mm Educational Films
Index to 35-mm Educational Filmstrips
☐ National Audiovisual Center, General Services Administration, Washington, D.C., 20409
United States Government Films
☐ Serina Press, 70 Kennedy Street, Alexandria, Va., 22305
Guide to Free-Loan Training Films (16-mm)
Guide to Government-Loan Films (16-mm)
Guide to Military-Loan Films (16-mm)
Guide to State-Loan Films (16-mm)
Guide to Foreign Government-Loan Films (16-mm)
☐ Westinghouse Learning Corporation, 100 Park Avenue, New York, N.Y., 10017
Learning Directory (multimedia listings by subjects and topics)

Now Apply What You Have Read

Examine the topic you had under consideration at the end of Chapter 4. Assume now that you are to continue with the planning and preparation of the audiovisual material related to this topic, and answer these questions concerning the three roles discussed in the section you have just finished reading:

1. Which roles would you fill? What are your qualifications?
2. Which parts of this book (skim it, or look at the table of contents) would you expect to be of greatest value to you in improving your qualifications for all of the three roles? Is any role beyond this book's objectives?
3. Would you ask for assistance in any of the three areas? Whom would you seek to fill the role of subject specialist? the role of communications specialist? the places on the technical staff?
4. How would you learn whether any audiovisual materials have already been prepared on your topic?

2. See also David Rawnsley, *A Comparison of Guides to Non-Print Media* (Stanford, Calif.: ERIC Clearinghouse on Media & Technology, Stanford University, November 1973).

6

EXPANDING FROM THE OBJECTIVES

Learn as much as you can about your subject, then develop an outline of the content in terms of the objectives.

In your preliminary planning you defined your objectives and your audience. Now consider the the subject matter on which your audiovisual materials will be based. Consult with your subject specialist, or, if you are handling the content yourself, do any necessary research work. Facts about a subject are often found through interviews, during visits to suitable facilities, and in the library. After this background work you can feel confident that your basic facts are correct and that you will include all pertinent information on your topic.

Prepare the Content Outline

From the data you have gathered prepare a content outline. This outline becomes the framework for your audiovisual materials. It consists of (1) basic topics that support your objectives, (2) factual information that explains each topic.

A word of caution: Remember the people who will be your audience—their interests and their limitations. Decide what information must be included in detail and what can be treated lightly; what you can suggest for additional study and what should be left out or considered for other audiovisual materials.

In the sequence of the instructional design, the examination of content follows the objec-

tives. At this stage you are not as yet concerned about specific materials. There is no gain in asking at this point whether a film or a set of transparencies, a recording, a printed program, or a combination of media will best serve the objectives. You must find out what content is required to support the objectives. Then you can make decisions about specific audiovisual materials.

Use Storyboard Cards

A good way of relating content to objectives is to connect the two visually. In a few pages we will examine the method of preparing a *storyboard* to visualize the treatment of a topic for an audiovisual material. This same technique has value now.

Write each objective on a 4×6 inch card or slip of paper. Tack or tape the cards to a wall for display. Then, from your notes on paper, make a second set of cards listing the content—the factual information related to each objective—and display these cards under or beside each appropriate objective card. At this stage, list all the available content relating to the objectives, without considering what you may use and what will be discarded.

It is advisable to use cards of one color for objectives and of a second color for the content.

An Example of a
Content Outline

```
         CONTENT OUTLINE—OUR WATER SUPPLY

  I.  Source of our water

      A.  Initially snow and rain along the western slopes of
          sections of the Sierra Nevada
      B.  Collected and transported as the Mokelumne River
      C.  Held in the proper reservoir

 II.  Treatment at the purification plant

      A.  Aeration
          1.  Spraying of water into the air
          2.  Adds or removes oxygen
          3.  Improves taste

      B.  Coagulation

          1.  Adding of alum to water
          2.  Causes small impurities to clump together
          3.  Takes 10–20 minutes

      C.  Sedimentation
          1.  Suspended impurities settle out
          2.  Removes 85% of all foreign matter
          3.  Takes about 3 hours

      D.  Filtration
          1.  Passing the water through beds of sand and gravel
          2.  Strains out unsettled suspended matter
          3.  Most straining action takes place in top 6 inches
              of sand

      E.  Disinfection
          1.  Adding of chlorine solution to water
          2.  Done after filtration is completed
          3.  Kills bacteria

III.  Distribution of water

      A.  Transmission pipes
      B.  Distribution reservoirs
      C.  Gravity flow of water

 IV.  Conservation of water

      A.  Each day 3,000,000 gallons used in our city
      B.  Less water collected now than formerly
      C.  Need to use water wisely and not wastefully
```

Later you can add additional cards for specific materials that relate to single objectives and items of content, or to groups of either.

You will find that using cards makes you free to experiment with the order of the ideas until they are in a logical sequence. What you start with as the first point may later become the last one. Additional objectives that occur as you organize can also be added easily at this stage, while anything that apparently disrupts the sequence can also, just as easily, be eliminated or relocated. Later, during the actual storyboarding and scripting, you may find need for further changes, but now you have a simple, natural guideline to follow.

It should be reemphasized that at this stage you include as much as possible about the content—facts, examples, locations, special reminders, and so forth. It will be easier to eliminate some points later than to search for them if needed. While you are listing content, visual ideas may come to mind. Note them also on cards.

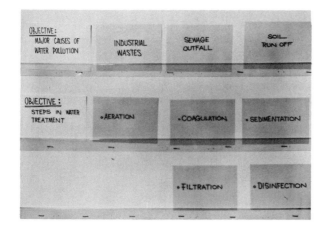

Once the content has been listed in relation to the objectives, you may consider this to be a *checkpoint* time—a time when you want to have other persons look over your progress and offer suggestions and help. Even though you may already have a team that includes subject consultants, it is a good idea to bring in other persons, not directly involved in the project, to examine your work objectively. They may find something important left out, or offer a comment that strikes a spark to give a direction you had not considered.

Often there is real benefit in asking one or more members of the potential audience group to review your planning as you proceed. The perceptions that they may have for your topic and its organization may differ appreciably from yours. Involve them at this checkpoint and others that will be indicated. Their suggestions can be of real value.

Review What You Have Done

Your content outline has been developed in the light of an idea, objectives, and audience. You are now ready to make decisions about the medium or media to carry the objectives and content. Ask yourself such questions as these:

☐ What medium (media) should be used?
☐ Is sound (narration, lip synchronization), necessary, or can a silent medium (films, slides, filmstrip) with titles, captions, and directions be used?
☐ Is motion important or can still pictures convey the ideas and information?
☐ Is there to be study by individuals or is the emphasis to be on group use?
☐ Is color important or will black-and-white be satisfactory?
☐ Will there be any problems in keeping the materials up to date?
☐ Will I be able to overcome any technical problems in preparation, or do I know where to get help if necessary?
☐ Will there be problems of duplication, distribution, or storage of the completed materials?
☐ Will budget and time permit a good job?
☐ What problems may be encountered when using the materials (facilities, equipment, size of group, and the like)?

Now consider the various media available to you—characteristics, best uses, advantages, disadvantages, and limitations. Then make choices to best serve your purposes.

Now Apply What You Have Read

1. Develop a brief content outline for the topic you previously selected. Consider the following questions:
   a. What research should you do on the subject?
   b. Have you included all important information, in the light of your purposes and anticipated audience?
   c. Do ideas for additional visual materials concerning other aspects of the topic come to mind for future consideration?
2. Relate the content to objectives on cards of different colors.

7

THE KINDS OF MATERIALS

Consider the specific contributions and special requirements of these eight audiovisual materials: photographic print series, slide series, filmstrips, recordings, transparencies, motion pictures, television and display materials, and multi-image/ multimedia. Then select those most appropriate to serve your objectives and content.

Notice the sequence that is being developed. First, establish *objectives* and consider your *audience;* then *organize the content* to fit your objectives. Now *select the specific audiovisual materials* and other experiences to carry through your purposes.

Why this sequence? Because audiovisual materials are channels through which content stimuli are presented to the learner—stimuli to motivate, evoke a response, inform, direct attention, evaluate, guide thinking, test for transfer, or whatever. Therefore, only after establishing *what it is that you wish to communicate* are you properly able to select the channel or medium through which the content will most likely elicit the proper response that serves the objective. Review the findings in Chapter 3, relating the effects of media on learning.

If motion is inherent in the subject, consider a motion picture; but if motion is not important, consider materials that demand simpler skills, less time, or less money, yet do the job equally well. To think further: a series of large photographs, which can easily be studied in detail, may be preferable to a filmstrip and less difficult to make. Also, consider using combinations of

media to serve your purposes: a series of transparencies that outline a process can be supplemented with a set of slides and the two used concurrently for effective instruction; or for motivational purposes, a dynamic three-screen presentation may be effective.

On the other hand, perhaps for practice or perhaps because you have certain equipment available, you may wish to prepare a specific material, possibly a series of slides or a motion picture. If this is your starting point, select a subject and establish purposes that will use the medium to its best advantage.

Any one or more of a number of audiovisual materials may be applicable to serve an objective and its content. The decision for selection may be based on your skills, equipment requirements, convenience, or cost. But each of the several types of audiovisual materials makes certain unique contributions to improving communications and subsequent learning. All require careful planning before preparation—some more than others. When selecting the ones to serve your purposes, examine all of them and become aware of their special characteristics and specific contributions to learning.

Photographic Print Series

A photographic print series may consist of drawings or photographs, in black-and-white or in color. Usually they are enlargements from camera negatives or direct prints with a Polaroid Land camera. They may include explanatory captions, and they may be accompanied with directions for their use. They lend themselves to display and to detailed self-instructional follow-up study, or they may be part of a programmed sequence.

Because photo series are normally used by individuals rather than by groups under direction, they need to be self-sufficient and self-explanatory; brief, concise captions impart this quality.

Slide Series

Slides are a form of projected audiovisual materials easy to prepare, hence they frequently serve as the starting effort in a local-production program. The pictures are generally taken on reversal color film, which is sent to a film-processing laboratory where the mounted slides are made up. Since they are ready for projection as the laboratory completes them, relatively little time goes into the mechanics of processing and mounting.

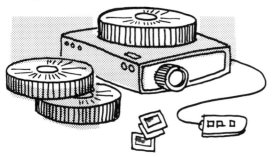

For many uses, any 35-mm camera will make satisfactory slides. But for filming some subjects, for close-up and for copy work, cameras with special attachments are required.

The standard slide dimensions are 2×2 inches. Since the slides are this small, they are easily handled and stored. Their sequence can

be changed, and slides can be selected from a series for special uses. But this flexibility entails some disadvantages. Slides can become out of order, can be misplaced (it is a common occurrence to leave the last slide in the projector!), and sometimes they are accidentally projected upside down or backwards. Most of these disadvantages can be overcome by the use of inexpensive trays and magazines, which store the slides and hold them during use. Also, automatic and remotely controlled projectors permit an instructor, while making his presentation, to make slide changes for himself. Tape recordings can be prepared to accompany slides and, with special recording equipment, slides can be shown automatically as the taped narration is played. The development of small, compact viewers also opens many possibilities for using slides with or without taped narration for self-instructional purposes.

Although 35-mm and 126-size films are most common for photographic slides, cameras requiring film of other sizes also can be used. In addition, Polaroid transparency film, available in two sizes for Polaroid Land cameras, produces completed slides in a few minutes.

Filmstrips

Thirty-five-mm filmstrips are closely related to slides, but instead of being mounted as separate pictures, the film, after processing, remains uncut as a continuous strip. You can make *double-frame filmstrips* using a standard 35-mm camera. Commercial sources usually supply *single-frame filmstrips* with about half the double-frame image area.

Filmstrips have the advantages of compactness, ease of handling for projection, and low cost for duplication when additional copies are needed. Since pictures are always in order, no wrong positioning can occur, as with slides. On the other hand, filmstrips are not flexible since rearrangement of pictures is not possible.

Filmstrips are more difficult to prepare than slides, and they present problems for a beginner. It is not advisable to film subject matter with a 35-mm camera and then use this film directly as a filmstrip. To do this would require extreme care to insure pictures that are consistent in composition and exposure. Usually, enlarged photographs, drawings, and titles are prepared and then photographed in sequence with a suitable 35-mm copy single-frame camera. Or, if you desire to prepare a color filmstrip, start with color slides or with color transparencies. Many commercial film laboratories will convert the slides or transparencies into filmstrip form.

Accompanying narration may be in the form of captions, filmed with the pictures, or separate tape or disk sound recording to supplement the projected picture. In addition to use with regular projectors, lightweight filmstrip viewers are widely available for independent study.

Tape Recordings

With the development of *language laboratories* and then the broadening of their use as *electronic learning laboratories* or *audio centers* to provide audio experiences in many subjects, tape recordings by themselves have become an important addition to the range of audiovisual materials. Recordings may be prepared for group or, more commonly now, for individual listening. Small, compact cassette recorders have made the use of audio materials easy and convenient. Increasing attention is being given to recordings, either by themselves or in combination with printed and projected materials, for self-instruction, often in study areas called *carrels*.

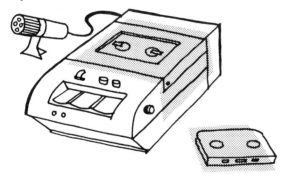

Recordings, for example, can provide brief responsive drill in mathematics or shorthand; can treat English grammar; or can provide language study involving the voice of an expert and allowing opportunities for the student to record his response and then listen to it for comparison with that of the expert. Recordings also can supply information or opportunity for appreciation

listening experiences or serve to lead students through a variety of other learning experiences as in the *audio-tutorial* method of instruction.[1]

But care must be exercised that recordings do not become vague and abstract textbook readings or lengthy verbal lectures. Correlation of the recordings with visual materials is often essential.

Recordings can reach the student directly as he listens in a classroom or as he handles the tapes and equipment in a study area. Recordings can be brought to him at a simple plug-in station, remotely on request via dialing, from a distance over telephone lines at the touch of a button, or at any location when the student uses a portable cassette recorder.

In addition to suitable listening and response facilities, tape-duplicating equipment is necessary when recordings will be used extensively.

Overhead Transparencies

Transparencies are a popular form of locally prepared audiovisual materials. The growing use of large transparencies is supported by the development of small, lightweight, efficient *overhead projectors* combined with simple techniques for preparing transparencies and by the dramatic effectiveness of the medium.

The projector is used from near the front of the room, with the instructor standing or seated beside it, facing the group. The projection screen is behind him, and room light is at a moderate level. Transparencies are placed on the large stage of the projector, and the instructor may point to features and make marks on the film. His work appears immediately on the screen. *Progressively disclosing* areas of a transparency and adding *overlay* films to a base transparency are special features that make the use of this visual medium effective in many subject areas.

Overhead projectors are especially useful for instructing large groups on all educational levels.

1. S. N. Postlethwait et al., *The Audio-Tutorial Approach to Learning* (Minneapolis: Burgess, 1972).

Investigate the range of techniques for preparing transparencies, and select the most appropriate ones for use. Some methods require no special equipment or training, while for others experience in photography and the graphic arts is necessary.

Motion Pictures

Motion pictures, whether 8-mm or 16-mm, are the most complex and can be the most costly of the audiovisual materials to be considered here. They may require costly equipment, skilled personnel, much time for preparation, and much money for materials and services. But for some purposes nothing surpasses the motion picture in effectiveness as a medium of communication. The motion picture should be considered whenever motion is inherent in a subject or when you wish to show relationships of one idea to another, to build a continuity of thought, or to create a dramatic impact.

Films need not be formal and lengthy productions. For some purposes a brief film shown completely in a few minutes is sufficient. It may treat a single concept, a problem situation, or a skill which is explained and applied. Such a film may be instructionally effective without elaborate titles or special motion-picture effects.

For many years educational films have been 16-mm in size, but with the development of super 8-mm cameras, a new era of inexpensive film production appears possible. The availability of both silent and sound continuous-loop and self-threading projectors can make the use of 8-mm films more widely acceptable and pertinent for individual and small-group study.

The next step is the use of 8-mm film as the medium for carrying both still-picture and motion-picture images in any sequential order or arrangement. Equipment for this purpose is available. A series of still/motion 8-mm films, designed for use with a simple hand viewer, is correlated with concepts and techniques in this book. See the description of the viewer and the films available in Appendix A. On page 289 is further discussion of this development.

People with limited knowledge of film production can accomplish various effective techniques, such as time-lapse and slow-motion photography, close-ups, photomicrography, and animation. But generally, someone who has experience in making films should be a member of the production staff if advanced techniques are to be used. Such a person can deal effectively and economically with problems of planning, filming, lighting, editing, title-making, and adding sound.

Television and Display Materials

Under this heading we group the audiovisual materials—graphics, photographs, slides, filmstrips, transparencies, and motion pictures—normally used on television. In addition, display boards and their materials are considered here—either for television use or to serve other instructional needs.

Display boards include felt, hook-and-loop, and magnetic surfaces, with materials backed appropriately for adherence and display on the board. They are most often used to progressively build elements of a presentation or to provide opportunities for students to participate overtly by selecting, arranging, or showing relationships among items displayed.

An instructional television program may, and usually does, employ a combination of visual materials. The success that television has gained in the educational field comes in part from the wise selection of the best aspects of all audiovisual materials and their proper utilization. Audiovisual materials for television are unlike other audiovisual materials in that they are not ends of production but contributions to the total televised presentation; their effectiveness must be assessed in terms of the support they give to the purpose of the entire presentation.

The choice of visuals depends not only upon the purposes to be served by the materials, but also on the ways they will be displayed and used on the program. The method of use will determine whether information should be presented, for example, as a slide for projection or as a large chart for use before the television camera. Ease of preparation, required skills, facilities, time, and material costs are other factors that influence choice.

Finally, the technical requirements of television—format and proportions, size, color, and contrast limitations—must all be considered as materials are selected and prepared.

Motion pictures and televised presentations have similar features. Essentially, both present an event in motion and with sound. But there are important features to consider about each media form, which can be either advantages or disadvantages when selecting a medium for production. For example, with television both picture and sound are recorded simultaneously—in synchronization. But for a motion picture, a camera and separate recorder may be required (there are some direct sound-on-film systems), and the process of combining sound with the picture during editing is both complex and time-consuming. Also, an important advantage of television is being able to immediately view what was recorded, erase, and rerecord if necessary. Each "take" on film requires fresh film, and you wait until after the film is processed to see the results.

On the other hand, television equipment generally is more expensive than motion-picture cameras and projectors. The need for color further increases the price of television recording and viewing equipment. For studio-level television production, the staffing and complexity of operation is much greater than for filming.

Through laboratory services (page 253) each medium can be converted to the other form with satisfactory quality: film to videotape in any size, or videotape to either 16-mm or 8-mm film.

So weigh these and other features of both television and motion pictures as you consider these media for use.

Multi-Image/Multimedia

If a single visual can do the job satisfactorily, avoid the temptation to try something different simply for the novelty of it. But combinations of visual materials are effective when used together for specific purposes—either concurrently or in succession.

When two or more pictures are projected simultaneously onto adjacent screens for group viewing, the term *multi-imagery* is used. Most often the coordinated images on two or three screens are slides with synchronized narration, music, and maybe sound effects. Brief motion-picture sequences or overhead transparencies may be shown along with slides for special impact or to carry appropriate information. Side-by-side images permit comparisons, relationships, perspective views, or multiple examples. Such multi-image presentations are often motivational by creating a high level of interest in a subject as well as by effectively communicating large amounts of information in a short time.

Multimedia refers to the sequential use of a variety of instructional materials in presentations, or the availability of a number of resources in learning packages, kits, or other self-study programs for individual students. For a classroom presentation, an overhead transparency could be used to introduce a unit, with a motion-picture

Summary of Characteristics of Audiovisual Materials   TABLE 7-1

MATERIAL	ADVANTAGES	LIMITATIONS	RELATIVE COST TO PREPARE[a] ORIGINALS DUPLICATES
Photographic print series	1. Permit close-up detailed study at individual's own pacing 2. Are useful as simple self-study materials and for display 3. Require no equipment for use	1. Not adaptable for large groups 2. Require photographic skills, equipment, and darkroom for preparation	$0.20 $0.15 per 8 × 10 inch black and white print $4.00 $4.00 per 8 × 10 inch color print (by processing laboratory)
Slide series	1. Require only filming, with processing and mounting by film laboratory 2. Result in colorful, realistic reproductions of original subjects 3. Prepared with any 35-mm camera for most uses 4. Easily revised and up-dated 5. Easily handled, stored, and rearranged for various uses 6. Increased usefulness with tray storage and automatic projection 7. Can be combined with taped narration for greater effectiveness 8. May be adapted to group or to individual use	1. Require some skill in photography 2. Require special equip- for close-up photography and copying 3. Can get out of sequence and be projected incorrectly if slides are handled individually	$0.35 $0.30 per color slide
Filmstrips	1. Are compact, easily handled, and always in proper sequence 2. Can be supplemented with captions or recordings 3. Are inexpensive when quantity reproduction is required 4. Are useful for group or individual study at projection rate controlled by instructor or user 5. Are projected with simple lightweight equipment	1. Are relatively difficult to prepare locally 2. Require film-laboratory service to convert slides to filmstrip form 3. Are in permanent sequence and cannot be rearranged or revised	$0.75 $0.02 per frame, black and white $3.00 $0.05 per frame, color (by processing laboratory)
Recordings	1. Easy to prepare with regular tape recorders 2. Can provide applications in most subject areas 3. Equipment for use, compact, portable, easy to operate 4. Flexible and adaptable as either individual elements of instruction or in correlation with programed materials 5. Duplication easy and economical	1. Have a tendency for overuse, as lecture or oral textbook reading 2. Fixed rate of information flow	*reel* *cassette* 300 feet—$2.00 C30—$1.75 600 feet—$2.50 C60—$2.00 1200 feet—$4.00 C90—$2.50 1800 feet—$5.50
Overhead transparencies	1. Can present information in systematic, developmental sequences 2. Use simple-to-operate projector with presentation rate controlled by instructor 3. Require only limited planning 4. Can be prepared by variety of simple, inexpensive methods 5. Particularly useful with large groups	1. Require special equipment, facilities, and skills for more advanced preparation methods 2. Are large and present storage problem	$0.40 $0.25 per single sheet of film
Motion pictures	1. May consist of complete films or short film clips 2. Are particularly useful in describing motion, showing relationships, or giving impact to topic 3. 8-mm film reduces cost for materials and services	1. May be expensive to prepare in terms of time, equipment, materials, and services	$7.50 $7.00 50 feet 8-mm color $9.50 $6.00 100 feet 16-mm

[a] Estimated cost of materials for a single unit. Time and special services would be in addition.

Motion pictures (continued)	4. Are useful with groups of all sizes and with individuals 5. Sound is easily added to magnetic film 6. May include special techniques for handling content 7. Insure a consistency in presentation of material	2. Require careful planning and some production skill 3. A changing field in which some present equipment may become obsolete	black-and-white $15.00 $12.00 100 feet 16-mm color· $0.03–$0.06 $0.03–$0.06 per 1 foot of magnetic striping
Television and display materials	1. Permit selecting the best audiovisual media to serve program needs 2. Permit shifting from one medium to another during program 3. Permit normally unavailable resources to be presented 4. Playback capability of video recording permits analysis of on-the-spot action 5. New-type display boards provide flexibility in displaying various kinds of objects and writing on surface	1. Do not exist alone, but are part of total television production 2. Must fit technical requirements of television 3. At times require rapid preparation of materials 4. Some display boards are expensive to make or purchase	Refer to the specific types of material above
Multi-image/ multimedia	1. Combine presentation of slides with other media forms for presentations 2. Use photographs, slides, filmstrips, and recordings in combination for independent study 3. Provide for more effective communications in certain situations than when only a single medium is used	1. Require additional equipment and careful coordination during planning, preparation, and use	Refer to each type of material above

sequence then showing generalized applications of the concept. This might be followed with a series of slides illustrating local examples of the concept. This is an example of multimedia uses in a presentation.

A learning package that contains a cassette recording, a filmstrip, a single-concept 8-mm film, and a printed worksheet, all designed to serve a set of objectives for a topic, is an application of multimedia for independent study.

The rationale behind the use of multimedia resources is two-fold. First, different media are necessary to serve different instructional purposes. A discussion of how to select specific media for instructional needs follows this section. Second, it is recognized that students have different learning styles, and alternative ways of studying with a variety of resources should be available to them. A foundation for both of these matters was set in the first chapter of this book, where the newer procedures in education received attention.

The eight types of audiovisual materials—photographic print series, slide series, filmstrips, recordings, overhead transparencies. motion pictures, television, and display materials—as well as multi-images and multimedia have different planning requirements and different degrees of complexity in preparation and use. Some require close adherence to all steps in the planning process, while others, such as photographs and transparencies, can be developed without strict procedure. Refer to the appropriate sections in Part 4 of this book for guidance as you study the planning steps in Chapter 8.

Selecting Media for Instructional Needs

In this chapter we have examined eight categories of audiovisual materials that can be produced locally. Table 7-1 compares the characteristics, advantages, limitations, and relative costs of each type. These summaries may be enough to assist you in making decisions about specific media to serve your objectives and content.

But many of us select media for use on the basis of what we are most comfortable with or what is conveniently available. The choice is a subjective one, often with little consideration to objective criteria for selection. Can more specific guidelines be established which could offer somewhat closer relationships between the various media and instructional requirements?

This question has been examined by various educational researchers. Their general conclusion is that most media can perform most instructional functions, while no single medium is likely to have properties that make it best for all purposes.

We should not leave the matter of media selection to those who make casual choices, nor can we wait patiently for the results of future research. We need some basis for making logical, educated guesses that will lead to practical media decisions. Fortunately, there are some efforts in this direction.

The most useful results are derived from a consideration of what Levie and Dickie term "media attributes."[2] These are the capabilities of a medium to show such things as motion, color, symbolic representation, simultaneous picture and sound, and so forth. The question of what media attributes are necessary for a given learning situation becomes the basis for media selection. After the appropriate media attributes have been specified, the medium, or group of media, which best incorporates these attributes can be identified.

Application of this approach to media selection has been attempted by some developers. Tosti and Ball identified six "dimensions of presentation" and broadly related media decisions to them;[3] while Briggs uses learner characteristics and the nature of learning involved in terms of Gagné's conditions (page 17).[4] More specific guidance can be obtained from the flow diagrams with leading questions developed by Bretz.[5] His questions point the way through levels, terminating in a particular medium or group of related media.

A similar practical approach for media selection can start with answers to three general questions:[6]

1. Which teaching/learning pattern (page 4)—presentation, individualized learning, or small group interaction—is selected or is most appropriate for the objective and the nature of the student group?

2. Which category of learning experiences—direct realistic experiences, verbal or printed word abstractions, or vicarious, sensory experience—is most suitable for the objective and instructional activity in terms of the selected teaching/learning pattern?

3. If sensory experience is indicated or selected, which attributes of media are necessary or desirable?

Upon answering the three questions, refer to the appropriate Media Selection diagram that follows on page 49. Each diagram is a sequence chart for a teaching/learning pattern. Questions which match media attributes to learner-objective needs are answered at various levels and lead to media choices.

Often the decision reaches a group of related media, such as still pictures. Each still-picture form—for example, photographs, slides, or a filmstrip—would provide equally effective instruction for an individual. The choice, then, is based on the most practical form to use, considering the relative merits of a number of empirical factors, such as those shown in Table 7-2.[7]

Finally, media decisions should be made not for a gross entity of learning as large as a *topic*, but rather for individual objectives that collectively make up the topic. Within a given topic, carefully designed combinations of media, where each performs a particular function, based on its attributes, and reinforces the learning effects of the others, may be required to achieve the kind of instruction for group or individual that is most effective.

2. Howard Levie and Kenneth E. Dickie, "The Analysis and Application of Media," in *Second Handbook of Research on Teaching* (Chicago: Rand McNally, 1973), pp. 858–82.

3. Donald T. Tosti and John R. Ball, "A Behavioral Approach to Instructional Design and Media Selection," *AV Communication Review* 17 (Spring 1969): 5–25.

4. Leslie J. Briggs, *Handbook of Procedures for the Design of Instruction* (Pittsburgh, Pa.: American Institute for Research, 1970).

5. Rudy Bretz, *The Selection of Appropriate Communications Media for Instruction* (Santa Monica, Calif.: Rand Corp., 1971).

6. Jerrold E. Kemp, "Which Medium?" *Audiovisual Instruction* 16 (December 1971): 32–36.

7. Adapted from Jerrold E. Kemp, *Instructional Design: A Plan for Unit and Course Development* (Belmont, Calif.: Fearon Publishers, 1971), p. 68.

Media Selection Diagrams

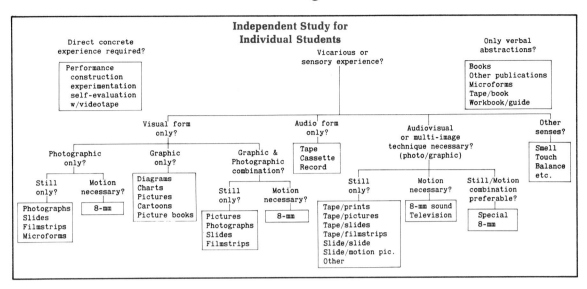

Independent Study for Individual Students

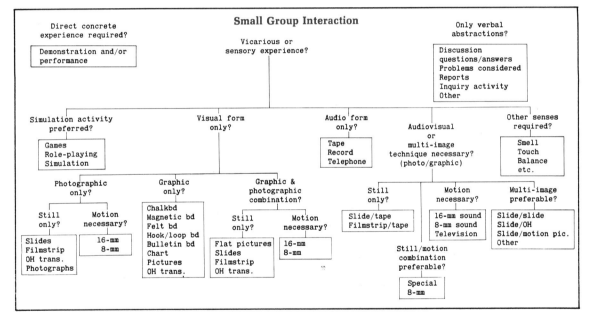

Small Group Interaction

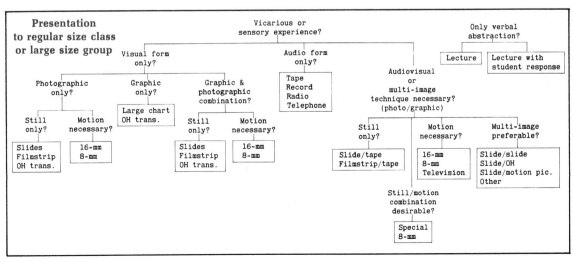

Presentation to regular size class or large size group

TABLE 7-2   Final Media Choice within a Category

	ALTERNATE MATERIALS		
CRITERIA	PHOTOGRAPHS	SLIDES	FILMSTRIP
Commercially available			
Preparation costs			
Reproduction costs			
Time to prepare			
Skills/services required			
Viewing-handling			
Maintenance-storage			
Student preference			
Instructor preference			

Now Apply What You Have Read

1. Of the eight types of audiovisual materials described in this section, which are of special value for: (a) individual study? (b) use with a large group?
2. Describe a multimedia use you might plan to make of two kinds of audiovisual materials in teaching a topic.
3. Refer to the Media Selection diagrams in this chapter on page 00 and choose a medium for these situations:
   a. Presentation to a group—visual diagram of an industrial-flow process developed progressively.
   b. Independent study—still color pictures with sound of architectural styles for 200 students to use in study carrels.
   c. Small-group interaction—visuals with motion and sound as a report on community recreational facilities.
4. In Question 2 following Chapter 4, you were directed to select a topic and to start planning for the preparation of an audiovisual material. What material would you now choose for use in developing this topic? Why do you think it is the most appropriate?

Answers to Review Questions

1. *Individual use*   *Group use*
   Photo print series   —
   Slide series   Slide series
   Filmstrips   Filmstrips
   —   Overhead transparencies
   Tape recordings   Tape recordings
   8-mm motion pictures   8-mm and 16-mm motion pictures
   Television   Television
                        Display materials
   Multimedia   Multi-images/Multimedia
2. Reader's activity
3. (a) Overhead transparency, (b) Color filmstrip, (c) Television recording
4. Reader's activity

8

MAPPING THE WAY

Prepare a descriptive synopsis of the content; then a storyboard; finally, write the script—a "map" for your production—and from it prepare the necessary specifications.

You have your content organized in terms of objectives and the audience. You are aware of the kinds of audiovisual materials you may consider for preparation, their characteristics and particular contributions, advantages, and limitations. And you have some empirical procedures for media selection. In putting all these together you must decide which materials can best communicate the content of specific objectives. Your plans may require that a single medium (film, slides, transparencies, or such) carry your message. Or, in the design approach, a number of media may be integrated, each serving one or more specific objectives and content.

Examine the cards you prepared listing objectives and content. Then decide on the medium or media to use.

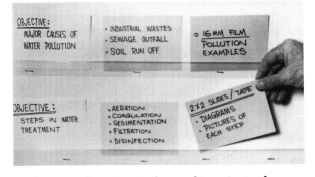

If more than a single medium is to be employed, make cards for each one and organize the objective and content cards with the appropriate medium cards. This plan will give you a visual reference to the flow and relationship of elements within the total topic. Now, start planning for production.

How do you handle the content? Should you start with the first item and plan to go systematically through the whole outline, making a picture for each heading and fact? Is it best to organize your script logically, or to build from the simple to the complex, regardless of the outline order?

There is no single best manner in which the details of the content outline can be transformed into meaningful and related pictures and words. Two approaches have been established through experience, but they are by no means the only sound ones. First, many successful materials carry an audience from the known to the unknown; they start with things familiar to the audience (perhaps by reviewing the present level of understanding) and then lead to as many new facts and new relationships as the material is meant to achieve. Second, many materials are successfully built around three divisions—the introduction, which captures the attention of the audience; the developmental stage, which contains most of the content and in effect tells the story (or involves the viewers in active participation); and, finally, the ending, which may summarize or review the ideas presented and suggest further activity.

51

Recall from Chapter 3 that there is evidence from research to show that detailed introductions and summaries in films, and probably in other audiovisual materials, do not add much to effectiveness. This finding may be particularly true of a series of integrated materials, each of which serves a specific objective. The single-concept film, illustrating a process, and the short tape recording of drill material are examples of the latter kinds of materials. A printed study guide or instruction sheet can introduce, relate, summarize, and direct student participation. The material itself contains just the essential facts, explanations, demonstrations, or whatever, without any embellishments.

Plan for Participation

A number of investigations of the effectiveness of audiovisual materials have shown the value of having the learner participate in some way during, or immediately after, the study of the material. These experiments, without reservation, have proven that *active participation definitely helps learning.* But most producers of audiovisual materials ignore this principle. Films, filmstrips, and sets of transparencies are designed primarily to present information and, within themselves, provide no opportunity or directions for other than passive activity—mentally or mechanically following the presentation. Hopefully, the treatment of the subject is so motivational that interest is maintained throughout. But often it is not. It is then left up to the teacher or presenter to plan for pre- and post-use activities (possibly with the help of study-guide suggestions).

The way to create participation is to make involvement an inherent part of the material itself. This is a key element of programmed materials—the learner is actively doing something as he studies.

Here are some suggestions for developing participation in audiovisual materials:

☐ Include questions, requiring an immediate written or oral response.
☐ Direct other written activity (explain, summarize, give other examples, and so forth).
☐ Require selection, judgment, or other decisions to be made from among things shown or heard.
☐ Require performance related to the activity or skill shown or heard.

These participation techniques often require a break in the presentation—having the student stop the projector to do something, or promoting immediate activity after studying a section of the material.

Also, be sure to plan for evaluation of the participation results and provide *feedback* to the student indicating the correct reply or a comparison of measurement for his level of accomplishment.

Write the Treatment

Carefully examine the example of a content outline (page 39) and for an idea of how you might develop the generalizations visually. Form several such ideas. Put them into written narrative form, as you might summarize a book or a motion picture. You will, however, work from the synopsis toward your motion picture or slide series or other material. Two or more treatments that handle the subject in different ways (informational, personal involvement, or dramatic) can be written so as to explore different approaches to the topic.

The treatment may combine the qualities of narration, personal involvement, and drama.

Writing the treatment is an important step since it causes you to think through your presentation, putting it in a sequential, organized form that you and others can follow easily.

Make a Storyboard

As you develop your story, *try to visualize the situations you are describing.* Remember, you are preparing an audiovisual material—with the emphasis on the word *visual.* Most people normally think in words, but now you may have to reorient yourself and learn to think in pictures—not in vague general pictures but in specific visual representations of real situations. Visualization can be aided by making simple sketches or by taking pictures (instant pictures with Polaroid film are ideal for this purpose) that show the treatment of each element or sequence. These sketches or pictures, along with narration notes, become the storyboard. Here is an example of a partial storyboard for *Our Water Supply,* using various techniques.

Put the storyboard sketches or pictures on cards, as was suggested for the objectives and content on page 38. Use 4×6 inch cards or 8½×11 inch paper. These proportions approximate the format of most visual materials, the pictures being wider than they are high. Use a card with an area blocked off for the visual and having space for narration notes or production comments.

Examples of Treatment

INFORMATIONAL TREATMENT—OUR WATER SUPPLY

Our water supply originates in the Sierra Nevada and flows through the Mokelumne River to a storage reservoir near the city. Then it enters the water purification plant, where the water is treated in five steps—aeration, coagulation, sedimentation, filtration, and disinfection. Laboratory tests are made to insure the water's high quality. After it leaves the plant it is sent to storage tanks and eventually to its many uses throughout the city.

PERSONAL-INVOLVEMENT TREATMENT—OUR WATER SUPPLY

What do we know about our water—where does it come from? how much of it is there? how is it made safe for our use? Two 15-year-old boys became curious about these questions while swimming one day. They checked in the school library and came across a pamphlet describing the city's water supply. They then made arrangements to visit the water purification plant. The supervisor took them on a tour. He showed them a large map, indicating that our water originates in the Sierra Nevada and then flows through the Mokelumne River to our city. In the treatment process the boys saw the aeration and coagulation tanks, the sedimentation basins, and the filter beds. They found out how chlorine was added to water as a disinfectant and also some of the tests made in the laboratory. With the information they read and the things they saw, the boys were now able to answer their own questions about our water supply.

DRAMATIC TREATMENT—OUR WATER SUPPLY

Water is indispensable—without it all living things die; fires cannot be extinguished; and many industries cease to operate. Nature provides our source of water. For our community it comes from the Sierra Nevada and reaches us via the Mokelumne River. But the amount is not unlimited. We must conserve it and use it wisely—otherwise desolation and lifelessness will result. And not only must we have water, but it must be pure water, free from disease-causing micro-organisms and impurities. Many diseases in man and animal arise from dirty and polluted water. Therefore we purify water. For our community, water treatment includes five steps —aeration, coagulation, sedimentation, filtration, and disinfection. Pure water and carefully used water contribute to life, growth, and good health for all living things.

COMBINATION TREATMENT—OUR WATER SUPPLY

Water serves us in many important ways. It is essential for all life on earth. Where does our water come from? How is it purified for our use? Our water supply originates in the Sierra Nevada and flows through the Mokelumne River to a storage reservoir near the city. Then it enters the water purification plant, where the water is treated in five steps— aeration, coagulation, sedimentation, filtration, and disin-fection. Laboratory tests are made to insure the water's high quality. After it leaves the plant it is sent to storage tanks and eventually to its many uses throughout the com-munity, where conservation and wise use of water are essential.

Every sequence should be represented by one or more cards. Include separate cards for possible titles, questions, and special directions (such as indications for student participation). It may not be necessary to make a card for all anticipated scenes. The details, like an overall picture of a subject followed by a close-up of detail within the subject, will be handled in the script that follows.

The storyboard is another important *checkpoint* stage in the development of your audiovisual material. Display it. Make it easy to examine.[1]

Reactions and suggestions from those involved in the project or from other interested and qualified persons are valuable at this point. These people may offer assistance by evaluating the way you visualize your ideas and the continuity of your treatment. Often people studying the dis-

played storyboard point out things that have been missed or sequences that need reorganization. Rearranging pictures and adding new ones are easy when the storyboard is prepared on sheets of paper or on cards.[2]

Develop the Script

Once the treatment and the storyboard continuity are satisfactorily organized, you are ready to write your detailed blueprint, the *script*. This

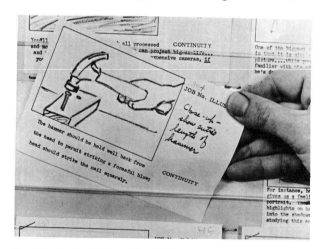

Storyboard in Use (Reproduced with permission from the Kodak pamphlet *Planning and Producing Visual Aids*)

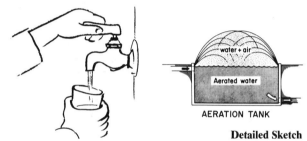

Simple Sketch

AERATION TANK

Detailed Sketch

35mm Contact Print (or 2″×2″ Slide)

Polaroid Print

Enlarged Photograph

Storyboard Card Containing Visual, Production Notes, and Suggested Narration (Reproduced with permission from the Kodak pamphlet *Planning and Producing Visual Aids*)

---

2. Plastic Planningstrips are available from Chicago Paper Box Co., 732 North Morgan Street, Chicago, Ill., 60622.

Ready made planning boards and printed cards are available from Medro Educational Products, P.O. Box 8463, Rochester, N.Y., 14618.

---

1. See *Audiovisual Planning Equipment*, pamphlet T-11, Eastman Kodak Company, for directions on constructing a storyboard.

script becomes the map that gives definite directions for your picture-taking, art work, or filming. The script is a picture-by-picture listing with accompanying narration or captions. As was indicated for storyboarding, *first* plan what will be seen, then what will be said or captioned. Write the script in a two-column format, placing camera positions and picture descriptions on the left half of the page and narration on the right, opposite the appropriate scene descriptions. (See the example below.)

The placement of the camera for each picture, with respect to the subject, should be indicated. If the subject is to be at a distance from the camera the picture is a *long shot* (LS); if the camera covers the subject and nothing more, a *medium shot* (MS); while a *close-up* (CU) brings the camera in to concentrate on a feature of the subject. Whether the scene is to be photographed from a *high angle* or a *low angle*, or *subjective* (from the subject's viewpoint, as over his shoulder) can also be specified. (For further information on camera positions, see page 235 in Chapter 23.)

An Example of a Script

SCRIPT—<u>OUR WATER SUPPLY</u>

	Visual	Narration Idea
1.	Main Title: <u>OUR WATER SUPPLY</u>.	
2.	CU Hand turning water faucet and filling a glass of water.	The water we take for granted —where does it come from? How is it purified?
3.	LS Snow-covered mountains.	It starts in the Sierra Nevada.
4.	LS Mokelumne River.	The Mokelumne carries it west.
5.	LS Upper reservoir.	It is held in the reservoir.
6.	MS Entrance to the water-treatment plant.	It is purified in our treatment plant.
7.	MS Aeration tank (overprint: <u>Aeration</u>).	The first step is to spray the water in the air.
8.	CU Spraying water.	This is aeration: air is mixed with the water.
9.	Diagram of aeration process.	Aeration improves the water's flavor.
10.	LS High Angle. Coagulation tanks (overprint: <u>Coagulation</u>).	The next step is coagulation, to start the removal of impurities.
11.	CU Mixing water in tank.	Here alum is mixed with the water.
12.	Diagram of coagulation process.	Impurities coagulate together to form large masses.
13.	LS High Angle. Sedimentation basins (overprint: <u>Sedimentation</u>).	Third step—sedimentation, the settling of impurities,
14.	CU Edge of tank as clear water runs over side into trough.	while clear water flows off at the top.

15.	Diagram of sedimentation basin.	Scrapers remove the settled impurities at the bottom.
16.	LS High Angle. Filtration beds (overprint: <u>Filtration</u>).	Then the water is filtered
17.	CU A single filter in operation.	through beds of sand and gravel.
18.	Diagram of a filter bed.	Make-up of filter beds—fine sand at top with progressively coarser gravel below.
19.	MS Chlorine gas tank.	Finally chlorine is added to kill bacteria.
20.	Diagram of chlorination process.	Chlorine is a disinfectant.
21.	MS Two chemists at work in laboratory.	Chemists check the quality of purified water at short intervals.
22.	Diagram. Total purification process—without labels.	Review the steps by questioning what takes place in each step of the treatment process and how each is accomplished.
23.	Repeat diagram in scene 22—with labels.	Review the steps by answering questions in scene 22.
24.	MS Low Angle. Large transmission pipe.	Transmission pipes carry water out of the plant
25.	LS Storage tank on hill.	to storage,
26.	Montage (group of pictures) showing uses of water—washing hands, animal drinking, irrigating field, cooking, fire fighting, etc.	and then to many important uses.
27.	MS A parched field.	Importance of water conservation.
28.	CU Hand turning off faucet with full glass beneath.	Use water carefully and not wastefully.

At this stage the narration or captions, indicated along the right-hand side of your script, need not be stated in final, detailed form. It is sufficient to write *narration ideas,* or brief statements, that can be refined later. Only when an explanation requires that a motion-picture scene be of a specific length must the narration be written carefully and in final form at this point.

Narration is important not only for the part it plays in explaining details as the *audio* of audiovisual; it also may call attention to relationships and indicate emphasis that should be given in some pictures (center of attention or camera position) when filming.

Be alert to problems that may arise with narration. If it is not related closely to the visual so as to reinforce the visual, the narration may interfere or inhibit learning. Review research evidence in Chapter 3 about the relation between visual and audio channels in audiovisual materials. See page 63 for further suggestions concerning writing narration.

On page 55 is an example of a script for *Our Water Supply,* developed chiefly from the informational treatment, with some details adopted from the other treatments.

Consider the Length

The content of an audiovisual material affects the time needed to present it. You need to have time in mind as the script takes shape. Any estimate at this early stage is inevitably loose and approximate, but an estimate is necessary.

How are you to forecast the time that will be needed? The following few facts, from experience, may offer some guidance:

☐ A projected slide or a filmstrip frame can hold attention for about 30 seconds (or it may remain on the screen for only a few seconds).

☐ A 12-inch disk recording, prepared at 33⅓ revolutions per minute to accompany a slide series or filmstrip, will permit a maximum playing time of 18 minutes on one side (a total of 36 minutes on both sides).

☐ The average motion-picture scene runs for 7 seconds; it may range from 2 seconds to 30 seconds or more.

You will collect many more such facts as you gain experience.

Even so, how are you to know whether the material, at whatever estimated duration, is too short, too long, or just right? There is no formula. A film or filmstrip or slide series or picture series must be allowed enough time to permit adequate development of the topic, as based on the purposes, but not be so long that it will lose its effectiveness. A single-concept film may run for 2 or 3 minutes, whereas an orientation film may require 15 to 20 minutes. A filmstrip for primary-grade children would ordinarily be shorter than one designed for high-school students. Also, available time must be considered—do not come up with a 15-minute film in a 10-minute program spot.

When you (and your team) appraise your script against the amount of time desirable or available, you may need to review it to see whether the needed time can be shortened, or the content divided into two or more outlines for a series of presentations.

Prepare the Specifications

You have prepared a map, the script. Now you face the questions: What specific things are to be done now, next, and thereafter until the audiovisual materials are ready to be used? What is to be bought, made, decided? The answers to these are the specifications.

An Example of Simple Specifications

```
        SPECIFICATIONS—OUR WATER SUPPLY

25-35 2 x 2 inch color slides
Two or three titles and four or five drawings for close-up
    photographic copy
Tape-recorded narration of 8-10 minutes duration
Materials to be prepared during last 6 weeks of first semester
    for use during second semester
All facilities and equipment available at no cost; most
    picture-taking at water-treatment plant

Budget:

Two rolls 35-mm 36-exposure Kodachrome II
    film, with processing ...........................$14.00

Two sets slide duplicates ............................ 18.00

Art supplies ......................................... 3.50

One roll 300 feet x ¼ inch magnetic recording tape ...... 2.00

Two C30 audio cassettes .............................. 3.50
                                                      _____
                                                       $40.50
```

The more complex the projected audiovisual material, the more numerous the specifications. Naturally they need to be organized and classified. Some classes of specifications have no bearing on some kinds of materials, while on others (slide series, filmstrips, motion pictures, multi-images) all may be needed. Here are some examples of specifications, with detailed and specific points that must be considered and choices that must be made:

☐ *Type of audiovisual material:* photo series, slides, filmstrip, recordings, transparencies, motion picture, television, display materials, or multi-images/multimedia
☐ *Material and size:* Kodachrome, diazo film, 8-mm or 16-mm, 5×7 inch prints
☐ *Length:* approximate number of photographs, slides, filmstrip frames, transparencies; running time for motion picture or tape recording

☐ *Sound:* tape-recorded narration, synchronous sound, magnetic-strip sound track; silent reading matter; titles, captions, labels
☐ *Facilities and equipment:* locations for filming, camera equipment and accessories, graphic and photographic supplies
☐ *Special techniques required:* high-contrast photography, color processing, copy work, time-lapse, animation, microphotography; art work, titles, diazo reproduction
☐ *Special assistance required:* for acting, filming, lighting, graphics, sound recording, film processing, printing, duplicating, secretarial
☐ *Completion date:* planned for or *must* be completed by when?
☐ *Budget estimate:* including film and other materials, equipment purchase or rental, film laboratory and other services, salaries (if applicable), overhead charges, and miscellaneous items.

Now Apply What You Have Read

1. Examine the sample treatments on page 35. Which one or ones do you consider the easiest to visualize as a script? Which treatments are verbally oriented, and which ones are visually oriented?
2. What is the recommended format for a script?
3. Show that there is more than one way of handling your topic's content. Prepare two brief treatments of the topic you selected on page 53, each having a different approach and giving a different emphasis to the topic. Keep in mind your audience and your purposes.
4. Consider the type of audiovisual material you would like to prepare. Does it fit the presentation of the content you have treated?
5. Sketch a few sequences of your storyboard on cards.
6. Prepare a script from the treatment and storyboard. Describe the scenes carefully, using letter abbreviations for camera positions. Write narration ideas if appropriate.
7. List the specifications necessary for your materials.

Answers to Review Questions

1. Informational treatment should be easiest to visualize.
   Verbal approach—dramatic treatment
   Visual approach—informational, combination, personal-involvement (last one most difficult)
2. Two-column format; visuals described on left and narration with other sounds on right.
3–6. Reader's activity.

9

MAKING THE PICTURES

Prepare a schedule for filming; then complete all art work and take pictures, keeping a record of all activities.

Now for the actual production.

Production is the point at which some people, unfortunately and mistakenly, start their work on audiovisual materials. It is difficult to convince some people that they need to do some thoughtful planning before making pictures. They may feel they do not have the time to plan, or that they are too knowledgeable about their subject to have to plan. Or they may be so taken with the mechanical phases of production (camera operation, sound recording, film editing, and so forth) that they have an insatiable urge to do something and see results *right now!* If you deal with such a person, you probably will not be able to influence him differently. Let him, then, go directly to production. Most often the results will easily show the fallacy of this approach and the added expense of unplanned production. Experience is sometimes the best teacher!

There is one situation in which unplanned picture taking may be necessary. See the discussion of *doucumentary* production on page 60.

You will generally find, in contrast to what results from precipitate picture taking, that planning and writing a script will enable you to visualize your ideas more clearly and that the final result will serve your purpose better because of its coherence and completeness. In the long run you will probably also save time and money by eliminating errors, reducing the need for retakes, and not forgetting scenes when picture taking.

Detailed graphic and photographic techniques for preparing specific audiovisual materials are presented in Parts 3 and 4 of this book. Some general practices (especially for making photographic print series, slide series, filmstrips, and motion pictures) are considered here.

Schedule the Picture Taking

Prepare a list, grouping together all scenes to be made at the same location, those having related camera positions at a single location, or those with other similarities. Then schedule each group for filming at the same time. Preparing and using this list will save you time. You will achieve further economies if you visit locations, check facilities, and gather items (props) for use prior to the time of filming. But remember—if you take pictures out of script order you must be especially careful to edit them back into their correct position and relationship with other scenes.

Take the Pictures

In general, the script outline of scene content should be followed. Sometimes, however, as you prepare to take a picture, it becomes evident that a script change is needed. If a single picture as planned does not convey the intent of the script,

Example of a
Filming Schedule

```
FILMING SCHEDULE—OUR WATER SUPPLY

At Water Plant

12/14

     Scene   6 — MS Entrance
            10 — LS High Angle Coagulation tanks
            13 — LS High Angle Sedimentation basins
            16 — LS High Angle Filtration beds
             7 — MS Aeration tank
             8 — CU Spraying water
            11 — CU Water in coagulation tank
            14 — CU Edge of sedimentation tank
            17 — CU Filter bed
           etc.

At School

12/16

     Scene   2 — CU Hand on faucet
            28 — CU Hand on faucet
           etc.
```

two pictures may be necessary. Don't hesitate to take them. Or, if you are uncertain about exposure, make an extra take of the same scene with different camera settings. Also, if desirable, repeat a scene, shooting it from a second position or with a change in action. In such cases, the entry on the record sheet (see page 61) should indicate *take 1,* then *take 2,* and so forth, *all of the same scene.* Be flexible in your picture taking. You spend less time and energy making adjustments at this time than you would spend retaking pictures later if they are found to be unsatisfactory—and you have extra pictures from which to make choices during editing.

When filming a motion picture, rehearse each scene before shooting. Rehearsals permit a check on the action so that the cameraman can "set" his shot and the actor can "feel" the action he is performing. For still pictures, carefully set the scene and check the appearance through the camera viewer before clicking the shutter.

There may be times when a *documentary* approach to all or portions of an audiovisual material is necessary. In such cases, pictures are taken of events as they happen, without preplanning or detailed script preparation. It is recommended that this approach be followed only for special cases (athletic events, large-group activities, meetings, spontaneous classroom activity, and other uncontrolled situations). Often two or more cameras are used and coordinated so as to capture all important action. (See the suggestions for *multicamera filming* on page 241. Many of

these recommendations apply to still-picture taking as well as to motion pictures.) The documentary technique puts an extra burden on the photographers, and the editing stage becomes extremely important for making decisions that may affect the final treatment of the subject (see page 246 for suggestions concerning preparing a script *after* documenting an activity on film). The producer of a documentary audiovisual needs greater experience and must give more attention to technical details than the producer of a planned and scripted material, since in a documentary production there can seldom be any retakes. The cameraman must think in sequences and not in individual shots. He must recall what went before and anticipate what will be happening and be ready to record it. Contrast to this the making of a preplanned audiovisual material in which all scenes are thought out in advance and content is controlled.

Keep a Record

Keep a careful record, a *log sheet,* of all pictures taken. It indicates the order in which scenes were photographed, and it includes data on exposure settings (unless a camera with automatic settings is used) and remarks about the suitability of the action. This record will be useful to you while evaluating picture quality and content when selecting scenes. These items are important:

Example of a Log Sheet

```
                        LOG SHEET

Title:  Our Water Supply          Date: 12/14
Film:   Kodachrome II Daylight    Location: Water Plant
Camera: Pentax #1
Meter:  Sekonic #2


              Light               Dis-
Scene  Take   Value   f/stop  Speed  tance    Remarks

  6     1     200      10     1/60   15 feet
  6     2     200      10     1/60   12 feet  low angle
 10     1     400      14     1/60   40 feet
 13     1     400      14     1/60   30 feet  poor composi-
                                               tion
 13     2     400      14     1/60   30 feet  better
etc.
```

☐ Scene number (according to the script)
☐ Take number (change each time the same scene is filmed)
☐ Light intensity (reading from light meter, if used)
☐ Camera settings (lens, shutter speed, and distance)
☐ Remarks (notes about the action, scene composition, and reminders for editing)

Permission for Pictures

Almost everyone has the right to control the use of pictures of himself or his property. If you are making audiovisual materials you must respect this right. If you fail to do so, you may expose yourself to personal, professional, or financial embarrassment. Specifically, a person may either permit you or forbid you to show pictures of himself, his children, or his property. It does not matter whether you show them free or for a compensation, to a large or small audience, or whether you show them yourself or turn them over to someone else to be shown.

Most people readily agree to being filmed and to having the pictures used, but you should protect yourself and your associates by having them *sign a release form*. (A suitable release form is shown below.) The release authorizing the use of pictures of a minor child must be signed by the parent.

A special kind of property that must be covered by a signed release is the property in copyrighted materials—commonly books, magazines, other printed matter, and commercial films. In

A Sample Release Form

```
                    Date:

I hereby give permission to (insert name of individual, group,
or institution making the audiovisual materials) to make
pictures of me, of my minor child (insert name of child), or
of materials owned by me and to put the finished pictures to
any legitimate use without limitation or reservation.

        Signature:

        Name printed:

        Address:

        City:                        State:

Project:

Director:
```

this case you must get the clearance from the owner of the copyright, *not* the owner of the object. (You may own this book; but you do not own the copyright in it—see the back of the title page.) You will be wise if you assume that books and the like are copyrighted, and seek clearance before you use pictures of them or parts of them in your audiovisual materials.

Currently the United States Congress is revising the copyright laws that were written in 1909. The draft law permits a teacher to make copies of recordings and other audiovisual materials for purely noncommercial teaching uses as long as the materials are for *use in the classroom,* whereas the 1909 law restricts this use. This is without restrictions. The proposed law does not permit the extension of this right of free reproduction to materials used other than by a teacher in *direct* classroom instruction. This means that copyrighted materials for use in motion pictures, slide series, filmstrips, recordings, or television cannot be reproduced without permission. This applies to materials designed for independent study by students, for use in audio listening centers, to be used by a teacher *other than the one preparing the material,* or whatever.

Since this book will be published before Congress completes its work on the new copyright bill, it is recommended that you check into the final requirements of the bill. Contact the Copyright Office in Washington, D.C. This will give you correct and complete information on copyright.

Now Apply What You Have Read

All activities discussed in this book up to now have been concerned with the planning phase of your audiovisual production. Now make pictures and prepare drawings. Refer to the how-to-do-it sections in Parts 3 and 4.

If appropriate:
1. Make a prefilming schedule.
2. Keep a log sheet.
3. Get clearances.

10

SELECTING AND ORGANIZING

Examine all drawings and pictures, select and arrange them into final order, and then match narration or captions to them.

Once the pictures are prepared you are ready for the concluding major step in the production process. During filming the pictures may have been taken out of script sequence, some scenes not indicated in the script may have been filmed, and more than one take may have been made of some subjects. During preparation of the script, the narration or captions were written in rough form or noted only as ideas. These changes and unfinished work give rise to the need for examination, careful appraisal, selection, then organization of all pictures, and the refinement of narration and captions. These activities become the all-important *editing* stage.

The Editing Process—Pictures

Using the script and the log sheets completed while filming, put all pictures in proper order. Inexpensive *contact prints* or *proof copies* of still pictures (page 108) or *workprint* from original motion-picture footage (page 253) can be used for editing.

Now choices must be made from among multiple takes of a scene. Examine all your work critically. You must be impersonal in your judgment and eliminate pictures that fail to make a suitable contribution to your specific purposes, and you must be firm in rejecting pictures that do not meet your standards of quality.

If you have made changes in the original script (page 55) by adding scenes or changing the sequence, rewrite the picture side to fit the edited picture version. Then complete the narration or caption side of the script as described below.

The Editing Process—Narration and Captions

Since your original script may have included only rough drafts or mere ideas for narration, there is need for further developing and rewriting the narration or captions in order to correlate words with the edited pictures.

As was indicated in explaining the storyboard on page 52, most of us think in words, and therefore we have a tendency to attempt to communicate with words more readily than with pictures. Even so, we comprehend things more effectively and retain information much longer when major ideas are presented visually in the form of pictures while being supplemented with written or spoken words. Words thus have an important part to play in your materials, but generally they should be secondary to the pictures. They can direct attention, explain details, raise questions, serve as transitions from one picture or idea to the next, and aid in preserving the continuity of the materials. If you find you have to use many words to explain what a picture shows, or to describe things not shown in a picture, perhaps the picture deserves another critical evaluation and possible replacement, or you may need to add a supplementary picture. *Let the pictures tell the greater part of your story.* If they do not, you will have a lecture with illustrations and you will fail to use the audiovisual medium at its best.

Keep in mind your anticipated audience and its background as you refine the narration. The audience will have bearing on the vocabulary you use and on the complexity and pacing of the commentary (page 33). Lengthy narration and long captions are detrimental to the effects of visual

Part of a Revised Script, with Pictures for Reference

OUR WATER SUPPLY

Visual	Slide	Narration
1. Main Title: OUR WATER SUPPLY.		
2. CU Hand turning water faucet and filling a glass with water.		The water we take for granted—do you know where it comes from? Is there enough for our continued use? How is it purified?
3. LS Snow-covered mountains.		The story of our water supply begins in the Sierra Nevada. When snow melts or rain falls,
4. MS Mokelumne River.		the Mokelumne River carries the water westward.
5. LS Upper reservoir.		A large amount is collected and held in the reservoir north of the city.
6. LS Entrance to the water-treatment plant.		The water is purified in our treatment plant. Each day 3,000,000 gallons are processed.

7. LS Aeration tank.

The process starts by spraying water into the air.

8. CU Spraying water (overprint: Aeration).

This is known as aeration: oxygen from the air is added to the water.

9. Diagram of aeration process.

AERATION TANK

As oxygen mixes with water it improves its flavor and also destroys certain types of bacteria.

10. LS High Angle. Coagulation tanks.

[and so on]

Now impurities must be removed from the water. In the coagulation tanks the chemical alum is added and mixed with water for 10-20 minutes.

[and so on]

materials. For example, the average narration should require viewing a slide for no more than 30 seconds; a filmstrip caption should be no longer than 15 or 20 words. The average length of a motion-picture scene is 7 seconds; individual scenes, depending upon action and narration required, range from 2 seconds to possibly 30 seconds running time.

Here are some suggestions for developing narration:[1]

☐ Narration should supplement the picture by making direct reference to picture content (directing attention, explaining details, providing transitions) rather than compete with the picture for attention by describing or discussing things not shown in the picture.

☐ Identify the picture subject being shown (especially if unusual) as quickly as possible with cue words or phrases. Identification that comes late in a written or spoken line may find the viewer lost in his attempt to understand what is being shown.

☐ Be sure to use proper grammar, words, and expressions. Keep sentences short and avoid

multiple clauses. Use simple, straightforward English as in conversation.

☐ Write enough to carry the picture as necessary—then stop writing.

☐ Have some pauses in narration, otherwise the audience will stop listening.

☐ Realize that one bit of narration can cover a number of pictures, and that narration can carry over from one scene to the next.

Formative Evaluation

As editing of both pictures and words continues, consider such questions as:

☐ Does the material satisfactorily serve the original objectives?

☐ Is there a smooth flow from one picture or idea to the next one?

☐ Does the narration aid in continuity and support the visuals?

☐ Is the material too long overall, requiring deletions?

☐ Have important points, not apparent before, been left out?

☐ Should some of the pictures be replaced or need additional ones be made?

☐ Is the material technically good?

1. Suggestions adapted from the *Aperture,* monthly publication of the Calvin Company, Kansas City, Missouri.

You may do better than quiz yourself. Here is another good checkpoint for an evaluation of your materials in terms of your objectives by other subject and audiovisual specialists, or even by a potential audience group. Show the edited visuals and read the narration or captions. A brief questionnaire for reactions and suggestions may be helpful.

This checkpoint is often called the *formative evaluation* step. Feedback and reactions may reveal misconceptions that are conveyed, shortcomings, or other needs for improvement. You can still make changes before your materials are in final form and reproduced for actual use. The final product will be a better one for your having done a careful formative evaluation.

An Example of a
Preview-Appraisal
Questionnaire

```
            OUR WATER SUPPLY

Purposes
1.  This set of slides is designed principally to explain steps
    in water purification and secondly to encourage conserva-
    tion of water.  How well do you feel these purposes are
    accomplished?
    _____

2.  Are there other purposes you believe these slides might
    serve?
    _____

Audience
1.  These slides and the narration are designed for ninth-
    grade science students.  Is the content appropriate?
    _____

    Are the pacing of the narration and the vocabulary
    appropriate?
    _____

Content and technical quality
1.  Has any important information been left out?
2.  Are there any errors or inconsistencies in the presentation?
3.  Would you suggest any reorganization?  If so, specify.
4.  Is the material technically acceptable?  Would you replace
    any slides?
    _____

    What is your rating of the slides and the narration in
    terms of the purposes to serve the indicated audience?

        Excellent      Good      Fair      Poor
```

Now Apply What You Have Read

1. This section mentions a checkpoint. In what previous sections were other checkpoints suggested? What purposes do such checks serve?
2. What procedures would you follow in editing your materials: (a) the pictures? (b) the narration?

Answers to Review Questions

1. Other checkpoints: content outline (page 40), storyboard review (page 54).
   To obtain reactions, suggestions, and help that might improve your audiovisual materials.
2. Reader's activity.

11

COMPLETING THE PROJECT

**Prepare titles and captions; then record narration
and reproduce materials into final, complete form.**

A few technical tasks remain before your materials are ready for the first formal showing. These include: making and filming titles and captions, recording narration on tape or on magnetic-striped film, and preparing final copies of photographs, slides, filmstrip, transparencies, or motion picture.

Prepare Titles and Captions

Titles serve to introduce the viewer to the subject. The *main title* presents the subject. *Credit titles* acknowledge contributions of those who participated in or cooperated with the project. *Special titles* and *subtitles* introduce individual sequences and may serve to emphasize or to clarify particular pictures. An *end title* gives your audiovisual material a completed appearance.

A little thought and some care in preparation and in filming will result in neat, professional-looking titles, captions, and labels. They should be simple, brief, easily understood, and large enough to be read when projected. Complex, vague, illegible titles confuse the audience rather than arouse its interest in an otherwise good production.

Other sections of this book will assist you in the preparation and the filming of titles and graphic materials:

☐ Making titles (page 123)
☐ Preparing artwork (page 111)

☐ Legibility standards for lettered materials (page 120)
☐ Photographic close-up and copy work (page 99)

Some materials, such as those to be less formally presented by integrated use within an instructional design, should not require extensive, formal titles. Keep these materials as simple as possible with an identifying number or brief title and incorporating captions, labels, questions, and directions as necessary. A formal end title may not be needed.

Record the Narration

Once the narration has been refined and, if possible, tested along with the visuals on a typical audience group, you are ready to record it on tape or on magnetic-striped film. Type the narration as full-width, triple-spaced pages for ease of reading. Mark places that will require cueing, pauses, and special emphasis (see the example). Then proceed to make the recording. See Chapter 17 for suggestions.

Final Photographic Work

If for your editing you used inexpensive proof copies of photographs or slides or a workprint of the motion picture, now prepare the final ma-

67

terials or have them prepared in the necessary number of copies. (See the appropriate sections in Part 4 for instructions.) Then check the final prints with the recorded sound. You are now ready for your first showing.

A final bit of advice: You have spent much time and, no doubt, have gone to some expense to prepare your audiovisual materials. Protect the time, money, and work against loss by preparing at least one duplicate set of all materials, both audio and visual, and file all the originals in a safe place for any future need.

A Part of a Narration to Be Read for Recording

NARRATION—OUR WATER SUPPLY

// Point at which cue will be given to start reading.
emphasis Underlined words are to be emphasized.
ㅇㅇㅇ Brief pause between phrases.

// The water we take for granted ㅇㅇㅇ do you know where it

comes from? Is there enough for our continued use?

ㅇㅇㅇ How is it purified?

// The story of our water supply begins in the Sierra

Nevada. When snow melts or rain falls the MO-KE-LUM-NEE

River carries the water westward.

// A large amount is collected and held in the reservoir

north of the city.

// The water is purified in our treatment plant. Each day

three million gallons are processed. The process

starts by spraying water into the air.

// This treatment is known as aeration: oxygen from the air

is added to the water. As oxygen mixes with water it im-

proves its flavor and also destroys certain types of

bacteria.

[and so on]

Now Apply What You Have Read

1. What tasks remain to be done in order to complete the project?
2. What procedures would you use with your materials to prepare titles, do art work, and make the narration?

Answers to Review Questions

1. Make titles, record narration, reproduce all materials.
2. Reader's activity.

12
WRITING AN INSTRUCTION GUIDE

Prepare a teacher's guide or correlated student guide for use with your audiovisual materials.

Materials for Classroom Use

If your audiovisual materials are designed for classroom or other regular instructional use, an *instruction guide* will offer suggestions and reminders for good utilization practice. Its purpose should be: (1) to help instructors prepare for successful use of the materials, and (2) to suggest related activities and problems for instructor and student consideration.

Such a guide may include:

☐ Information about the materials—type, length, date of preparation, source for loan, rent, or sale, rental or sale price
☐ Statement of objectives materials are intended to serve
☐ Enumeration of intended audience(s)
☐ Subject area or topic to which materials are related
☐ Description of content
☐ Key words, terms, or expressions
☐ Preparatory questions, problems, and activities for instructor and students
☐ Participation activities for instructor and students during actual use
☐ Follow-up questions, problems, and activities after using the materials
☐ Correlation of the materials with references and other instructional materials

Also, there are advantages to preparing hand-out materials for distribution to a group at the time your materials are presented. Such information may relieve members of the audience of the need to take notes or to copy information that is being presented, thus permitting them to give all their attention to your presentation. Such handout, prepared and duplicated in advance of their anticipated use, may include:

☐ An outline of the presentation
☐ Detailed information or how-to-do-it directions concerning matters being presented
☐ Sources for items referred to
☐ Bibliography of references for future consideration by the audience

Materials for Use within an Instructional Design

If your audiovisual materials are designed for use within an instructional design or in correlation with a series of other printed and visual materials for independent study by students, there is little need for a guide of the traditional type. Most of the elements of such a guide are part of the instructional program itself.

Students may receive directions that lead from audio and visual materials to reading materials to activities. Questions, problems, and

**A Part of an
Instruction Guide**

INSTRUCTION GUIDE—OUR WATER SUPPLY

A set of 31 2 x 2 inch color slides with 8 minutes of taped
narration. Available on loan from the Audiovisual Center.

Purposes:
1. To learn the five steps in the purification of our local
   water supply.
2. To recognize the scientific principles that apply during
   the treatment process.
3. To practice the conservation of water (secondary purpose).

Audiences:
Primary: Ninth-grade general-science classes.
Secondary: High-school chemistry classes.

Related topic:
Community health services.

Content: (words underlined represent new vocabulary)
   Our water supply originates in the Sierra Nevada and flows
through the Mokelumne River to a storage reservoir near the
city. Each day 3,000,000 gallons are purified in the treatment
plant. Treatment requires five steps: First, aeration as the
water is sprayed into the air. Oxygen mixes with the water
to improve its flavor. Second, coagulation to remove
impurities. [and so on]

Questions for group discussion before seeing the slides:

   (Instructor or student committee should preview slides and
tape before class.)
1. Do you know the source of our water supply?
2. Do you believe the quantity of water is unlimited?
3. Why must water be purified?
4. How do you think water is purified? [and so on]

Participation during viewing:
   Plan to stop the tape after slide 24 and review the details
of each purification step. Slide 25 will review and reinforce
the total process.

Follow-up questions and activities:
1. Conduct laboratory demonstrations of each step in the
   process.
2. Find out how other communities purify their water.
3. Prepare a display to describe health dangers from polluted
   water.
4. In what ways can water be conserved at home and at school?

Correlation with references and other instructional materials:
Davis, Burnett, and Gross, Science: A Story of Discovery,
   pp. 124–27.
Water (a booklet), East Bay Municipal Utility District,
   Oakland.
Water Supply, 16-mm sound color motion picture, 12 minutes
   (M 2120).
Wonderland of Science: Purifying Drinking Water, filmstrip,
   46 frames (F2499).
[and so on]

other participation activities are introduced. Evaluations are provided. Therefore, the student's general guide sheet, along with specific correlated instructions, information, and summaries, serves as a continuous guide for the materials as they are used.

A Student
Study-Guide Sheet

COMMUNITY HEALTH UNIT—ACTIVITY #6

Following the class viewing and discussion of the film Water Purification you are ready for an examination of our local water supply. Be prepared to:

    a. Point out on an area map the source of our water supply and trace how it gets to our city.

    b. List and write a definition of the steps in the purification of our water.

1. For background, read the booklet Water by the East Bay Municipal District.

2. Study the slide series and tape recording Our Water Supply.

3. Complete the diagram of the purification process on the next page.

4. Prepare for the laboratory exercise demonstrating each step in the process.

[and so on]

Now Apply What You Have Read

1. What elements of an instructional guide for group use of your materials would you consider using?
2. If your materials are for individual study, develop the student guide sheet.

13

USING AND EVALUATING YOUR MATERIALS

Plan your presentation and use by checking facilities and rehearsing; then make your presentation and evaluate the results.

Now . . .

You are ready to use your materials with the intended audience. You—and your team—have spent much time in planning and in preparation, and now, in order to insure a successful reception, it is important that you arrange for the mechanics of the presentation and also make the materials meaningful to the audience, whether your materials are for use with a group or for individual study.

Here are some pointers that may make **this** and subsequent uses successful:[1]

☐ If you are not familiar with the room in which the materials will be used, try to visit it in advance. Check for electrical outlets, screen placement, seating arrangements, viewing distances, and appropriate placement for the projector. Also, find out how the room lights are controlled.

☐ Arrange for necessary equipment—projector, tape recorder, stands, screen, extension cord, adapter plugs, and extra projection lamp.

☐ Provide for the proper physical comfort of the group—ventilation, heat control, light control, and other conditions.

☐ Provide for distribution of hand-out materials, if appropriate.

☐ Rehearse your use of the materials (if possible in the setting in which they are to be used).

☐ If necessary, find out who will assist you with projection and other services, and instruct him accordingly.

☐ Arrange materials for use in proper sequence and in proper position.

☐ Prepare the group for viewing the materials. Refer to the instruction guide described in Chapter 12.

☐ Make your presentation, using good projection techniques (centering of the image on the screen, focus, sound level, and the like).

☐ After the presentation, discuss the materials and, if possible, provide for related activities (see the instruction guide).

☐ Judge audience reactions and consider any revisions for subsequent presentation.

Finally, evaluate the effectiveness of your audiovisual materials. Recall that a suggested checkpoint during the final stage of production was to get reactions from colleagues and from a student group for improving the materials at that time (page 66). Now after use encourage reactions from those viewing and using the materials. Determine changes in audience behavior in terms of the purposes originally established (page 31)

---

1. For suggestions on good projection practices, see *Audiovisual Projection*, pamphlet S 3 (Rochester, N.Y.: Eastman Kodak Co.)

through observing specific actions by members of the audience, and by administering performance or written tests based on your initial project objectives. These results will allow you to answer the question, How well do the materials do the job for which they were designed?

Here are suggestions for items to include when evaluating the effectiveness of your audiovisual materials:

☐ How well do students accomplish the objectives upon which the materials are based?
☐ Do reactions indicate the materials are appealing to students?
☐ If the materials do not meet the criteria of the objective(s), or lack appeal, what revisions can be made?

☐ Are the arrangements for use of the materials convenient for instructor and students (applicable to independent study)?
☐ What were the development costs (professional and staff time, materials, services)?
☐ What are the operational use costs (staff time, materials, facilities use)?

On the basis of the responses to these questions, revise the materials as necessary. Repeat the evaluation periodically to maintain a standard of effectiveness. Keep the materials up-to-date by adding or substituting new content when appropriate and eliminating the obsolete. Only by revision will your audiovisual materials be kept timely and maintained at your standards of quality and effectiveness.

Now Apply What You Have Read

1. Assume you are ready to use your materials. List all the factors you should consider in preparation for use.
2. How would you evaluate the effectiveness of your materials?

14

IN SUMMARY

The successful planning and production of audiovisual materials follows a logical sequence. For some types this is a detailed step-by-step procedure; for others it may be simplified and brief. Also, the degree to which any materials are formally completed (including titles, music, duplicates, laboratory services, and the like) is determined by the specific purposes to be served. For example, a short film designed to develop a single concept for direct instruction might be used with limited editing and without titles or special laboratory services.

A checklist and outline of steps is given in tabular arrangement in Table 14-1. It covers all possible steps; but your purposes and the treatment you give the subject may permit you to omit some of these steps. The numbers in the various columns refer to pages containing a discussion of the things to be done at each step. The planning and production of audiovisual materials for instructional television, multi-imagery, and multi-media generally follow the recommendations for each category column in Table 14-1. Study these pages as you plan specific materials.

Summary of Planning Steps for Audiovisual Materials   TABLE 14-1

STEP	PRINT SERIES	SLIDE SERIES	FILM-STRIPS	RECORD-INGS	TRANS-PAR-ENCIES	MOTION PICTURES	DISPLAY MATE-RIALS	MULTI-IMAGE MULTI-MEDIA
Planning								
1. Express your idea	31	31	31	31	31	31	31	31
2. Develop the objectives	31	31	31	31	31	31	31	31
3. Consider the audience	33	33	33	33	33	33	33	33
4. Get some help	36	36	36	36	36	36	36	36
5. Prepare the content outline	38	38	38	38	38	38	38	38
6. Select the medium	42	42	42	43	43	44	44	45
7. Write the treatment	—	52	52	—	—	52	—	52
8. Make a storyboard	—	54	54	—	—	54	—	54
9. Develop the script	54	54	54	54	—	54	—	54
10. Prepare the specifications	57	57	57	57	57	57	—	57
11. Schedule the picture taking	59	59	59	—	—	59	—	59

STEP	PRINT SERIES	SLIDE SERIES	FILM-STRIPS	RECORD-INGS	TRANS-PAR-ENCIES	MOTION PICTURES	DISPLAY MATE-RIALS	MULTI-IMAGE MULTI-MEDIA
Production								
12. Take the pictures	166	172	186	—	—	234	—	277
13. Process the film	168	176	186	—	—	253	—	—
14. Make work copies	168	—	—	—	—	253	—	—
15. Edit the pictures	168	176	—	—	—	254	—	—
16. Edit narration and captions	63	63	63	63	63	63	—	—
17. Prepare artwork, titles, and captions	167	174	185	—	199	252	267	278
18. Record narration	—	180	191	153	—	259	—	278
19. Prepare final copies	168	177	190	160	202	258	267	—
Follow-up								
20. Write the instruction guide	70	70	70	70	70	70	70	70
21. Prepare for use of the materials	73	73	73	73	73	73	73	73
22. Use the materials	73	73	73	73	73	73	73	73
23. Evaluate for future use	73	73	73	73	73	73	73	73
24. Revise as necessary	74	74	74	74	74	74	74	74

PART 3

FUNDAMENTAL SKILLS

15

PHOTOGRAPHY

Advances in cameras, films, processing, and other aspects of photography can free you from many once essential tasks. While recognition is given in this chapter to many newer developments, an understanding of the fundamental elements of photography will help you to make choices and decisions that can result in high-quality visual materials, prepared with a sense of pleasure and satisfaction.

Your Camera

Although cameras can be classified into groups according to picture size or operating characteristics, all cameras are basically similar and include five essential parts:

A. Lens
B. Light-tight enclosure
C. Lens diaphragm and shutter
D. Film-support channel
E. Viewfinder

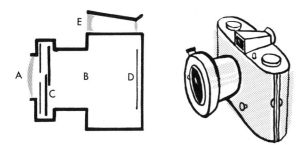

In addition, all cameras except the simplest have some means for changing the distance between the lens and the film plane in order to focus the image on the film. The more expensive kinds have features and attachments that offer greater capacity and versatility when filming. These include methods of changing lens-diaphragm openings, shutter speeds, and focus. Adjustable diaphragms and shutters are desirable because they can be adapted to changing light conditions and to different kinds of subjects. Lens quality differs over a wide range and has important bearing on the price of a camera.

AUTOMATIC-SETTING CAMERAS

This group consists of cameras having a built-in exposure meter to measure the intensity of the light reaching the lens from the subject toward which the camera is aimed. The meter is coupled to the diaphragm of the lens and automatically adjusts the opening according to light intensity. Once the camera is set for the type of film being used, proper exposure adjustments for many conditions are automatically made. Since most automatic-setting cameras have only one shutter speed, picture-taking under low light conditions or for fast action may be limited.

Thus, with automatic-setting cameras you are **79**

relieved of making adjustments for light changes and can concentrate on picture content, composition, and the relation of one picture to another. Such cameras are available in 35-mm cassette and cartridge-loaded (Instamatic-type) 110 and 126 film sizes.

SMALL-FORMAT CAMERAS (35 mm)

This is the most widely used type of camera for preparing visual materials, principally as slides for slide series and conversion to filmstrips. Color and black-and-white prints can also be made from appropriate 35-mm negatives.

These cameras have either *window-type viewfinders* or a *prism and mirror* system that allows the subject to be framed and focused through the camera lens for more accurate viewing. The latter type of camera is called a *single-lens reflex* and is especially convenient for close-ups and copy work. Lenses and shutters of higher-priced cameras can be adjusted over a wide range of settings, which broadens the possibilities for taking pictures under varying conditions.

Quick operation is a feature of 35-mm cameras, and there is an economy with film in that many exposures can be made on a single roll before reloading. For more details on the characteristics of 35-mm cameras, see page 170.

MEDIUM-FORMAT CAMERAS

These cameras use a larger size film (generally 120) than 35-mm cameras, thus providing $2\frac{1}{4} \times 2\frac{1}{4}$ inch or $2\frac{1}{4} \times 2\frac{3}{4}$ inch slides or black-and-white negatives. The larger size may be preferable when considerable enlargements are required. One disadvantage of this slide size is the higher cost and, often, the unavailability of projectors.

There are two subcategories in this group. Both focus the image, when viewing, on a ground glass surface. One has a *single lens,* with a mirror that reflects light to the ground glass. The mirror moves upward to clear the film plane just before the shutter opens as in a 35-mm single-lens reflex camera. The other is a *twin-lens* camera. Its lower lens (*A*) is for taking pictures, while the upper one (*B*) carries light rays to the ground glass. The parallax problem caused by the separation between viewing and filming positions (page 99) is a limitation of the twin-lens camera when close-ups are being made.

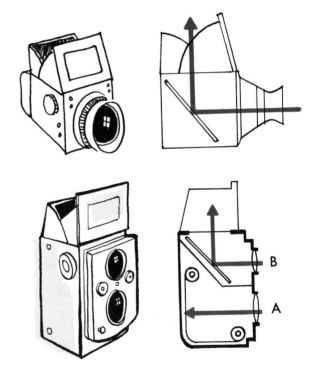

The method of viewing the subject as it appears on the ground glass of these larger-format cameras can be an advantage because the image is generally the same size as it will appear on the film, although on certain cameras it may be reversed left to right. Image size may be especially important when accurate composition or careful positioning of a subject for a multi-image slide presentation is required.

LARGE-FORMAT CAMERAS

These cameras include press- and view-type cameras in many sizes. They use cut sheets of film rather than rolls, thus permitting single pictures to be taken and immediately processed. The larger negative permits extreme enlargement and ease of retouching. These are ideal cameras for copywork and close-up photography since accurate viewing and focusing take place on a ground glass surface directly in line with the lens.

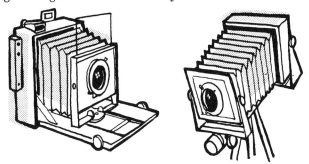

On page 214 the preparation of photographic overhead transparencies with a sheet-film camera is described.

POLAROID LAND CAMERAS

Most models of this camera have features similar to those found on automatic-setting types. The outstanding feature of all Polaroid Land cameras is that the film is developed and prints are made in the camera, thus eliminating the need for darkroom work and letting you see the results of your picture-taking almost immediately. Prints in both black-and-white and color, and large-size slides in black-and-white, can be produced in a matter of seconds.

Polaroid film consists of light-sensitive negative film and a nonsensitive positive stock (paper or film). To the latter are affixed sealed pods, one for each picture, which contain developing chemicals. After a picture is taken, a pull on the tab (or motorized movement) advances the film, rollers squeeze the developer from a pod, allowing gelatinlike material to spread between the negative and positive stock. Development takes place quickly. The result it a print or slide ready for use.

MOTION-PICTURE CAMERAS

The same features and functions essential in the operation of other cameras are necessary in all 8-mm and 16-mm motion-picture cameras. The differences are in the threading of film and its movement through the camera, or within a cartridge, and the action of the shutter behind the lens. See page 227 for more details on the characteristics and operation of motion-picture cameras.

Now, Review What You Have Learned About Camera Types:

What type of camera would best fit each situation?
1. Used to produce a quantity of color slides.
2. Used to make greatly enlarged close-up pictures of small objects on pieces of film.
3. Simplest for a young person to use, since settings are controlled in the camera.
4. Used to quickly and easily prepare photographs immediately after the pictures are taken.

5. Used as a roll-film camera for accurately viewing a subject in same size and appearance as it will be filmed.

6. Aim this camera at a subject and it adjusts its own lens for the immediate light conditions.

Note: Answers to review questions can be found at the end of the chapter.

Camera Lenses

If you have an inexpensive still-picture camera, you probably have only the standard lens that came with it. But many of the higher-priced cameras permit removal of the original lens and its replacement with other lenses for special purposes. An 8-mm motion-picture camera commonly has a *zoom* lens, which in effect is a series of lenses within one housing. With a 16-mm motion-picture camera, either a zoom lens or a complement of other lenses or both may be available. There are advantages in using different lenses to film various subjects under certain conditions.

The major feature of a lens (and within a zoom lens) is its *focal length*. This term refers to the distance measured from the center of the camera lens to the film plane within the camera when a subject at a far distance (infinity) is in focus.

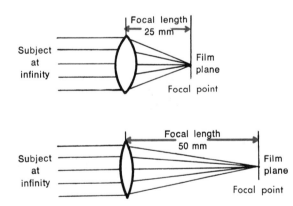

Lenses of different focal lengths form different-size images on film (when the camera is used from the same position). As you substitute a lens for another one having a *longer* focal length, a *larger* image is projected to the film. Thus, on the film you record only a portion of the image you had with the first lens. If you use a lens of *shorter* focal length, a *smaller* image reaches the film and you record a *greater* area of the subject.

The focal length of a lens is measured in millimeters (mm). A "normal" focal length has been established for various cameras. For the lens of a 35-mm camera the normal focal length is 50

mm. For an 8-mm motion-picture camera it is 13 mm. A lens with a *larger* or *longer* focal-length number than that of the normal lens is called a *telephoto* lens. A lens with a focal-length number *smaller* or *shorter* than the normal lens is called a *wide-angle* lens. For a 35-mm camera this relationship holds true:

Field with Wide-Angle Lens (28 mm)

Field with Normal Lens (50 mm)

Field with Telephoto Lens (135 mm)

Wide-angle Lens   **Normal Lens**   **Telephoto Lens**

View of Same Subject from Same Position

In summary, as compared with a normal lens, a *longer*-focal-length lens has a *larger* millimeter number and is called a *telephoto* lens; while a *shorter*-focal-length lens has a *lower* millimeter number and is called a *wide-angle* lens.

A zoom lens includes the focal-length feature of all three lenses as a continuously variable setting for your selection.

By selecting from lenses with different focal lengths, you can take pictures more easily under difficult conditions. For example, a wide-angle lens is useful when you cannot move far enough away from a subject to shoot with a normal lens.

When you cannot get close to a subject or do not want to, a telephoto lens may be helpful.

Also, recognize that some unusual optical impressions can be caused by both wide-angle and telephoto lenses. A person viewing a wide-angle picture may feel he is farther away from the subject than he actually is and experience an exaggerated feeling of depth. With extreme wide-angle lenses, objects close to the camera will appear changed in perspective, often distorted.

A telephoto lens may give the impression of compressing the distance between objects in a scene so that the foreground and background elements appear very close together.

Now, Review What You Have Learned About Camera Lenses.

1. Make a sketch to illustrate the meaning of focal length for a lens. Label the parts.
2. What numerical measure is used to indicate focal length?
3. Into what three groups are lenses placed?
4. Which lens would you select for each situation:
   a. General picture-taking of a group of children at play
   b. General scene in a factory showing as much of the equipment as possible
   c. As close a view as possible of a track start on the field when filmed from the grandstand
   d. Two by two inch slide of a bird in a nest which is in a bush at some distance
5. Into what group(s) would you place the lens(es) you have with your camera?

Note: Answers to review questions can be found at the end of the chapter.

Camera Settings

If you have an automatic-setting camera, you may feel you have little need to recognize and understand the purposes for the settings made on an adjustable camera. But your camera may allow you to override the automatic feature and, for special situations, make settings to insure correct exposure. For example, when filming a *back-lit* subject (sun or other light source *behind* the subject, with much of the subject in shadow), or when making close-ups of an object on a light-colored background, you face situations in which the general exposure determined by the camera may be incorrect.

There are three essential settings on adjustable cameras. The amount of light that enters a camera is controlled by the *lens diaphragm* and the *shutter,* working together. The *lens diaphragm* controls the *amount* of light that can reach the film; the *shutter* controls the *length* of time the light can reach the film.

LENS DIAPHRAGM

Light enters a camera by passing through the lens. The intensity of light entering is controlled by a metal diaphragm, which is located either directly behind the lens or between two elements of the lens. The diaphragm acts somewhat like the iris of an eye. It is always open, but its size can be changed to control the intensity of light passing through the lens.

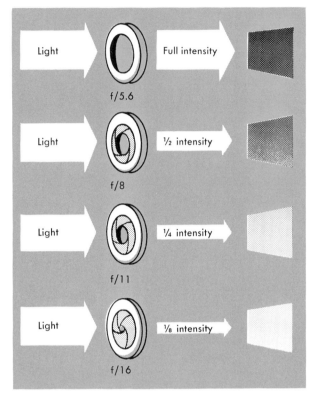

Lens-diaphragm settings are indicated by a series of numbers—4, 5.6, 8, 11, 16, . . .—called *f/ numbers* or *f/ stops. The larger the f/ number the smaller the opening.* A lens setting of f/11 admits only *half the amount of light* passed by an f/8 setting.

Thus, adjacent numbers in the series admit light in the proportion of 2 to 1 (permitting the passage of *twice as much light* or *half as much light*).

An f/number expressed the relationship between the local length (page 82) and the diameter of the lens aperture opening. Thus, for f/11 the opening has a diameter one-eleventh of the lens focal length.

SHUTTER SPEED

A second camera setting is the shutter speed. The camera shutter is similar to the eyelid as it closes and reopens rapidly. In the camera the shutter remains closed until opened to permit the lens to "see."

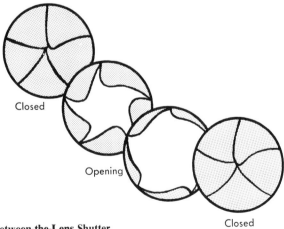

Between-the-Lens Shutter

The most common type of shutter is placed between elements of the lens and consists of thin pieces of metal that can be moved to allow light to pass for various lengths of time. The other method of permitting light to reach the film is

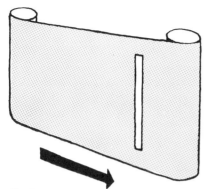

Focal-Plane Shutter

with a cloth or metal curtain located just in front of the film plane. The curtain has a slit in it, and at the instant the picture is taken the curtain moves across the film at a selected speed to expose the film to light.

Generally, shutter speeds are measured in fractions of a second: ½, ¼, ⅛, 1/15, 1/30, 1/60, 1/125, and so on. On the camera they are printed as whole numbers instead of fractions. A shutter speed of 1/60 second is *slower* than a speed of 1/125 second, admitting light for *twice as long a time*.

Thus, adjacent speeds are in the proportion of 2 to 1 (permitting the entrance of light for approximately *twice as much time* or *half as much time* —1/60 twice as much as 1/125; but 1/60 half as much as 1/30).

ter speed of 1/60 or 1/125 is suggested. But when a moving subject is to be filmed, the choice of a shutter speed is dependent on the speed of movement, the distance from camera to subject, and the direction of movement relative to the camera.

Since both the adjacent lens-diaphragm settings and the adjacent shutter speeds are in the 2-to-1 proportion, they may be used in various combinations to allow the same amount of light to reach the film. As you will see, the selection of such combinations is important to obtain specific effects.

FOCUS

The third setting on many cameras is for focus. With your camera you may have to estimate the distance from camera to subject and set an indicator accordingly. Or your camera may include a built-in *rangefinder* coupled to the lens, which, upon proper adjustment, automatically sets the lens for the correct subject-to-camera distance.

Distance scale

On older cameras, shutter speeds are graduated in another series of fractions of a second, as . . . 1/25, 1/50, 1/100, and so on. The principle of 2-to-1 proportion holds for these graduations also.

On your camera you may have many speeds from which to select. For general scenes, a shut-

The rangefinder may be either of two kinds: *superimposed image* or *split-field*. The former will show two images unless the focus is correct, at which point the two images are superimposed to make a single image. The split-field rangefinder will show two half-images, one below the other, unless the focus is correct, at which point the two halves are matched together to make a complete image.

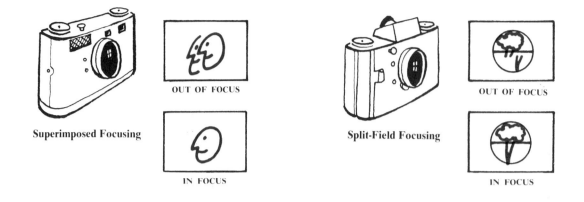

OUT OF FOCUS

Superimposed Focusing

IN FOCUS

OUT OF FOCUS

Split-Field Focusing

IN FOCUS

DEPTH OF FIELD

While lens-diaphragm openings and shutter speeds work together to admit various amounts of light into the camera, lens-diaphragm openings and distance settings can also be coordinated to get sharp pictures.

out

in focus

Plane of focus

in focus

out

In this scene the camera is focused at 8 feet, but children both closer and farther away than 8 feet also appear sharp. This distance from the closest sharply focused point to the farthest spot in focus is the *depth of field* of the lens at the *f*/number used. To get a sharp picture, a photographer must have his subject in this field.

Of the total depth of field within a scene, about ⅓ is included ahead of the point of actual focus and about ⅔ beyond the point of focus. Therefore, to get the maximum value from the depth-of-field factor, focus your camera lens on a point that is about one-third of the way into a

scene. If your camera gives you more exact information, use it.

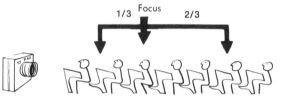

1/3   Focus   2/3

Your camera may include a depth-of-field scale adjacent to the focusing ring. Refer to this scale to determine quickly the depth of field for any combination of lens setting and distance to the plane of focus. The illustrations that follow show how this scale is to be read in combination with the distance scale on the focusing ring. Note that its graduations are like those on the lens-setting scale: 4, 8, 16, 22 (the 2.8, 5.6, and 11 points are omitted for legibility in the scale used in the illustration). It should be easy to observe the two important facts. First, whatever the lens setting, it provides greater depth of field at far distances than at near distances. Second, whatever the distance, it provides greater depth of field at higher-numbered lens settings than at lower-numbered ones (see page 84).

The focus is set for a little less than 9 feet. If you change the lens setting to *f*/16, the field will extend from a little more than 5 feet to something more than 20 feet; if you change the lens setting to *f*/4, the limits of the field will be about 7 feet and about 10 feet.

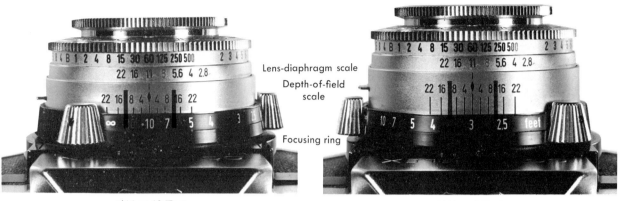

ƒ/11 at 10 Feet   *ƒ/11 at 3 Feet*

The depth-of-field scale is graduated both to left and to right of a zero marker with numbers corresponding to the ƒ/ scale. Some graduations are omitted to permit making the numbers large and clear. At left, the focus (white numbers on black) is set for 10 feet, the lens setting at ƒ/11. Reading the focus scale opposite the two 11 points (between 8 and 16) on the depth-of-field scale shows that the field extends from about 6½ feet in front of the camera to almost infinity. At right, with the same lens setting but with the focus at 3 feet, the two 11 points on the depth-of-field scale indicate that the field extends from a little more than 2½ feet to a little more than 3½ feet in front of the camera.

By using this relationship between lens setting, distance, and depth of field, you can often get exactly what you want into your picture.

To get a greater depth of field, use a smaller lens-diaphragm opening (that is, a higher ƒ/ number). The illustration shows how the depth of field, at whatever distance the camera is focused, will be increased by setting the ƒ/ number up from 4 to 16, for example (see page 86).

In order to get the maximum depth of field (for close-up work or for scenes requiring extreme depth), use a large ƒ/ number (small lens-diaphragm opening—perhaps ƒ/16).

To reduce the depth of field (perhaps to throw part of a subject or an undesirable background out of focus), use a small ƒ/ number (large lens-diaphragm opening—perhaps ƒ/4).

Depth of field also has a relationship to the focal length of lenses. Pictures shot with wide-angle lenses have *greater* depth of field than those filmed with either normal or telephoto lenses. You can film a scene with a subject very large and close to the camera in the foreground and still have distant background objects in sharp focus.

A telephoto lens has much less depth of field. Consequently, the distance from subject to film should be carefully measured to insure focus, especially for close-up scenes. See page 230 for

Scene with Maximum Depth of Field—ƒ/16

Scene with Limited Depth of Field—ƒ/4

further consideration of depth of field for various focal-length lenses used in motion pictures.

In summary: On adjustable cameras three settings must be made—lens-diaphragm opening (f/number), shutter speed, and distance. Study their relationships carefully and learn how to use them. Also, remember when taking pictures to:

☐ Hold the camera steady.
☐ Use a tripod whenever shutter speeds slower than 1/30 second will be used.
☐ Squeeze the shutter release, rather than punch it.
☐ Keep the light over your shoulder, rather than let it shine toward the camera lens.

Now, Review What You Have Learned About Camera Settings:

1. If a lens setting of $f/8$ permits a certain amount of light to pass into a camera, then how much light does a setting of $f/5.6$ admit?
2. What shutter speed would you select to "stop" the action of (a) a person diving off a board, (b) a car driving past at 25 mph, or (c) a child walking by you?
3. If $f/11$ and 1/125 second are correct exposure settings, but you want to increase the depth of field by two $f/$ stops, what camera settings would you now use?
4. What is the depth of field indicated on the lens on page 85?
5. Does a lens setting of $f/4.5$ permit *greater* or *less* depth of field as compared to one set at $f/11$?

Note: Answers to review questions can be found at the end of the chapter.

The Film

Selection of film is determined by a number of factors:

☐ Kinds of subjects, such as general scenes, action shots, or close-ups of fine details
☐ Lighting conditions, such as daylight, floodlights, flash, or low-level room light
☐ Use for materials, such as enlarged photographs, slides, or transparencies

In addition, choices are based upon characteristics of different films, including:

☐ Degree of light sensitivity (film speed or exposure index, see explanation following)—*slow* films, such as Kodachrome II Daylight (index 25), Kodalith Ortho Type 3 (index 6); *moderate-speed* films, such as Ektachrome-X (64) and Plus-X (125); *fast* films, such as High Speed Ektachrome (160), Tri-X (400)
☐ Size of film grain
☐ Useful exposure range to reproduce a range of tones from highlights to shadows

The terms *film speed, exposure index,* and *ASA* (American Standards Association) *speed* refer to the degree of light sensitivity of a film. They are used interchangeably and are scaled by a number assigned to each film. The number is a relative one; it applies to specified light conditions. A film with a speed of 100 requires less light for proper exposure than one with a speed of 64, and vice versa.

The data about films in Table 15-1 are correct at the time of writing; but changes and new developments are to be anticipated. Check carefully the data sheet packaged with your film for the latest assigned exposure index and other details (see page 91).

BLACK-AND-WHITE FILM

Black-and-white films are inexpensive, easy to use, and simple to process and print. Their primary use is in making enlargements, as for photographic picture series. Black-and-white films can also serve for slides, filmstrips, photographic transparencies, and motion pictures.

COLOR NEGATIVE FILM

Color negative film is versatile since it may serve as negative for color prints, for black-and-white prints, and for positive color slides. On a color negative the colors of the subject are complementary to their normal appearance (yellow in

TABLE 15-1　Characteristics of Some Widely Used Films

FILM	EXPOSURE INDEX (ASA)	LIGHT SOURCE	SUGGESTED USE
Panatomic-X	32	any	Copying fine detail for extreme enlargements (black-white)
Kodalith Ortho Type 3	6	flood	Copying high-contrast black-and-white print and artwork
Tri-X	400	any	Subjects under low light conditions (black-and-white)
Kodacolor II negative	80	daylight or blue flash	General purposes to prepare color prints and/or slides in quantity
Kodachrome II Professional Type A	40	flood	Close-up and copy work for color slides
High Speed Ektachrome Daylight	160	daylight or fluorescent	Fast action or dimly lit subjects for color slides

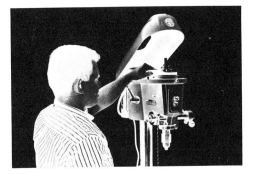

Negative

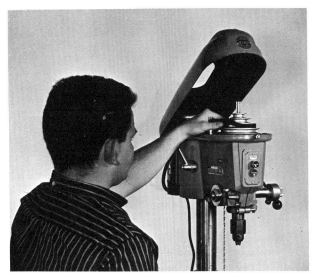

Enlarged Print

Black-and-White Slide

place of blue, magenta for green, and cyan or blue-green for red). Kodacolor and Ektacolor are the principal color negative films available. The negative color films, available in sizes for most cameras, are more expensive than black-and-

white, but they can be processed with prepared kits, thus reducing the cost when a number of rolls are handled. Also, new processes are on the market that simplify the developing and printing of color film.

Color Negative

Color Slide from Color Negative

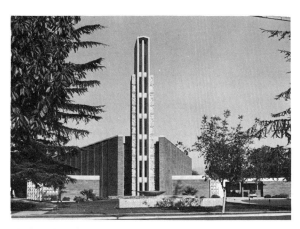

Black-and-White Print from Color Negative

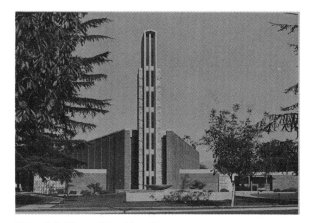

Color Print from Color Negative

COLOR REVERSAL FILM

After exposure and processing, color reversal films become positives—slides, filmstrips, or motion pictures. In processing, the image on the film is *reversed* to make a positive picture.

Color reversal films are supplied in sizes for 35-mm, 110, and 126 (the latter two for Instamatic-type) cameras and for standard roll-film cameras. They are available in a range of film

speeds and in various types, each type designed for a specific light condition—daylight or photoflood. The light supplied by these sources differs in "color temperature," a characteristic measured in degrees Kelvin (°K). Therefore, each film type has an emulsion for a specific color temperature, such as 6000°K (daylight) or 3400°K (photoflood). Frequently, correction filters can be employed to permit use of a film under lighting conditions that differ from its Kelvin rating.

2×2 inch (35-mm Film)

2×2 inch (126-size Film)

110-size Film

2×2 inch (35-mm Half Frame)

Now, Test What You Have Learned About Film:

1. Most reversal color films are available in two types. The selection of the type to use depends on what major factor?
2. If you wanted to have both color slides and enlarged color prints from the same subject, what film would you select to use?
3. What does the number 125 mean when referred to as the ASA rating?
4. What is the reason for selecting a film with an exposure index of 160 in preference to one with an index of 64?

Note: Answers to review questions can be found at the end of the chapter.

Correct Exposure

How do you put together information about f/numbers, shutter speeds, and film characteristics to get correct exposure? The simplest method is to refer to the data sheet packaged with the film, on which a table gives you *general* guides to proper exposure.

OUTDOOR EXPOSURE GUIDE FOR AVERAGE SUBJECTS	Set shutter at 1/200 or 1/250 second and lens opening at:			
	f/22	f/11	f/8	f/8
	BRIGHT OR HAZY SUN* (DISTINCT SHADOWS)	CLOUDY BRIGHT (NO SHADOWS)	HEAVY OVERCAST	OPEN SHADE
	Exposure Values			
	17	15	14	14
*For back-lighted subjects, use f/11 or EV15.				

But what about situations involving particularly dark- or unusually light-colored subjects or backgrounds? What corrections should you make when the sun is behind the subject rather than over your shoulder? How do you determine camera settings when doing copy work or when using floodlights? These are common problems and their solutions may require more information than that provided by the data-sheet tables alone.

Typical Film-Information Sheets

USING A LIGHT METER

The most accurate method for determining exposure is with the use of a photographic light meter. All such meters consist of three main parts: a photoelectric cell, a light-level scale, and a camera-setting scale (see page 92).

The Incident-Light Method

The Reflected-Light Method

Light strikes a photoelectric cell which converts the light energy into electrical energy.

The light level is shown by the movement of a needle over a scale.

Then proper camera settings are indicated on the dial scales.

Light is measured by an exposure meter in either of two places: at the place where the subject is or at the place where the camera is. The *incident-light method* measures the light where the subject is, with an *incident-light meter* at or near the subject's position and pointed toward the camera. The *reflected-light method* measures the light where the camera is, with a *reflected-light meter* at or near the camera's position and pointed toward the subject. Another way of describing the two methods is to say that the incident-light method measures the light that *falls on* the subject whereas the reflected-light method measures the light that *comes off* the subject (see page 91).

Some meters measure light by only one of these methods; many have attachments or components that permit measurements to be taken in either way.

The exposure meter measures light through its photoelectric cell and electronic circuit. You then use this measurement to compute lens opening and shutter speed, employing scales on the instrument. Follow these steps:

1. Note the exposure index of the film you are using (as 500 for Super Anscochrome) and set the meter's exposure-index scale at this number.

2. Take your light-level reading and note the light level indicated by the needle.
3. Adjust the movable scale until its pointer points to this light level.
4. You will now find lens openings and shutter speeds matched on two dials. Select the pair you will use.

The two illustrations below present examples of the appearance of exposure meters after they have been set as directed above.

Since shutter speed and lens opening work together, as has been explained, to admit the proper amount of light to the film, correct exposure is

Reflected-Light Meter

Incident-Light Meter

shown by any paired values for *f*/ number and shutter speed. Can you read the paired figures in the two illustrations? If you find *f*/16 paired with 1/30, then other pairs will be *f*/11 at 1/60, *f*/8 at 1/125, *f*/5.6 at 1/250, and so on.

Now, which pair to choose? Your selection is based upon answers to two questions:

1. How much movement is there in the scene? (Recall the examples of shutter-speed selection on page 85; the faster the motion, the higher the necessary speed.)
2. How much depth of field is desired? (Recall the discussion of depth of field, page 86; for greater depth of field, use a setting with larger *f*/number).

Now apply some of these relationships. Can you explain why the particular exposure settings were selected for these three examples?

ƒ/11 at 1/60 Second

ƒ/4 at 1/500 Second

ƒ/22 at 1/15 Second

A good exposure meter is a worthwhile investment. Use it *carefully* for correct exposure determinations.

☐ When using an incident-light meter, hold it in the center of the scene and aim the white cone toward the camera.
☐ When using a reflected-light meter, aim it at the subject, especially for exterior scenes. Do not tip the meter and record too much light from the foreground or from the sky.
☐ Average the readings of a reflected-light meter taken from various objects in a scene; avoid taking readings with a reflected-light meter from very bright or very dark parts of the scene.
☐ With an incident-light meter, when a subject is back-lighted (that is, when the sun or other light source is behind the subject and parts of the subject facing the camera are in shadow), open the lens to one additional *f*/ number beyond that indicated on the meter.
☐ When filming under photoflood lights, follow the additional suggestions for using a meter that you will find on page 96.
☐ When doing close-up and copy work, make use of the exposure information on page 101.
☐ Follow other suggestions found in the instruction manual accompanying your light meter.

Keep a careful record of light and subject conditions, choice of exposure, and the quality of resulting pictures. From this record you can judge how well your meter is serving you and establish the modifications you must make in using it.

A final word about automatic-setting cameras. On such cameras an exposure meter is coupled directly to the lens, and as light strikes this meter it automatically sets the lens opening (*f*/ number) to correspond to a preselected shutter speed. This lens-opening setting will be satisfactory *provided two requirements are fulfilled:*

☐ The light must come over your shoulder as you take the picture.
☐ The meter must not be measuring any unusually bright or unusually dark large areas (such as a white shirt or a background) that are unimportant to the picture (these could cause underexposure or overexposure of the main subject).

Automatic-setting cameras are almost foolproof—but your own experience should guide you to vary the camera setting under certain conditions.

Now, Test What You Have Learned About Determining Exposure:

1. What three numbers, relating to exposure, can be determined from a film-data sheet? Which two can be used directly to make camera settings and which one is for a setting on a light meter?
2. What two settings are required on a light meter before determining exposure?
3. When these two settings are made on the meter, what pair of numbers result?
4. According to the setting illustrated on the incident-light meter on page 92, if a subject requires extreme depth of field what camera shutter speed would you use? (First, would you select $f/4.5$ or $f/32$?)
5. The type of light meter on which the measurement of light intensity is not affected by the color or other characteristics of the subject itself is the ———.

Note: Answers to review questions can be found at the end of the chapter.

Artificial Lighting

Often, good exposures can be made under available light, and even under unfavorable lighting conditions, on the high-speed films that are available—some of them with an exposure index greater than 1000. Even so, it is necessary at times to provide lighting in place of, or in addition to, the normal light in the area. Such artificial light is either flash light or flood light.

PHOTOFLASH LIGHTING

Notice the difference in brilliancy and in shadow detail between two otherwise identical photographs, one taken with the natural available light and one with added photoflash light.

WITH NATURAL LIGHT   WITH FLASH LIGHTING ADDED

Flash cubes or electronic flash units are one way of creating your own light. Even in sunlight, flash lighting can be used to add light to shadow areas. A flash is most useful for lighting relatively small areas or for lighting larger ones that have light-colored backgrounds. The light fall-off from flash is so great that the background, if it is too far behind the subject (over 8 feet or so), will appear undesirably dark. Conversely, if flash is used too close to a subject, the subject may appear too light or washed out.

DISTANT BACKGROUND   NEAR BACKGROUND

Flash Lighting and the Background

The exposure for taking pictures under flash lighting is determined by referring to tables in the literature and using a formula. The tables appear on the film-information sheet, on the flashcube box, or in the instructions with your electronic flash unit. There may be some discrepancy in the recommended *guide number* among these sources. In such a case, use the information on the package or electronic unit in preference to that from other sources.

In using the tables, you take into account the film, the flash source, and the shutter speed to be used; these enable you to find the guide number. Then, using this number and the *flash-to-subject distance,* you compute the lens setting from the formula:

$$\text{lens setting} = \frac{\text{guide number}}{\text{distance}}$$

Note the data with the sample picture, and the use of these data in computing the $f/$ number.

Kodachrome-X film,
  exposure index 64
Flash cube
Shutter speed 1/125
  second $\text{lens setting} = \dfrac{45}{10} = 4.5$
Guide number 45
Distance 10 feet (flash $\text{lens setting} = f/4.5$
  to subject)

(Note: $f/4.5$ would be set between the 4 and 5.6
"click stops" on your lens.)

When using other lighting, you may adjust
exposure by increasing the shutter speed and the
lens setting, but you are less freely able to make
such changes when using flash lighting because
the duration of flash is brief and is not controlled;
hence the shutter speed is substantially fixed and
is a component of the exposure guide number.

For unusual flash techniques (bounce lighting, use of multiple flash, reducing flash intensity
for extreme close-ups), see the special references
for flash photography on page 295).

PHOTOFLOOD LIGHTING

Classrooms, offices, and many other areas are
usually well illuminated by fluorescent lights.
Frequently this available light is sufficient for
many filming purposes, with high-speed color film
or with moderate-speed black-and-white films.
Because color films respond differently to various
light sources, fluorescence may cause unusual effects. Test your film to determine any variations
in color rendition and film speed (for example,
tests show that High Speed Ektachrome daylight-
type film, under certain classroom fluorescent
lights, at an exposure index of 80 and using a
FLD filter over the lens, gives highly acceptable
results).

If supplementary or controlled lighting is necessary, consider using photographic floodlamps.
They may be essential for motion-picture photography; even for still photography floodlights
are often better than flash since you see exactly
what effect the lights are creating (reflections,
heavy shadows, or uneven lighting) and can make
corrections before taking pictures.

Two major types of photoflood lamps are
available. The traditional incandescent-filament
lamp, with wattages of 250, 500, or 1000 in a
hemisphere-shaped reflector, is widely used. Recent advances in lamp technology have made
available small tubular units consisting of quartz
filaments and filled with iodine vapor. These
quartz-iodine lamps provide a very bright, narrow ribbon of light and project an extremely even
illumination. People appearing in scenes in which
the quartz-iodide lamps are used should be
warned not to look directly into the light as the
brightness of the source can cause eye discomfort.

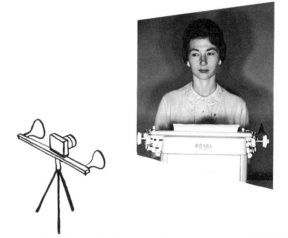

Floods placed close to the camera will light
the subject only from the front side. Such lighting results in a flat, shadowless subject with
heavy background shadows, usually undesirable.

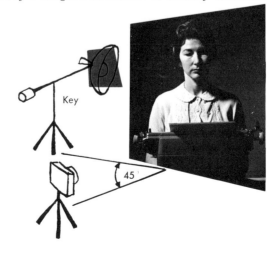

It is better to place one light about 45° to the side of the camera, somewhat closer to the subject, and higher than the camera. This becomes the *main,* or *key, light.* It substitutes for the sun, which shines on an outdoor scene. Therefore it should be the brightest light source (either by wattage or closeness to the subject).

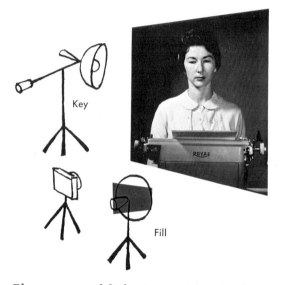

Place a second light (or two) beside the camera (on the side opposite the main light) and at camera height. This light serves to soften shadows created by the key light, thus bringing out more detail in the subject. It is called the *fill light.*

Some light from the key may fall on the background, but a third light (or two), aimed evenly at the background, will illuminate it, thus separating the subject from the background and giving the scene some depth. This is the *background light.* Always keep the subject at least 2 or 3 feet away from the background to minimize heavy shadows created by any lights.

These three lights—key, fill, and background —form the basic lighting pattern for good indoor lighting. The key as the brightest one is often *twice* the light intensity of the fill light (key-light to fill-light ratio 2 to 1); for example, light-meter readings of 100 for key light and 50 for fill light. (For close-up scenes, to soften shadows, the intensity of the fill may equal that of the key light —key to fill ratio 1 to 1.) One or more background lights may be set to illuminate the background evenly with a meter reading one-half to one stop lower than the general reading within the scene. Sometimes a spotlight (or photospot) is used as an *accent light* to highlight a person or an object in the scene.

Use your light meter for balancing lights and determining exposure. You can use one or more of four methods:

1. Move an incident-light meter through the scene (aimed at the camera). Adjust lights by changing positions until the lighting is even, then determine the exposure.
2. Take readings with a reflected-light meter held at various parts of the scene and average them.
3. Take a reading with a reflected-light meter from a neutral gray card (Eastman Kodak's neutral test card) held in the scene.
4. Take a reading with a reflected-light meter from a face or hand in the scene and then use twice the indicated exposure (that is, a lens opening one $f/$ number lower, since the flesh tone is somewhat brighter than the over-all scene should be. (For example, for a reading from the face of $f/8$ at 1/60 second, use $f/5.6$ at 1/60).

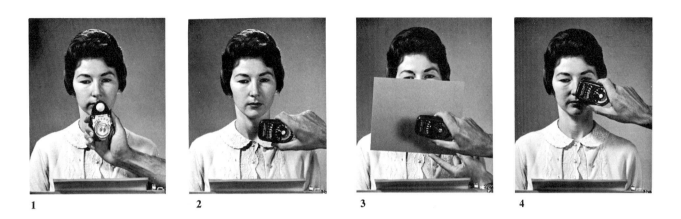

1   2   3   4

Now, Test What You Have Learned About Lighting:

1. Are flashcubes effective for lighting *small* or *large* areas?
2. Apply the correct formula to determine $f/$ number: flashcube guide number for film is 100, distance of camera to subject is 6 feet.
3. In a scene including people and large objects, what are some disadvantages of using lights placed only right beside the camera?
4. What is meant by the expression, "key to fill ratio is 2 to 1"? Is this an acceptable ratio to create moderate but not harsh shadows?
5. What method would you use for determining exposure under floodlighting?
6. Explain the positioning and purpose served by each light—accent, background, key, and fill. In what order is each set for use?

Note: Answers to review questions can be found at the end of the chapter.

Picture Composition

The effectiveness of your visual materials is strengthened by careful arrangement of elements within each picture, be it a still or motion picture. Although composition is a matter of personal choice, some principles should be kept in mind:

☐ Have only one major subject or center of interest in a scene. Do not clutter a picture or make it tell too much. Eliminate or subordinate all secondary elements and focus attention on the main one.

☐ Because viewers have no way of judging the

size of unknown objects in pictures, it is important to include some familiar object for comparison.

☐ If action or movement is implied in a picture, allow more space or picture area in the direction of the action rather than away from it.

☐ Try not to be static from one scene to another by shooting from the same relative camera position or angle. Plan to vary camera positions. Changing angles creates a dynamic impression and gives variety to composition.

☐ Place the center of interest near to but not directly in the physical center of the picture area. By making the picture slightly unsymmetrical you create a dynamic and more interesting arrangement.

☐ Include some foreground detail to create an impression of depth (principally in long-shot exterior scenes). Foregrounds help to balance the picture and to make it interesting.

☐ In black-and-white photography similar tones may blend together. Have the color of the center of interest contrast with the background and surrounding objects.

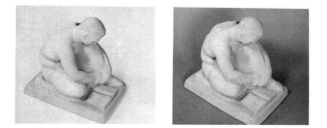

☐ Keep the background simple. Eliminate confusing background details by removing disturbing objects, by putting up a screen to hide the background, or by throwing the background out of focus (using a smaller f/ number, thus controlling the depth of field).

☐ Most visual materials normally have a horizontal format. If possible, plan your content for this format. Try not to mix vertical photographs or slides with horizontal ones in a series if there is a possibility that they might be used in a filmstrip, a motion picture, or on television.

☐ Finally, use common sense in composition. Ask yourself, What am I trying to accomplish with this picture or scene? Then pick what appears to be the best angle and the best distance for the camera. If necessary, view the scene from two or three positions and make pictures from each one for future selection.

Study the suggestions for composition of graphic materials on page 113. Many of these principles also apply to photographs, slides, and motion-picture scenes.

Now, Test What You Have Learned About Picture Composition:

Following is a group of six pictures (scenes); each one composes the same subject differently. Which one do you prefer? Why?

Note: Answers to review questions can be found at the end of the chapter.

Close-up and Copy Work

In photography it is often necessary to photograph subjects closer than a camera is normally used, such as for titles, reproductions of charts and pictures, and for close-ups of subject details.

Your camera may be unsatisfactory for such close-up work unless you can make adjustments and allowances in two respects: focusing and viewfinding.

VIEWFINDING AND PARALLAX

The viewfinder on some roll-film cameras is lo-cated above the picture-taking lens. In such cameras the viewer and the taking lens do not see exactly the same area; the difference is of the kind that you perceive when you look at a book with each eye alternately closed. But your eyes can move individually to compensate for some of the difference; the two lenses on your camera cannot do so. This is the phenomenon of *parallax*. The different areas that the taking lens and the viewfinder see are illustrated in two pictures on page 100.

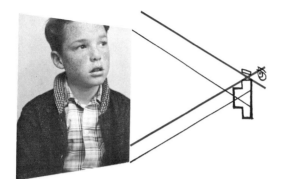

Camera with Window-Type Viewfinder—Parallax Results in Cutting Off a Portion of the Subject

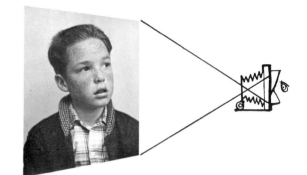

Camera with Ground-Glass Surface behind the Lens—No Parallax Problem

View cameras and single-lens reflex cameras permit through-the-lens viewing of the subject. It is viewed directly through the taking lens and focused on a ground glass. These cameras are preferred for close-up and copy photography.

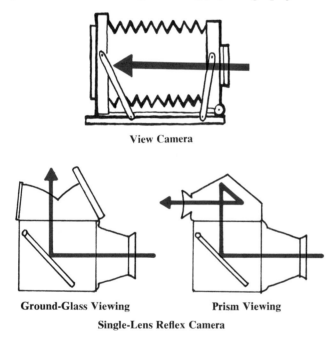

View Camera

Ground-Glass Viewing   **Prism Viewing**

Single-Lens Reflex Camera

If your camera does not have such built-in features or special attachments to deal with the parallax problem, it is difficult but not entirely impossible to do close-up and copy work. You can use framing and copying aids to be described shortly. Using them, however, requires some understanding of the problems of close-up focusing and exposure determination.

FOCUSING AND EXPOSURE

Cameras are adapted for close-up photography (picture-taking close to the subject, often under 2 feet) by one of four devices:

☐ A lens specially made for close-up focusing, which maintains a flatness of field and does not distort lines in a subject (some manufacturers call this a *macro* lens).
☐ The camera is built with bellows that can be used to lengthen the lens-to-film distance.
☐ The camera permits the use of separate extension tubes or bellows that lengthen the lens-to-film distance.
☐ A close-up attachment can be mounted on the lens to change the optical character of the lens system.

Extension Tubes

Bellows

When you use bellows or extension tubes for close-ups, you are using the same lens that you would use to take pictures at normal distances. But exposure calculation must be adjusted because of the increased distance between lens and film. The exposure for close-ups under these conditions is found by the usual exposure-meter procedure plus an additional computation. The additional computation takes into account the

Retaining ring

Close-up lens

Adapter ring

Camera lens

opening up the diaphragm of the lens 2 $f/$ stops (to give exposure of $f/4$ at 1/60 second) or by reducing the shutter speed one-fourth (to give exposure of $f/8$ at 1/15 second.

To insure best focus and maximum depth of field when working close, use a larger $f/$ number where possible. Select camera settings with a shutter speed faster than 1 second to avoid the unusual reactions of some films to longer exposure times.

The majority of cameras can be adapted for close-up work with one or more supplementary lenses (close-up attachments) placed in a retaining ring and attached over the regular lens. With this method no compensation for exposure is required as with tube or bellows extension.

The effectiveness of close-up attachments with some adjustable cameras is shown in Table 15-2.

TABLE 15-2
Close-up Attachments and Camera-Subject Settings

WIDTH OF SUBJECT (INCHES)	DISTANCE, CAMERA TO SUBJECT (INCHES)	POWER OF CLOSE-UP LENS	DISTANCE SETTING ON CAMERA (FEET)
$26\frac{1}{2}$	39	1+	infinity
$11\frac{1}{2}$	$15\frac{1}{2}$	2+	6
6	8	3+	2

focal length of the camera lens (which is printed or engraved on the lens housing) and the amount of extension of the bellows or tubes. The formula can be used for measurements either in inches or in metric units. It is:

$$\frac{\text{increased-exposure}}{\text{factor}} = \frac{(\text{length of extension})^2}{(\text{focal length of lens})^2}$$

The application of this formula to a specific problem is illustrated:

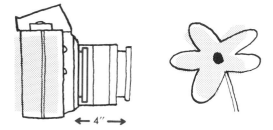

← 4″ →

Focal length of lens; 50 mm or 2 inches
Length of extension; 100 mm or 4 inches
Normal exposure; $f/8$ at 1/60

Using the formula with the distances in inches gives:

$$\text{increased-exposure factor} = \frac{4^2}{2^2} = \frac{16}{4} = 4$$

Therefore exposure must be 4 times the normal exposure. This increase can be accomplished by

USING A COPY STAND

It is difficult to do copy work if you are using a camera without built-in parallax-correction features. But with patience and some skill, simple devices can be constructed or purchased and used to insure proper viewing for close-up work.

A series of home-made or commercial focal frames simplifies framing and focusing.[1]

Focal Frame in Use

_____
1. For details on constructing and using focal frames see *Close-up Pictures with 35-mm Cameras*, pamphlet AB-10 (Eastman Kodak Co.).

An adjustable copy stand, which holds your camera at various heights for different-size copy materials, is very versatile. Vertical stands are more serviceable than horizontal ones because of the difficulty of securing books in a vertical position.

Constructed Wooden Stand Made According to Directions in *A Simple Wooden Copying Stand for Making Title Slides and Filmstrips,* **pamphlet T-43 (Eastman Kodak Co.)**

Commercial Copy Stand

Portable Slide-Production Copy Kit (Visualmaker) from Eastman Kodak Co.

Here is a method for establishing camera and subject positions for filming flat materials of various sizes, using a copy stand with a camera that does not include through-the-lens viewing:

1. Attach the camera to the stand.
2. Open the camera lens fully (to the smallest f/ number).
3. Open the shutter (use the T or the B setting).
4. Open or remove the camera back.
5. Place an appropriate close-up attachment over the lens.
6. Set a piece of ground glass, frosted plastic, or tracing paper in the camera at the film position. Make certain the material is cut to fit over the opening and will lie flat. You will view and focus on this surface.

7. Set the material to be copied on the stand under the camera and switch on the lights.
8. Fill the image area with an image of the subject by moving the camera up and down on the stand. Focus, as necessary, by adjusting the distance setting on the lens. The image will be *upside down* as compared with the copy position.
9. When the picture is framed properly and sharply focused, mark the camera position on the stand and make a record of the distance setting indicated on the focusing ring for the close-up attachment used. See the illustration

for marks of camera position; letters or numbers can be used.

10. On the base of the copy stand outline the area being photographed and relate it (by letter or number) to the camera position and the distance setting.

11. Repeat steps 7–10 for subjects of various sizes. Thus you rule on the stand platform a series of areas, and you relate them to corresponding camera positions, distance setting, and close-up attachments.

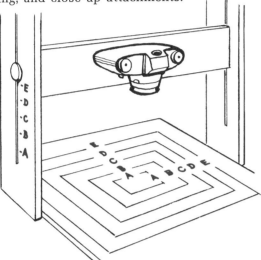

12. Return the camera to normal (remove the material for focusing, close the shutter, and replace the back).

13. Thereafter, with film in the camera, use the marked positions and the recorded distance settings for copying flat materials of various sizes; it will not be necessary to use the viewfinder.

SUGGESTIONS FOR CLOSE-UP AND COPY WORK

☐ Use a tripod or a sturdy stand to steady your camera.

☐ Use either photoflood lamps in reflectors or lamps with built-in reflectors. For copying set the lamps evenly at 45° angles to each side of the camera and at a sufficient distance to avoid uneven lighting, reflections, or "hot spots." Check for evenness of lighting with your meter.

☐ When copying from a book or other source that does not lie flat, hold the material in position with a sheet of nonreflecting glass (available from photo-supply, art-supply, or hardware stores).

☐ For close-up filming of three-dimensional subjects, avoid most shadow areas by using *flat lighting* (that is, use a key-to-fill light ratio of 1 to 1).

☐ Use a meter to determine exposure. An incident-light meter gives a direct reading when placed in the position of the subject or material. If you use a reflected-light meter, read either from a gray card (Eastman Kodak's neutral test card) or from a sheet of white bond paper held against the main portion of the subject. Because such paper reflects a large portion of the light, a reading from it will be *5 times too high*. To correct for this high reading, divide the exposure index of the film by 5 and set your meter at the closest value (example: Kodachrome II Type A, exposure index 40, set meter at 40 ÷ 5, that is, at 8).

☐ Select camera settings with lens-diaphragm opening of $f/11$ or $f/16$ to insure adequate depth of field (but note the exception on page 101 in order to keep the shutter speed faster than 1 second).

☐ *Remember:* You must have the copyright holder's permission to reproduce copyrighted materials (see page 61).

FILMING TITLES

Titles are handled as is other copy work.

If a mask was used to frame the original art work, align the camera on the copy stand to take in the open area of the mask (see page 112). Remove the mask. Then proceed with routine copying of materials made to its size and format.

If a mask was not used to prepare the lettering, adjust picture size by raising or lowering the camera. Keep in mind that acceptable legibility requires lettering size to be a minimum of one-fiftieth the height of the projected area. (See page 120 for description of legibility standards.)

Titles to appear over a special background as *white-letter overprints* may require double exposure (see page 131 for preparation of art work). First film the background slightly dark (½ to 1 *f/* stop underexposed). Then, on the same negative without advancing the film, expose the lettering. Many cameras permit double-exposing, but check yours before trying this technique.

Now, Test What You Have Learned About Close-up and Copy Work:

1. Of the cameras described at the beginning of this chapter (page 79), with which ones would you expect to have a parallax problem in viewing?
2. If a close-up lens is used over the regular camera lens, need there be a calculation for change in exposure? Would this also be true if a bellows extension was used?
3. In close-up work is a *larger* or *smaller* *f/* number desirable? Does this mean that a *slower* or a *faster* shutter speed is used? Therefore, a tripod or stand *is* or *is not* essential?
4. Explain how a reflected-light meter can be used with a sheet of white paper to determine exposure for copying. In such a situation, what setting for exposure index (film speed) is made on the meter for Ektachrome-X film having a rated exposure index of 20 (tungsten)?

Note: Answers to review questions can be found at the end of the chapter.

Processing Film

You may choose, for convenience, to send exposed film to a commercial film-processing laboratory for developing and even for printing. But in recent years the processing of both black-and-white and color film has been greatly simplified by easy-to-handle equipment and easy-to-follow methods.

FACILITIES AND EQUIPMENT

☐ Light-tight room or light-free closet for film loading (a daylight-loading tank eliminates this need)
☐ Sink with running water and counter-top working area
☐ Clean, ventilated area for film drying
☐ Roll-film developing tank with one or more reels for the film size being used or one or more tanks and film holders for cut film
☐ Prepared chemicals for processing film
☐ Graduate or other calibrated measuring container and a funnel
☐ Thermometer
☐ Timer or watch with second hand
☐ Three to six stoppered bottles, preferably of brown-tinted glass

BLACK-AND-WHITE FILM

Practice loading an old roll of film onto the reel of your tank (see suggestions on the instruction sheet with the tank) until you can do it smoothly.

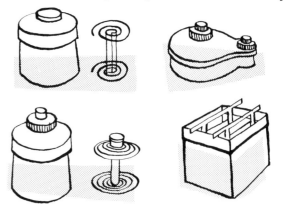

Then, *in the dark,* load and thread the film to be processed. Place the reel in the tank and cap it. From here on do all processing under normal room light.

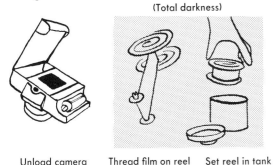

(Total darkness)

Unload camera   Thread film on reel   Set reel in tank

The purpose served by each step in the process is:

- [ ] *Developer*—acts upon the exposed silver chemicals in the film that have been affected by light during picture-taking, depositing the silver as tiny grains to form the black silver image of the negative.
- [ ] *Rinse*—removes excess developer from the film.
- [ ] *Fixer*—sets the image by changing the remaining undeveloped silver chemical so that it may be removed.
- [ ] *Washing*—removes all chemicals that may cause discoloration of the negative or deposits on its surface.

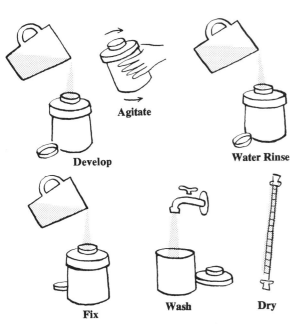

Agitate

Develop   Water Rinse

Fix   Wash   Dry

Refer to the information sheet packaged with your film for recommended developer and for specific processing instructions. Follow all direc-

tions, especially those for time and temperature controls.

Judge the quality of your negative by these points:

- [ ] A good negative will have a considerable amount of detail, even in its very darkest and lightest portions, unless these portions represent parts of the picture which were themselves entirely lacking in detail.
- [ ] A good negative will be transparent enough, even in its very blackest areas, so that you can read a newspaper through it.
- [ ] A good negative will have no part of the picture quite as clear as the borders of the film.

COLOR NEGATIVE FILM

Kodacolor and Ektacolor films can be processed by a film laboratory or with a color processing kit. Processing time in a tank is under 1 hour with careful timing and critical temperature control (the first step requires a constant temperature of $75°F \pm \frac{1}{2}°F$ and the remaining 9 steps permit a $4°F$ range).

1. **Developer** (14 minutes) 2. **Stop Bath** (4 minutes) 3. **Hardener** (4 minutes)

4. **Wash** (4 minutes) 5. **Bleach** (6 minutes) 6. **Wash** (4 minutes)

7. **Fixer** (8 minutes) 8. **Wash** (8 minutes) 9. **Wetting Agent** (1 minute) 10. **Dry**

COLOR REVERSAL FILM

All color reversal films, except Kodachrome, can be "home" processed. Kodachrome is handled only by authorized processing laboratories. As with color negative films, processing kits allow handling of one or more rolls in normal room light with the film in a light-tight tank during the initial part of the process. Here again, temperature and timing must be carefully maintained. As an example, the procedure for Ektachrome roll film (process E-4) is illustrated.

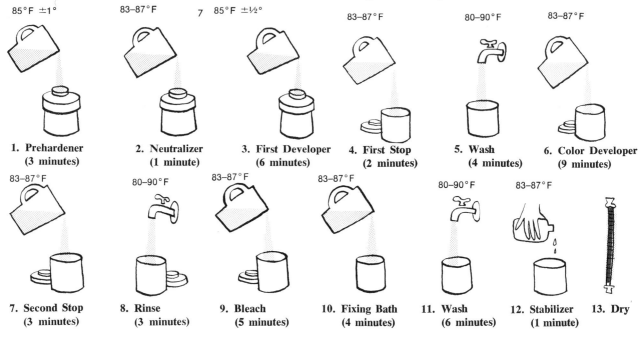

85°F ±1°	83–87°F	7 85°F ±½°
1. Prehardener (3 minutes)	**2. Neutralizer** (1 minute)	**3. First Developer** (6 minutes)

83–87°F — **4. First Stop** (2 minutes)   80–90°F — **5. Wash** (4 minutes)   83–87°F — **6. Color Developer** (9 minutes)

83–87°F — **7. Second Stop** (3 minutes)   80–90°F — **8. Rinse** (3 minutes)   83–87°F — **9. Bleach** (5 minutes)   83–87°F — **10. Fixing Bath** (4 minutes)   80–90°F — **11. Wash** (6 minutes)   83–87°F — **12. Stabilizer** (1 minute)   **13. Dry**

Making Prints

For successful contact printing and enlarging you need to know about:

☐ The selection of contact and enlarging papers (printing papers are classified by speed, weight, finish, contrast, color of image, and base material)
☐ Exposure—length of time for contact printing; lens-diaphragm opening and length of time for enlarging
☐ Processing chemicals and times
☐ Washing, drying, and finishing

More detailed information about printing will be found in the references on page 295. Your photo-supply dealer can advise you on equipment, printing papers, and chemicals.

The negative is used to prepare a positive print on paper or film. *If the print is to be the same size as the negative, the process is contact printing, but if the print is to be larger than the negative, the process is enlarging.*

After the print material is exposed to light, the photographic paper from either contact printing or enlarging follows the same general chemical treatment as for film—develop, stop, fix, and wash (for a paper print, a paper developer is used in place of the film developer).

A two-step *rapid-processing* method for paper is becoming popular. This method takes only a

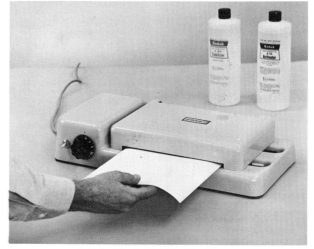

Unit for Photo-Stabilization Process

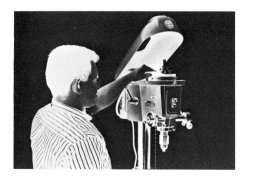

Negative

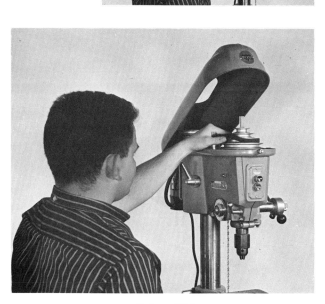

Contact Print

is automatically accomplished in a matter of seconds. Although the resulting print will not fade for a long time, it is recommended that for greater permanence, a print processed by this method be fixed in regular hypo and then thoroughly washed and dried. In addition to various kinds of photographic papers, high-contrast and continuous-tone sheet films are available for use in the photo-stabilization process.

Printing color negatives, while requiring particular care and a great deal of time, has been simplified, and for some products requires fewer chemicals than formerly. For further details refer to the instructions packed with processing chemicals and color printing paper.

FACILITIES AND EQUIPMENT

The standard equipment and materials for a darkroom consist of the following:

- ☐ A darkroom 6×8 feet or larger, equipped with running water, counter-top workspace, storage, and electrical outlets
- ☐ A contact printer or printing frame
- ☐ An enlarger with easel and timer
- ☐ A print washer or tray siphon
- ☐ A print dryer
- ☐ One or more sets of trays (three to a set) in various sizes (8×10 inches, 11×14 inches, and so on)
- ☐ Clock, tongs, and miscellaneous small items
- ☐ One or more safelights (with color filter based on printing paper to be used)
- ☐ Photographic contact and enlarging paper
- ☐ Prepared chemicals for developer, stop bath, and fixer

Enlarged Print

few seconds for developing and fixing exposed paper. It also eliminates the need for an extensive darkroom and most equipment, other than the enlarger and processing unit. In this method, known as *photo-stabilization,* part of the developing agents required are built into the photographic paper. The paper is carried automatically in timed sequence by a system of rollers, first through the developer and then through a *stabilizer* bath. The paper emerges damp-dry. The stabilizer arrests development and stabilizes the image (the chemistry is similar to, but not exactly the same as, fixing with hypo). Thus, processing

If a photo-stabilizer unit is used, the three trays are eliminated; the sink and even the darkroom itself can be reduced appreciably in size.

CONTACT PRINTING

This method is particularly useful for rapid preparation of *proof sheets* from negatives. A whole roll of negatives (12 to 36) can be printed at one time on a sheet of contact paper (8×10 inch). From these contact prints, negatives can be selected for enlargements.

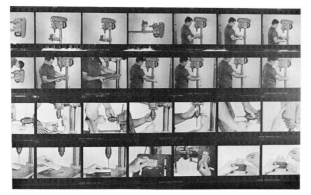

Place the negative (emulsion, or *dull side, down*) on top of a sheet of photographic contact paper (emulsion, or *shiny side, up*); cover them with glass and expose the pack to light. Or use a contact printer with a pressure platen and a built-in lamp for exposing. Develop the paper. The resulting print will be the same size as the negative.

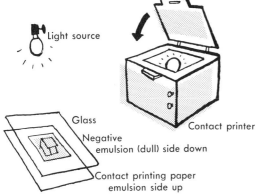

Light source

Glass

Negative
emulsion (dull) side down

Contact printer

Contact printing paper
emulsion side up

ENLARGING

Place the negative in the enlarger and project it through the lens onto a sheet of enlarging paper. Make tests on strips of paper before preparing the final prints.

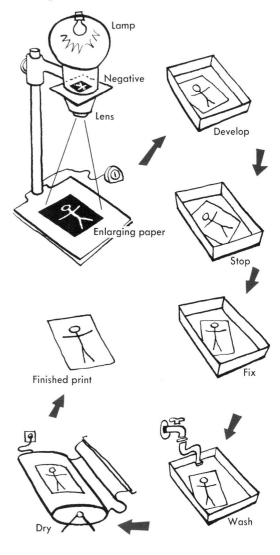

Lamp

Negative

Lens

Develop

Enlarging paper

Stop

Fix

Finished print

Wash

Dry

Now, Test What You Have Learned About Processing Film and Making Prints:

1. What are the four steps necessary to develop black-and-white film and the purpose of each step?
2. What are some characteristics of a good black-and-white negative?
3. In what ways and with what materials do the four steps in tray processing of black-and-white photographic paper differ from those in developing of black-and-white film?
4. Sketch your own layout for a darkroom, showing location of the equipment and necessary supplies.

5. What purpose is often served by making contact prints of a roll of black-and-white negatives?
6. What are two advantages of using the photo-stabilization process for processing paper over the regular tray process?
7. What is the major difference in film processing procedure between color negative and color reversal processes?

Answers to Review Questions

CAMERA TYPES (PAGE 81)
1. 35-mm camera
2. Sheet-film camera
3. Automatic-setting camera
4. Polaroid Land camera
5. Twin-lens reflex camera
6. Automatic-setting camera

CAMERA LENSES (PAGE 83)
1. Reader's activity, page 82.
2. Millimeters
3. Wide angle, normal, telephoto
4. (a) Normal, (b) wide angle, (c) telephoto, (d) telephoto
5. Reader's activity

CAMERA SETTINGS (PAGE 88)
1. Twice as much
2. (a) 1/500 second, (b) 1/250 second, (c) 1/125 second
3. f/22 and 1/30 second
4. 3⅓–5 feet
5. Less

FILM (PAGE 91)
1. Type of light source (sunlight, photoflood, or other)
2. Kodacolor or Ektacolor negative film
3. Indicates the relative light sensitivity of the film; higher number for greater sensitivity (faster film)
4. For use under lower light levels or to film faster action

EXPOSURE (PAGE 94)
1. Film speed, f/stop, shutter speed; f/stop and shutter speed; film speed
2. Film speed and light-level indication
3. f/stop and shutter speed
4. f/32 and ⅛ second
5. Incident-light meter

LIGHTING (PAGE 97)
1. Small areas.
2. f/16.
3. Flat shadowless lighting on the subject with heavy background shadows.
4. Incident meter reading of key light, measured at the scene, is twice that of the fill light. Yes, this is an acceptable ratio.
5. Check the four methods described on page 97.
6. **a.** Key—main light on subject; 45° to side of camera and placed higher than camera.
b. Fill—lighten shadows created by key light; at camera position on other side from the key.
c. Background—lighten background, reduce shadows on background and give some depth to scene; aimed at background from side.

d. Accent—highlight or outline the subject and separate from background; above the subject, aimed down.

PICTURE COMPOSITION (PAGE 99)

Generally No. 4 would be preferable because of the careful framing.

CLOSE-UP AND COPY WORK (PAGE 104)

1. All lenses that have separate window-type viewers.
2. No. Calculation is necessary if a bellows is used.
3. Larger number (that is, smaller opening). Slower. Tripod essential.
4. Divide 20 by 5. Set meter at film speed of 4.

PROCESSING FILM AND MAKING PRINTS (PAGE 108)

1. Developer—causes chemical change to form black silver image on film.
   Rinse—stops action of developer.
   Fixer—sets the image on the film.
   Wash—removes all chemicals.
2. See list on page 105.
3. Paper developer instead of film developer in first step, others the same.
4. Reader's activity.
5. You can examine photographs to select best negatives for enlargements.
6. Faster processing and requires less print handling and darkroom space.
7. A single developer step is used in color negative processing, while with color reversal processing, after the first developer, a color developer is used which brings out the positive image. Eventually the negative image is bleached out.

16

GRAPHICS

In preparing your audiovisual materials you may find it necessary to:

☐ *Plan* art work and titles in terms of size, proportions, and principles of design.
☐ *Draw* illustrations, diagrams, cartoons, and title backgrounds.
☐ *Color* art work to clarify details or to give emphasis and add attractiveness.
☐ *Letter* titles, captions, and labels that comply with recognized legibility standards.
☐ *Mount* photographs, pictures, and related materials for durability, ease of handling, and attractive display.
☐ *Protect* the surface of materials to insure long use when handled.
☐ *Reproduce* materials on paper for distribution, using the most appropriate of a number of methods.

This chapter treats each of these areas with details and techniques.

The success of many audiovisual materials can be attributed in large measure to the quality and effectiveness of the art work and related graphic materials. These are achieved through organizing preliminary thoughts, careful planning, and applying the techniques outlined in this chapter.

Many persons who develop audiovisual materials have little or no professional art background. They need not, therefore, prepare amateurish and poor-quality graphic materials. First, they can consider a number of common-sense practical suggestions and guiding principles, then apply them as the need arises. Second, there are a number of easy-to-use manipulative devices that, with little practice, will insure semiprofessional-quality results.

Planning Art Work

Your art work must be planned with consideration for the size and dimensions of the working area, for the proportions of your visual materials, for design and layout features, for backgrounds, and for the resources, skills, techniques, materials, and facilities that you can employ.

SIZE OF WORKING AREA

Decide on a size for your art work that meets these requirements:

☐ Lettering and drawing can be done easily.
☐ Parallax and close-up difficulties in the camera, if there are any, can be easily overcome when copying (see page 99).
☐ The art work is easy to store.

The minimum dimension that is likely to meet these requirements is 10×12 inches; therefore use cardboard of this size or larger. You can cut boards 11×14 inches without waste from standard-size 22×28 inch sheets, which can be had in

8-ply or 14-ply thickness. Commonly used working areas, on boards of either size, are 6×9 inches and 9×12 inches; minimum lettering sizes for these areas are suggested on page 122. Compose within the proper proportions (see below) of your selected audiovisual materials, and provide generous margins around the sides of all work.

The end papers inside the front cover of this book contain recommended mask sizes for filmstrips and slides. The end papers inside the back cover have diagrams for masks to use with overhead transparencies and motion-picture formats.

If many scenes require art work and lettering, standardize your size and prepare a mask with a cut-out of the proper working area. The mask will serve as a margin and as a frame when you view the prepared art work and will also be useful as a guide for positioning art work and camera during copying.

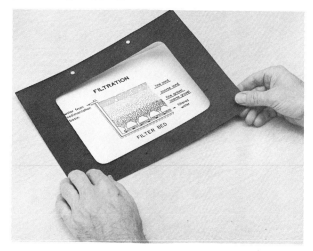

If titles, labels, or diagrams must be placed one over the other or over a background, you need equipment to hold them in *alignment,* or *register.* If you need to make only a few such graphics, you may be able to work on an ordinary

drawing board with thumbtacks. If you have any quantity of work, a *register board* will save time. Use a two- or three-hole punch to perforate your drawing materials at the edge, and put two or three pegs or pins in the drawing board to fit these perforations snugly while allowing the work to lie smooth and flat. This register board can be used both during preparation of the materials and also when filming the final assembly. A two- or three-ring binder may serve instead of a register board for work that does not require precise alignment.

PROPORTIONS OF AUDIOVISUAL MATERIALS

☐ Photographs—commonly 4 to 5, but may vary depending on size for final use.

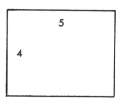

☐ Slides

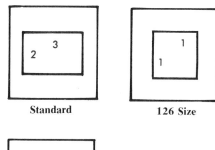

Standard   **126 Size**

Half-Frame   **110 Size**

☐ Filmstrips

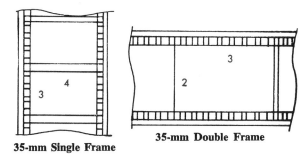

35-mm Single Frame   **35-mm Double Frame**

☐ Overhead transparencies—usually 4 to 5

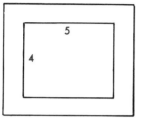

☐ Motion pictures

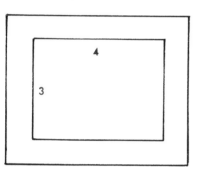

☐ Television format

DESIGN AND LAYOUT

Examine some of the graphic materials that are a common part of your everyday world—magazine advertisements, outdoor billboards, animated cartoons, television titles and commercials, and so on. You can find many ideas for designing your own materials by studying the arrangement of elements in such commercial displays.

You may be planning a title for a slide series, for a filmstrip, or for a motion picture; or your plans may deal with art work for a chart, a diagram, a poster, or even an instructional bulletin board. In these and other planning situations you should be aware of certain design principles and visual design tools. Then be prepared to apply those that can help you.

Design principles include: simplicity, unity, emphasis, and balance.

Simplicity

Charts, graphs, and diagrams suitable for page printing may not be suitable for projection. They may include large amounts of information and be acceptable in a printed report or for a manual, but these permit detailed, close-up study, which is not usually possible with projected materials. A cutting from a publication, used in a slide, might be so complex that it would be confusing. Therefore, evaluate the suitability of all items you consider for inclusion in your visual materials and try to limit your selection or design to the presentation of one idea at a time.

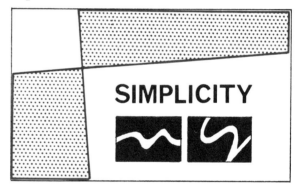

Generally speaking, the fewer elements into which a given space is divided, the more pleasing it is to the eye. Subdivide or redesign lengthy or complex data into a number of easy-to-read and easy-to-understand related materials. Limit the verbal content for projected visuals to 15 or 20 words.

Drawings should be bold, simple, and contain only key details. Picture symbols should be outlined with a heavy line. The necessary details can be added in thinner lines since they should appear less important. Many thin lines, particularly if they are not essential, may actually confuse the clarity of the image when viewed from a distance.

Finally, for simplicity use simple, easy-to-comprehend lettering styles and a minimum of different styles in the same visual or series of visuals.

Unity

Unity is the relationship that exists among the elements of a visual when they all function together. It can be achieved by overlapping elements, by using pointing devices like arrows, and by employing the visual tools (line, shape, color, texture, and space) described on page 115.

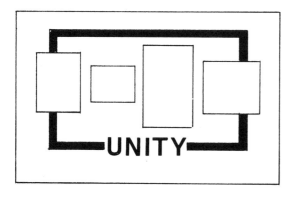

Emphasis

Even though a visual treats a single idea, is simply developed, and has unity, there is often the need to give emphasis to a single element—to make it the center of interest and attention. Through the use of size, relationships, perspective, and such visual tools as color or space, emphasis can be given to the most important elements.

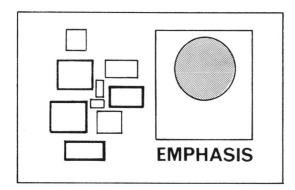

Balance

There are two kinds of balance—formal and informal. Formal balance is identified by an imaginary axis running through the center of the visual dividing the design so that one half will be the mirror reflection of the other half. Such a formal balance is static.

Informal balance is asymmetrical; the elements create an equilibrium without being static. It is a dynamic and more attention-getting arrangement. It requires more imagination and daring by the designer. The informal balance may have an asymmetrical or a diagonal layout.

For titles, a symmetrical balance of lettering is formal in effect and is desired for many uses. It requires accurate positioning of letters and extra care when filming to insure even margins (equal side margins, but a somewhat greater area at the bottom than at the top).

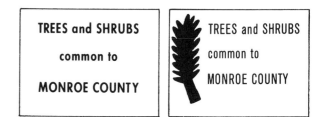

Informal arrangements, when appropriately combined with sketches or pictures, make attractive titles. Such arrangements eliminate the problem of centering but not the problem of accurate positioning.

Try various arrangements before doing the final lettering.

The *visual tools* that contribute to the successful use of the above design principles include line, shape, color, texture, and space.

Line

A line in a visual can connect elements together and will direct the viewer to study the visual in a specific sequence.

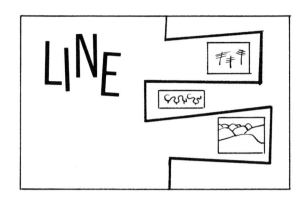

Shape

An unusual shape can give special interest to a visual.

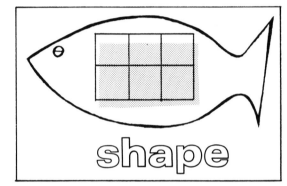

Space

Open space around visual elements and words will prevent a crowded feeling. Only when space is used carefully can the elements of design become effective.

Texture

Texture is a visual element that may serve as a replacement for the sense of touch and can be used in much the same way as color—to give emphasis or separation, or to enhance unity.

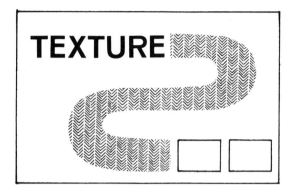

Color

Color is an important adjunct to most visuals, but it should be used sparingly for best effects. Apply it to elements of a visual to give separation or emphasis, or to enhance unity. Select colors that are harmonious together because colors that are dissonant (of equal intensity and complementary on the color wheel, like orange—blue and red—green) create annoyance in the audience and consequently interfere with a clear perception of the message.

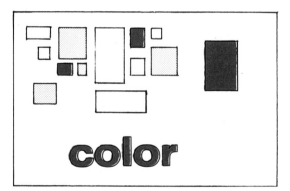

Consider using both the four design principles and the five visual tools as your art work, titles, and other graphic materials.

Now, Review What You Have Learned About Planning Art Work:

1. What is a satisfactory size for a working surface on which to prepare art work?
2. Which audiovisual materials have a 4 to 3 proportion? Which a 3 to 2 proportion?
3. Enumerate the four principles of design and the five visual tools for design.

Note: Answers to review questions can be found at the end of the chapter.

Illustrating

In addition to photographed subjects, your script may require illustrations made as original drawings or as copies of available pictures. If you have an art background, you will have little difficulty in preparing such illustrations. If you do not have this ability, you can resort to a number of easy-to-apply methods.

USING READY-MADE PICTURES

Pictures from magazines, from free or inexpensive booklets, or from similar sources can serve your needs for some illustrations. If you maintain a file of clipped pictures (*tearsheets*) on various subjects, you may have suitable pictures as called for in your script. At times, part of a picture or combined sections of two or more pictures may be needed. Mount pictures on cardboard (see page 132) and add lettering if it is appropriate (see page 121). And remember, always, that such pictures may be copyright and to use them you need the permission of the copyright holder (see page 61).

For certain general uses *clip-book* pictures are ideal. Clip books on many subjects are available commercially (see the list on page 300 for sources). Each book contains a variety of black-and-white line drawings, on paper or on translucent material. These may be cut from the page or, frequently, duplicated; pictures or copies are then combined with suitable lettering in paste-ups (see page 144) to make titles or visuals. To use these, photograph them using high-contrast film (page 214) and print the negative as a slide or transparency on film (page 215) or as a print on photographic paper (see page 108).

If a picture cannot be used directly or easily reproduced, you can place a sheet of translucent tracing paper over the picture and outline the main lines with a pencil. Then transfer the tracing to a cardboard or other material by backing the tracing paper with a sheet of carbon paper and tracing over the lines.

ENLARGING AND REDUCING PICTURES

There are a number of machines, simple devices, and hand techniques you might consider using to change the size of available diagrams. We will examine five of them.

A small picture on a single sheet or in a book can be enlarged by using an *opaque projector*. Place the paper or book on the holder of the projector and attach a piece of cardboard to a wall. Adjust the size of the projected picture to fit the required area on the cardboard by moving the projector *closer* to the cardboard (*to be smaller*) or *farther away* from the cardboard (*to be larger*) and focusing as necessary. Then trace the main lines of the projected picture with pencil. After completing the drawing, ink in the lines using pen and ink or a felt pen. This is one of the easiest and quickest ways to enlarge a picture.

If a transparency or a slide of the original diagram is available or can be made by one of the processes to be described later in this book, an overhead projector or a slide projector can be used to make an enlargement.

But also with the *overhead projector*, large pictures can be *reduced* to fit $8\frac{1}{2} \times 11$ inch or other formats. This technique uses the overhead projector in reverse fashion as compared to its normal enlarging use. The original, large diagram is attached to a wall and a light (floodlight or a slide projector) is aimed at it. Sufficient light must be reflected from the diagram through the lens of the projector to be visible on a white sheet of paper placed on the projection stage. Move the lens up and down to focus the image on the paper. Control the size by moving the whole projector closer to the wall or farther from it. Sketch the visual over the image on the sheet of paper.

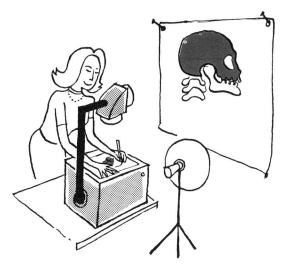

Another device, especially designed for enlarging and reducing art work, is the *photo modifier.* It resembles a large view camera (page 100) with a ground glass back against which tracing

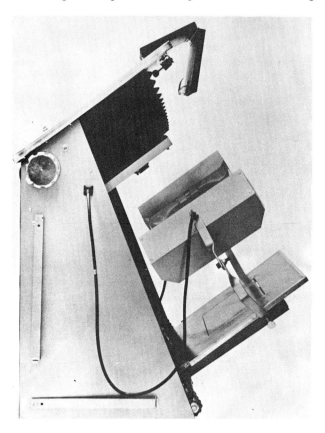

paper can be taped. The size of the original picture can be reduced or enlarged in accurate proportion by moving the device and then focusing the image by adjusting the bellows. Perspective can be changed and distortion created by tilting the ground-glass surface or the front lens.

A *pantograph* also may be used to enlarge or reduce pictures. It is operated by setting a fulcrum pin, tracing the lines of the picture with one point, and reproducing them in the desired proportion (larger or smaller) with a pen or pencil at another point.

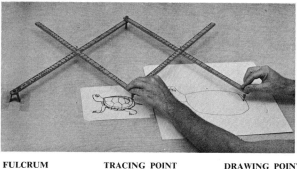

FULCRUM   TRACING POINT   DRAWING POINT

By using the *squaring method,* a picture can be proportionally enlarged or reduced or even elongated and distorted purposefully. First, prepare a grid on acetate or translucent tracing paper. The size of each square is determined by the size and detail in the picture (use at least four or five squares in height or width to cover the picture). Then make a second grid with squares

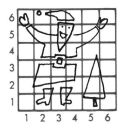

proportionally larger or smaller than the first one (for a 2× enlargement the squares of the second grid should be twice the dimension of those of the first grid). Place the first grid over the picture and copy the relative position of each line onto a piece of translucent paper placed over the second grid. Finally, transfer this drawing to cardboard or other material using carbon paper.

If you want a copy relatively higher or wider than the original, use rectangles instead of squares on your copy grid—tall or wide according to your wishes for the changed picture.

Now, Review What You Have Learned About Illustrating for Visual Materials:

1. What is a clip-book and how is it used?
2. List four methods for changing the size of illustrations and compare them as to ease of use, time and equipment required, and probable quality of results.

Note: Answers to review questions can be found at the end of the chapter.

Coloring and Shading

The attractiveness of a black-and-white line drawing is greatly enhanced by the addition of shading or coloring.

Using certain color combinations or coloring selected parts will contribute emphasis and even clarification to a complex diagram. For example, since yellow and orange are colors of high visibility, black lines on a yellow or orange background will command more attention than black on white.

Those who have art backgrounds may be able to use such techniques as wash drawing and air brushing; even those with limited training may consider using several simple techniques.

FELT PENS

When strips of felt are cut, beveled to an edge, and mounted in a holder, they become printing and drawing tools called *felt pens*. Colored lines of various thicknesses can be made. Some felt pens are refillable and need not be discarded when the ink supply runs out. Both permanent and wash-

able inks are available for use in felt pens, and they come in a variety of colors. Felt pens are useful for coloring small areas. Since the colors are transparent, apply them carefully; each overlapping stroke deepens the tone and may produce uneven coloring in large areas.

COLORED PENCILS AND CHALK

Ordinary colored pencils, when handled with care, can produce pleasing color effects. Keep the pencil sharp, but hold it at a flat angle when stroking, being sure to work back and forth in only two directions. After coloring an area, rub over it with a small piece of blotter or with a stump of rolled paper. Rubbing helps to spread the color evenly over the whole area.

Chalk (often dampened with water) can be used in much the same way as pencils, although chalk adheres better to a coarse surface like construction paper. To prevent smudging of either pencil- or chalk-colored art work, spray a fixative coating over the surface.

SPRAY-CAN PAINTS AND AIR-BRUSHING

Paint in pressurized cans can be used to apply color to areas on a visual. This technique is also used to color cardboard around three-dimensional letters which are removed, after spraying, to reveal the unpainted image of the letters. By controlling the distance between the spray can and the surface to be sprayed, either a spatter effect or an even paint coverage can be achieved. Protect parts of the visual not to be colored by covering with paper attached with masking tape.

Carefully controlled color spraying can be done with an *air brush* attached to a compressed-

air line or to a pressurized-air can. By adjusting the air-brush nozzle and depressing the control knob the spread of spray is controlled. As with the spray-can paints, it is necessary to cover parts of a visual around the area to be colored.

COLOR AND SHADING SHEETS

Prepared color and shading sheets are excellent for use on areas of any size. They are available in a wide range of patterns and colors, both transparent and translucent. They will adhere to all surfaces.

Translucent color sheets have an adhesive wax backing, which makes them partially opaque. Such sheets should be used to color art work prepared on cardboard. Transparent color sheets are prepared with a clear adhesive backing so the color will project brilliantly when applied to a transparency or to other visuals for projection.

The shading or color is printed on a thin plastic sheet, which has an adhesive backing. This in turn is protected with a backing sheet. To work with these sheets, use a razor blade or a very sharp knife and follow the procedure illustrated.

1. Place a sheet of the selected material over the area to be shaded or colored.
2. Lightly cut a piece slightly larger than the area to be colored or shaded. (Try not to cut through the backing sheet.)
3. Peel the cut piece from the backing.
4. Place the cut piece of adhesive-backed material over the area and rub to adhere.
5. Cut to match the area, using lines in the diagram as guides.
6. Peel off the excess pieces of the coloring or shading material.

When applying color to acetate for transparencies:

☐ Adhere the color piece to the underside of the transparency so it can not be damaged during use.
☐ Place the color piece in place on one line of the visual and ease it into place, smoothing by hand so no trapped air or wrinkles result.
☐ Use care so as not to cut through the acetate when trimming the color to match a line.
☐ Do not slip off the line being traced since the blade cut will be visible as a dark mark when projected.

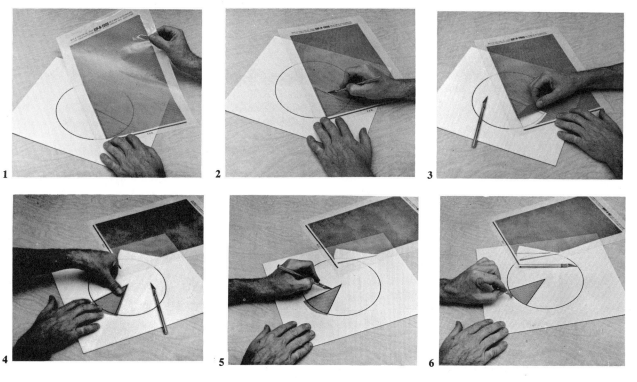

Now, Review What You Have Learned About
Coloring and Shading:

1. How does the use of felt pens compare to the use of spray paints for coloring moderate-sized areas?
2. When using a color adhesive sheet why is it *not* proper to cut through the color sheet *and* the backing sheet when first cutting the piece for use? Also, why should you *not* cut the piece to be used the exact size at first?
3. Of the coloring methods described, which one might be selected to carefully tint a large, irregular area.

Note: Answers to review questions can be found at the end of the chapter.

Legibility Standards for Lettering

The legibility of the words, numerals, and other data that an audience is expected to read is frequently neglected during the planning and preparation of visual materials. This neglect is especially common since simple and quick methods have become available for duplicating typewritten and printed materials. But it is very important that planners give proper attention to legibility—hence to methods of lettering, sizes of letters, and styles of lettering. These matters physically control the amount of information that can be presented in one visual unit. Reciprocally, the psychological limits on amount of information affect the choices in respect to lettering. Keep in mind, therefore, the methods for dividing lengthy or complex data into a sequence of visuals (page 199); see the discussion of layout and design earlier in this chapter.

The suitability of lettering is further complicated by a number of other factors—characteristics of the projection room, such as its shape; the type of screen surface (rear-screen transmitted projection is not as brilliant as front-screen reflected projection and will require larger lettering for legibility); the brightness of the projection lamp to be used; and the amount of ambient or outside light that cannot be controlled.

If your audiovisual materials are designed for use in a specific room, then take into account as many of these factors as possible in deciding on lettering sizes. But no one can predict or be prepared for all eventualities in viewing situations. Often visuals must be presented under less than ideal conditions; therefore, it is advisable that *minimum standards* be recognized. As a general guide, select minimum lettering size for *all* materials so that any member of an audience, seated at an anticipated maximum viewing distance, can easily read titles, captions, and labels. If you do not heed this advice, you are likely to find members of the audience losing interest in your presentation because they cannot read the lettered information.

To assist with good legibility, the following guidelines are recommended:

☐ Select a readable letter style, like a sans-serif or gothic type, in which all letters are easily recognized with a minimum of confusion. Avoid script letter styles because they are difficult to read.

MANY BUYERS	A Sans Serif-Letter
MANY BUYERS	A Condensed Sans Serif
MANY BUYERS	A Modern Letter with Serifs
Many Buyers	A Script Letter
𝔐𝔞𝔫𝔶 𝔅𝔲𝔶𝔢𝔯𝔰	An Old English Letter

Some Common Lettering Styles Arranged According to Their Legibility (Most Legible at Top and Decreasing Downward)

☐ Use capital letters for short titles and labels, but for longer captions and phrases (six words or more) use lower-case letters with appropriate capitals since the lower-case letters are more easily read.

A HISTORY **OF OUR CHURCH**	**The Forty Most Common** **Deciduous Trees and Shrubs** **in Vernon County**

☐ Allow 1½ letter widths for the space between words and 3 widths between sentences. Too much or too little space again makes reading difficult.

☐ Space letters *optically*. Equal measured distances between all letters do not look equal. *Make spaces look equal*, regardless of measurement.

CAPITAL CAPITAL

Good   Poor

☐ Separate lines within a caption so that adequate white space is left for ease of reading —about 1½ times the height of the lower-case letter *m*, measured from an *m* on one line to an *m* (or comparable letter) on the next line.

San Jose State College,
the first public institution
of higher education in
California, was founded
in 1857.   **Too Close**

San Jose State College,

the first public institution

of higher education in

California, was founded

in 1857.   **Too Far**

San Jose State College,
the first public institution
of higher education in
California, was founded
in 1857.   **Good**

☐ Contrast the lettering in color on tone with the background so that separation contributes to good legibility

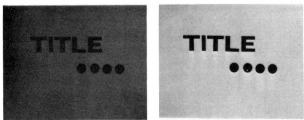

| **Black Lettering on Blue Background** | **Red Lettering on Yellow Background** |

NONPROJECTED MATERIALS

For display materials follow these recommendations:

MAXIMUM ANTICIPATED VIEWING DISTANCE	MINIMUM LETTER HEIGHT (LOWER-CASE LETTER M)
8 feet	¼ inch
16 feet	½ inch
32 feet	1 inch
64 feet	2 inches

Capital letters, alone or with lower-case, should be correspondingly larger than the recommendations above because they are less legible.

PROJECTED MATERIALS

For slides, filmstrips, transparencies, and motion pictures, minimum letter size also is based on the maximum anticipated viewing distance. This maximum, as a standard, is accepted as being *8 times the horizontal dimension of the picture on the screen* (that is, 8W). Thus, for a screen 6 feet wide, filled with a picture, the maximum viewing distance of 8W is 48 feet.[1]

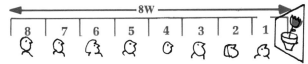

Rear-screen projection does not permit as bright or as contrasty an image as does front projection. For suitable legibility, lettering half again as large as for front projection is required for rear-screen projected materials.[2]

The maximum viewing distance for television, in terms of the screen size, is greater, being 14W. As you might expect, minimum letter size for television is therefore greater.

Minimum letter sizes are recommended in Table 16-1 (page 122).

Although the recommended lettering heights in Table 16-1 are minimum, larger or bolder lettering is often advantageous (following the 8W formula). This is not only for legibility, but also

1. The 8W recommendation is by the Eastman Kodak Co. (see reference in n. 2 below). One noted authority in the field of planning and designing facilities for audio visual communication, Gerald McVey, advises a 6W rather than the forementioned 8W formula. See his *Educational Facilities: Man, Media and the Learning Environment* (Boston: Department of Media and Technology, Boston University, 1974).

2. For further description of many of these processes, *Large Group Instruction*, University Facilities Research Center, University of Wisconsin, Madison, 1964.

TABLE 16-1   Minimum Letter Sizes for Viewing Distances of Various Audiovisual Materials.

MEDIUM	MAXIMUM VIEWING DISTANCE	MAXIMUM RATIO OF LETTER HEIGHT TO HEIGHT OF ART-WORK AREA	MINIMUM LETTER HEIGHT (LOWER-CASE LETTER M) FOR AREA 6 × 9 INCH
Slides Filmstrips Transparencies Motion pictures	8W	1 to 50	$\frac{1}{8}$ inch
Television	16W	1 to 25	$\frac{1}{4}$ inch

Adapted from *Legibility: Artwork to Screen*, pamphlet S-24 (Eastman Kodak Co., Rochester, N. Y.) See the Legibility Calculator in this pamphlet for application to various distance situations.

to increase the impact and emphasis of the lettering, thus improving learning and retention.

As the table suggests, captions for slides to be used on a screen 6 feet wide in a room 48 feet or 8W deep, prepared within a 6×9 inch work area, would require lettering at least .125 inch, or

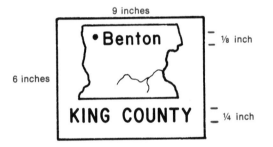

⅛ inch in height. This is 1/50 times the vertical dimension of the working area.

You can make a rough test of the legibility of lettered materials for projection by first measuring the width of the art work in inches, then dividing this number by 2 and placing the material that many feet away from a test reader. If he reads the lettering easily, then for normal conditions the material, when projected, will be legible. But don't trust yourself as a test reader if you prepared the lettering or know how it should read —your memory may help your vision too much.

The recommendations for insuring legibility of visual materials are only for your guidance. Be alert to special conditions in any situations— seating arrangements, light level, image brightness, and so forth. These may require larger images or bolder lettering to insure satisfactory legibility.

Now, Review What You Have Learned About Legibility Standards for Lettering:

1. What is the single most important reason why legibility standards must be considered for projected materials?
2. How might you relate the degree of legibility to quantity of information possible in a visual?
3. What are four guidelines that will contribute to good legibility in lettering?
4. What is the minimum letter size for materials displayed at the front of an average-sized classroom—30 feet deep?
5. What is the minimum size for lettering used in the direct preparation of a transparency (7½ inches vertical dimension)?
6. Should visuals for television use be lettered larger, smaller, or the same size as materials for regular classroom use?
7. Does rear-screen projection require larger or smaller lettering than comparable front-screen projection?

Note: Answers to review questions can be found at the end of the chapter.

Lettering for Titles

However good the photography and picture content of visual materials, their effectiveness is enhanced by well-appearing titles, captions, and labels. Neat lettering, simple designs, and attractive colors or background patterns all add a professional touch to your materials.

Titles generally require large, bold letters. Since there are relatively few major titles, their letters may be hand-drawn, or set individually in place by hand. But such methods may be too slow for preparing captions that consist of many words; here other lettering techniques are appropriate, adequate, even better. You need to know and select techniques with regard to the results needed and the time available for preparation of your materials.

Some remarks follow concerning nine specific lettering techniques. Many more techniques exist, and still more will be devised by ingenious workers using new ideas and new materials. No one technique is necessarily the best for any lettering job. You need to evaluate as many of them as you can—for your own needs, in respect to availability, cost, ease of use, time required for preparation, and resulting quality.

BOLDFACE TYPEWRITER LETTERING

Lettering typed on a boldface typewriter is good for captions requiring many words. It is satisfactory for titles and subtitles. Its legibility is

 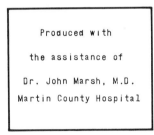

superior to that of the pica or elite type on regular office typewriters unless the latter is photographed and enlarged. Use paper of good quality, whether white or colored, and a carbon-paper ribbon or a well-inked cloth ribbon. Have the type clean and strike the keys firmly and uniformly to get sharp, even, black impressions.

THREE-DIMENSIONAL LETTERS

Three-dimensional letters are manufactured in cardboard, wood, cork, ceramics, and plastics, and are available in plain backs or pin backs. They are excellent for main titles, and when pho-

tographed with side lighting they give shadow effects and three-dimensional effects. Costs vary widely according to kind and size. Surfaces can be tinted with paint or water colors. Position the letters against a T-square or on a guideline and adhere temporarily with rubber cement.

CONSTRUCTION-PAPER PUNCH-OUT LETTERS

Inexpensive ready-to-use letters, cut out of white or colored paper, in many styles, colors, and sizes, are easy to manipulate and are satisfactory for bold titles. They can be placed over

any background. To align them neatly, use a T-square or lightly rule a guideline on the mounting material. Arrange the letters and attach them with a small amount of rubber cement or other adhesive. Finally, erase the guideline.

GUMMED-BACK PAPER CUT-OUT LETTERS

Manufacturers supply complete alphabets of cut-out letters with gummed backs. They are similar in effect and method of use to other cut-out

letters, and are suitable for titles and labels on many types of backgrounds. Position the letters on guidelines, then fix them on the background after moistening the adhesive on the back with a sponge dipped in water. Be careful not to get water on the front side of letters because some colors run.

DRY-TRANSFER LETTERS

These letters have sharp, clean edges much like those printed from good type, and are easy to handle. They come in sheets of many sizes, styles, and colors. They are excellent for titles and labels—on many types of backgrounds.

Dry-transfer letters are printed on the back of the sheet and each sheet is backed with a protective sheet of paper. It is important to keep this backing sheet behind the letters except when exposing a portion of the letter sheet for use.

Follow this procedure in using dry-transfer letters:

1. Slip the backing sheet below or above the row of letters having the letter to be used.
2. Position the letter by aligning the printed line under the letters over the guideline drawn on the mounting surface.
3. Burnish (rub) the entire letter to the mounting surface with the round part of a pen, or other blunt object on which you can exert pressure without tearing the paper.
4. Slowly pull the sheet of letters from the mounting surface. The letter will remain transferred.
5. After all letters have been transferred, replace the backing sheet behind the letter sheet. Then erase the guideline from the mounting surface.

Dry-transfer letters are also available in transparent colors for direct use on transparencies. When they are adhered to acetate, a clean transfer results with no adhesive residue appearing around the letter.

If a dry transfer letter must be removed from paper or cardboard, this can be done by firmly sticking a piece of masking tape on the letter. Then carefully pull the tape up. A new letter can be adhered in the same place.

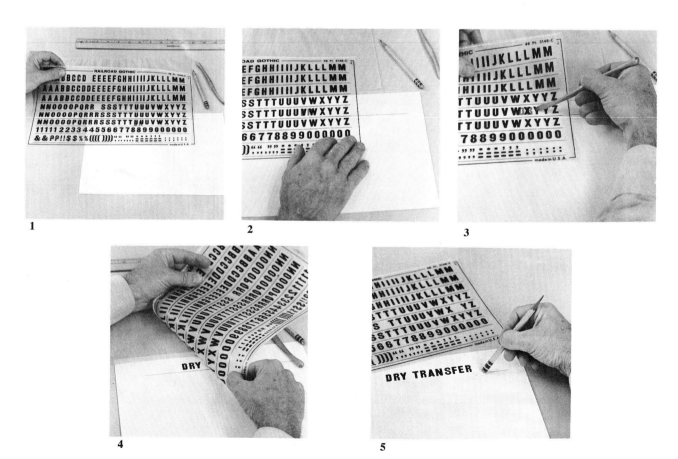

FELT-PEN LETTERING

The use of the beveled-edge felt pen for coloring has been described on page 118. These pens can also be used for lettering. For successful results:

- ☐ Hold the pen firmly in a "locked" or set position in the hand.
- ☐ Make no finger or wrist movement. *All* movements should consist of arm movements.

Sharp-tipped nylon pens make a thinner mark than the beveled-felt pens. They are easier to use and are good for quick lettering on all surfaces. The inks in some make permanent marks, but most have water-based inks.

Always replace the cap on a felt or nylon pen as soon as you are done using it. Since their inks dry quickly, uncapped pens will dry out, resulting in a hardened unserviceable tip. If this happens, soak the tip in lighter fluid (permanent-ink pen) or in water (water-based-ink pen).

STENCIL LETTERING GUIDES (WRICO SIGNMAKER)

Stencil lettering guides are offered in a variety of styles and sizes. The better ones can be used, after a little practice, to produce neat and attractive lettering, even in lengthy captions. They are thus satisfactory, in skilled use excellent, for all

lettering needs. Some stencils are designed to be raised off the background and positioned against a metal guide. A special pen is used, which fits and follows the letter outline in the plastic stencil.

Lettering from ½ inch to 4 inches in height can be made with the *Wrico Signmaker* unit. It consists of a *stencil guide,* a *brush pen* or special *felt pen,* and a *guide holder* to raise the guide from the paper.

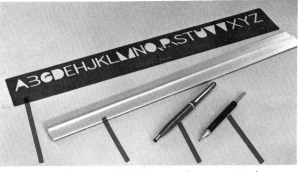

Stencil guide   Guide holder   Felt pen   Brush pen

A stencil guide has this kind of label printed on the lower center part:

(WRICO)
GUIDE No. AVC 100
USE WITH BRUSH PEN C or FELT PEN NCF

These labels give such information as:

AV—letter style (other styles have codes A, D, BF, T, MS).
C—*capital* letters on stencil.
L—*lower-case* letters on stencil.
N—*numbers* on stencil.
Letter size—Wrico Signmaker stencils are based on a code of 100 for 1 inch, 75 for ¾ inch, and the like.
Pen size—Brush pens are coded *A* to *E,* with size *A* making the thinnest line. Felt pens are coded *AF* to *EF,* with size *AF* making the thinnest line.

1. The letter for the size of a Wrico brush pen is stamped near the tip; on the felt pen the letter is stamped on the barrel. Each stencil guide requires a certain pen size for proper use as indicated on the guide.

2. On the back of the guide holder is an indication of which side to use as based on the pen

size the stencil requires. This difference in elevation (look at the edge of the guide holder) is necessary in order to raise the stencil from the paper and avoid the possibility of smearing ink while lettering.

WRICO GUIDE HOLDER No. 18
Use LOW side for guides requiring Brush Pens A and B and Felt Pen BF.   ↑

Use HIGH side for guides requiring all other Brush Pens or Felt Pens.

High side   Low side

3. Align the guideholder on the work. Set the stencil on the guide holder.

4. Hold the brush pen vertically and depress the plunger from the top. You can then see the grooves of the metal "brush" which will hold the ink.

5. Hold the metal collar (located above the black handle shaft) and turn the black shaft so the tip of the brush is flush with the outer tip of the pen. If the brush protrudes beyond the tip, it will scratch the paper. If it is recessed inside the tip, ink will not flow to the paper.

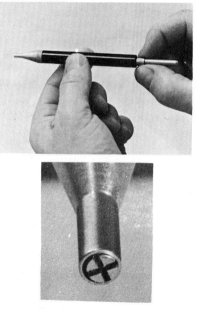

Brush Flush with Tip

   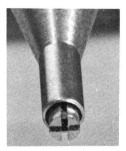

Brush Recessed   **Brush Out too Far**

6. To fill the pen, depress the plunger, immerse the exposed brush portion so that it goes below the ink surface, then release the plunger. Enough ink is held in the grooves of the brush to make a few letters. Try not to dip the outer tip of the pen itself into the ink but only the extended brush part.

7. Hold the pen in a *vertical position* so that the tip is flat on the surface. Move the pen in this position.

8. Judge letter spacing according to what looks good. You will improve with practice. When practicing, don't just copy the alphabet; for practice in spacing, letter words.

9. Start near the middle of a stroke and work to the ends. Keep the pen moving to eliminate the globs of ink that collect and fatten ends of strokes and other places where the pen pauses.

Poor · Good

10. Go over a letter to make even, crisp lines and get into the corners of the stencil to complete the edges.

Poor · Good

11. When lettering is completed, wash the brush pen under running water. Dry with paper toweling. Do not leave ink in the pen to dry. Always cap a felt pen after use.

STENCIL LETTERING GUIDES (WRICOPRINT)

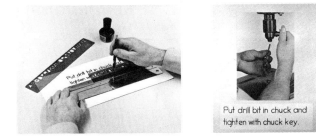

Put drill bit in chuck and tighten with chuck key.

For lettering ½ inch tall and *smaller*, use the *Wricoprint* unit. It consists of three parts—a *lettering guide*, a *pen*, and a *lettering pad*. The principle of using the Wricoprint is similar to that of the Signmaker, although the parts are different and the pen is filled in another way.

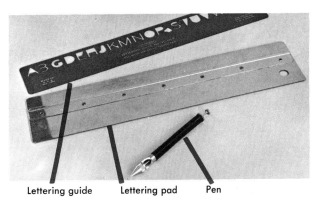

Lettering guide · Lettering pad · Pen

A Wricoprint guide has these labels printed on the lower center and side:

(WRICOPRINT)

LETTERING GUIDE No. VC 1/2 P
USE WITH WRICO LETTERING PAD

FOR USE WITH
WRICO PENS No.
3-3A-4-4A-5-5A

These labels give such information as:

V—letter style (the other style is S = slant).
C—*capital* letters on guide.
L—*lower-case* letters on guide.
N—*numbers* on guide.
Letter size—Wricoprint-guide sizes are given in fractions of inches, as ½ (inch), ¼ (inch).
Pen size—Wricoprint pens are coded 3 to 7, with size 3 making the *thickest* line.

1. The number for the size of a Wricoprint pen is stamped near the tip.

2. Fill the well near the tip with a few drops of ink.

3. Pull or push the plunger knob at the top of the pen to start ink flowing. Pushing the plunger in reduces the ink flow (the needle end of the plunger fills the flow channel), and pulling it back increases the ink flow (the needle moves back, opening the channel).

4. Test the pen on paper. Adjust the plunger for a *moderate* flow of ink.
5. Hold the pen in a vertical position with the tip flat on the surface.

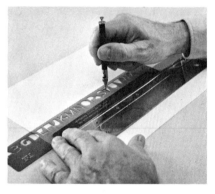

6. Go over a letter to make even, crisp lines.

FOUR   FOUR
Poor   Good

Another stencil-type guide for smaller size lettering, similar to Wricoprint, is the *Koh-i-noor Rapidoguides* and pens. The unit consists of a plastic stencil guide having raised edges and a rapidograph pen, which is held vertically as the point follows the letter cut-out in the guide.

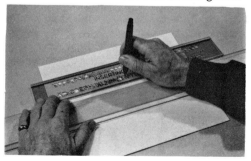

TEMPLATE LETTERING GUIDES (LEROY)

Lettering templates are excellent for all lettering needs, especially for captions of many lines. Although more expensive than stencils, they permit faster work and can give higher-quality lettering. The pens come in ranges from fine to very bold, and are used in a tripod scriber, one leg of which follows the letters grooved in the template.

The most common template equipment is the *Leroy* brand. It consists of a *template,* a *scriber,* and a *two-part pen.*

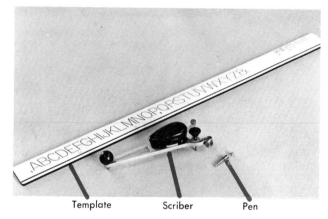

Template   Scriber   Pen

A Leroy template has this label printed in red in the right corner:

The label gives such information as:

3240—letter style.
CL—*capitals, lower-case* (and numbers) on the template. Capitals are usually on one side, with lower-case and numbers on the reverse side. Larger templates and special ones have only the capitals and numbers or the lower-case on a single template.

Letter size—Leroy lettering templates are coded with 1000 = 1 inch (350 = ⅓ inch).

Pen 4—Both parts (the well and the plunger) are numbered. Lower-numbered pens make thinner lines.

1. Set the template against a T-square (taped to the working surface).
2. Set the pen firmly into the hole in the scriber arm and tighten the screw on the side.
3. Fill the well of the pen with two or three drops of ink.
4. Set the butt end (the arm with the round ball) of the scriber into the long black groove under the letters of the template.
5. Place the scriber arm with the point into the letter groove.
6. Lower the pen to the surface and guide the scriber with little pressure.
7. After completing a letter, lift the pen from the surface and slide the template to position the next letter.

The following additional details are useful in proper lettering with the Leroy device:

☐ Judge letter spacing by eye, according to what looks correct.

☐ Start ink flowing by stroking the pen on scrap paper. Sometimes it is necessary to raise the plunger part of the pen a few times for ink to reach the tip.

☐ Adjust the vertical screw on the scriber, just behind the pen, so it touches the paper lightly to permit a steady flow of ink from the pen while lettering.

☐ Start near the center of a stroke and work to the ends. Keep the pen moving to eliminate the globs of ink that collect and fatten ends of strokes and other places where the pen pauses.

☐ When you finish using a Leroy pen, remove it from the scriber, separate the two parts, and wash them.

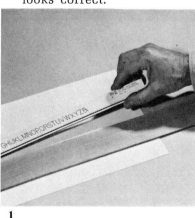

1

2

3

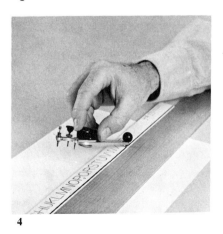

4

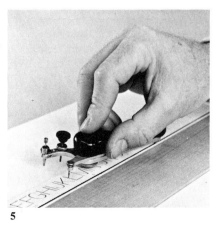

5

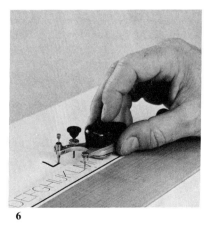

6

☐ Use a reservoir pen in place of the standard Leroy pen. The plastic cylinder holds a large supply of ink which eliminates the need to refill the pen constantly during use. The reservoir pen is available in all sizes.

☐ Some Leroy scribers are adjustable. A screw on the underside can be loosened and the two arms spread apart. This permits making slanting letters of various degrees.

☐ Larger size templates (about or larger than size 500) require the use of a different scriber.

PHOTOCOMPOSING-MACHINE LETTERING

High-quality professional lettering is often done from type, either by setting metal type or by using a *cold-type* machine to photographically set type on sensitized paper. A photocomposing machine is of the latter type. It is a quick and efficient way to do lettering for titles, transparencies, and publications. Pictured are representative types of photocomposing machines.

Varitype Headliner

Strip Printer

The printing letters, numbers, and symbols are prepared as high contrast negatives (clear letters on an opaque black background) on photographic film, sometimes sealed in thick plastic for protection. Letters are contact printed (page 108) onto the photographic paper which moves through the machine beneath the letter stencils. Numerous styles and sizes of lettering are available. Prices of machines vary greatly, depending on their versatility and manual or automatic features. Here is how the Headliner works:

1. Each letter to be made is selected, in turn, and *contact* printed onto photographic paper or film (by exposure to light, in the machine).
2. The paper or film is then processed, either in the machine or in trays in a darkroom.
3. The completed lettering is then ready for use (often for paste-up work (page 144).

1

2

3

Now, Review What You Have Learned About Lettering Methods:

1. What rules guide the holding and using of a beveled-tip felt pen?
2. How do you line up and space punch-out letters?
3. What purpose is served by the backing sheet with dry-transfer letters?
4. What method of lettering might you select to prepare a caption of 12 words?
5. What are the required parts to letter with a Wrico Signmaker unit? How do they differ from the Wricoprint parts?
6. What size lettering will each of these make: Wrico Signmaker 150, Wricoprint ¼, Leroy 240?
7. How does filling a Wricoprint pen differ from filling the Wrico Signmaker brush pen?
8. What is the proper position during use for the brush pen? for the Wricoprint pen?
9. What parts are required to do Leroy lettering?
10. Compare the lettering methods described in this section in terms of best uses, time and skill to use, cost of equipment if required, and quality of results.

Note: Answers to review questions can be found at the end of the chapter.

Backgrounds for Titles

Select backgrounds that are appropriate to the treatment of the subject in color and design and do not distract attention from the title or detract from its effect. Such backgrounds will be inconspicuous in color and design, yet will contribute to the mood or central idea of the topic. Cool colors (blue, gray, green) are preferred for backgrounds, and warm colors (red, orange, magenta) for titles and visuals over the background.

For backgrounds you may consider plain, colored, or textured papers; cardboards of various finishes and colors; cloth, wood, or other unusual materials like wallpaper samples, or pictures and photographs. Rich colors give maximum contrast in black-and-white and pleasing effects in color. But do not let the background design or extremes of color interfere with legibility or with the purpose of a title or diagram.

SPECIAL TECHNIQUES

For most uses, prepare simple titles directly on the background material. But for special purposes, you can make *overlays* and place them over the background before filming. Overlays are particularly useful when several titles or diagrams must appear over the same background. Lettering for overlays can be in black, in white, or in color.

BLACK OVERLAY LETTERING

☐ Adhere punch-out letters, cut-outs, or dry-transfer letters directly to the background (page 124).

☐ Make regular black-line transparencies by heat process (page 208), diazo method (page 204), or photography (page 214) and overlay them on the background.

WHITE OVERLAY LETTERING

Prepare white letters on black nonreflecting cardboard. Then, during filming, double-expose the film to record first the background and then the white title (page 104).

COLOR OVERLAY LETTERING

☐ Use colored dry-transfer letters directly on the background or on clear acetate.

☐ Make single color diazo transparencies (page 204).

☐ When more than one color is needed on a title, prepare multicolor diazo transparencies or multicolor paper copies.

For applications of these techniques in preparing titles, see the section on Titling for Slides on page 174.

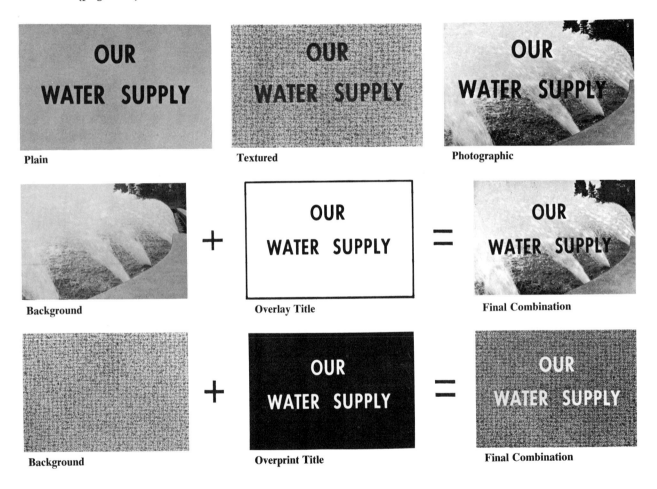

Plain   Textured   Photographic

Background   +   Overlay Title   =   Final Combination

Background   +   Overprint Title   =   Final Combination

Mounting

A variety of techniques can be considered for mounting art work and for preserving finished visual materials and commercially-available pictures, maps, charts, and so forth. These techniques have various characteristics: final results are temporary or permanent; special equipment may or may not be required; heat may or may not be required; and sealing may be on cardboard, cloth, or other surfaces. Because of the variety of these methods, you should evaluate them in terms of your needs and select the most appropriate for use.

The methods to be described on the following pages include:

☐ Rubber cement mounting—temporary or permanent

☐ Dry mounting on cardboard—with press and hand iron

☐ Dry mounting on cloth—to fold or roll

RUBBER CEMENT METHODS

Mounting with rubber cement is a simple procedure that requires no special equipment. It will accomplish temporary or permanent mounting.

Temporary mounting is useful for making paste-ups (page 144) of line drawings and accompanying lettering that are to be photographed rather than used directly. There are four steps:

1. Trim the material to be mounted.
2. With rubber cement, coat the back of each piece to be mounted.
3. Place the coated pieces cement-side down on the cardboard, while the cement is wet. They can be moved as necessary to get exact position and alignment, or picked up and repositioned.
4. Allow the cement to dry before using the paste-up. Rub away any visible cement.

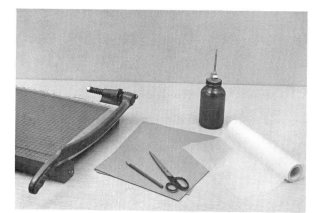

Rubber-Cement Mounting Requires These Tools and Materials: Trimmer or Scissors, Cardboard Backing, Pencil, Rubber Cement in a Dispensing Jar, Wax Paper

1

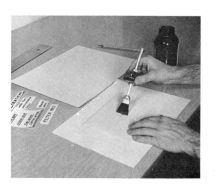

4

2

3

Permanent mounting is not truly permanent, but materials thus mounted with rubber cement will adhere for long periods. There are twelve steps in the procedure.

1. Trim the picture or other piece to be mounted.
2. Place the picture on the cardboard backing; make guide marks for each corner.
3. Coat the back of the picture with rubber cement.
4. Coat the marked area on the cardboard with rubber cement.
5. Allow the cement to dry on both surfaces.
6. Overlap two wax-paper sheets on the cement-covered cardboard after the cement is dry.
7. Align the picture on the guide marks as seen through the waxed paper.
8. Slide out one sheet of waxed paper.
9. Smooth the picture to the cardboard on this exposed cement.
10. Remove the second waxed sheet.
11. Smooth the remainder of the picture to the cardboard.
12. Rub excess cement away from the edges of the picture.

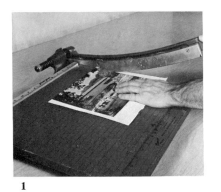

1

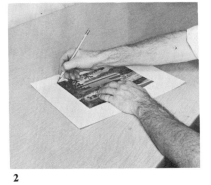

2

3

4

5

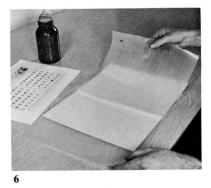

6

7

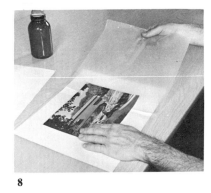

8

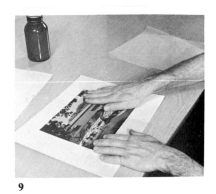

9

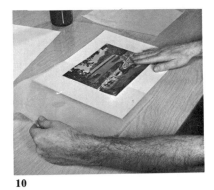

10

11

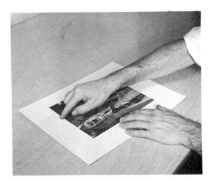

12

Consider these additional details when using the rubber-cement methods of mounting:

☐ Make guide marks in corners on mounting board lightly in pencil so they are not noticeable after the mounting is completed. Erase the obvious ones.

☐ Make sure the brush is adjusted in the lid of the cement jar so the bristles are below the cement level in the jar.

☐ Cement should flow smoothly from the brush. If it thickens it will collect on the brush and fall in lumps. Add a small amount of rubber-cement thinner and shake the jar well.

☐ If colored cardboard is to be used, test the cement on a sample, as rubber cement may stain the surface.

☐ Apply cement with long sweeping strokes of the brush. Move moderately fast as cement dries quickly.

☐ Keep the lid on the dispenser jar tightly closed when not in actual use.

☐ In the permanent method, the cemented surfaces can be considered dry when they feel slightly tacky.

☐ The sulfur in rubber cement may react with the silver in a photograph to stain the face of the picture a yellowish-brown color.

DRY-MOUNT METHODS (ON CARDBOARD)

This is a fast method, resulting in permanent and neatly mounted materials. It is particularly useful when a number of pictures are to be mounted. The mounting material is *dry-mount tissue*—a tissue paper coated on *both sides* with a heat-sensitive adhesive. When heat and pressure are applied, the adhesive is activated. Upon cooling the adhesive forms a strong bond between the picture and the cardboard.

Thus the cooling phase of the process is particularly critical when preparing a successful dry mount. To insure a satisfactory result, immediately after the heating and pressure phase, place the mount under a weight to allow cooling to take place undisturbed. The liquified adhesive hardens to form a firm, even seal between the picture and its backing.

Either an electric hand iron or a dry-mount press is used to provide heat and to exert pressure. (The Masterfax unit, shown on page 143, can also be used to dry mount smaller materials.)

The Seal product *Fotoflat* should be used with a hand iron set at *rayon* or *low*. With the dry-mount press use Eastman Kodak's dry-mount tissue or Seal's *MT5* and set the thermostat at 225° F and the tacking iron on *medium* heat.

A shortcoming of the dry-mount method is the possibility that bubbles of steam may form under a picture when heat is applied. Most bubbles can be eliminated by predrying the cardboard and picture. If bubbles do appear after mounting, puncture them with a pin and then reapply heat and pressure. Unfortunately, when bubbles do form, the paper may stretch, resulting in a wrinkle.

Here is a comparison of the hand-iron and dry-mount-press methods for dry mounting:

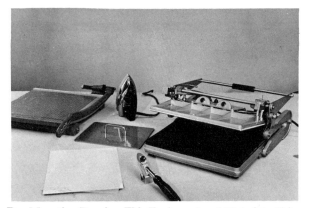

Dry Mounting Requires This Equipment and Materials: Trimmer; Cardboard Backing; Sheets of Dry-Mount Tissue; Hand Iron or Dry-Mount Press and Tacking Iron; Metal Weights

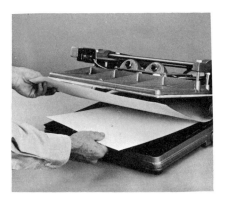

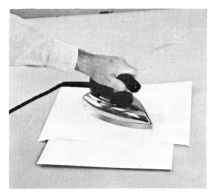

1. Preheat both the picture and cardboard for 10 seconds to remove moisture from them.

2. Adhere the dry-mount tissue to the back of the picture by touching the iron directly to the tissue. Always protect the table top with paper.

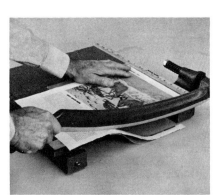

3. Trim the picture and the tissue together on all sides.

4. Align the picture on the cardboard.

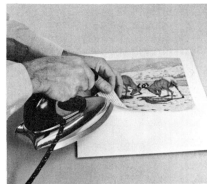

5. Tack the tissue to the cardboard in two corners.

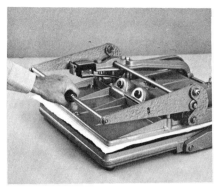

6. Cover the picture with a clean sheet of thin paper. Seal the picture to the cardboard with heat and pressure for 15 seconds. With the hand iron, maintain a slow circular motion.

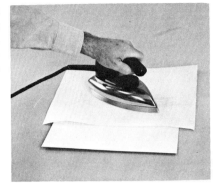

7. Cool the mounted picture under a metal weight for one minute or more.

The Completed Mount

Consider these additional details when dry-mounting:

☐ If more than one sheet of tissue must be used, butt the edges together; do not overlap them.

☐ If a mounting is too large to be sealed in the dry-mount press at one time, seal it in sections. Make sure successive areas in the press are overlapped so none of the picture is missed.

☐ When using the hand iron there is a tendency to move the iron quickly across the paper covering the picture. Properly, a moderate amount of pressure should be exerted with the iron, and it should be used from the center of the picture outwards with slow movements so all parts receive heat and pressure for about 5 seconds.

☐ When pressing is completed, *quickly* place the mount under a weight for cooling. This is when actual sealing takes place. A metal weight, which absorbs heat quickly, is preferred.

☐ When color photographs are to be mounted, extreme care must be taken because the delicate photographic emulsion can be easily damaged. Temperature, pressure, and press time are more critical. Seal brand ColorMount tissue is designed for mounting the newer resin-coated photographic papers at 200° F. Follow instructions with the ColorMount material.

In addition to mounting complete rectangular pictures, cut-outs around pictures can be made to eliminate unnecessary details. Be sure to tack tissue to back of the picture before cutting it out. Then follow the same procedures as described for regular dry-mounting to mount a cut-out picture.

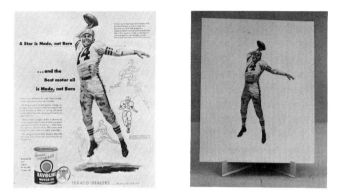

Pictures that extend across two pages in a magazine require special handling. The pages must be spliced together so neither a clear line or picture separation is visible where they are joined. Follow these steps:

1. Remove the picture from the magazine by cutting or take out the staples.
2. Trim the edge to be joined on each part of the picture. Remove as little paper as possible.
3. Tack dry-mount tissue to the back of one part, leaving part of the sheet of tissue overhanging the edge to be joined.
4. With the picture face up, align the edges to be joined and touch them together tightly. Make sure there is protective paper under the picture and tissue.
5. With a small piece of paper over the joined splice, tack the second part of the picture to the tissue in two or three places. Remember, the picture is face up.
6. Tack additional tissue if necessary to the back of the picture to cover it entirely. Always butt pieces of dry mount tissue together, do not overlap them.
7. Then finish the mounting as with a regular dry-mounted picture—trim, tack to cardboard, seal with the press or iron, and cool immediately under a weight.
8. If a slight white line shows at the joined splice, darken it lightly with soft lead or colored pencil.

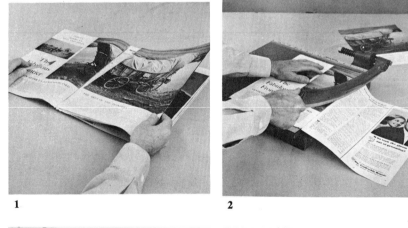

1

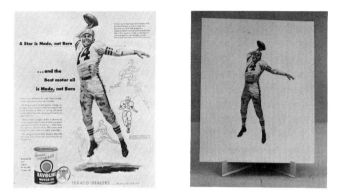

2

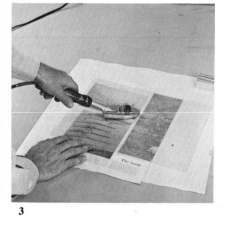

3

4

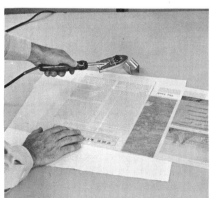

5

6

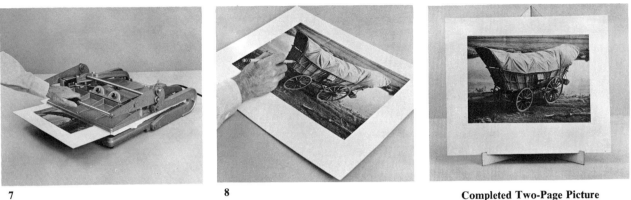

7   8   **Completed Two-Page Picture**

DRY MOUNT METHODS (ON CLOTH)

For some purposes, such as booklets or turn-over charts, photographs or visual materials may require a pliable backing. In such cases a dry-mount cloth (Chartex) can be adhered to the back of the materials to give them durability and still maintain flexibility. The adhesive is a coating on one side of the cloth, which is ironed on the back of the materials or applied with a dry-mount press. Large materials can be mounted so as to be rolled or folded. Follow these steps:

1. Set the dry-mount press at 225° F., the tacking iron at *medium,* and the hand iron at *rayon*.
2. Dry the chart in the press or with the hand iron. Besides removing moisture from the paper, this treatment will flatten folds in the chart.
3. **Chart to be rolled**
   a. Place the chart face-down on a sheet of clean paper.
   b. Cover the back of the chart with sufficient cloth. Place the adhesive coating (smooth side, on inside or roll) against the back of chart.
   c. Tack the chart to the cloth in one large spot.

d. Cut the cloth to match edges of chart or leave excess cloth all around for a cloth margin. Plan for 2 or 3 inches of extra cloth at the top edge for grommets or eyelets.
e. If you have left a margin, fold the cloth and tack it to the edge of the chart along the full length of each side. Slit the cloth at the corners so adjacent pieces can be overlapped. *Do not* leave any cloth exposed or unfolded, as the adhesive side will stick to other surfaces during sealing.
f. Cover the chart with paper and seal in the dry-mount press or with the hand iron. Apply heat to each section for at least 5 seconds. Cool under a weight.
g. Check for bubbles or wrinkles. Reiron or repress as necessary.
h. Add gummed eyelets or grommets to the upper cloth margin. Place them 3 inches in from the outer edge. Add an additional one or two toward the center of the margin for large charts.
i. If it is difficult to get a rolled chart to open fully for use, attach a wooden strip to the lower edge of the cloth as a weight.

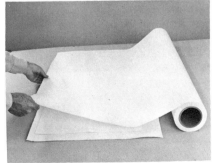

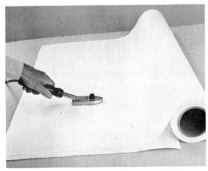

3a   3b   3c

3d

3e

3f

Completed Cloth-Backed Mount (Rolled)

4. **Chart to be folded**
   a. Cut the chart into suitable sections.
   b. Dry each section in the press or with the hand iron.
   c. Spread the cloth on sheet of clean paper with the adhesive coating (smooth side, on inside of roll) placed upwards.
   d. Arrange the cut sections of the chart on the cloth. Leave ⅛ inch (or less) between the sections.
   e. Tack each section to the cloth from the top side through a piece of paper.
   f. Follow steps *d* through *h* as above.

4a

4b

4c

4d

4e

Completed Cloth-Backed Mount (Folded)

Protecting the Surface (Laminating)

The face of a photograph or other mounted material to be handled a great deal needs protection. A clear plastic spray can be applied, but an even better and more permanent protection is achieved by sealing a clear plastic laminating film over the face of the picture. A dry-mount press set at 270°F. adheres this film to a mounted picture in a few seconds. To get satisfactory results may require some practice, and it may be necessary to increase the pressure by putting cardboard or a sheet of thin masonite into the press.

The following steps apply to laminating a previously dry-mounted picture.

1. Set the dry-mount press at 270° F. and the tacking iron on high.
2. Dry the mounted picture in the press for 10 seconds.
3. Extra pressure is required for laminating. Put a piece of heavy cardboard or masonite (smooth face to the mount) on the rubber pad of the press. Always place materials in the press on *top* of the cardboard or masonite.
4. Cut a piece of laminating film (Seal-lamin) to cover the entire mount surface (front and back if desired).

5. The adhesive side of the film is on the inside of the roll. Tack the film to the mount in one spot with a piece of paper placed between the film and the tacking iron.
6. Trim excess film so none overhangs the mount edge.
7. Smooth the film over the mount. Cover it with a sheet of paper. Seal the assembly in the press for at least 15 seconds.
8. Immediately after removing the picture from the press, cool it under a metal weight for 1 or 2 minutes.

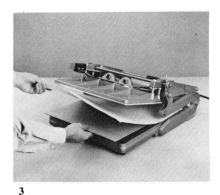

3

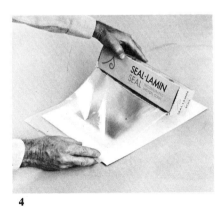

4

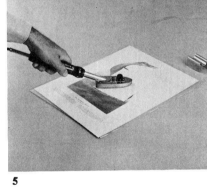

5

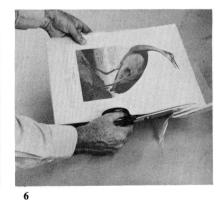

6

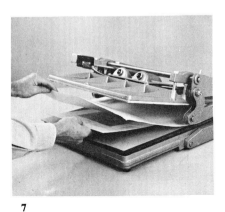

7

8

Completed Laminated Mount

Consider these additional details when laminating:

☐ If bubbles appear under the lamination film they are due to moisture in the picture or cardboard expanding to form steam. Place the mount back in the press for about 45 seconds and cool again.

☐ It may be helpful, instead of cooling under a weight, to rub firmly over the affected area with a wadded handkerchief.

☐ If bubbles persist, break them with a pin and press again or rub by hand again. Because of bubbles, the film may stretch, resulting in a wrinkle.

☐ If unmounted pictures are laminated (to protect and display both sides of a sheet), seal one side with film, as above. Then repeat the process on the second side.

☐ If materials to be laminated are wider than the roll of film to be used (11 inch, 20 inch, and 22 inch rolls are available, butt adjacent pieces together. Seal each piece in turn, in the press.

☐ Thin three-dimensional objects, such as leaves, can be laminated easily to cardboard. Before starting, secure the object in place with rubber cement.

☐ When laminating glossy photographs, follow the above procedures, but with these changes:
Set the thermostat on the press at 325° F.

Wipe the surface of photograph with cotton moistened in rubbing alcohol. Allow thorough drying before laminating. Preheating the photograph is unnecessary.

Apply additional pressure in the press with an extra piece of cardboard or masonite.

Protect face of picture with a sheet of thin paper.

Maintain pressure in the press for at least 1 minute. Cool immediately under a weight.

In addition to using the dry-mount press, other units are designed especially for laminating. They are used either cold or with heat.

☐ A *cold* lamination unit requires adhesive-backed acetate. The machine consists of motor-driven rollers that apply strong pressure to the acetate and picture as the two are drawn between the moving rollers.

Translifter (National Adhesive Co.)

☐ A *heat* lamination unit feeds thin film over the picture between heated, motor-driven rollers and results in an excellent laminated picture. With the use of two rolls of acetate, mounted on the machine, both sides of a picture, or two pictures back-to-back, can be laminated at the same time.

GBC Laminator (General Binding Corporation)

Now, Review What You Have Learned About Mounting and Surface-Protection Methods:

1. What are two differences between *temporary* and *permanent* rubber-cement mounting methods?
2. For what two reasons is wax paper used in the rubber-cement permanent method?
3. What is the principle of mounting with dry-mount tissue?
4. Why is tissue tacked to the back of the picture *before* the latter is trimmed to size?

5. What procedure is used if bubbles appear under a completed mount?
6. Compare three methods—rubber-cement permanent, hand iron, and dry-mount press in terms of speed of process, ease, equipment, cost, and quality of mount.
7. What two variations of the regular dry-mount procedure are used when a two-page picture is mounted?
8. How do you decide whether to mount a map on cardboard, on cloth to be rolled, or on cloth to be folded?
9. Why should cloth either be trimmed flush with the chart edge or turned as a border before sealing it to the chart?
10. What are two variations of the regular dry-mount procedure when covering a mounted magazine picture with laminating film?

Note: Answers to review questions can be found at the end of the chapter.

Multipurpose Equipment

It is an accepted axiom that a piece of equipment should be designed to serve only one primary function. When it is adapted to perform a number of functions, it may not do any of them very well. But because of the interrelation of various graphic techniques, certain pieces of equipment can very satisfactorily do a number of things.

As was shown previously, the dry-mount press can be used to dry-mount, to laminate, and (as will be seen on page 212), to make picture-transfer transparencies.

Another unit, the Masterfax, can perform five important reproduction and production functions —make paper copy reproductions of printed sheets, prepare spirit masters for further duplication (page 144), dry-mount, laminate, and make transparencies.

The Masterfax is a flat-bed thermal unit, similar in method of use to the equipment described for heat-process transparencies on page 208. Two features of this machine are important, and both

contribute to good-quality reproductions. First is the infrared lamp that provides the heat and exposure by moving past the stationary materials, rather than having the materials rotate around the lamp. Second is the "vacuum blanket" in the lid, against which a pump creates a vacuum guaranteeing extremely tight contact between the original material and the paper or film for reproduction.

For the mounting and laminating procedures, set the exposure dial at the red mark (for the longest possible exposure). For other procedures, adjust exposure setting as instructed or according to experience. Before use, warm up the machine with one exposure.

Materials are assembled on the glass surface of the Masterfax unit in the following ways (and they must not extend beyond the glass), to prepare:

☐ Paper copies—original sheet (image down) on reproduction paper (sensitive side down) on glass surface
☐ Spirit masters—original sheet (image down) on carbon sheet (carbon side down) on master sheet on glass surface
☐ Mounting—cardboard on dry-mount tissue on picture on black bonding sheet on glass surface
☐ Laminating—laminating film (adhesive side down) on picture on laminating film (adhesive side up) on black bonding sheet on glass surface
☐ Laminating—dry-mounted picture (face down) on laminating film (adhesive side up) on black bonding paper on glass surface
☐ Transparency—original sheet (image down) on heat sensitive film (coating down) on glass surface

Masterfax (Ditto/Bell & Howell)

Making Paste-ups

When materials are prepared for offset printing, or sometimes for photographic print series, slides, or transparencies, the lettering and the visuals (in the form of black-ink line drawings) are made separately. Each part is then *pasted* onto paper or cardboard in proper arrangement. The result of this procedure is termed a *paste-up*. For example, before printing, a paste-up was made for each page in this book.

Pasting-up is done by putting rubber cement on the back of each piece, as in temporary mounting (page 133). This method permits moving the piece for alignment before the cement dries and the piece adheres firmly.

Wax can also be used as a backing adhesive for paste-ups. It is applied with a hand-operated roller or a mechanical coating unit. Wax backing permits ease of alignment, a tight seal between copy and paper, and elimination of some of the

clean-up problems that rubber cement presents.

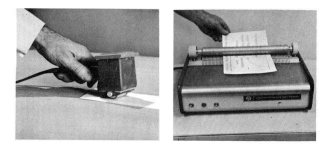

Paste-ups are useful in preparing titles and diagrams for all types of visual materials. By using high-contrast film to photograph the paste-up (page 214), the visible separation lines between each piece and the background paper are avoided. Print the resulting negative in the visual form you need (see facing page).

Reproducing Printed Matter

When audiovisual materials are prepared, there is often the need for accompanying reading matter for use by teachers and students. Also, for individual learning activities, duplicates of study guides, instructional sheets and photographic-print picture series may be required. A number of reproduction processes can be utilized. Each one serves a particular need and has certain requirements, advantages, and limitations. We will examine eight commonly used methods.[1]

SPIRIT DUPLICATION

A master is prepared with colored carbon sheets placed in contact with the back side of the master paper. Impressions are made on the front side of the master by writing, typing, or drawing. At the same time a carbon impression is deposited on the back of the master sheet. Up to five carbon colors may be used to prepare one-color or multi-color paper copies.

The carbon transferred to the back of the master is an aniline dye, soluble in methyl alcohol. In the spirit duplicator, alcohol. In the spirit duplicator, alcohol is spread over the duplicator paper. When the master comes in contact with paper,

some of the dye is deposited on the paper, producing a printed copy.

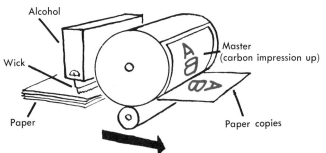

1. For further description of many of these processes, see Dennis Pett, *Copying and Duplicating Processes,* Audio-Visual Center, Indiana University, Bloomington, 1973.

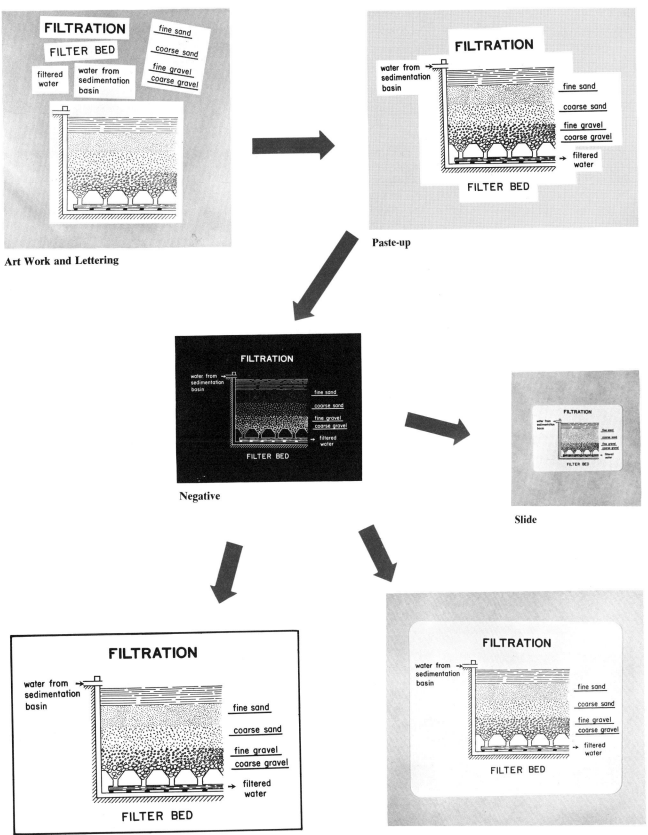

Art Work and Lettering

Paste-up

Negative

Slide

Print

Transparency

STENCIL

One printing application of the stencil process is *mimeograph*. The stencil consists of a sheet impregnated with a waxlike substance that does not allow ink to penetrate unless the coating is broken or pushed aside by a stylus or by the force of a typewriter type, thus leaving openings for ink to pass through.

In the machine, ink flows through a cotton pad onto and through the stencil wrapped around a rotating cylinder. Blank paper, pressed against the stencil by a rubber cylinder, absorbs the ink. By using separate stencils and reruns of the paper, more than one color can be put on the same sheet.

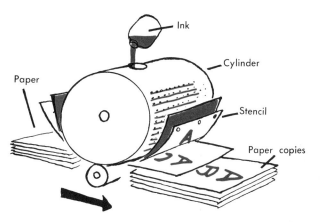

Care must be exercised in preparing the stencil, and the operation of the machine takes some special experience. Quality is similar to good reproduction by the spirit method, but somewhat less than that from offset printing since in mimeographing the ink is absorbed by the porous paper and has a tendency to spread.

Electronic scanning machines are sometimes used to reproduce printed sheets onto stencils by the action of electric sparks without any hand work. The resulting printed copies from such stencils are of textured quality.

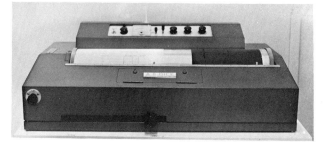

Electronic Scanning Mimeo

DIAZO

Inexpensive paper copies can be made from translucent master diagrams by the same process described for making transparencies (page 204). The paper products of this process are called *white prints* and have blue or black lines on white paper, as opposed to *blueprints* with their white lines on blue background. The latter are still widely used for making large plans and engineering drawings on paper. The diazo method requires a translucent (tracing paper or matte film) or transparent (clear film) master sheet with opaque markings for reproduction. The diazo machine

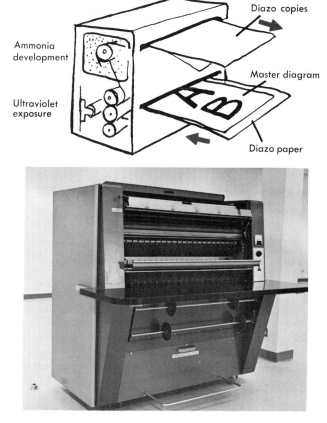

has two separate sections. In the first, light-sensitive paper is exposed through the master to ultraviolet light. In the second section, fumes of ammonia develop the exposed image on the paper.

This method is essentially a hand operation, as the master comes out of the machine after each exposure for reinsertion with a new sheet of diazo paper. Some diazo machines will reproduce masters up to 42 inches wide and of any length. Except for large sheets, the process is not efficient for runs of more than 10 copies. Exposure of printed sheets to direct sunlight will cause some fading of the image. Reproductions of half-tone printed pictures and continuous-tone photographs can be made satisfactorily on certain diazo papers.

THERMAL

This process is represented by the Thermo-fax (3M Company) equipment and materials. It requires a master drawn or typed sheet (on any kind of paper) exposed in contact with thermal paper to heat generated by an infrared lamp. The processing time is only a few seconds, and no development time is required. The thermal paper costs about $0.05) a sheet. This process is widely used to prepare transparencies as well as paper copies (page 208).

A major limitation of the thermal process is that master drawings or printing must consist of heat-absorbing material (pencil, black ink, or carbon-depositing items); markings made by dyes (spirit copies, ordinary ball-point pens, colored inks) are not reproducible. The average thermal paper used is not durable and the image is not very sharp. But for quickly making a few copies for temporary reference, this process is fine.

The thermal process is also useful for making *spirit masters* from printed sheets for normal spirit duplication (as with Masterfax machine page 143). A special backing sheet with a waxed carbon surface, attached to a thin master sheet, is fed through the thermal machine with the original printed sheet. The resulting master will permit up to 100 paper copies. Prepare the thermal master in this way:

1. After removing the thin separating sheet, place the master on the original printed sheet with the thin master sheet on top.
2. Put the sheets into plastic carrier.
3. Set the thermal copy machine as instructed.
4. Run the carrier through the machine.
5. Separate the carbon sheet from the master sheet. A strong impression on the back of the master will insure good reproduction copies.

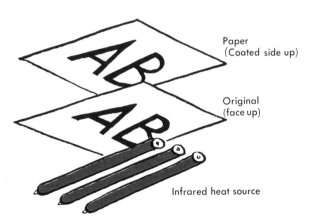

Paper
(Coated side up)

Original
(face up)

Infrared heat source

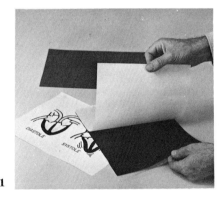

1

2

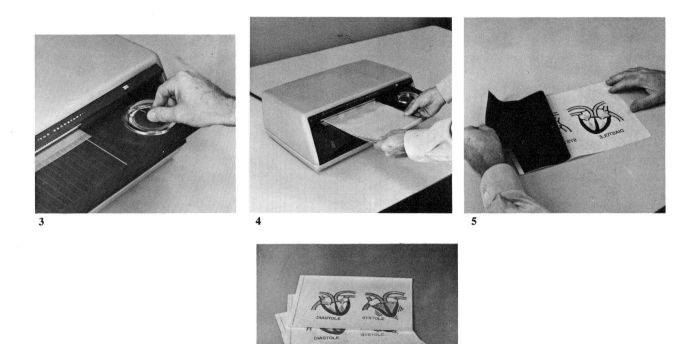

3   4   5

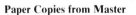

Paper Copies from Master

ELECTROSTATIC

There are two related processes under this category. Both require charged surfaces that are effected (discharged) by light. The charged area will hold a substance to create the image.

In *xerography,* a selenium-coated plate, which is photoelectrically sensitive, is given an electrical charge. The original to be duplicated is exposed to light, with the white area (and gray portions of photographs) reflecting light to the charged plate. The light that reaches the selenium-coated surface dissipates the electric charge, leaving a charge only in the image area. The copy paper (any ordinary bond paper) is charged, and a toner (a fine black powder) is transferred to it from the selenium surface. Finally, the copy paper is heated to fix the powder permanently to the image area.

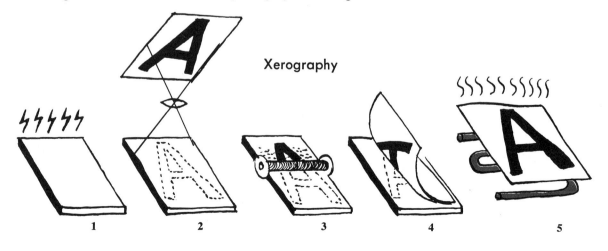

Xerography

1   2   3   4   5

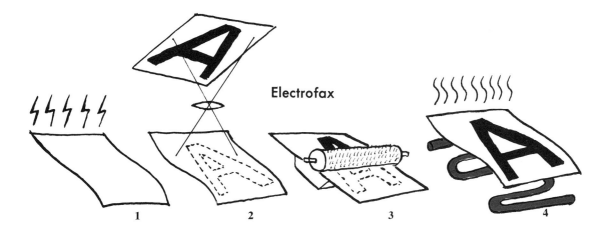

Electrofax

1   2   3   4

1. Positive electric charge is placed on selenium-coated plate.
2. Image of original is projected onto plate to form latent image.
3. Negatively charged powder *toner* is dusted onto selenium plate.
4. Sheet of paper is placed over plate and receives positive charge.
5. Final copy is heated to fuse image into paper.

A related method, the *electrofax* process (RCA trademark name), requires the use of a special copy paper coated with zinc oxide, discharging of the coating by light, and collection of charged toner on its surface.

1. Uniform electric charge is placed on copy paper.
2. Image of original is projected onto charged paper to form latent image.
3. Powder *toner* is brushed onto paper, where it adheres to image area.
4. Toner is fused to paper with heat.

The electrostatic machines are easy to operate but expensive to purchase (some are leased on a per copy charge). Copies are of fair to good quality.

LETTERPRESS PRINTING

The most widely used form of *relief printing* is letterpress. This method transfers ink from a raised surface (the image areas) to the paper. The raised surface may range from an artistic woodcut, to metal type, to fine photoengravings. The paper normally used has a very smooth finish and can hold very fine detail. Letterpresses range from

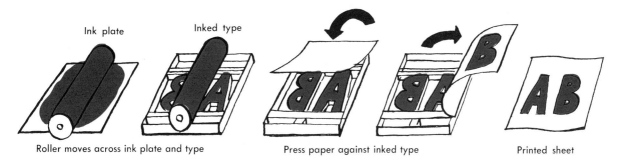

Ink plate   Inked type

Roller moves across ink plate and type   Press paper against inked type   Printed sheet

Letterpress

small hand-fed units to those that print in multi-color at up to 800 feet per minute.

A print shop or duplicating department must set the type or prepare the plates and operate the equipment.

OFFSET PRINTING

The basic principle of offset is that grease (ink) and water do not mix. The printing plates have ink-receiving (greasy) image areas and ink-repelling (watery) nonimage areas. Plates are prepared directly on paper or aluminum with special pencils and typing ribbons, by thermal or photocopy methods, by the electrostatic process, or photographically using the same high-contrast film as for transparencies (page 214). A water roll on the press coats the plate with a thin layer of water; where there is an image the grease in the image repels the water but allows the ink, which is oily, to adhere. The ink is then *offset,* or transferred, to a cylinder covered with a resilient rubber "blanket." The ink image from the blanket is then tranferred to paper.

The offset process is extensively used for educational and commercial printing. It requires expensive equipment and trained personnel.

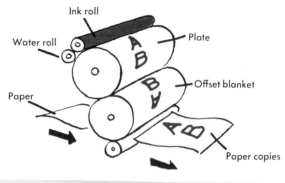

Now Review What You Have Learned About Reproducing Printed Matter:

1. What mounting technique, previously described, is used in doing paste-ups?

2. Which reproduction equipment should you select for each job? (In addition to the textual material, refer to Table 16-2 on page 151.)
   a. Inexpensive preparation of 100 copies in two colors.
   b. Single-sheet duplication; copies all colors.
   c. Original drawing on tracing paper; requires four inexpensive copies.
   d. Usual reproduction of printed materials in quantity, like pages for this book.
   e. Ink passes through openings cut in stencil.
   f. Can prepare spirit masters from printed originals.

Answers to Review Questions

PLANNING ART WORK
(PAGE 115)

1. 6×9 inches or 9×12 inches
2. 4 to 3—35-mm single-frame filmstrip, 8-mm and 16-mm motion pictures, television format
   3 to 2—standard 35-mm slide and 35-mm double-frame filmstrip
3. Principles—simplicity, unity, emphasis, balance
   Tools—line, shape, color, texture, space

Summary of Reproducing Processes   TABLE 16-2

METHOD	PRINCIPLE	REPRODUCTION SPEED AND APPROXIMATE MATERIAL COST		EVALUATION
Spirit	Carbon impression on master transferred to paper with alcohol	Moderate	Master $0.08 Paper $3.00/ream	Master easily prepared; operation simple; good for up to 150 copies in multicolor
Stencil	Ink passes through openings in waxlike stencil and is picked up by paper in contact with stencil	Moderate	Stencil $0.30 Paper $3.00/ream	Care needed in making master; machine more complex than spirit; each color requires separate operation; quality slightly better than spirit; long run easy; clean-up takes time
Diazo	Expose sensitized paper to ultraviolet light through translucent master; develop in ammonia	Slow	Paper $0.06 per $8\frac{1}{2} \times 11$ inch sheet	Easy operation; good for few copies; image affected by sunlight; duplication of photos possible; translucent master required
Thermal	Expose sensitized paper with master to infrared light	Fast	Paper $0.05–$0.08	Rapid, easy reproduction for few copies; quality fair; won't copy all colors; image affected by heat; produces spirit masters
Electrostatic Xerography	Charged selenium drum discharged by light; toner powder collects on charged paper for image	Moderate	Paper $0.07	Can copy anything; fair to good quality; machine cost high; operation simple after adjustments
Electrofax	Charged, coated, light-sensitive paper discharged by light; collects charged toner to form image			
Letterpress	Ink from raised type transfers to paper	Fast	$3.50 per 100 copies	Excellent reproduction of fine detail and tone gradations; typesetting can be time consuming
Offset	Ink adheres to image on plate; transferred to blanket and then to paper	Very fast	Plates: $0.15–$3.50 Copies: $4.00 per 100	Inexpensive plates and rapid preparation of plates of some types; quality excellent; operation requires technician; clean-up time lengthy

ILLUSTRATING (PAGE 118)
1. Numerous black-and-white high-contrast line drawings on one or a number of subjects in booklet or sheet form
2. Reader's activity

COLORING AND SHADING (PAGE 120)
1. Spray paints are quicker to use and provide a more even covering, but time is required for masking and protecting areas not to be sprayed with a color.
2. It is too hard to separate the color sheet from the backing sheet unless a "lip" remains for insertion of a blade. If a piece is cut to exact size it is very difficult to line it up exactly over area to be covered. Cutting it larger allows some margin when placement is made.
3. Air brushing.

LEGIBILITY STANDARDS (PAGE 122)
1. So they can be read easily by audience at an anticipated maximum distance.
2. Legibility decreases as quantity of information increases.
3. Use capital letters for short titles; lower case for six words or more.

Space letters optically (as they look proper to you).
Allow 1½ letter widths between words and twice as much between sentences.
Separate adjacent lines about 1½ times a lower-case letter.
Contrast letter color with background color.
4. 1 inch.
5. About ⅕ inch high.
6. Larger.
7. Larger.

LETTERING FOR TITLES (PAGE 131)

1. Hold pen firmly in hand, make only arm movements.
2. Against a T-square or a lightly ruled line.
3. Protects back of letter sheet from dirt and inadvertent pressure that may transfer letters.
4. Wricoprint, Koh-i-noor Rapidoguide, or Leroy.
5. Signmaker—large guide holder, brush pen, guides.
   Print—small lettering pad, lettering pen, guides.
6. 150—1½ inches.
   ¼ —¼ inch.
   240—¼ inch.
7. Wricoprint pen—ink added to well with dropper.
   Wrico Signmaker pen—pen plunged into ink bottle.
8. Vertical.
9. Template, scriber, pen, or reservoir pen.
10. Reader's activity.

MOUNTING AND PROTECTING SURFACES (PAGE 142)

1. Coat only one surface and put two surfaces together for temporary mounting. Coat both surfaces and allowing them to dry for permanent mounting.
2. You can see guide marks through it; it does not adhere to rubber cement.
3. A heat-sensitive adhesive is coated on both sides of tissue paper.
4. So both picture and tissue can be accurately trimmed together.
5. Puncture bubble with a pin, reapply heat and pressure.
6. Reader's activity.
7. The edges of the picture to be joined are trimmed *before* the dry-mount tissue is tacked to the back; tacking the second piece of the picture is done with the picture face-up.
8. For cardboard or cloth, size is the deciding factor. Choose rolling or folding on the basis of convenience of use.
9. So there is no exposed adhesive that might stick to the working surface or to the dry-mount press.
10. The dry-mount press is set at 270° and extra pressure is necessary, so a sheet of cardboard or masonite is used in the press.

REPRODUCING PRINTED MATTER (PAGE 150)

1. Temporary rubber cement method
2. (a) Spirit, (b) electrostatic, (c) diazo, (d) offset press, (e) mimeograph, (f) thermal

17

RECORDING SOUND

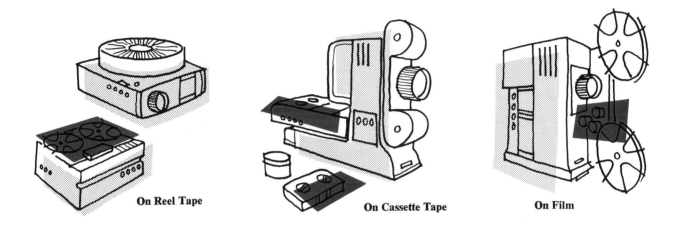

On Reel Tape   **On Cassette Tape**   **On Film**

Recorded sound can be used as individual tape recordings, or in conjunction with the visuals when a slide series, a filmstrip, or a motion picture is prepared. The recording can be on a reel of tape, a tape cassette, or on motion-picture film.

Plan to make your recording when picture editing is completed and after the narration has been refined (see page 63). First typewrite the narration in a form that will be easy for the narrator to follow. The illustration on page 68 with its narrow page and marks for cueing and special attention is recommended.

The Narrator and the Script

Choose one or more persons who speak clearly and who can read the script in a conversational tone while still communicating with proper feeling and expression. Generally men's voices are more easily understood on a recording than are women's. Have the narrator study the script carefully. The script should have markings indicating where points are to be emphasized. You should verify the pronunciation of proper names and special terms, and indicate it in the script. The script should have all cueing places plainly marked. See the sample narration script, page 68.

Music and Sound Effects

Research evidence indicates that background music is not essential to effective communications with audiovisual materials. In some instances, indeed, it interferes with the message. But for other purposes it may help in creating a desirable mood and in building continuity. Music as background for titles will assist projectionists to set the volume level for the narration that follows. When music is used under narration, maintain it at a low enough level so it does not interfere with the commentary or compete with the picture for the viewer's attention.

Select musical recordings carefully. Semi-classical pieces that are descriptive and maintain an even tempo and volume are more desirable than popular or classical selections, which may dominate the picture. If your audiovisual materials are to be distributed and sold, permission must be obtained for the use of copyrighted music. A number of commercial music libraries, for a fee, make available selections of all types for recordings (see page 308 for a listing).

Sound effects, which add a touch of realism, also are available commercially. If you do not want these commercial effects or cannot find them you can record actual sounds on tape, or create sound effects (see page 296 for a book on this subject). Sound effects on tape can later be transferred to the final tape or to the magnetic film recording.

Recording Facilities

Good-quality recordings are made in an acoustically treated and soundproofed room. Where possible use a room having some wall drapes and carpeting. Do not try to "deaden" the room entirely, as it would be difficult for the narration to sound vibrantly alive in such a room. When desirable facilities cannot be found, improvise a recording booth in a corner of a room with some drapes or blankets to reduce sound reflections. Then record after normal working hours to eliminate extraneous noises.

When you record sound on magnetic-striped motion-picture film the projector is the recorder and the microphone is attached to it. Thus particular care must be taken to eliminate as much projector noise as you can. The narrator and microphone must therefore be separated from the projector. To achieve this separation, use the most effective of several methods that may be feasible:

☐ Put the projector and the narrator in separate rooms, preferably with a glass window or door in the partition between them.

☐ If no transparent partition is available between two rooms, project the picture through an open doorway and use the wall as a sound barrier between the projector and the microphone.

☐ If only one room is available, make a partition to shield the microphone from the projector, using a blanket or other sound-absorbing material.

When selecting a room in which to record, keep in mind the fact that the microphone cannot distinguish between the sound coming from the narrator's voice and any ambient noise—the projector, a ventilating fan, or sounds you can hear from outside the room. Any of these extraneous sources can cause undesirable background noise on the recording. Furthermore, an annoying hum, caused by 60 cycle electrical interference, may be picked up by the microphone and recorded on tape. This is often caused by the close proximity of fluorescent lights or high voltage (220 volt) power lines.

Keep these facts in mind when selecting a suitable recording facility.

Recording Equipment

Even though final audio material may be used with a cassette tape recorder, it is preferable to make the original recording on a ¼ inch tape with a reel-to-reel recorder. The quality will be better and it will be easier to edit the tape, if necessary.

A tape recorder of average quality and price (about $200) or slightly better can be used to make the recordings for slides or for a filmstrip. The operating principles of all recorders are the same, whether their controls are actuated by buttons, by knobs, or by levers.

If you have a choice of microphones, select one of good quality. The *dynamic* microphone is capable of reproducing a wider range of tones and is thus preferable to the crystal or ceramic types included with most tape recorders.

Check the instruction manual that should accompany your recorder if you encounter any questions about the way to operate it.

If only voice is to be recorded, a tape speed of 3¾ inches per second (ips) is satisfactory. Music, however, requires higher fidelity than voice; if it is to be included, the tape should be run at 7½ ips.

Music or sound from a disk can be transferred to a tape in either of two ways. The better of the two methods avoids the use of the microphone and produces sound of superior quality.

In the preferable method, a *patch cord* is used to connect electronic components of the record player and the tape recorder. If the record player has the necessary jack, the cord can be run from the record player's *speaker output* to the tape recorder's *phono input*. If there is no speaker output, use *alligator clips* to connect the record player's *speaker terminals* to the recorder's *phono input*.

The alternative and inferior method is to record through the microphone; undesirable room noises may be picked up by this method. If you must use the microphone, set it on a pillow or a blanket in front of the speaker of the record player, at a distance of 1–2 times the diameter of the speaker.

Music, sound effects, and voice can be mixed during the original recording by setting the microphone beside the speaker of a record player as the voice recording is made. Control the volume on the record player to bring the music in or to fade it out.

Better quality and control are obtained by using an electronic *mixer* to add music and sound effects after the original voice recording is completed. A *dubbing* (copy) of the narration is made, through the mixer, onto a second tape. Record-

From the Speaker Output to the Phono Input

With Alligator Clips on the Speaker Terminals to the Recorder Phono Input

ings also are added to the second tape through the mixer, and in this way voice and music can be blended by controlling volumes and fading one in and the other out or under. Separate channels on the mixer are required for each sound component. The use of a mixer is particularly important when adding music to a voice recording being made on magentic-striped film.[1]

Another method for adding music and sound effects to a voice narration is by using a *stereo tape recorder*. With a stereo recorder, separate recordings can be made on each of two tracks which move in the same direction. Thus, you record your narration on one track, go back to the beginning, listen to the narration through a headset, and record music and sound effects on the second track in proper relationship to the narration. If mistakes are made, the music or effects can be redone without erasing the narration. Then the two tracks can be played together or both dubbed to another recorder as a single composite sound track. This procedure requires a stereo tape recorder with *separate* record controls for *each* channel.

Magnetic Recording Tape

There are many kinds of magnetic tape for use in making recordings. Which type is best to use?

Your tape choice depends largely on how you plan to use your recording. The best guidepost is recording time per reel (at your chosen recording speed).

For comparatively short programing, 1½-mil acetate tape offers the advantages of low cost, low print-through (signal transfer from layer-to-layer), and long life. It provides recordings of excellent quality.

For longer programs, a 1-mil tape is preferred. It provides 50 percent more recording time than the 1½-mil tape on a reel of the same size. Tapes of this thickness are available in both acetate and polyester (mylar) backings. Acetate is recommended for economy, while polyester provides extra strength and protection against breakage, especially for repeated uses.

The longest available playing time is provided by ½-mil polyester tape. Tape this thin usually is *tensilized*, a process which protects it from excess stretching during use. Some tape recorders will not handle this extra-thin tape; consult the instructions with your machine.

Table 17-1 shows maximum recording time for two-track tape recorders *recording* on *both sides* at 7½ and 3¾ ips. Use half of the time shown for a recording made on only one half of the tape.

TABLE 17-1

Recording Times for Various Tape Lengths

| TAPE | REEL SIZE (INCHES) | TAPE LENGTH (FEET) | RECORDING TIME MINUTES | |
			AT 7½ IPS	AT 3¾ IPS
Standard	3	150	7.5	15
1.5-mil	5	600	30	60
acetate	7	1200	60	120
Long-play	3	225	12	24
1-mil acetate	5	900	45	90
or				
1-mil mylar	7	1800	60	180
Extra-long-play	3	300	15	30
0.5-mil	5	1200	60	120
mylar	7	2400	120	240

Preparation for Recording

The quality of a recording depends primarily on proper microphone use and on regulating volume level. Follow these practices:

☐ If possible, attach the microphone to a stand so it cannot be handled or moved during recording.

☐ If a stand is not available, set the microphone on a table with a sound-absorbing towel or blanket under the microphone.

☐ Determine by test the best distance from the narrator's mouth at which to place the microphone (about 10 or 12 inches) and have him speak across the front of it rather than directly into it.

☐ Make a volume-level check for each voice to be used. Select a moderately high volume setting, but one below the distortion level. This setting permits greater flexibility for controlling volume during playback.

☐ Be sure to turn off fans and other apparatus that make noises which may be picked up by the microphone.

1 See *Basic Magnetic Sound Recording for Motion Pictures*, publication S-27 (Eastman Kodak Co., Rochester, N. Y.)

☐ Set the script on a music or other stand so the narrator will not have to handle the script too much or lower his head while talking. Change pages quietly to avoid possible paper rustle.

☐ Have a glass of water nearby for the narrator to "lubricate" his throat if necessary.

Recording Procedure

Three people are necessary to make a recording: the narrator, a cue giver—someone familiar with the timing of the narration in relation to the pic-

tures, and a person to operate the recorder or projector.

Seat the narrator at a table with microphone and his narration script before him (each sheet separate so it will not make shuffling noises when moved). Stand the person to give cues behind the narrator ready to watch the projected pictures. He will indicate when each section of the narration is to start by tapping the narrator on the shoulder. The third person operates the recorder and the projector.

Experience shows that the best recording takes place in the first one or two tries. As the narrator repeats he loses spontaneity and may make more frequent errors. Rehearse the presentation and then make the recording. Then play the recording back, checking the narration with the script to make sure that nothing has been left out, that no words are mispronounced, and that there are no extraneous noises.

Synchronizing Narration with Visuals

During recording, a low musical tone or door chime, a brief bell or buzz signal, or a tap created by striking an object like a drinking glass can be recorded to indicate slide or filmstrip frame changes. The best source for a controlled tone or signal is an electronic audio "tone generator"; 440 cycles per second for ½ second, keyed from a push button, is most acceptable. The unit is attached to the input of the tape recorder and activated by the button according to the script.

Since audible signals are often distracting and may be annoying to the viewer, an inaudible signal should be used to control picture changes whenever the necessary equipment is available for recording and playing back. Some program units create a low-frequency signal below the hearing threshold. The unit is attached to the input of a monaural tape recorder and the signal recorded on the same track with the narration. When the tape is played back with the programmer in circuit between the recorder and the slide projector, the recorded signal from the tape triggers a mechanism in the programmer, which activates the slide projector to change a slide. Thus slide changes take place automatically according to the signals on the narration track.

A preferred method of synchronization is with a stereo tape recorder. As indicated previously, two tracks can be used concurrently for synchronizing sounds—one with narration, music, and so forth, and the other carrying the control signal. But only the first track is fed into the speakers and heard by the audience. The signal on the control (second) track activates the slide projector in synchronization with the narration. Almost all quality stereo recorders can be used in this manner. Some recorders even have built-in programmers for generating the signal. See Chapter 25 for further explanation of methods for synchronizing narration with visuals.

If the resulting audio and visual materials are to be used by students studying independently, consider indicating slide or frame changes verbally along with some identification of the forthcoming picture, like—"turn to frame 12," or "now, the next slide of the city hall." When audible or inaudible control signals are used, it becomes possible for the student to inadvertently get the picture and sound out of synchronization and thus lose the meaning or continuity of the message being communicated. Furthermore, the signal method of controlling the advance of pictures eliminates the opportunity of going back to review either the narration or the picture. By verbally indicating changes and identifying the visuals, the student is free to go back to rehear or resee any material and then to easily move ahead with picture and sound synchronized.

Tape Editing

After the recording is completed, tape editing may be necessary to remove slight imperfections, rearrange elements into a more cogent order, add tape for lengthening pauses, or even to substitute a corrected bit of narration. Before editing starts (which requires cutting the tape), it is a good idea to make a quality dub and store the original recording safely away. This will protect you if an incorrect cut is made while editing.

If the original recording is made on cassette equipment, it is necessary to make a copy on an open reel of tape. There is no practical way to cut and splice the thin, narrow tape in cassettes. Follow these steps for successful tape editing:

1. Listen to the recorded tape, listing spots to be edited (use the index counter on the recorder to note locations on the tape).

2. Replay the tape and stop at the first spot.
3. Pinpoint the spot to be edited by moving the tape manually back and forth across the playback head.
4. Carefully mark cutting points on the base or shiny side of the tape. Use a fine-tipped felt pen or a chine-marking (grease) pencil.
5. Cut the tape; remove the felt-pen or grease-pencil marks; then splice the ends together or add tape as necessary.
6. Repeat the same procedure at the next editing spot.

The editing procedure is impractical for magnetic-striped motion-picture film, which cannot be cut without damage to the picture area. For film it is necessary to rerecord until the sound track is correct.

Tape Splicing

Splicing is best and most conveniently done with a tape-splicing block. This is a piece of metal that holds a short length of recording tape in precise alignment while you use a single-edge razor blade to cut the tape at a 45° angle, following slots cut in the block to guide the razor and then apply the splicing tape. The 45° cut makes a strong splice and provides some sound overlap between spliced pieces as they pass over the playback head of the recorder. Use a sharp blade to make straight, clean cuts. Follow this procedure when splicing:

1. Set one piece of tape, with shiny (base) side up, firmly in the splicing channel so it just passes the cutting groove.
2. From the other side, do the same with the second piece.
3. Draw the razor blade across the 45° cutting groove to cut both pieces of tape at the same time. Remove the top waste end of tape.
4. Cover the cut with one 1-inch piece of splicing tape.
5. Rub firmly with a fingernail or nonmetallic burnisher.
6. Draw the blade along both edges of the splicing channel to trim any excess splicing tape extending beyond the edges of the magnetic tape.
7. Examine the splice for strength.

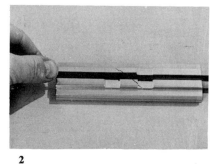

1

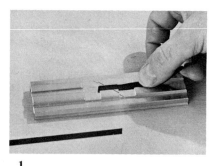

2

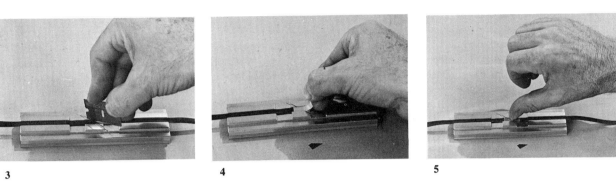

3   4   5

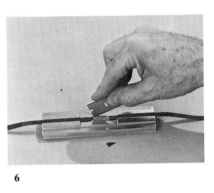 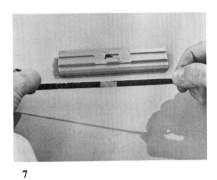

6   7

If you have no splicing unit, follow this procedure:

1. Line up the tape ends, shiny sides up and overlapping, then cut through both tapes at a 45° angle.

2. Butt the cut ends exactly together.
3. Cover the cut with splicing tape and rub firmly with a fingernail or nonmetallic burnisher.
4. Trim off the excess splicing tape.
5. Examine the splice to see if it is properly and soundly made.

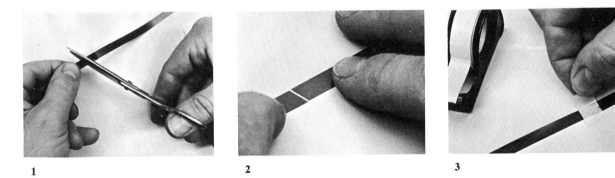

1   2   3

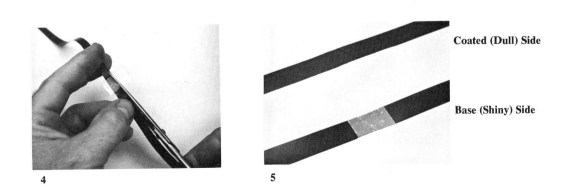

4   5

Coated (Dull) Side

Base (Shiny) Side

Preservation and Duplication

When your editing has been completed, with all sound and signals on the tape, it becomes the *master* recording. Make a dubbing of it, and file the original.

When a slide series or a filmstrip is to be duplicated in quantity, the recording must also be duplicated. High-speed equipment is available for making any required number of tape copies—either reel or cassette. A commercial recording laboratory can prepare the required number of 10- or 12-inch disk recordings from the final tape. Disk recordings are the least expensive method of quantity duplication, although the trend is toward use of cassette recordings.

Time-Compressed Speech

Normal speaking rate is 150–200 words per minute (wpm). An educated person reads printed material at 300–500 wpm. Therefore, the thought processes within the human brain can function much faster than information is presented aurally to an individual. One way of closing this gap between speaking rate and potential degree of assimilation is to speed up the speech rate. The technique of increasing the word rate of recorded speech *without* distortion in vocal pitch (to avoid the "Donald Duck" speech effect) is called *time-compressed, rate-controlled,* or *accelerated speech.*

Various speech compressors are on the market. They are of two basic kinds. One type employs a *sampling* method, which deletes brief segments of the speech signal by turning the recording off periodically during reproduction of the original tape recording. Interrupting the speech momentarily (10 or more times per second) can increase the word rate appreciably while still allowing the speech to be understood satisfactorily. Other compressors apply a *selective* method which shortens pauses and vowel sounds (which have a greater period of duration than consonants) while retaining all consonants.

There is research evidence that speech compressed up to 50 percent (from 175–275 wpm) is understandable and can appreciably shorten the communication and learning time for a given message. But for many uses, especially those requiring understanding of technical material, compression of 10–30 percent is preferred by students.[1]

There are many potential uses for time-compressed speech. It can save time when an individual wants to scan a recording rapidly (like leafing through pages of a book) to review a speech or lecture, to reduce boredom by keeping students alert and concentrating while studying recorded material, and, most important, to shorten the time necessary when listening to a recording.

Now, Apply What You Have Learned About Recording Sound:

1. Consider the recording facilities available to you. What arrangements would you make to insure the best possible tape recording?
2. How would you prepare a recording so as to include music from a disk, along with the narrator's voice?
3. What are the most desirable practices for proper microphone placement and use?
4. What method would you use to add an audible signal to a tape recording for indicating slide changes?
5. How would you use a stereo tape recorder as a "mixer" for combining narration and music?
6. What is one disadvantage of a synchronous sound/slide presentation when used for independent study?
7. Explain the procedure for removing a portion of a tape recording and inserting a substitute part.

---

1. Such evidence is reported and summarized in numerous issues of a newsletter published during the years 1968–1973 by the Center for Rate Controlled Recordings, University of Louisville, Louisville, Ky.

8. What equipment, materials, and procedures would you use for splicing tape?
9. What is one principle on which time-compressed speech is based?
10. Give a possible application for compressing speech.

Answers to Review Questions

1. Reader's activity.
2. Reader's activity, review page 155.
3. See list on page 156.
4. Reader's activity, review page 157.
5. Reader's activity, review page 155.
6. Student may accidently get the sound and picture out of sync and proceed along not knowing it; student cannot go back to review a part of either sound or picture without being very careful not to lose sync.
7. Carefully locate the very beginning and end of the new and the to-be-replaced pieces of tape; mark each end with a grease pencil; cut out the section to be replaced; splice in the new section.
8. Reader's activity, review page 158.
9. Sampling method—recording turns off periodically to delete brief parts.
   Selective method—shortening pauses and vowel sounds.
10. Reader's activity.

PART 4

PRODUCING YOUR AUDIOVISUAL MATERIALS

18
PHOTOGRAPHIC PRINT SERIES

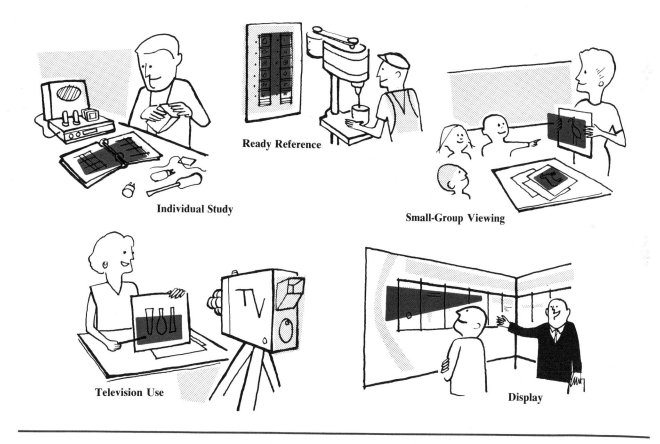

Individual Study

Ready Reference

Small-Group Viewing

Television Use

Display

A photographic print series consists of photographic prints prepared from black-and-white or color negatives. The preparation of photographic prints involves four main steps: (1) taking pictures, (2) processing film, (3) editing and making prints, and (4) preparing prints for use.

A print series may convey information, teach a skill, or affect an attitude through individual study, small-group viewing, ready reference, display, or television use.

Before taking pictures always consider this planning check list:

☐ Have you clearly expressed *your idea* and limited the topic (page 31)?
☐ Have you stated the *objectives* to be served by your print series (page 31)?
☐ Have you decided that a photographic print series is an appropriate *medium* for accomplishing the objectives (page 47)?

☐ Which of the five methods of use shown above fits your plans? (Perhaps your print series supplements other audiovisual materials for follow-up detailed study.)

☐ Have you considered the *audience* which will use the print series and its characteristics (page 33)?

☐ Have you prepared a *content outline* (page 38)?

☐ Have you sketched a *storyboard* or prepared a *script* as a guide to picture-taking (page 52)?

☐ Have you considered the *specifications* necessary for your print series (page 57)?

☐ Have you, if necessary, selected other people to assist you with the preparation of materials (page 36)?

The information in Part 3, Chapters 15 and 16, on photography and graphic techniques is basic to the successful preparation of photographic print series. As necessary, refer to the page references indicated with the following topics.

Taking Pictures

YOUR CAMERA

You can prepare a print series successfully with any camera—from a simple automatic-setting type to the large-format kinds. A Polaroid Land camera is particularly useful for the rapid preparation of either color or black-and-white small tory for self-study materials. For enlargements size photographs. Such photographs are satisfac- 8×10 inch or greater, a camera with a good-quality lens is preferable because the negatives prepared with some simple cameras are incapable of producing good enlargements. If you are selecting a camera for purchase, consider the characteristics and advantages of each category described on page 79.

Carefully study the three settings that are made on adjustable cameras—lens diaphragm, shutter speed, and focus. Understand the purposes for each, the relation of one to another and to depth of field; then determine how each setting is made on your own camera. These settings have been discussed and explained in this book on page 83.

ACCESSORIES

You may find need for:

☐ A photographic light meter to determine exposure accurately (page 91)

☐ A tripod to steady the camera (When filming at shutter speeds slower than 1/30 second *always* use a tripod.)

☐ A flash unit or photoflood lights for indoor scenes (page 94)

☐ A close-up attachment to photograph subjects at close range and to do copy work (page 99)

☐ A cable release to eliminate any possibility of jarring the camera during long exposures

☐ Wide angle and telephoto lenses in addition to the normal camera lens (page 82)

FILM

Factors pertinent to the choice of film are discussed on page 88.

Many photographers limit themselves to using a few general films, or even one, for most purposes. This practice enables a photographer to become familiar with the behavior of his film. Some of the most useful black-and-white films are briefly described in Table 18-1.

The variety of color negative films from which photographs can be made is limited. Kodacolor and Ektacolor are the most common. From them not only color prints but also color slides and black-and-white prints can be prepared.

EXPOSURE

Correct exposure is based on proper camera settings for the film to be used and on the conditions under which pictures are to be taken. Simple cameras require good light conditions because the settings are limited or the lens and shutter are preset. For other cameras, film-information sheets indicate general exposure for average conditions (page 91).

LIGHTING

The proper use of artificial light is essential for many good photographs. The overall, even, almost shadowless fluorescent light found in many areas is ideal for black-and-white pictures, even with films of moderate speed.

To boost the level of light striking the subject and then reflecting to the camera, flashcubes or electronic flash units can be used. They are handy and easy to operate, especially when small areas must be illuminated. Make sure that your camera is synchronized with the flash (at the recommended shutter speed); then apply the information on page 94.

TABLE 18–1
Commonly Used Black-and-White Films

FILM	EXPOSURE INDEX (ASA)	CHARACTERISTICS/USES
Professional copy (sheet film)	12	Extra fine grain for copy work; whites and full range of grays reproduce well
Panatomic-X	32	Fine grain for copy work; and making extreme enlargements
Plus-X Pan	125	Moderate speed, all-purpose film
Super Panchro Press Type B (sheet film)	250	Moderate speed, all-purpose sheet film
Tri-X	400	Fast, medium grain; for use under low light levels

For more carefully controlled lighting and for larger areas, use photoflood lamps. They are available in various sizes and are used with separate metal reflectors unless they have built-in reflectors. In place of regular photoflood lamps, consider using the highly efficient *sealed quartz lamp* of approximately 1000 watts.

Avoid flat lighting created by placing lights beside the camera only. Instead, establish a lighting pattern involving a key light, fill lights, and supplementary background and accent lights. Study the purposes and placement of these lights and exposure determinations as described on page 95.

CLOSE-UP AND COPY WORK

When a picture series requires a large or enlarged view of a subject, it is not always necessary or advantageous to take the picture close up; a negative or a portion of a negative can be enlarged in making the print. (This flexibility is an advantage of having negatives.) But close-up picture-taking may give sharper images or better perspective. Close-up photography presents problems of parallax, viewfinding, focusing, lens diaphragm setting, exposure timing, and lighting; solving these problems requires knowledge and use of special equipment and attachments. The problems and solutions are discussed and explained starting on page 99.

When copying flat materials with either a single-lens reflex or a sheet-film camera, you view the subject directly through the camera lens. Ma-

terials can be placed on a stand, the camera set on a tripod, and lights adjusted as shown on page 102. But with other cameras, in order to overcome the problem of parallax when copying, use a focal frame or a simple copy stand. Suggestions for constructing and using such a stand are on page 102.

A reminder—remember to obtain a release when preparing to use copyrighted materials (see the form on page 61).

TITLES AND ILLUSTRATIONS

Since most print series are designed for study by individuals, there is need for explanatory titles, captions, labels, and possibly diagrams in addition to photographs. Titles should serve the purposes noted on page 67 and captions may need refinement according to the suggestions. Then:

1. Word each one so that it is brief and communicative.
2. Select materials or aids for appropriate lettering (page 123).
3. Prepare the lettering, keeping in mind the final proportions of your photographs, using simple yet effective design features and appropriate backgrounds (page 113).
4. Use close-up copy techniques to photograph each completed title (page 99).

Prepare captions, labels, and *overprint* titles by first making an 8×10 inch or larger print from the subject negative (page 108). In planning the composition be sure to provide light areas where black lettering will appear or darker areas to support white lettering. Then select an appropriate method for doing the lettering from among the special techniques described on pages 123. Film the final title according to suggestions on page 104. Print each title negative along with others in the picture series.

When preparing illustrations:

1. Plan the artwork (page 113).
2. Select suitable backgrounds (page 131).
3. Use appropriate illustrating, drawing, and coloring techniques (page 116).
4. Use close-up copy techniques to photograph each illustration (page 99).

COMPOSITION

A well-composed picture tells one story or points out only one specific detail. Plan for simplicity of composition and clarity and sharpness of detail.

The actual size and placement of a subject

within the picture frame can be decided during enlargement printing. But as you plan and photograph each scene keep in mind the general suggestions for good composition on page 97.

SCHEDULING AND RECORD KEEPING

As you plan to take your pictures, make a list of scenes that can be filmed conveniently together. Then schedule each group. Organizing the work thus will save time and facilitate your picture-

taking. See the example on page 60.

Then, as you prepare to shoot pictures, consider the suggestions on page 59. Keep a record of the scenes filmed, the number of times each is taken, the camera settings used, and any special observations. Develop a form similar to the sample log sheet on page 61.

Be alert to the matter of copyright limitations as explained on page 60. Remember to obtain a release from persons appearing in your pictures. See the sample form on page 61.

Processing Film

It may be desirable to send exposed film to a processing laboratory for developing. Color negative film is frequently handled in this way since the procedure is long, requiring careful time and

temperature controls. But processing black-and-white film is easy and fast, requiring a minimum of equipment and facilities. The procedures are outlined on page 104.

Editing and Making Prints

Selections must be made from among the many pictures taken—some are in addition to those called for in the script or are substitutes; others are multiple takes of the same scene but differ in composition and exposure. First make *contact prints* or small enlargements (up to 4×5 inches) of all usable negatives (page 108).

Examine the prints, choosing those of highest quality that fit or supplement each scene in the script. Refer to the log sheet prepared during picture-taking for assistance in making choices. Make your final selection and assemble the prints, titles, and illustrations in sequence.

Now complete final or master enlargements of proper size and number.

Regular darkroom tray processing may be satisfactory for one or a few copies. If a number of prints will be needed, consider using the photo stabilization method with its processor as described on page 108. For a large quantity of prints here are alternatives for duplication:

☐ Diazo paper copies from translucent master photographs (page 146)
☐ Electrostatic paper copies (page 148)
☐ Commercial reprints for volume above 250 copies (source, page 149)
☐ Screened negative and plate for offset press run (page 150)

Preparing Photographs for Use

The final task is to prepare your picture series for attractive display or for ease of use by individuals and for durability.

PROTECTING

Protect the surfaces of photographs and other mounted materials that will be handled a great deal.

☐ Coat them with a clear, fast-drying plastic spray.
☐ Seal a mylar laminating film over the face of the picture (page 141)
☐ Place photographs in acetate folders for use and for filing in loose-leaf binders.

MOUNTING

Mounting photographs on cardboard protects them and assures long service. Use the dry-mount method described on page 135. Give particular attention to the special instructions and recommended materials for use in mounting color photographs, if a flexible backing is desirable, as for a turnover chart or a small booklet, mount the photographs on a cloth backing as shown on page 139.

In a series for use by individuals, separate photographs should be attached together. Cloth sheets can be stapled (cover staple points with tape), while cardboard pieces can be bound with inexpensive plastic loops (punch the cardboard and insert the loops) or spiral binding. See the examples following.

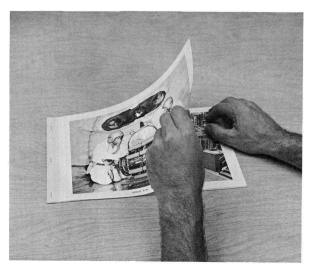

Stapled Cloth Booklet

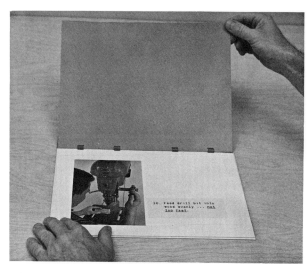

Plastic Loops

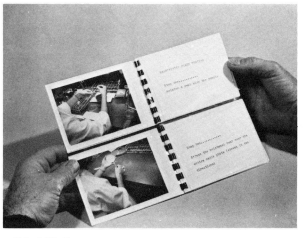

Spiral Binding

DISPLAYING

If your picture series is to be displayed for ready reference, or will be part of an exhibit, make use of the principles of design and the suggestions for layout on page 113.

Photographs can be attached to the display surface with a variety of adhering aids, some of which are not visible from the front side when applied to the back of each corner.

One of the most effective techniques is to use masking tape through which thumb tacks are punched from the adhesive side. Then press the tape to the picture backing, *on the back side.* Three or four such tape-tack units can hold fairly large and heavy display materials to a wall.

Thumb Tack Punched through Masking Tape

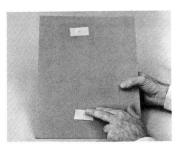

Tape-Tack Units on Back of Mounting

If the same materials are to be displayed over and over again, consider using gummed-backed cloth hooks or setting eyelets in the cardboard (available from art-supply or stationery stores). These can be used with straight pins or hooked to small nails permanently set in the display board.

Other useful adhering aids not visible from the front side of a display, are:

- ☐ Double-sided tape that has pressure-sensitive surfaces on both sides
- ☐ Regular masking tape cut in 1-inch strips and looped on itself with the adhesive-side out
- ☐ A puttylike adhering plastic (Plasti-tak) that is activated by stretching and kneading
- ☐ Temporary rubber cement mounting (page 133) for light weight materials on stiff backing

Gummed Hooks

Eyelets

Now, Review What You Have Learned About
Producing a Photographic Print Series:

1. What minimum planning is necessary as you prepare to make a print series?
2. What picture-taking equipment would you use?
3. How will you process the exposed film?
4. What is meant by "editing the contact prints"?
5. What is your procedure for making photographic enlargements?
6. In what form will you prepare the photographs for use?

Answers to Review Questions

1. Idea, objective, audience, content, storyboard
2. Reader's activity, page 164.
3. Reader's activity, page 104.
4. Selecting the negatives for enlargement printing
5. Reader's activity, page 168.
6. Reader's activity, page 168.

19

SLIDE SERIES

Individual Study   **Group Viewing**   **Television Use**

A slide series consists of transparencies, usually in color for projection, all mounted in square frames, usually 2×2 inches.

A slide series may convey information, teach a skill, or affect an attitude through individual study, group viewing, or television use.

Before making slides always consider this planning checklist:

☐ Have you clearly expressed *your idea* and limited the topic (page 31).

☐ Have you stated the *objectives* your slide series should serve (page 31)?

☐ Have you considered the *audience* which will use the slide series and its characteristics (page 33)?

☐ Have you prepared a *content outline* (page 38)?

☐ Have you written a *treatment* to help organize the content and then sketched a *storyboard* to assist in your visualization of the content (page 52)?

☐ Have you decided that a slide series is an appropriate medium for accomplishing the purposes (page 47)?

☐ Have you prepared a *scene-by-scene script* as

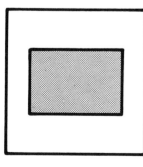

35 mm

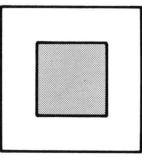

126

Half Frame
(single-frame filmstrip)

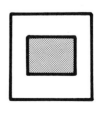

110

a guide for your slide-making (page 54)?

☐ Have you considered the *specifications* necessary for your slides (page 57)?

☐ Have you, if necessary, selected other people to assist you with the preparation of materials (page 36)?

The preparation of a slide series involves four main steps: (1) taking pictures, (2) processing film, (3) editing slides, and (4) preparing the slides for use.

The information in Part 3, Chapters 15 and 16, on photography and on graphic techniques is basic to the successful preparation of a slide series. As necessary, refer to the page references indicated with the following topics.

Taking Pictures

YOUR CAMERA

Most of the cameras described on page 79 can be used to prepare slides and color films are available for use with them. Those cameras with adjustable lens settings (f/numbers), shutter speeds, and attachments for focusing are especially useful since their flexibility enables you to record various subjects under almost any light and action conditions.

The majority of slide series are made with 35-mm and 126 cameras. There are two major types.

☐ One with a *window viewfinder* through which you see a picture slightly different from the one that the camera will record. This difference becomes greater as the camera gets closer to the subject. (Study the parallax problem described on page 99.)

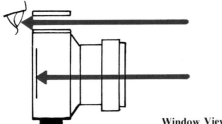

Window Viewfinder—Parallax

☐ The other (single-lens reflex camera) with a *reflecting mirror* and a prism which permits you to accurately view the same picture that the lens transmits to the film—regardless of the distance from camera to subject.

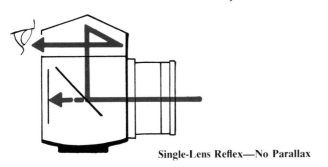

Single-Lens Reflex—No Parallax

The single-lens reflex camera is preferable for picture-taking in which framing is critical, as in close-up and copy work. With some difficulty most other 35-mm cameras can be adapted for close-up photography (see page 100).

Carefully study the three settings that are made on adjustable cameras—lens diaphragm, shutter speed, and focus. Understand the purposes of each, the relationship of one to another and to depth of field, and determine how each setting is made on your camera. These matters have been discussed and explained on page 83.

ACCESSORIES

You may find need for:

☐ A photographic light meter to determine exposure accurately (page 91)

☐ A tripod to steady the camera (When filming at shutter speeds slower than 1/30 second *always* use a tripod.)

☐ A flash gun or photoflood lights for indoor scenes (page 94)

☐ A close-up attachment to photograph subjects at close range and to do copy work (page 99)

☐ A cable release to eliminate any possibility of jarring the camera during long exposures

FILM

Select a reversal film to prepare slides when only one or a few copies will be needed. If many copies will be required, use a color negative film if it is available for your camera. In addition to considering the factors explained on page 88, select film on the basis of:

☐ The main light source that will strike the subject (daylight or photoflood; see the note about fluorescent lights on page 95)

☐ The anticipated light level (low, moderate, high)

☐ The desired sharpness of reproduction

☐ The desired reproduction of colors

TABLE 19-1   Commonly Used 35-mm Color Films

FILM	TYPE	EXPOSURE INDEX (ASA)		USE
		DAYLIGHT[a]	PHOTOFLOOD[a] (3400°K.)	
Kodacolor-II	—	80	25 (80B)	Negative for prints and slides
Kodachrome II	Daylight Type A	25 25 (85)	8 (80B) 40	Slow speed good color resolution for copy work and well-lit subjects
Kodachrome-X	Daylight	64	20 (80B)	Moderate speed, similar to Kodachrome II in other respects
High Speed Ektachrome	Daylight Type B	160 80 (85B)	50 (80B) 125 (3200°K.)	High speed for subjects under moderate available light

[a] Numbers in parentheses are filters recommended for converting film to use with other than recommended light sources.

☐ The expected number of pictures to be taken (based on 35-mm 20- or 36-exposure cassettes or rolls)

☐ The manner of film processing (by film laboratory or by yourself)

The data about films given in Table 19-1 are correct as of the time of writing; but changes and new developments can be anticipated. Carefully check the data sheet packaged with your film for the latest assigned exposure index and other details.

EXPOSURE

Correct exposure is based on proper camera settings for the film used and for the light conditions under which pictures are to be taken. Film information sheets provide general exposure data for average conditions (page 91). For proper exposure, reversal color films permit only a narrow range of camera settings, limited to from ½ to 1 f/stop on either side of the correct setting; therefore use a photographic light meter to determine exposure accurately. Follow the recommendations on page 92.

LIGHTING

As indicated in Table 19-1, color films are designed for use with specific light sources. Select your film accordingly, although with a proper light-balancing filter a film can be used under other than the recommended light conditions. When such filters are used, the exposure index of the film is reduced (example: Kodachrome II Type A with exposure index 40 when used outdoors requires a No. 85B filter and the exposure index is reduced to 25). Refer to the film information sheet packaged with each roll for detailed information about light-balancing filters.

For many slide subjects the use of artificial lighting is necessary. To boost the light level, flashcubes in reflectors or electronic flash units can be used. They are handy and easy to operate, especially when small areas must be illuminated. Make sure that your camera is synchronized (at the recommended shutter speed) with the flash. Then apply the information and formula on page 94).

For more carefully controlled lighting use photoflood lamps. They are available in various sizes and are used with separate metal reflectors or have reflectors built into them. In place of regular photoflood lamps, consider using highly efficient *sealed quartz lamps* of approximately 1000 watts. Avoid flat lighting created by placing lights beside the camera only. Instead, establish a lighting pattern involving a key light, fill lights, and supplementary background and accent lights. Study the purposes and placement of these lights and methods for determining exposure with them as described on page 95.

CLOSE-UP AND COPY WORK

Close-up and copy techniques are often very useful when preparing color slides. Your script may call for close-ups of objects, for details in a process, or for copies of maps, pictures, and diagrams. For these purposes, as has been mentioned, the single-lens reflex camera is the more suitable by reason of its accuracy in viewing. Refer to page 100 for guidance; these deal with viewfinding, parallax, focusing, lens openings, exposure timing, and equipment and attachments that you may need for this special kind of photography. They also suggest procedures for copying flat materials and for constructing and using a simple copy stand.

A reminder—always remember to obtain a release when preparing to use copyrighted materials; see the form on page 61.

TITLES

Titles should serve the purposes noted on page 67. Be sure to take account of the legibility standards for projected materials (page 120) as you select lettering sizes for titles, captions, and labels. Then:

1. Word each title so it is brief *and* communicative.
2. Select materials or aids for appropriate lettering (page 123).
3. Prepare the lettering and artwork (page 111), keeping in mind the correct proportions of your slides (page 112 and inside front cover), using simple yet effective design features (page 113), and selecting appropriate backgrounds (page 131).
4. Use close-up copy techniques to photograph each completed title on color film (page 99).

You can prepare titles on black-and-white film and then color them quickly and with ease to make negative or positive slides:

To make a negative slide:[1]

1. Prepare lettering and art work in black-on-white paper or on cardboard (if necessary use the paste-up technique on page 144).
2. Film the title. Use either 35-mm Eastman Kodalith or 35-mm Eastman High Contrast Copy film. The Kodalith film is preferable, and its use is described on page 214.
3. Process according to instructions; when dry, swab the emulsion (dull) side of the negative with transparent water-color dye or with a colored felt pen.
4. Mount the film in a cardboard frame for use.

To make a positive slide, prepare white lettering (dry-transfer letters) on black paper and film as above, or:

1. Follow step 1 as for making a negative slide.
2. Follow step 2 as for making a negative slide.
3. Contact print the negative onto a piece of high-contrast cut film (page 215).
4. After developing, fixing, and washing, dip the positive into concentrated transparent water-color dye, then hang it to dry. The clear film background will absorb the dye evenly.
5. When the positive is dry, mount it in a cardboard frame for use.

Special titles, captions, or labels can be added to prepared color slides. In composing such slides, be sure to provide light-colored areas where black lettering will appear and darker areas to support clear lettering.

To add black lettering to a slide:

1. Prepare a high-contrast negative and then a positive on cut film as in making a positive slide. Do not color the background.

2. Seal the slide and this positive in the same mount between glass covers.

To place white or clear lettering on a pictorial slide, double-expose the original subject and the

lettering on the same frame of film. (Check your camera's instruction booklet to determine whether double exposure is possible before applying this method.) Then:

1. Prepare lettering in white on nonreflecting black paper or cardboard.
2. Film the subject slightly darker than normal (½ *f*/stop underexposed) so that the lettering will stand out.
3. Then cock the camera *without advancing the film.*
4. Film the lettering with normal exposure and then advance to the next frame.

You can use various methods, according to the materials you have to work with, for superimposing colored letters on a slide. Here are several:

☐ Place colored letters directly on an original flat picture, then copy the picture and lettering together as a slide. The letters most useful for this method are the dry-transfer letters described on page 124.
☐ Place a diazo-colored transparency of the lettering over the original flat picture, then copy the combination as a slide. For information about diazo transparencies, see page 204.
☐ Make a high-contrast positive of the lettering on film and use this as a master to prepare a diazo-colored 35-mm slide (page 205). Then align and seal the diazo slide in the same mount with the prepared color slide.

To put colored lettering on a colored background, prepare the lettering on a color background according to one method described below and film:

☐ Use colored lettering on colored paper, cardboard, or suitable background material.
☐ Use a diazo-colored transparency (page 204) over suitable colored background.
☐ Use the Multicolor diazo process (page 207) to prepare lettering and contrasting background colors on one sheet.

Another easy way to prepare simple slide titles is to draw directly on clear or frosted film. See the description of how to prepare a filmstrip on acetate, page 189. The same techniques apply to slide-preparation. Use a blank cardboard slide mount to outline, on paper, the inside dimensions within which the title should be drawn. After preparing, drying, and spraying the title, mount the piece of acetate as described later in this chapter.

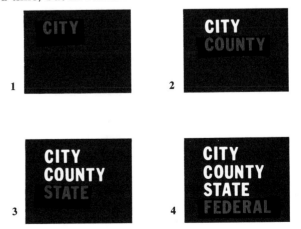

A variation of the *progressive disclosure* technique, used with overhead transparencies (page 219), can be applied to slides. Use this method if a series of titles or a list is to be shown, one at a time, but in cumulative order.

Prepare the total list on white paper, then use the *negative slide* method for preparation as described previously. Frame the entire list, then cover all items but the first one with a sheet of white paper. Film the first item. For the second picture, uncover the second item and film the two that are exposed. Repeat with three items uncovered, and so forth. The result will be a series of slides, each one revealing an additional title or item on the list.

After the slides are completed, use felt pen to color the words comprising the list. Use a different color for each new item introduced on a slide. In this way the new item will stand out and be separated from the prior items on the list.

ILLUSTRATIONS

For preparing illustrations and diagrams:

1. Plan the art work in terms of the slide proportions (page 112).
2. Select suitable backgrounds (page 131).
3. Use appropriate illustrating, drawing, and coloring techniques (page 111).
4. Use suitable copy techniques to photograph each illustration as a slide (page 99).

COMPOSITION

Composition must take place in the viewer of your camera when you film each scene; therefore study the general suggestions for good composition on page 97. As you select subjects, keep in mind the proportions of .the slides you are preparing.

If you can, prepare all slides with a uniform format—preferably horizontal.

SCHEDULING AND RECORD KEEPING

As you plan your slides, make a list of scenes that can conveniently be filmed together. Then schedule each group. Organizing the work thus will save time and facilitate your picture making. See the example on page 60.

Then, as you prepare to make slides, consider the suggestions on page 59. Keep a record of the scenes filmed, the number of times each is taken, the camera settings used, and any special observations. Develop a form similar to the sample log sheet on page 61.

Remember to obtain a release from the persons appearing in your pictures. See the sample release form on page 61.

For some purposes you may use a *documentary* approach for preparing a slide series. This means that you shoot slides treating a topic or event *without* having previously done much, if any, planning. Upon examining the resulting slides you *then* develop your script for them. See further discussion of the documentary method on page 246.

Processing Film

One advantage and convenience in using reversal color film is that after exposure, a roll can be sent to a film-processing laboratory (through your local photo dealer). The slides are returned mounted in cardboard frames ready for projection. But, if desired, many color films (GAF, Ektachrome, and color negatives) can be processed with kits of prepared chemicals. Time can thus be saved between filming and seeing the completed slides; moreover, if a number of rolls are ready at about the same time, money can also be saved. The requirements and some of the cautions that must be observed when processing both reversal color films and color negative films are outlined on page 105. Maintaining temperature with little variation is most important.

Editing Slides

Selections must be made from among all the slides—some are in addition to those called for in the script or are substitutes; others are multiple takes of the same scene but differ in exposure and composition.

Place all slides on a light box or other illuminated area for ease of inspection. Discard those so indicated on the log sheet prepared while filming. Examine the slides; eliminate the poorer ones until the remaining selection is limited to those of highest quality that fit or supplement the prepared script. Now revise the script as necessary and, if spoken or recorded commentary is to accompany the slides, refine it. Refer to the suggestions on page 63.

With the editing finished, your slide series is nearing completion. It may be advisable at this time to show the series and to read the narration

to other interested and qualified persons. For suggestions for developing a questionnaire to gather

reactions and suggestions which may help you to improve your slide series, see page 65.

Preparing Slides for Use

Slides can be mounted in commercial cardboard frames, in plastic mounts, or between glass plates. The glass seems advisable for protection when slides are to be handled a great deal or are to be used with older types of projectors that may not preheat the film, resulting in buckling and changes in focus on the screen.

But there are drawbacks to glass-mounted slides:

☐ They are heavier than cardboard or plastic mounts, and more expensive.
☐ They require more time when mounting.
☐ The glass may break if slides are dropped.
☐ Moisture often collects under the glass, or even mildew.
☐ Glass-mounted slides may not fit into some holders or slide magazines.

Moreover, slides may not need the protection of glass. In modern projectors they are removed from magazines or trays and returned to them mechanically during projection, and thus are touched by the hands only when being filed or rearranged in the magazines.

Regardless of whether you mount in cardboard plastic or between glass, always protect the surface of film being handled by wearing thin cotton gloves (generally used when editing motion-picture film).

MOUNTING IN CARDBOARD FRAMES

Use these tools and materials: cotton gloves, hand iron, cardboard mounts, gummed-back thumbspots, scissors—and the film to be mounted.

Materials for Mounting in Cardboard Frames

1. Cut the film along the frame line between the pictures.

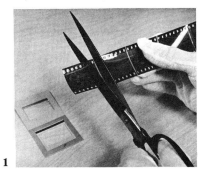

1

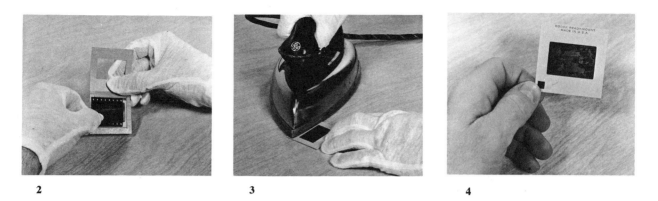

2   3   4

2. Align the film in the mount.
3. Using an electric iron (set at "low"), seal all four sides.
4. Put a thumbspot in the lower-left-hand corner (as you view the slide correctly).

If a large number of slides is to be mounted in cardboard, a faster method than using the hand iron may be preferred. A relatively inexpensive slide-mounting press (source, page 303) consists of 2×2 inch heated pressure plates. The folded mount, holding a 35-mm film frame, is placed between the pressure plates, which are then tightly closed. After a few seconds the plates are opened and the sealed slide drops out.

Seary Brand Slide-Mounting Press

MOUNTING IN PLASTIC FRAMES

A variety of plastic slide frames are available for mounting slides. With one-piece frames, the film is placed in one section, the other part folded over and secured. Other types consist of separate parts that are snapped in place to hold the film.

Check your photo supplier and other commercial sources (page 303) for specific kinds of plastic slide mounts.

MOUNTING IN GLASS

At one time slides were sealed in glass with slide-binding tape. This preparation required much hand work; eventually, also, the tape might loosen or become sticky. Moreover, some projector trays or magazines do not accommodate tapebound slides. More recently, with the availability of metal and plastic frames into which the film and glass slip easily, mounting slides in glass can be accomplished quickly and with little effort.

Get together these materials and equipment: soft brush, razor blade or scissors, paper mask, glass plates, frames, and the film to be mounted. The procedure shows the use of the Eastman Kodak metal frame.

1. If the film is in a carboard frame, cut the cardboard and remove the film.
2. Dust each piece of glass.
3. Align the film in the paper mask (silver side up).
4. Set the film under the paper tabs.
5. Dust the film on both sides.
6. Place the mask with the film between the glass plates.
7. Slide the sandwich (upside-down) into the metal frame to complete the mounting.
8. Add a thumbspot to the lower-left-hand corner (as you view the slide correctly).

Fold-Over Frame

Snap-Together Frame

Thumbspots, punched from gummed-back labels, help you to arrange slides correctly for viewing and for projection.

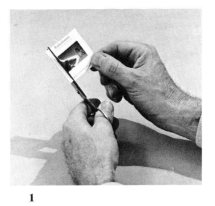

1

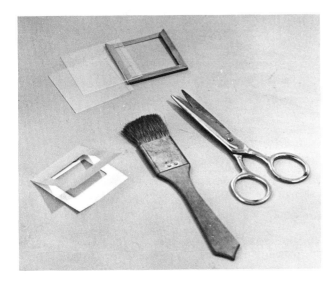

Materials for Mounting in Glass

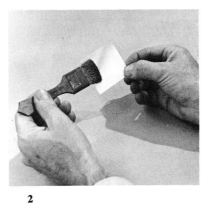

2

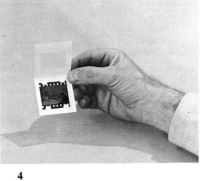

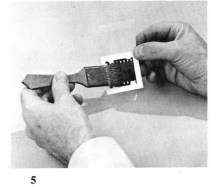

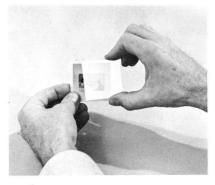

3

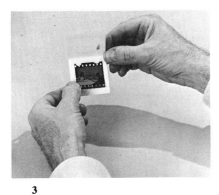

4

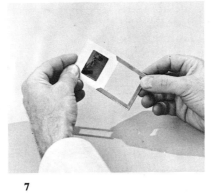

5

6

7

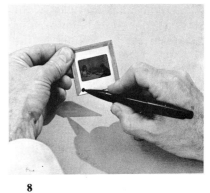

8

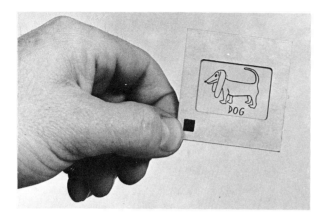

Thumbspot in <u>Lower Left Corner</u> When the Slide Is Viewed Correctly

Thumbspot in <u>Upper Right Corner</u> When the Slide is Correctly Positioned for Projection in a Carousel Projector Tray

Recording Narration

Narration can be used with a slide series in the following ways:

☐ As informal comments while slides are projected
☐ As formal reading of narration as slides are projected
☐ As recorded narration with an audible signal to indicate slide changes
☐ As recorded narration with an inaudible signal which electronically controls slide changes (requiring either a special programing unit connected between the tape or record sound unit and the slide projector, or a tape recorder with built-in programmer)

If a tape-recorded narration is to be prepared, refer to earlier suggestions concerning the selection and duties of personnel, recording facilities and equipment, and recording and tape-editing procedures (Chapter 17).

Duplicating Slides

If the number of duplicate slides that will be needed is known before photographing begins, then all duplicates can be made as high-quality originals when the original subjects or materials are photographed. Should additional sets be required after photography has been completed, a film-processing laboratory can make duplicates of the original slides.

Some people successfully project slides onto a matte-surface screen and then photograph the image to make duplicates. Careful exposure and film-color balance to match the color temperature of the projection lamp are important. (Use film balanced for photoflood light.) A slide made by this latter method will have more undesirable contrast (deeper and darker shadows and whiter highlight areas) than the original slide, and some loss of original color. This and other slide-duplicating techniques are described in *The Fourth Here's How Techniques for Outstanding Pictures*, publication AE-85 Rochester: Eastman Kodak Co., pp. 26–36.

The most successful method of slide duplication is with a specially designed slide-duplication unit. It consists of a camera, with an appropriate

Repronar Slide-Duplication Unit

close-up lens, mounted vertically over a translucent glass plate that holds the original slide to be copied. Behind the glass plate is an electronic flash unit. Exposure information is printed on the vertical bar holding the camera.

A regular 35-mm single-lens reflex camera can be attached to another slide-duplication unit (Bogen Illumitran). It includes a built-in meter for accurate exposure determination.

Filing Slides

Initially most slides are stored in the small 20- and 36-exposure boxes in which they are received from the processing laboratory As quantities of slides are accumulated, some type of filing system becomes advisable so that individual slides can be located easily. Develop a numerical filing system and consider the illustrated filing methods.

For visual reference purposes, numbered groups of slides can be placed on a light box, photographed on black-and-white film, and the negative printed to 8×10 inches. This sheet, with its numbered slide pictures, can be referred to when slides are being selected for a presentation or other use. Then, using the numbers, the slides are located in the storage file. Each topic in a file can be treated in this way and the slide picture sheets filed for reference in a notebook. This method is preferable to having to take each slide from a file and look at it when deciding on a selection.

Slide Box

Slide Cabinet

Plastic Sheet

Projector Tray

Slides on Light Box

Sheet of Photos of Slides in Notebook

Selecting a Projector

Simple slide projectors require the operator to insert each successive slide in a holder, feed it by hand into the projector, remove it by hand, and so continue with each slide in the series. The process is slow and requires much care to keep slides arranged properly. The operator must be alert for focus change as heat from the projection lens causes cardboard-mounted sides to buckle. The operator using such a projector must give undue attention to mechanics and can scarcely conduct a narration or give a lecture in addition.

For most slide projectors, adapters are available for attaching magazines or tray-fed low-cost slide-changing units, either hand-operated or remotely controlled from a distance through an electric cord with a push button (operated by the speaker once the machine is switched on). Many projector models preheat slides in the magazine to maintain correct focus, and are completely automatic, even permitting wireless remote control (including focus as well as slide changing). Such units eliminate all the problems inherent in the hand placement of slides—inversion, wrong sequence, or off-cue changes. Magazines for some projectors have capacities as high as 140 slides, thus permitting a long program to be set up in a single loading.

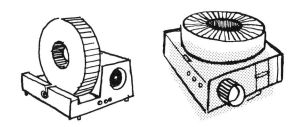

Magazine projectors offer further advantages with respect to the preservation, care, and storage of slides.

☐ Slides are protected from frequent handling and thus need not be protected by glass.
☐ Slides can be quickly removed from magazines for examination and resequencing. Unless so removed, they are always in proper order and in proper position for projection.
☐ Magazines and trays are easily handled and stored.

Automatic slide-projector and tape-recorder combination units offer the added feature of being able to put an inaudible signal on the tape which, at the proper instant, will set off a relay that causes a slide change. Such a unit accomplishes automatic projection of slides, correlated with narration. Separate "programming units" for use with many tape recorders (may require stereo units) and slide projectors (having remote-control outlets) also permit this operation (see the list on page 306). See the discussion related to multi-image synchronized presentations on page 279.

For individual use of slide series, a number of compact viewers that magnify or project the slide image from the rear onto a translucent screen may be used. More sophisticated models include sound playback units using tape cassettes which electronically control slide changes and permit the viewer to stop the tape while studying the slide image.

In summary, there are available:

☐ Projectors requiring hand placement of slides —can be used with separately operated tape recorders.
☐ Projectors with hand-operated or remotely controlled changing units having slides in magazines or trays—can be used with separately operated tape recorders.
☐ Combination or separate projectors and tape recorders—with inaudible-signal automatic slide-changing features or attachments.
☐ Hand or table viewers for individual use—can be used with separately operated tape recorders.
☐ Automatic projection viewers for individual uses—some with synchronized sound playback attachments.

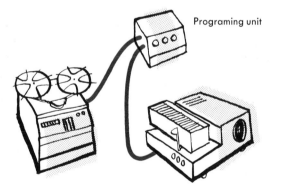

Programing unit

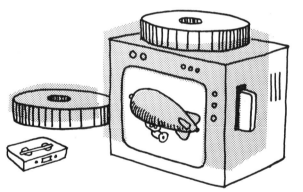

Techniques of Projection

One advantage of using slides in trays or magazines is the ease with which a showing can be "programmed." This means that you decide not only the order of using slides, but also when you want to transfer the attention of the audience to other matters (participation activities, discussion, or whatever) by interrupting the projection. To accomplish the latter insert 2×2 inch pieces of cardboard or solid-color-tone slides in the tray at places where the screen should be dark with no image. Then when a blank falls into projection position the light rays from the lamp are interrupted and the screen goes dark. When the audience is ready for the next slide, projection can smoothly start—the blank is removed and

PLAN

the next regular slide is shown. This technique is particularly effective as you end a topic and shift to another one.

Slides lend themselves very readily to *multi-image* projection, either as two or more slides projected simultaneously, or along with other media. Overhead transparencies and motion pictures are media which, for some purposes, can be effectively correlated with slides. See Chapter 25 for detailed information on multi-image techniques.

Preparing to Use Your Slide Series

With the completion of the slide series and of your preparations for using it, consider the advisability of developing an instruction guide as described on page 70.

Remember that the success of your slide series will depend not only on its content and quality, but also on the manner in which you introduce and show it to an audience. As you prepare for the first showing, if your materials are designed for group use, follow the suggestions on page 73.

Now, Apply What You Have Learned About Preparing Slide Series:

1. What size film does your slide-making camera use?
2. Is your camera a window-viewfinder or a single-lens-reflex type? What are the advantages or limitations of it?
3. What film or films would you select for use? Why have you made your choice(s)?
4. What method of making slide titles would you use in each situation:
   a. A general main title having black lettering on a colored background?
   b. "Overprinting" a word on a prepared slide?
   c. A series of three titles to be shown progressively as negative slides with colored words?
5. What factors do you consider in making choices during editing of slides?
6. Assuming your slides will be handled a great deal, how would you protect them?
7. How would you proceed to prepare duplicates of some original slides?
8. What method of filing your slides might you use?
9. What equipment is available for your use in synchronizing slides and tape recording?

Answers to Review Questions

1. Reader's activity, page 79.
2. Reader's activity, page 172.
3. Reader's activity, page 173.
4. Page 174.
5. Improper subject treatment, poor technical quality (exposure, focus, composition, etc.)
6. Reader's activity, page 177.
7. Reader's activity, page 180.
8. Reader's activity, page 181.
9. Reader's activity, page 182.

20
FILMSTRIPS

Group Viewing

Individual Study

A filmstrip consists of a series of illustrations and photographs on 35-mm film, in sequence, prepared for projection.

A filmstrip can convey information, teach a skill, or affect an attitude through individual study or through group viewing.

Before making pictures always consider this planning check list:

☐ Have you expressed your *idea* clearly and limited the topic (page 31)?

☐ Have you stated the *objectives* the filmstrip should serve (page 31)?

☐ Have you considered the *audience* which will use the film strip (page 33)?

☐ Have you prepared a *content outline* (page 38)?

☐ Have you decided that a filmstrip is the *most appropriate medium* for accomplishing the objectives and handling the content (as opposed, possibly, to a series of slides) (page 47)?

☐ Are you aware of the difficulties that must be overcome in making a filmstrip (page 186)?

☐ Have you written a *treatment* to help organize the material and then sketched a *storyboard* to assist in your visualization of the content (page 52)?

☐ Have you prepared a *scene-by-scene script* as a guide for your picture-taking (page 54)?

☐ Have you considered the *specifications* necessary for your materials (page 57)?

☐ Finally, if necessary, have you selected other people to assist you with the preparation of materials (page 36)?

Types of Filmstrips

There are two types of filmstrips, both on 35-mm film: the single-frame and the double-frame. Most filmstrip projectors will show either.

SINGLE-FRAME FILMSTRIPS

The most common type of filmstrip, standard in commercial preparation, is the *single-frame* filmstrip. It consists of pictures about 18×24 mm positioned on 35-mm film so that the long dimension runs across the film. The proportion of this single-frame picture is thus nearly, though not exactly, 3 to 4.

To prepare this type of filmstrip a single-frame 35-mm camera is necessary. Single-lens reflex models are available, which, in addition to use for direct filming, are best for copying photographs, art work, or even slides for filmstrip production.

In commercial production of single-frame filmstrips, a precisely aligned 35-mm motion-picture camera, held on an animation stand to permit rapid changes in position, is used.

DOUBLE-FRAME FILMSTRIPS

Pictures on a *double-frame* filmstrip are of the same size as those on 2×2 inch slides, that is, 24×36 mm. The long dimension runs in the lengthwise direction on the film. The proportion of this double-frame picture is nearly, though not exactly, 2 to 3.

A standard 35-mm camera is used to prepare the double-frame filmstrip, either directly from original subjects or as a copy of prepared illustrations.

With some filmstrip projectors you can remove the filmstrip mask from the aperture so a double-frame filmstrip might be projected. But this equipment is becoming less available. Also, the great majority of small filmstrip viewers used for independent study will accept only single-frame filmstrips. Therefore, double-frame filmstrips can be used only under limited conditions and there seems little value in preparing them.

Special Considerations When Planning a Filmstrip

During planning, in addition to the usual steps on page 184, consider these special factors that influence good filmstrip results:

☐ Treat the filmstrip as an entity, with continuity among frames, rather than as a series of separate disconnected pictures.

☐ A filmstrip need not be limited to a single visual medium. It can consist of photographs, art work, diagrams, charts, or graphs in any combination. Select the appropriate medium to best serve each scene in your script.

☐ Variety in the pace of a presentation is important. If narration is to be used, vary the timing of it from frame to frame. Captions also should vary from a few words in some frames to as many as 15 or 20 words if required.

☐ Recall the value of including student participation in materials designed for individualized learning (page 52). Passive viewing of lengthy sequences is undesirable.

☐ Be certain the selection and quality of pictures are all acceptable and the sequence order is firm. Changes cannot be made once the filmstrip is prepared. Consider try-out in slide-form before conversion to filmstrip.

Difficulties to Overcome

There are several ways of making filmstrips, all of which present certain difficulties that must be understood and faced.

Making a filmstrip requires a camera with an accurate film-transport mechanism, extreme care when filming, and a great deal of patience on your part. Most important is the need for accurate alignment and registration so that the film is advanced exactly the same amount from one frame position to the next. Very few cameras, other than expensive professional ones, provide this accurate movement. Minor variations between frames may not be too serious, as slight adjustments can be made in framing during projection, but you should be aware of this problem.

Any error made while filming—wrong picture order, improper composition, or wrong exposure, will require reshooting the entire filmstrip (with the same risks repeated). Therefore you must take care and use a systematic procedure. Follow the script carefully, and keep an accurate record of pictures taken and exposures used.

Frequently it is desirable to print a small number in the lower corner of each frame for reference purposes. This is particularly important when a filmstrip is to be used for independent study. Frame numbers are added when the original filmstrip is made from slides or when duplicating the original. The numbers, appearing white on the frame, are prepared by double-exposure—first the scene and then a high-contrast negative (see page 214) containing the number in proper frame location (usually lower-right corner). While double-exposing is possible with many 35-mm cameras, the need to do it properly for each frame as it is shot, and the care for placement of the number, makes this a difficult technique to accomplish outside of a film laboratory unless specialized filmstrip-production equipment is available.

The length of the filmstrip you can make is limited by the length of the film available for your camera. A normal 36-exposure roll of 35-mm film can result in a strip of 30 double frames or 60 single frames, leaving a few frames for leader and trailer. Longer filmstrips require special camera attachments or the services of a film laboratory.

The difficulties extend to duplicating filmstrips as well as to making them. Duplicating an original filmstrip requires special equipment, and it is best to leave this reproduction process to a qualified film laboratory.

The information in Part 3, Chapters 15 and 16, on photography and on graphic techniques is basic to the successful preparation of filmstrips. As necessary, refer to the page references indicated with the following topics.

Making a Filmstrip by Direct Filming

For beginners, the direct-filming procedure is *not* recommended (consider, instead, making a slide series, which can be converted into a filmstrip or projected as slides). But an experienced photographer, if he observes care as to standardized procedure, details, and uniformity of pictures, can prepare a satisfactory color filmstrip by filming scenes directly with a regular or single-frame 35-mm camera.

Remember! Direct filming will produce a *double-frame filmstrip* unless a single-frame camera is used. Hence, shoot all scenes with the regular camera in horizontal position—a double-frame filmstrip projector will not properly project vertical pictures. With a single-frame camera all pictures are taken as the camera is held vertically.

For direct filming, use a color reversal film (GAF, Ektachrome, or Kodachrome). Balance for nonrecommended light conditions by using the proper filter (page 173).

Exposure is a critical factor in direct filming, inasmuch as one poor picture will require refilming of the entire series. Carefully study the three settings that are made on adjustable 35-mm cameras: lens setting, shutter speed, and focus. Understand the purposes of each, the relation of one to another and to depth of field; and determine how each setting is made on your camera. Then relate these settings to the determination of exposure. The three settings have been discussed and explained in this book on page 83.

In direct filming, you must shoot titles, close-ups, and copy work at the proper points in the sequence. Prepare the titles and copy work in advance, and make ready for the close-up shots. To guarantee the best chance for success in directly making a filmstrip, plan carefully. A detailed storyboard (page 52) is a necessity. Refer to it as you prepare to film each scene.

Finally, if you send the film to a laboratory for processing, be sure to indicate that it is to remain as a strip and is *not* to be mounted as slides.

Making a Filmstrip from Slides

The easiest method for preparing a filmstrip is to prepare slides and copy them onto 35-mm film. Make a regular 2×2 inch color-slide series, including titles and captions, as explained in Chapter 19.

Remember! All the slides must be in horizontal format.

The time before conversion is the time for editing and also for any tryout or review-evaluation. It may be advisable to show the series and to read any planned narration to other interested and qualified persons. For suggestions about a questionnaire to gather reactions and suggestions, see page 65.

You can transfer your slides to 35-mm film for a filmstrip by using a single-frame 35-mm single-lens reflex camera equipped with a proper close-up attachment and attached to a copystand. The slides to be copied are placed over a simple light box or other back-lighted surface.[1] Align the camera perpendicular to the slide. A small bubble level is helpful in doing this.

Use a reflected light-meter to determine exposure. You may wish to shoot a roll of test film, exposing for various camera-lens settings, to be certain the correct exposure for your set-up is determined.

If a regular 35-mm camera is to be used, it is necessary to copy two slides at the same time, as this camera is of the *double-frame* type. The procedure is similar to that described for copying illustrations in the next section. Study the suggestions there and construct a mask to hold *two* pieces of 35-mm slide film (remove the film from the cardboard mounts) to be photographed.

Commercial slide copy units (see page 180) include attachments for converting 35-mm slides to filmstrip form.

Recall that the format of a 35-mm slide (3 to 2) differs from that of a single-frame filmstrip (4 to 3). Therefore in copying slides, *cropping*, or loss of part of the slide area, must be recognized. To be prepared for this loss, reproduce the cropping guide shown. Place the guide under a slide. Within the rectangle is the approximate area (depending on the aperture of your camera) of the slide that will be converted to the filmstrip frame. By examining a few slides you will realize that the subject for each slide must be composed so that important objects or action are not close to the side edges or they may be lost during conversion to filmstrip.

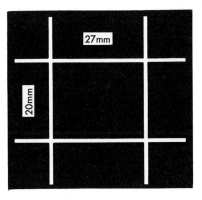

If you start with 126-size slides (square format), cropping is necessary at the top and bottom for adjusting to the 4 to 3 ratio.

Commercial film laboratories, equipped with special copy facilities, can convert slides into single-frame filmstrips at varying costs. Some laboratories do a satisfactory job for under $0.30 per frame (see sources on page 207), while high-quality professional service may cost $3.00 to $5.00 per frame. Most filmstrip preparation starts with 35-mm slides, although some original materials are filmed on either 4×5 inch Ektachrome sheet film or as 2¼×2¼ inch slides. These larger areas permit sharper reproduction; simplicity in addition of captions, labels, and other markings; easier control of color (through color and contrast masking at the laboratory); and generally better overall quality as compared to starting from the smaller 35-mm slide. The versatility of 35-mm originals can be increased by making color prints (4×5 inch size) from each slide, then retouching each print, overlaying lettering, and adding frame numbers. The prints are then copied onto film as described in the next section.

1. For constructing a simple light box see; *Producing Slides and Filmstrips*, publication S-8 (Rochester: Eastman Kodak Co.), p. 25.

Making a Filmstrip by Copying Illustrations and Photographs

One common method for making a black-and-white or color filmstrip from original materials is to prepare the illustrations and photographs in proper size and format and mount each on cardboard. Add titles, captions, and labels. Then send the complete set of these *filmstrip flats* to a film processing laboratory for conversion into a filmstrip, or copy the prepared flats yourself, in sequence, on 35-mm film.

Follow the recommendations for preparing a picture series when making photographs (page 165) and the suggestions for making titles and captions (page 65), in keeping with standards of legibility (page 120).

The size of each enlargement and illustration depends on the type of filmstrip to be prepared or on the 35-mm camera to be used for copying:

☐ For filmstrip flats to be converted by a film laboratory, use the *single-frame mask* size as your guide in composing all illustrations, photographs, and titles. The proportion is 3 high by 4 wide (6×8 inches), and an outline of it is printed inside the front cover of this book.

☐ For filmstrip flats to be copied with a single-frame camera, also use the *single-frame mask* size.

☐ For filmstrip flats to be copied with a standard 35-mm camera to make a *double-frame filmstrip*, prepare your materials to fit within the *double-frame mask size*. The proportion is 2 high to 3 wide (6×9 inches), and an outline of it is printed inside the front cover of this book.

☐ For filmstrip flats to be copied with a standard 35-mm camera to make a *single-frame filmstrip*, prepare your materials to fit within the openings of a special *two-illustration mask*. The dimensions of this mask are shown inside the front cover of this book. The mask permits the placing of two illustrations under the camera at one time. The proportions of the mask openings are near 3 high to 4 wide (2¾×4 inches).

When using the above mask be sure each picture is located at the proper mask opening.

Follow these suggestions as you make ready and film your materials:

1. Before you convert the illustrations and photographs into your filmstrip, be sure to edit them carefully. Also, you may want to try the set out by showing them and reading any planned narration to other qualified and inter-

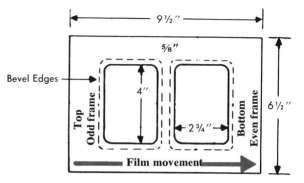

Two-Opening Mask for Copying Single-Frame Filmstrip with Standard 35mm Camera (adapted from "Photographic Production of Slides and Filmstrips," publication S-8, Eastman Kodak Company). See full-scale outline inside front cover.

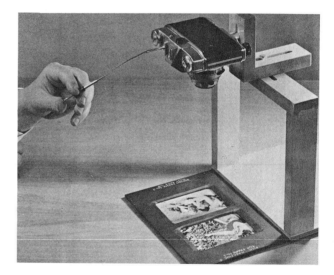

Camera Position for Photographing Single Frames with Standard 35mm Camera. The camera takes two frames on each exposure. (Reproduced with permission from the Kodak pamphlet "Simple Ways to Make Slides and Filmstrips.")

ested people. Revising pictures or captions at this point is less expensive than revising them after the filmstrip has been made. For suggestions about a questionnaire to gather reactions and suggestions, see page 65.

2. When all illustrations, photographs, and titles have been prepared, using the appropriate mask cut from cardboard as a guide for precise positioning and mounting, number each piece in sequence for filming. Keep the numbers in a corner of the projection area, but have them clear and uniformly placed (the lower right corner is the usual location).

3. Prepare to copy the flats on a copy stand (page 101).

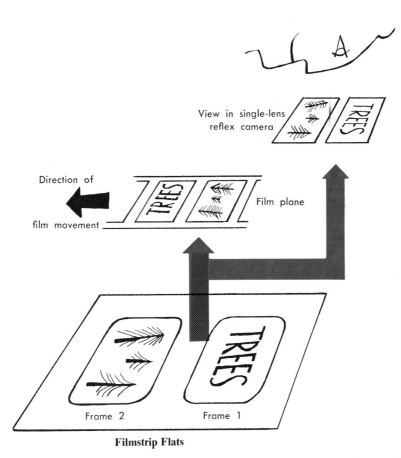

View in single-lens reflex camera

Direction of film movement

Film plane

Frame 2

Frame 1

Filmstrip Flats

4. For black-and-white use a fine-grain film such as 35-mm Kodak Panatomic-X (available in 20- and 36-exposure rolls) or 35-mm Kodak Direct Positive Film (available only in 100-foot rolls, which must be spooled into cassettes). Shoot five or more frames as a test. Process either film with a Kodak Direct Positive Film Developing outfit to a reversal or positive filmstrip (this procedure is quicker and more satisfactory than making a negative and then printing a positive from it—see the instructions with the film and developing outfit).[2] Examine the test print for exposure, framing, alignment, and focus. Repeat the test as necessary. For color use Kodachrome 64 or Ektachrome-X reversal film.

5. Shoot the total picture series to make a master filmstrip. Leave five or six black frames (by clicking the camera shutter with hand held over the lens) at the beginning as leader, and after the end title as trailer. If only a few copies of the filmstrip are needed, repeat the filming and developing procedure. (*Always photograph all filmstrip material in one working period.* Do not be distracted by other activities.)

Making Filmstrips by Drawing on Acetate

It is possible to write and draw directly on film, thus preparing a hand-made filmstrip. This can be a useful and enjoyable activity for students since no camera or other special equipment is needed as they express their ideas in visual form.

Such a filmstrip can be prepared on either one of two 35-mm film surfaces.

ON CLEAR ACETATE

Rolls or lengths of clear 35-mm film can be purchased from many film-processing laboratories. Other teaching-materials supply sources may stock the clear film. Follow this procedure to make a filmstrip:

1. On paper, prepare an outline of a series of filmstrip frames, carefully delineating the working area within each frame. Use a **strip** of 35-mm film for a guide. Each frame includes

---

2. Panatomic X is not a reversal film but is used as such in this method. See *Black and White Transparencies with Panatomic-X Film,* pamphlet F-19 (Rochester: Eastman Kodak Co.).

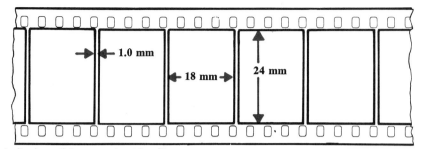

four sprocket holes and has an inside dimension of 18×24 mm.

2. Make a number of copies of this lay-out sheet. Use them to sketch in the diagrams and words that will comprise the filmstrip. This becomes the *storyboard* for the filmstrip.

3. Tape a length of clear 35-mm film exactly over the storyboard. Allow three or four clear frames at the beginning as leader. Then draw and letter over the sketches using fine-tipped felt pens (black and colors). If water-based pens are used, corrections can be made by carefully removing the ink marks with a damp cloth. With permanent-type pens, the marks can only be removed with a chemical solvent. Leave three or four blank frames at the end as trailer.

4. Allow the markings to dry. Spray the complete strip lightly on the inked side with a clear plastic spray to protect the lines and areas.

ON FROSTED ACETATE

When acetate is lightly abraded or scraped, the surface loses its transparent appearance and becomes fosted. It now has a fine "tooth," which will take ordinary pencil markings. Thirty-five-mm frosted acetate is available only from certain distributors.[3]

The same procedure as for planning and pre-

paring filmstrips on clear acetate is followed with frosted acetate. In addition to fine-tipped felt pens, number-2 lead lencils and colored drawing pencils can be used on the frosted surface. Sharpen the pencils frequently during use to maintain a sharp writing point. Work carefully, because erasures and wash-offs tend to remain as blemishes or ghost images on frosted acetate.

Spraying the frosted surface with a clear plastic coating after the filmstrip is prepared protects the pencil and pen marks, and also makes the translucent frosted surface more transparent. This allows for better transmission of light and a brighter projected image.

Duplicating a Filmstrip

Preparing more than a few copies of a filmstrip by shooting each one from the original photographs or slides is impractical. It is advisable to have duplicates made from the master filmstrip by a film laboratory providing such service. Two methods are employed in making duplicates. Good quality copies can be made directly from an original filmstrip. Such a service is charged on either a per frame basis ($0.20), or on a per foot basis ($0.45 in quantity). There are

16 frames per foot on a 35-mm single-frame filmstrip.

The second duplication method is used when large numbers of high quality strips are needed. A negative ($0.50 per foot) is made from the original and copies ($0.25 per foot) run from it.

See the list of film laboratories providing the services described here (page 207). Inquire about special services to fill your needs.

Upon completion, roll each filmstrip with the emulsion (dull) side on the inside to insure proper handling when projected. Store it in a filmstrip can (source on page 303) and label the can with the title.

---

3. A major source for frosted 35-mm film is Hudson Photographic Industries, Inc., Irvington-on-Hudson, N.Y., 10533.

Correlating with Narration

If narration is to accompany the filmstrip, refine it to fit the visuals (suggestions on page 63). Narration and supplementary comments can accompany filmstrip projection as:

☐ Informal comments and instructions for participation

☐ Formal reading of narration

☐ Recorded narration on tape with an *audible* signal to indicate frame changes

☐ Recorded narration with an *inaudible* signal which electronically controls frame changes and requires a combination tape unit and projector

If a tape-recorded narration is to be prepared, refer to earlier suggestions relating to the selection and duties of personnel, recording facilities and equipment, and recording and tape-editing procedures (Chapter 17). Inexpensive duplicate disk and cassette recordings can be made as necessary, from the master tape. Sources for this service are given on page 308.

Preparing to Use Your Filmstrip

With the completion of the filmstrip and of your preparations for using it, consider the advisability of developing an instruction guide as described on page 70. Consider also correlating the filmstrip with other materials for use in an instructional program.

Remember that the success of your filmstrip will depend not only on its content and quality, but also on the manner in which you introduce and show it to an audience or integrate it with other materials for independent study. As you prepare for your first showing, if your materials are designed for group use, follow the suggestions on page 73.

Now Review What You Have Learned About Producing Filmstrips:

1. Does your camera permit the preparation of a single-frame or a double-frame filmstrip?
2. For what reasons is it not advisable to make a filmstrip by direct filming?
3. What are three special considerations when planning a filmstrip?
4. What does "cropping" mean as it refers to slides for use in a filmstrip?
5. Which method of filmstrip preparation would you select to use? What steps in production does this entail?

Answers to Review Questions

1. Reader's activity, page 185.
2. Any error requires reshooting the entire strip. All pictures must be taken in sequence, and this may entail much more time in moving back and forth from one location to another as well as the difficulty of adding captions and titles at proper places.

3. Have continuity among pictures; possibly mix diagrams, drawings, photographs, and other visual forms; vary the timing of narration to provide variety in pacing.
4. Deciding what areas of the edge of a slide to eliminate when copying.
5. Reader's activity, page 186.

21
TAPE RECORDINGS

Class Listening   **Group Use**   **Individual Study**

Tape recordings can be used by themselves to convey information, provide drill and practice, teach a skill, test learning, or serve as the study guide for an *audio-tutorial* lesson, and they can also be used in conjunction with visual materials.

The latter use is described with specific audiovisual materials in other chapters of this book. This chapter considers tape recordings, by themselves or as the study guide, for instructional purposes.

Planning a Recording

If recordings are simply oral duplications of reading matter or contain information that could be read more readily and probably more quickly, then recordings have little to offer as carefully designed, thoughtful, and exciting instructional materials. But if recordings are for small-group and independent study, as part of instructional packages, in which students set their own pace, and participate actively, then such recordings can be thought provoking, making positive, creative contributions to instruction. In the audiotutorial method, since the recording becomes the central element of the instructional package, planning is essential.[1]

Planning a tape recording (or series of recordings) requires the same care as the planning of other audiovisual materials, and should follow this sequence.

- ☐ Establish objectives (page 31)
- ☐ Consider audience characteristics (page 33)
- ☐ Develop the content outline (page 38)
- ☐ Correlate with other media and learning experiences
- ☐ Prepare the script (page 54)
- ☐ Write the worksheet (page 71)

Instructional recordings designed for small-group or individual use must be self-teaching, without direct supervision by the teacher. Therefore a worksheet or other materials for the stu-

1. S. N. Postlethwait, J. Novak, and H. Murray, *The Audio-Tutorial Approach to Learning* (Minneapolis, Minn./ Burgess Publishing Co./72).

dent should be furnished for use with the recording. The worksheet provides directions for using the recording and has places for responses to questions, for solutions to problems, and for activities initiated on the tape.

The tape portions of the lesson should be structured to contain the following:

☐ A motivational portion that introduces the lesson, lists the objectives, and indicates any special preparation required (unless these are provided in the worksheet).

☐ Instead of initially preparing the script on paper, record the necessary information on tape, then type out the material, edit the script, and rerecord in final form. Use an informal conversational tone with simple, direct phrases.

☐ Avoid the possibility of a "mind-drift" by the listener. Frequently change the rhythm of the presentation (change in voice pacing and emphasis, add other sound effects like music, give directions for participation activities, and

so on). Most audio programmers recommend that about *10* minutes is the maximum continuous time that a high-school student can pay attention to a single topic or concept. Naturally, this is shorter for elementary-grade students. Therefore, divide your subject into subtopics or limited objectives so that each element can be accomplished in a reasonable period of time.

☐ Explicit instructions for participation work, which may include completing readings, viewing visual materials, observing demonstrations or displays, carrying out other activities, and completing worksheet exercises, problems, and self-checks

☐ Pauses of sufficient length (or instructions to turn off the recorder or 4–5 seconds of music) to allow for completion of responses or performance of activities.

☐ Indications of correct responses for immediate feedback

☐ Summary and/or instructions leading to other materials or activities

Preparing a Recording

In some ways preparing recordings as instructional resources by themselves is easier than combining recordings with visual materials. In addition to the recording itself, the latter require attention to synchronization and pacing with the visuals.

The procedures for making recordings are presented in Chapter 17. Follow those steps that are important in your situation, especially with regard to:

☐ Recording facilities and equipment
☐ Selection of magnetic tape

☐ Recording procedure
☐ Mixing with music and other effects
☐ Tape editing and splicing
☐ Synchronizing narration with visuals or printed materials
☐ Duplicating the recording in sufficient copies for use
☐ Preservation and storage

Also, consider the possible value in using a time-compressed-speech technique (page 161) for presenting information, for rapid scanning or reviewing recordings.

Now, Apply What You Have Read About Planning and Preparing Tape Recordings:

1. If recordings are planned as part of an instructional package, with what other materials or experiences might you correlate a recording?

2. What planning steps will you follow in developing a recording for group or individual use?

3. Of the procedures described in Chapter 17, which ones will you study for help in making the recording?

4. How will you make duplicates of your recording for use?

Answers to Review Questions

1. Textbooks, articles, and other printed materials; any projected or nonprojected visual materials; laboratory, field work, or other direct experiences
2. Objectives, audience, content outline, correlation with other media and experiences, script, accompanying study guide or worksheet
3. Reader's activity
4. Reader's activity, page 160.

22
OVERHEAD TRANSPARENCIES

Large Groups   **Average-Size Classes**   **Small Groups**

Transparencies are large slides for use with an overhead projector from the front of a lighted room. They project a large, brilliant picture.

Transparencies can visually present concepts, processes, facts, outlines, and summaries to small groups, to average-size classes, and to large groups.

A series of transparencies is like any other

audiovisual material in requiring systematic planning and preparation. Before you actually set about making your transparencies, therefore, always consider this planning check list:

☐ What *objectives* will your transparencies serve (page 31)?
☐ What factors are important to consider about the *audience* that will see the transparencies (page 33)?

☐ Have you prepared an *outline* of the content to be included (page 38)?
☐ Are transparencies an appropriate medium to accomplish your purposes and to convey the content (page 47)? Might they be combined with other media for even greater effectiveness (page 45)?
☐ Have you *organized the content* and made *sketches* to show what is to be included in each transparency (page 52)?

Features of Overhead Projection

When showing visual materials with an overhead projector, you can make your presentation effective by using these techniques:

☐ You can show pictures and diagrams, using a pointer on the transparency to direct attention to a detail. The silhouette of your pointer will show on the screen.

☐ You can use felt pen or a special pencil to add details or mark points on the transparency during projection.

☐ You can control the rate of presenting information by covering a transparency with paper or cardboard and then exposing the data when you are ready to discuss each point.

☐ You can superimpose additional transparent sheets as overlays on a base transparency so that you separate processes and complex ideas into elements and progressively present them.

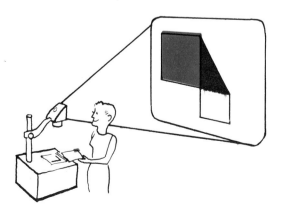

☐ You can move overlay sheets so as to re-arrange elements of a diagram or a problem.

☐ You can simulate motion on parts of trans-parency by using the effects of polarized light on special plastic with a polaroid spinner. (See sources on page 304.)

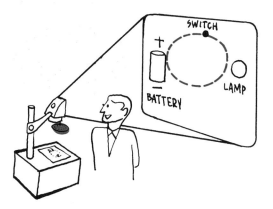

☐ You can show three-dimensional objects from the stage of the projector—in silhouette if the object is opaque, or in color if an object is made of a transparent color plastic.

☐ You can duplicate inexpensively on paper the material to be presented as transparencies. Distributing copies to the class or audience will relieve them of the mechanics of copying complex diagrams and outlines.

☐ You can simultaneously project other visual materials (slides or motion pictures) that illus-trate or apply the generalizations shown on a transparency.

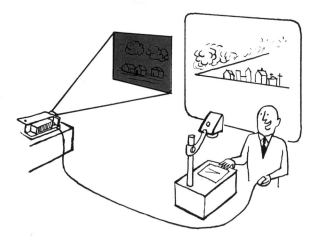

Evidence from research studies reported in Chapter 3 indicates the value of student partici-pation during learning. Develop some transparen-cies that involve the learner by requiring the com-pletion of parts, replies to questions, or solutions to problems. Or, provide students with paper copies of the content of transparencies and in-structions for activities relating to your presen-tation.

Dimensions of the Working Area

The area of the stage (the horizontal glass surface) of most overhead projectors is 10×10 inches. The entire square can be used for the transparency, but it is better to avoid the extreme

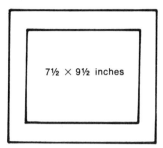

7½ × 9½ inches

edges. Also, since a square is less attractive for most purposes than a rectangle, it is well to work

within a retangle having a height-to-width ratio of about 4 to 5. Thus a convenient transparency size, made on 8½×11 inch film, is 7½×9½ inches. This is normally projected with the 9½ inch dimension horizontal because it is difficult to view some parts of vertically oriented transparencies in rooms with low ceilings or with suspended lighting fixtures.

You can buy cardboard or plastic frames with the opening cut in them, or you can make your own from 6- to 10-ply cardboard. An outline of the open area of a frame is printed inside the back cover of this book.

Whatever the size of the mask opening you plan to use, prepare all art work, pictures, and lettering to fit within this opening or to have its proportion if size changes are to be made by photographic or other enlargement or reduction.

Necessary Skills

DESIGN AND ART WORK

Limit the content of a transparency to the presentation of a single concept or a limited topic. Do not try to cover too many points in a single transparency. A complex transparency may be confusing to the viewer and thus lose its effectiveness. Design a series of transparencies rather than a crowded single transparency.

As you plan diagrams and outlines or captions and labels for your materials, consider the applications of:

☐ Planning the design and artwork (page 113)
☐ Illustrating and coloring techniques (page 116)
☐ Legibility standards for lettering projected materials (page 120)
☐ Lettering materials and aids (page 123)

If you select diagrams and printed materials from books or magazines to convert to transparency form, be alert to certain limitations:

☐ The format will probably be vertical rather than horizontal as recommended above.
☐ The quantity of information included in printed materials may be more than can properly be presented in a single transparency.
☐ Materials printed in a book, to be read and studied close-up at the reader's own pacing, may be too dense and thus not suitable for projection and group use.

interrelationship of key operations

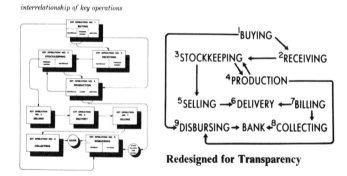

Original Subject

Redesigned for Transparency

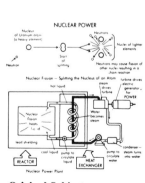

Original Subject

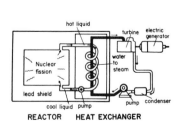

**Divided into Parts for Series
of Transparencies**

☐ Finally, realize that copyright may impose limitations and it may be necessary to request permission for certain uses (page 61).

Therefore, at first glance some printed materials may look suitable for use, but may in actuality be too small, too detailed, and even illegible as transparencies.

ADDING COLOR

The addition of color to parts or areas of a black-line transparency will clarify details or give emphasis to the content of a diagram. Use color purposefully.

Color must be transparent and can be applied in various ways:

☐ Use sharp-tipped felt pens directly on a transparency to write and draw lines (see page 118).
☐ Use broad-tipped felt pens to color areas on a transparency. Color may be applied as a solid area, although overlapping strokes build up layers of color and these irregularities become visible. Felt pens can also be used to color by applying parallel lines, as in hatching, or by making dots, as in stippling.
☐ Use diazo films (page 204), which are available in a number of colors. They give even, rich coloring effect.
☐ Use transparent color adhesives, available in a wide range of colors and black-and-white shading patterns. Color adhesives can be applied to areas of any shape, and a number of colors can be used on a single transparency sheet. Add the color to the *underside* of a transparency. Follow the instructions on page 119 for using color adhesives.

MAKING OVERLAYS

One of the most effective features of overhead projection is the *overlay technique*. As indicated on page 201, problems, processes, and other forms of information can be divided into logical elements, prepared separately as transparency sheets, and then shown progressively for effective communication.

In preparing a transparency in overlay form, first make a sketch of the total content. Decide which elements should be the *base (projected first)* and which elements, from the original sketch, will comprise each overlay. Make separate *masters* for the base and each overlay. Then prepare a transparency from each master, using one or more of the techniques described in the following pages.

When mounting the final transparent sheets, attach the base to the underside of the cardboard frame and the overlays to its face on the appropriate sides (see page 219 for details in mounting).

To insure proper alignment of all layers of the final transparency, carefully *register* the master drawings to the original sketch and also each piece of film to its master when printing. Do this by placing a guide mark (+) in each of two corners (outside the projected area) on the master exactly over the marks on the original sketch; or, preferably, use punched paper and film aligned on a register board (page 112).

Now, Review What You Have Learned About
Planning Transparencies:

1. Of all the features of overhead projection, which ones seem of most value to you?
2. Should you plan transparencies to be viewed horizontally or vertically, or does it matter? Reasons?
3. What are the inside dimensions of a standard transparency mount?
4. How might you plan one or more transparencies that require student participation during their use?
5. For what reasons might it *not* be advisable to use available printed pages as transparencies?
6. For what reasons might you use coloring on a transparency?
7. What should be the minimum letter size used on transparencies?
8. What lettering aids might you use in preparing transparencies?
9. To insure proper alignment, when preparing to make overlays, what procedure is followed?

Note: Answers to review questions can be found at the end of the chapter.

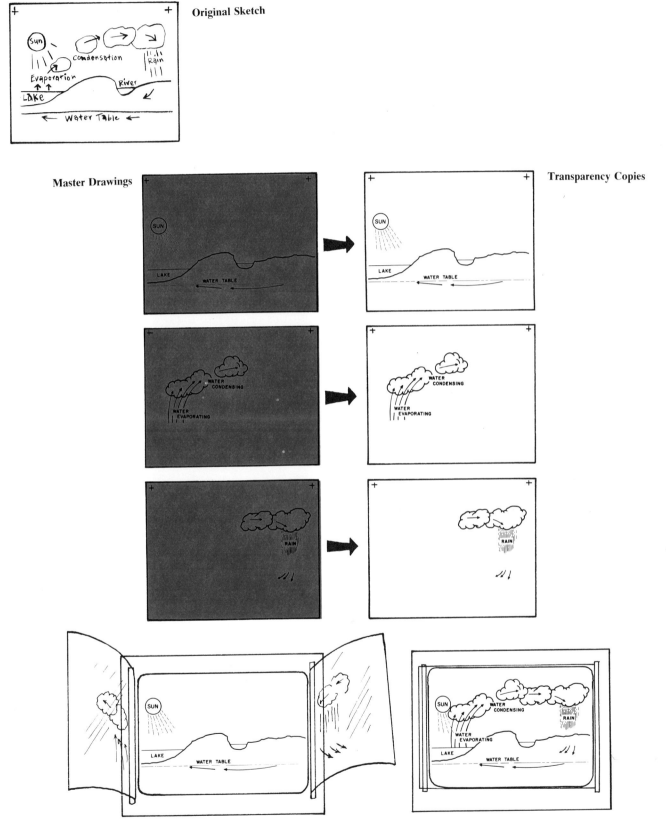

Original Sketch

Master Drawings

Transparency Copies

Mounted Transparency

Preparing Transparencies

Many processes have been developed for preparing transparencies. They range from very simple hand lettering or drawing to methods requiring special equipment and particular skills. Of these, the most practical and proven techniques are considered here. The methods are grouped as follows:

1. Making transparencies directly on acetate
   a. On clear acetate with felt pens
   b. On clear acetate with tapes and dry-transfer letters
2. Making transparencies as reproductions of prepared diagrams
   a. With the spirit duplicator
   b. On diazo film
3. Making transparencies as reproductions of printed illustrations—with no size change
   a. On heat-sensitive film
   b. On electrostatic film
   c. As a picture transfer on pressure-sealing acetate
   d. As a picture transfer on heat-sealing acetate
4. Making transparencies as reproductions of printed illustrations—with size change
   a. High-contrast subjects
   b. Halftone and continuous-tone subjects

Which method or methods to use? First, consider those most appropriate to your purposes, the subject matter, and the planned use for the transparencies. Your final decision should be based upon accessibility of equipment and materials, on your skills and available time, and, certainly not of least importance, on your standards for quality. Refer to Table 22-1, Summary of Methods for Preparing Transparencies, page 218.

Finally, ask yourself these questions as you start your preparations:

☐ Is the layout of the subject simple and clear?
☐ Have you checked the accuracy of content details?
☐ Will this be a single-sheet transparency or should you consider using overlays to separate elements of the subject—or might masking and uncovering of parts be effective?
☐ Will you plan to write some information on the finished transparency in addition to what is presented? (It is often more effective and attention-getting to add details or key points to an outline or diagram as the transparency is used, or to involve the audience with activities relating to the transparency during use.)
☐ Is color important to the subject and treatment? If so, how should it be prepared?
☐ Is it satisfactory to do the lettering freehand, or should you consider using a lettering aid, like a boldface typewriter, dry-transfer letters, Wricoprint, or a Leroy set (see page 123)? Remember to make lettering large enough for easy viewing—⅕ to ¼ inch minimum size.[1]
☐ Will duplicates of the transparency be needed for other users?
☐ Will paper copies of the content of the transparency, or related information, be needed for distribution to the audience before or after seeing the transparency?

Making Transparencies Directly on Acetate

With these simple techniques transparencies are prepared quickly. They are not durable. For repeated use, neater and more permanent methods are advisable. But use these techniques for trying out your visuals; then, if necessary, make revisions before redoing them in permanent form.

On paper, outline the boundaries of the opening in the mount that you will use. Still on paper, make a sketch or position an illustration for tracing. Then, using the appropriate tools below, put your drawing or tracing on acetate. Complete the transparency as directed later in this section.

ON CLEAR ACETATE WITH FELT PENS

Materials and tools: clear acetate sheets (.005–.010 inch thick preferred); a cardboard mount; fine-tipped and broad-tipped felt pens in colors.

See page 125 for a discussion of types and characteristics of felt pens. As indicated on page 118 under Coloring, the fine-tipped felt pens are designed for drawing lines and writing, while the broad-tipped ones are useful for coloring areas. All felt pens produce transparent colors and are therefore suitable for transparency preparation. The permanent-type inks require a plastic cleaner or other solvent (such as lighter fluid) for removal. Marks made with water-base felt pens can be removed with a water-dampened cloth.

To protect the surface of a transparency made with washable inks, cover it with a clear sheet of acetate.

---

1. Sarah Adams et al., "Readable Letter Size and Visibility for Overhead Projection Transparencies," *AV Communication Review* 13, no. 4 (Winter 1965): 412–17.

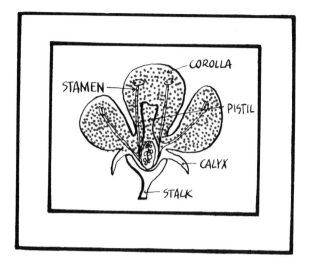

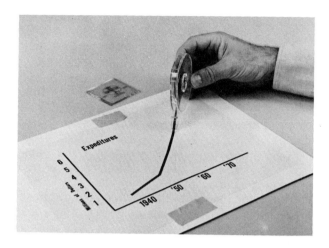

Some inks tend to run slightly; therefore use pens lightly. Also, colors may not take to the acetate evenly; therefore consider using a stippling method (small dots of ink) to color large areas.

ON CLEAR ACETATE WITH TAPES AND DRY-TRANSFER LETTERS

Materials and tools: clear acetate sheets; a grid or graph paper; rolls of transparent-color tapes or patterns; sheets of transparent-color dry-transfer letters.

Charts, graphs, and similar diagrams can be prepared quickly using tapes and dry-transfer letters. The tapes are available in various widths, colors, and black-and-white patterns. The letters and numerals are the dry-transfer sheets decribed on page 124, but with two differences—the colors are transparent, and no wax is visible around a letter after it is transferred to the acetate.

Use a grid sheet or graph paper under the acetate as a guide for placement and alignment of tapes and letters. When cutting strips of tape to length on the acetate, avoid making cut marks on the acetate—they will project as dark lines.

Now, Review What You Have Learned About Transparencies Made Directly on Acetate:

1. Are all felt-pen colors suitable for use on acetate?
2. How can you remove the markings of a permanent felt pen?
3. Do felt pens cover areas evenly?
4. How would you protect from smearing a transparency that has been made with water-base felt pens?
5. What is special about the dry-transfer letters used on transparencies?
6. What is the warning offered when using a blade to ut color tapes on a sheet of acetate?

Note: Answers to review questions can be found at the end of the chapter.

Making Transparencies As Reproductions of Prepared Diagrams

To make transparencies as reproductions requires the preparation of one or more master drawings on appropriate paper and then the duplication of these drawings on transparent material. The spirit-duplicator and diazo methods are described immediately hereafter. In addition to these, the methods of copying on heat-sensitive film and on electrostatic film, described in the next section, are suitable for making transparencies from original diagrams.

WITH THE SPIRIT DUPLICATOR

Just as in making paper copies from a master with the spirit duplicator, a sheet of frosted (matte) acetate can be run through the machine. The acetate will pick up color carbon from the master, resulting in a translucent-type transparency. A benefit of this technique is that inexpensive paper copies of the subject can be made at the same time for distribution to the class.

Materials, equipment, and tools: sheets of frosted (matte) acetate, 8½ × 11 inches, having a fine tooth (which picks up the color better and allows good transmission of light); cardboard mount; spirit duplicating masters (with colored carbons); duplicating paper; a spirit duplicating machine; ball-point pen and lettering aids; clear plastic spray.

1. Prepare the duplicating master in the same way used for making paper copies; use colored carbons as appropriate.
2. Attach the master to the drum of the duplicating machine, cause fluid to flow to the wick, and adjust pressure.
3. Feed some paper through the machine; when a good image is being transferred, send through a sheet of acetate (matte side up).
4. The acetate will pick up the image from the master just as the paper did.
5. Allow the image to dry. Then carefully coat the frosted side with clear plastic spray to transparentize and protect the image. Use the spray carefully to flood the surface lightly and evenly. Too much spray will cause color to run, while too little spray gives a splattered appearance. (See warning, page 213.)
6. After the spray coat is dry, mount the transparency for use.

There may be some difficulty in feeding the frosted acetate sheet through the spirit duplicator. The smooth surface of the acetate can cause slippage against the feed rollers. Experience has shown that you can push the acetate sheet into the machine, up against the drum, and it will then catch easier than if you depend on the feed rollers for transport. Also, owing to the attraction of static electricity charges after it passes through the machine, the acetate may stay on the drum, over the master, rather than move straight to the take-up tray. If it clings, carefully remove the acetate sheet from over the master so as not to smear the image.

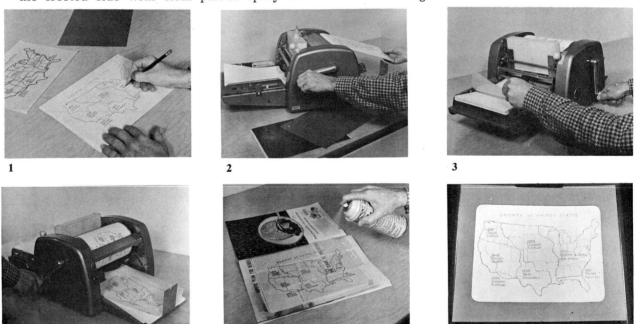

ON DIAZO FILM

Diazo films have been designed especially for the preparation of brilliantly colored transparencies. The term *diazo* refers to the organic chemicals, *diazo salts,* that, along with *color couplers,* are coated on acetate. If the coating on the film is exposed to ultraviolet light, it is chemically changed so that no image will appear. But if the coating is *not exposed* to ultraviolet light and is *developed* in an alkaline medium, like fumes of commercial ammonia (ammonium hydroxide), the diazo salts combine with the color coupler in the film to form a colored image. By using various color couplers during manufacture, any one of about 10 colors can be coated on acetate.

When film, or a section of a sheet of film, is first exposed to ultraviolet light and then developed in ammonia, color appears only in those sections *not* affected by the ultraviolet light. Thus exposure to ultraviolet light *prevents* the color coupler from uniting with the diazo salts to form a visible color.

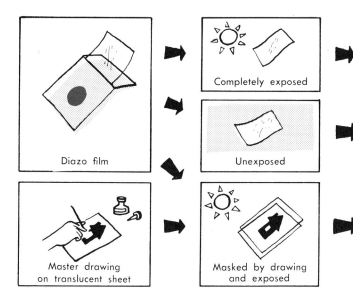

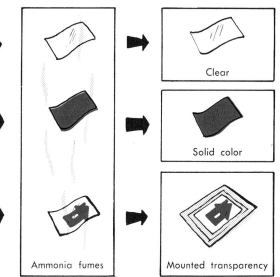

Four simple experiments can be performed to aid in understanding the principle of the diazo process as explained above:

1. Take a sheet or piece of diazo film from its storage box and immediately place it in a jar of ammonia vapor.
2. Expose a sheet of diazo film to sunlight (3–5 minutes) or to another ultraviolet-light source and then develop it in the ammonia jar.
3. Cover a sheet of diazo film partially with opaque paper, expose as in experiment 2, and develop in ammonia.
4. Prepare an *opaque* line drawing on a sheet of tracing (translucent) paper; place it in contact with a sheet of diazo film; proceed to expose the two (light source—drawing—diazo film, in that order) and then develop.

Now, refer to the previous diagram and explain why the color appears on the film or does not appear for each experiment.

To prepare a diazo transparency, therefore, put lettering or drawing on a translucent sheet and expose it in contact with the diazo film to ultraviolet light; then develop the film in ammonia vapor. The opaque marks on the master diagram prevent the ultraviolet light from affecting the film next to them, hence color appears in these areas when the film is developed in the ammonia.

Materials, equipment and tools: translucent tracing paper; cardboard mount; diazo film of selected color; black drawing ink; pen and lettering aids; diazo reproduction unit—ultraviolet-light printer and ammonia-vapor developer.

1. From a sketch, prepare a master drawing on translucent paper using black inks or other materials that make opaque marks.
2. Cover the drawing with a sheet of diazo film.
3. Place the drawing and film in the ultraviolet-light printer. (Note the correct order: light below, drawing, film on top.)

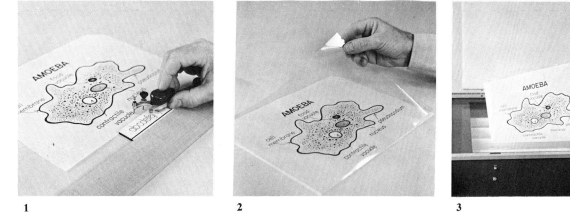

1   2   3

4 5 6

4. Close the cover, and set the timer for proper exposure time.
5. After the exposure time has elapsed, transfer the exposed sheet of film to the container of ammonia vapor.
6. In a short time the image will appear. Keep the film in the ammonia until the color appears fully. (Overdevelopment is not possible.)

The transparency image may be too *light,* or *faint,* for projection; if so, print it again with a new sheet of film, *reducing* the exposure time. A *faint* diazo transparency has been *overexposed.*

If, on the contrary, the transparency shows some *unwanted tones* in the background, print it again with a new sheet of film, *increasing* the exposure time. A *muddy* diazo transparency with unwanted background has been *underexposed.*

In practical use, a number of different brands of diazo reproduction equipment (including ultra-violet-light printer and ammonia-vapor developer) is available. With each, the principle of diazo reproduction is the same.

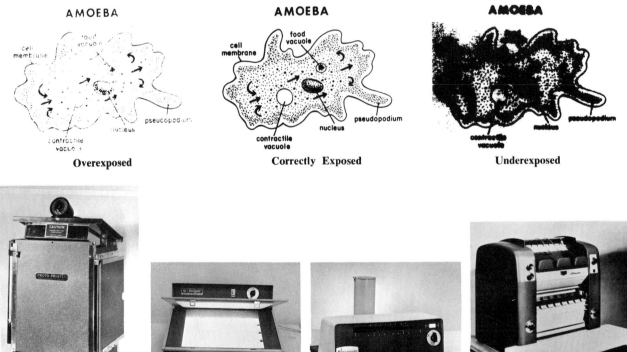

Overexposed

Correctly Exposed

Underexposed

Protoprinter
(Tecnifax Corp.)

Visual Aid Printer
(VariTyper Corp.)

Mercury
(Keuffel & Esser Co.)

Ozamatic
(General Aniline and Film Corp.)

Of key importance to the success of the diazo process is the paper used in making the master. Ultraviolet light must pass through the paper in those areas that are *not* to result in color on the film, while opaque marks are *necessary* on the master to block the ultraviolet light from reaching the film in order for color to appear. Thus for the master a transparent film or translucent paper is essential. Tracing paper, commonly used for engineering and drafting work, is highly translucent and is recommended. Select a grade with a fine fiber texture and use the same kind for *all* masters. If you change your master paper you may also change the correct exposure and thus waste film until the correct exposure is redetermined.

Another factor for success in the diazo process is the quality of the opaque marks made on the tracing paper. Black India ink makes good opaque lines. Pencils and typewriter ribbons are often not suitable.

The diazo process requires attention to a number of details and permits use of a number of effective techniques both in preparing the master and in modifying the transparency. Among these are:

☐ Exposure time in the printer is critical, but development time is not. Film must be developed long enough to obtain maximum color and can be removed from the ammonia any time thereafter.

☐ As many transparencies as are needed can be made from the one master drawing.

☐ For distribution to an audience, copies of the master drawing can also be made by the diazo process on inexpensive diazo paper.

☐ If areas of a transparency are to be in solid color, attach construction or other opaque paper in proper place on the translucent master. It will entirely block the ultraviolet light and result in a rich, even colored area.

☐ If more than a single color is needed on one sheet of diazo film, areas can be colored by applying one or more pieces of color adhesive material (see page 119).

☐ A heat-process transparency (next process) can be used as the master for color diazo work.

☐ Diazo films do not have a long shelf life. Keep unopened packages under refrigeration until ready for use. Allow the film to reach room temperature before use.

☐ If an ink spot or other imperfection must be removed from the translucent master, the paper can be cut and the spot removed. The resulting hole in the paper has no effect on exposure or on the final transparency.

☐ Minor mistakes on the master can be corrected before the diazo film is exposed. Use a translucent tape (Scotch No. 810) that will not block ultraviolet light.

☐ On one brand of diazo film (Multicolor by VariTyper Corporation or Charles Bruning Corporation), more than a single color can be produced on a sheet of film. In this method, after exposure of the master and film to ultraviolet light, various color couplers are applied to areas of the image on the film to form any of five colors. In addition, both sides of the film are coated, permitting not only the coloring of intersecting lines and words, but the combining of two colors to form a third (a blue on one side and yellow on the other will produce a green area). The company also makes diazo-coated cardstock that is excellent for preparing slide, filmstrip, and motion-picture titles in colors.

Cut the error out of the paper or acetate master carefully with a sharp blade

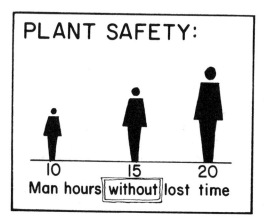

Insert the correction. Make it on similar paper and fix it in place with the tape. Do not overlap the edges of the paper

Now, Review What You Have Learned About Transparencies As Reproductions of Diagrams:

1. Can you use color carbons, other than purple, when preparing a spirit master for a transparency?
2. Which side of the frosted acetate should be upward when run through the spirit duplicator?
3. What technique can be used to insure that the acetate will pass through the duplicator?
4. Why is the spirit transparency sprayed after preparation?
5. Explain in your own words the principle of the diazo process.
6. What material is used as a master in the diazo process?
7. How would you prepare a master requiring a solid color to cover a large area?
8. What is the order in which materials are placed in the ultraviolet-light printer?
9. Which is critical for time—ultraviolet exposure or ammonia development?
10. If the lines on a diazo transparency are very weak, does this condition indicate *over-* or *under*exposure? Would you expose for a *shorter* or *longer* time?

Note: Answers to review questions can be found at the end of the chapter.

Making Transparencies As Reproductions of Printed Illustrations—with No Size Change

Of the four methods described under this heading, the first two can be used either with printed line drawings or with original drawings prepared in black ink on white paper. The two described thereafter can be used with illustrations printed on clay-coated paper. Whatever method is being considered, keep in mind the following:

☐ Permission may be necessary to reproduce copyrighted materials (page 61).
☐ Legibility standards for projected materials should be observed when printed items are considered; most materials printed on paper are for close-up study and are not directly suitable for overhead projection (page 199).

ON HEAT-SENSITIVE FILM

This is a rapid process. It is completely dry, and transparencies are ready for immediate use. Heat from an infrared-light source passes through the copy film to the original. The words and lines on the original must be prepared with "heat absorbing material," such as carbon-base ink or a soft lead pencil. These markings absorb heat, and the resulting increase in temperature affects the film, forming an image on it within a few seconds.

Several brands of thermal copy machines are available. In each, the principle of thermal reproduction is the same. Most carry the original and film on a belt or between rollers around the infrared-light source. In one type (the Masterfax), the

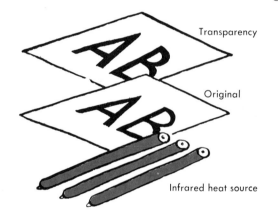

Transparency

Original

Infrared heat source

original and film lie flat and the infrared-light tube moves under them (page 143).

The film to make basic transparencies in these machines is of two types:

☐ Heat-process film placed in direct contact with the master drawing (3M Co. product)
☐ Ordinary acetate and a sheet of special carbon paper are placed in contact with the master drawing

Materials, equipment, and tools: printed or original material on paper; a cardboard mount; heat-sensitive projection film; copy machine.

1. Set the control dial as directed (usually at the white indicator). Turn on the machine if necessary.

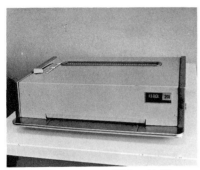

Master Transparency Maker (A.B. Dick Co.)

Secretary (3M Co.)

Masterfax (Ditto Co.) (page 143)

1

2

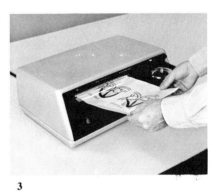

3

2. Place the projection film (with the notch in the upper right corner) on the original material.
3. With the film on top, feed the two into the machine.
4. When the two emerge, separate the film from the original.

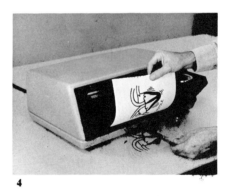

4

The transparency image may be *too light,* or *too faint,* for satisfactory projection; if so, print it again with a fresh sheet of film, *increasing* the exposure time (that is, with the machine running at *slower* speed). A faint heat-transfer transparency has been *underexposed.*

If, on the contrary, the transparency is *too dense,* or if there is *unwanted background tone,* print the transparency again with a fresh sheet of film, shortening the exposure time (that is, with the machine running at *faster* speed). An *overdense* heat-transfer transparency has been *overexposed.*

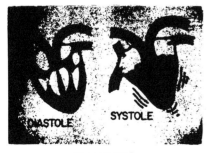

Overexposed

Correctly Exposed

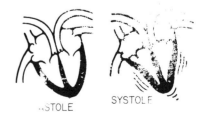

Underexposed

The thermal process requires attention to a number of details and permits the use of a number of effective techniques:

☐ No special paper is required for the preparation of original printing or master diagrams.

☐ Original materials for thermal reproduction should be prepared with black India ink, soft lead pencil (like the test marker used on an IBM card), or large-size typewriter having a carbon-paper or well-inked cloth ribbon. Black printing inks are satisfactory, but inks of other colors, regular ball-point pens, and spirit duplicated copies (purple) are not suitable for thermal reproduction.

☐ If using India ink, make sure the ink is completely dry before the master is run in the copy machine.

☐ If you are uncertain about correct exposure or about the reproduction quality of a diagram, use test strips of the thermal film before exposing a whole sheet. Cut four to six vertical strips from one piece of film, being sure to clip a corner of each for proper placement on the diagram.

☐ In addition to black-image film, various colored-image, tinted (color background for black image), and negative films (black background with clear or colored image) are available. But there is some evidence that better visual acuity is achieved with clear-background transparencies than with colored backgrounds.[2]

☐ Another thermal-process film, called Transparex (Agfa-Gavaert), is developed in water after exposure in contact with the original diagram in a thermal copy. Using the company's processor, the transparency emerges dry, ready for use. This film has a higher resolution than other thermal-film products.

☐ Clear plastic bags used in the home, when cut and opened flat, are suitable for making an inexpensive thermal transparency. The resulting white image is opaque to light when projected with an overhead projector. Because this is an adaptation of a product not made for this purpose, only gross detail will reproduce on the film sharply.

☐ Add color to areas on a transparency with felt pens (page 118) or use color adhesive material (page 119).

☐ A thermal transparency, because of its opaque image, can serve as a master for the previously described diazo process.

———
2. Richard L. Snowberg, "Bases for the Selection of Background Colors for Transparencies," *AV Communication Review* 21 (Summer 1973): 191–207.

ON ELECTROSTATIC FILM

The latest reproduction method—the *electrostatic process*—makes use of electrical charges. In this method, specially coated electrically charged and light-sensitive film is used. The original sheet or page is exposed to light, which is reflected from the white parts, but not from the printed or drawn image, to the electrostatic film. Where the light strikes the paper the coating is discharged. The remaining charged areas (where the image will be) then collect a charged *toner* (a fine black powder), which, upon deposit, results in a visible, opaque image.

With appropriate film (sources, page 305), most Xerox copy machines can be used to prepare transparencies. The resulting images are not as sharp or black as those made by other transparency methods. For a further description of the xerography process see page 148.

AS A PICTURE TRANSFER ON PRESSURE-SEALING ACETATE

In this process the inks of printed pictures (color or black-and-white, on *clay-coated paper*) adhere to specially prepared acetate to make a transparency of the picture. The picture and the acetate are sealed together with heat and/or pressure, then submerged in water to dissolve the clay coating and soak the paper free from the inks. The inks remain on the acetate. A plastic coating applied after the acetate is dry transparentizes and protects the picture side.

A similar method that employs equipment is explained next after this.

Materials and tools: picture printed on clay-coated paper; sheet of Con-tact brand *clear* adhesive-backed shelf paper (available from hard-

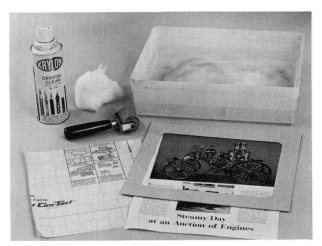

ware and houseware stores); wooden roller (used in craft work); tray of water; wad of cotton; clear plastic spray; cardboard mount.

1. Test the selected picture for clay coating by rubbing a moistened finger over a white area of the page, outside the picture. A white deposit on the finger indicates the presence of clay.
2. Separate the adhesive-backed acetate from its backing sheet.
3. Carefully adhere the acetate to the *face* of the picture.
4. Use a roller or other tool to apply pressure over the entire surface. Roll or rub in all directions.

5. Submerge the adhered picture and acetate in a pan of cool water.
6. After 2–3 minutes, separate the paper from the acetate. The inks of the picture and some clay adhere to the acetate.
7. With wet cotton, rub the image side (ink side) of the acetate to remove the clay. Be sure to loosen all the clay. Then rinse the transparency in clear water.
8. Blot the transparency between sheets of paper toweling or hang it to dry.
9. When the transparency is dry, coat the picture side with plastic spray to transparentize and protect the image by flooding the surface lightly and evenly. (See warning, page 213.)
10. When the spray coating has dried, mount the transparency for use.

1

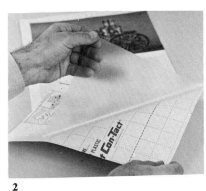

2

3

4

5

6

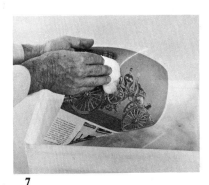

7

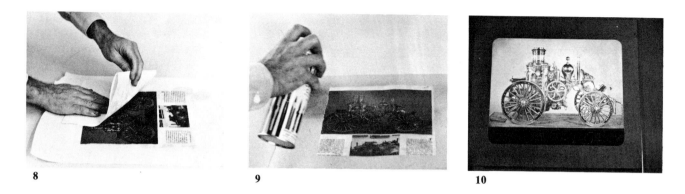

8   9   10

A pressure-roller laminating machine can be used to seal the picture to adhesive-backed laminating film.

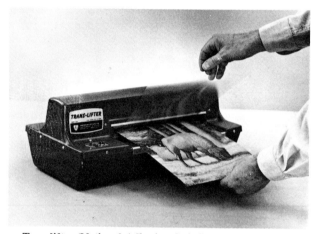

Translifter (National Adhesive Co.) Cold-type Laminator

Suggestions for avoiding problems when making a picture transfer include:

☐ Select bright pictures with sharp color contrasts for best-looking results.
☐ Keep the surface of the picture to be used as clean as possible because dirt, dust, and oil from fingers can prevent the ink from adhering to the film.
☐ Do not trim the picture before starting. Allow excess paper around the picture for film overlap.
☐ Cut the acetate so none will extend beyond the edge of the paper. If the film laps beyond the page it will stick to the table.
☐ Applying pressure to the acetate and picture is important to insure a good seal. Use a roller on both sides and in all directions. If a roller is not available, any blunt tool, like the back of a comb wrapped in a handkerchief, can be used.
☐ If a transparency does not fit the standard cardboard frame, cut a piece of cardboard with the necessary opening.

☐ Among the magazines from which successful picture transfers have been made are *Better Homes and Gardens, Cosmopolitan, Holiday, National Geographic, Newsweek, Sports Illustrated, Sunset, Time,* and *U.S. News & World Report.*

AS A PICTURE TRANSFER ON HEAT-SEALING ACETATE

This method is, in principle, the same as the proceeding pressure-sealing one. In this one, heat is used, and a dry-mount press is required to provide the heat and pressure. Use either Seal brand Transpara-film or Seal-lamin laminating film (page 141). The latter is much thinner, but less expensive.

Materials and equipment: picture printed on clay-coated paper; Seal film; pair of glossy metal plates; piece of flannel; tray of water; wad of cotton; plastic spray; cardboard mount; dry-mount press; timer.

1. Set the dry-mount press at 270°F.
2. Test the picture for clay (as in the preceding process).
3. Insert the metal plates in the dry-mount press and preheat the flannel between the plates to drive out moisture.
4. Dry the picture in the press on the flannel between the metal plates.

5. Remove the metal plates, flannel, and picture from the press and set the top metal plate to one side. The flannel should remain on the shiny side of the bottom metal plate, the picture face-up on the flannel. Cover the picture with a sheet of film, coated side down.

6. On top of the film set the other metal plate, shiny side down, and place the complete sandwich in the press. Have two pieces of thick cardboard on the base to increase the pressure.

7. Shut the press and apply heat for two minutes.

8. Follow steps 5–10 of the previous process on page 211.

9. The resulting transparency.

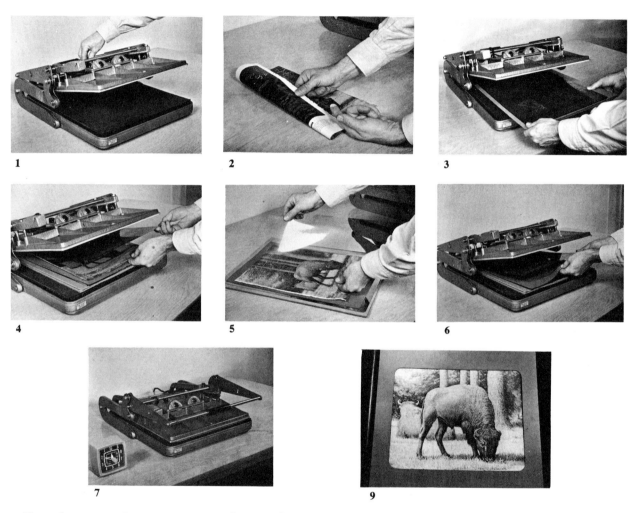

Note the suggestions on page 212 for avoiding problems when making a picture transfer. In addition to those listed, for this process allow the picture and film to curl naturally when removed from the dry-mount press. They will straighten out when cooled or in water.

The flat-bed thermal unit, the Masterfax (page 143), exerts great pressure as well as heat and also can be used with laminating film to prepare picture-transfer transparencies. Follow the same procedure as described for laminating on page 141.

The heat lamination unit described on page 142 can also be used to make high-quality picture-transfer transparencies. With this machine, if you have a page with useful pictures on both sides, apply the laminating film to both sides. Then carefully split the paper so that each picture, with its adhering film, is separated. Follow the regular procedure described above to make a transparency from each picture.

There is increasing concern with the pollution and health hazards of propellants used in pressurized spray cans. Instead, consider using thin coatings of floor or furniture wax, applied with cotton or a soft cloth in this and other processes requiring such sprays. Experiment with available brands to select a product that covers the picture surface easily, dries quickly, and shows little streaking or visual imperfections when projected.

Now, Review What You Have Learned About Making Transparencies As Reproductions of Printed Illustrations:

1. What is the main thing to check when preparing or selecting a diagram to be made into a heat-process transparency?
2. Is the kind of paper for the master important in the heat process?
3. If lines on a heat-process transparency are very weak and thin, is the film *over-* or *underexposed*? The next time, must you *slow down* or *speed up* the machine?
4. How might small areas be colored on a heat-process transparency?
5. Which process might be used to reproduce a printed diagram having three colors?
6. What is the first step in preparing to make a picture transfer from a picture?
7. How is pressure applied in both picture-transfer methods described?
8. Why must all the clay be removed from the transferred picture?
9. What is the difference in the use of the dry-mount press for a picture transfer and regular dry mounting?

Note: Answers to review questions can be found at the end of the chapter.

Making Transparencies As Reproductions of Printed Illustrations—with Size Change

To change the size of an illustration requires a camera and application of photographic methods. The following two techniques are basic ways of using photography to prepare overhead transparencies. Both use the same easy-to-handle film, but require different developers.

Before proceeding, review the following:

☐ Legibility standards for projected materials when printed items are considered for reproduction (page 120)
☐ Permission to reproduce copyrighted materials (page 61)
☐ Use of your camera, especially with reference to:
 Sheet-film cameras, if available (page 81)
 Camera settings (page 83)
 Correct exposure (page 91)
 Close-up and copy work (page 99)
☐ Processing film (page 104)
☐ Making prints (page 106)

Two processes are used: one for *high-contrast* subjects, the other for *halftone* subjects. Here are examples of the two kinds:

High-contrast film is used to make the transparencies, both for high-contrast and halftone subjects. High-contrast film is preferable to common orthochromatic sheet films for transparencies because it is easier to work with, has a clear base for projection, can produce more saturation in gray shades, and dries quicker by reason of being thinner.

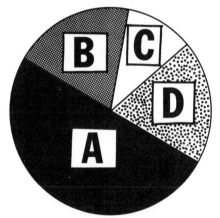

High Contrast: Lines, dots, or solid areas, with the paper between these unprinted

Halftone: Printed picture consisting of uniformly spaced dots, which blend together and convey shades of gray. The dots in this picture can be separated by the eye only under high magnification.

HIGH-CONTRAST SUBJECTS

Use this process to prepare transparencies from line prints and other high-contrast subjects.

Materials, equipment, and tools: subject for reproduction; 35 mm or sheet-film Kodalith (Professional Line Copy), or equivalent from other manufacturers; appropriate film developer, stop bath, fix; cardboard mount; press or view camera or 35-mm single-lens reflex camera; camera accessories; film holders; copy stand; lights; darkroom facilities for film developing, printing, and enlarging under red safelights.

The high-contrast process has four steps:

1. Film the subject, using high-contrast film. (For exposure determination, film speed of Kodalith Ortho Type 3 is 6.)

2. Process the film to a negative under a darkroom red safelight, using a recommended high-contrast developer.

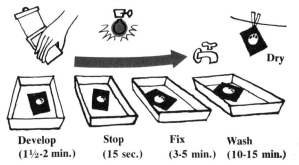

| Develop (1½-2 min.) | Stop (15 sec.) | Fix (3-5 min.) | Wash (10-15 min.) |

3. Opaque the negative to eliminate clear spots, paste-up marks, or unwanted printed areas.

4. Enlarge the negative onto an 8×10 inch or larger sheet of the same high-contrast film, and process the film in the same chemicals as in step 2. (See below.)

5. Dry and mount the transparency for use.

Other suggestions:

☐ Prepare a negative rather than a positive transparency by contact printing the original camera negative onto a piece of high-contrast film and then using this positive in the enlarger to make a negative transparency. Color clear areas of the final transparency with felt-pen colors. Or, if a copy camera 8×10 inch or larger is used, the negative prepared with it can be used directly as a transparency.

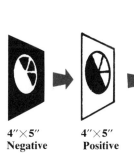

4″×5″ Negative **4″×5″ Positive**

Enlarged Negative Transparency

☐ If a number of transparencies are to be prepared at one time, consider using the *photo-stabilization* method with the appropriate high-contrast film and a rapid processor unit (page 107).

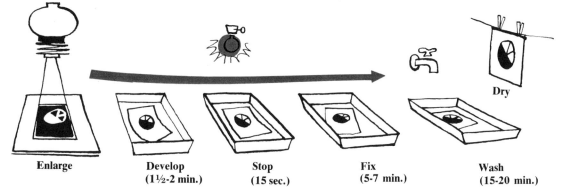

| Enlarge | Develop (1½-2 min.) | Stop (15 sec.) | Fix (5-7 min.) | Wash (15-20 min.) |

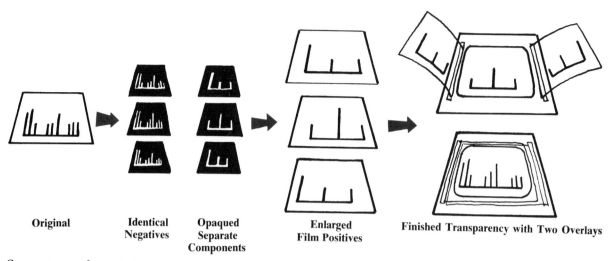

Original   Identical   Opaqued   Enlarged   Finished Transparency with Two Overlays
           Negatives   Separate   Film Positives
                    Components

☐ Separate a subject into its components for preparing overlays by making a number of negatives of the subject equal to the number of overlays needed. Block out all but necessary areas on each negative by opaquing. Print each one, in the enlarger, onto a separate sheet of high-contrast film.

☐ Add color to areas on a transparency with colored adhesives. Apply it to the base (shiny) side of the transparency (see page 119).

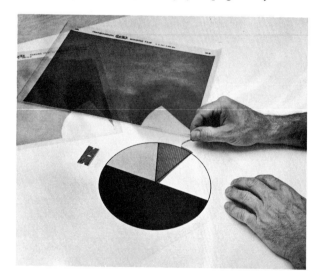

☐ Add special stressed plastic to areas of a transparency and use it in conjunction with a rotating polarizing disk (page 198) to create simulated motion or other unusual effects—an on-and-off blinking motion, an effect of turbulence, a swirling effect, a rotating effect, a flow effect, and a radiation effect. The plastic material is most easily applied to negative transparencies for which careful cutting is not important. See sources for this material and special equipment on page 304.

☐ Prepare a large (8×10 inches or greater) high-contrast negative and *reverse it*, after development, to a positive transparency. Doing this requires using an etch bath and then permits coloring the positive image with transparent dyes.[3]

☐ Use high-contrast transparencies as masters for reproduction by the diazo process to make additional transparencies in color (see page 204).

HALFTONE AND CONTINUOUS-TONE SUBJECTS

In this category of subjects are halftone illustrations printed in books and magazines, photographs, and original works of art which contain shades of gray varying from white to black. Be sure to recognize the difference between such subjects and high-contrast subjects, which consist only of black marks on white paper.

A Halftone (or Continuous-Tone) Subject

---

3. For a detailed explanation of this process, see *Making Black and White or Colored Transparencies for Overhead Projection*, pamphlet S-7, Eastman Kodak Co.

Although high-contrast film is used primarily for reproducing line subjects, it can be adapted to prepare continuous-tone transparencies from negatives of halftone and continuous-tone subjects. It is necessary to change the developer used in the first processing step from the normally used high-contrast developer to a regular photographic paper developer (Dektol or equivalent), diluted 1 part to 12 parts of water.

Materials and equipment: halftone or continuous-tone subject for reproduction; regular continuous-tone black-and-white film (see page 167), film developer, high-contrast sheet film, paper developer, stop bath, fixer, cardboard mount; camera and darkroom accessories.

1. Prepare a negative of the subject using regular black-and-white film.

2. Process the film as recommended (page 104).
3. Enlarge the negative onto a sheet of high-contrast film. Make tests, because correct exposure time will be less than when enlarging a regular high-contrast negative or enlarging onto photo paper.
4. Process the film under a red safelight in *paper developer* (diluted 1 to 12 with water). Development proceeds rapidly and should be completed in 1½ minutes. Completion is indicated by the appearance of the full image on the base side of the film, but judge quality only under white light. A rich, dense image is the best for projection. The use of stop bath, fixer, and wash are the same as in the regular high-contrast process.

Transparency of Continuous-Tone Subject

Most of the transparency-making techniques already described, except for the picture-transfer methods, start with masters that result in high-contrast transparencies (black or colored lines on a clear background). The quality of continuous-tone transparencies made by these methods is generally fair to poor. The results of the method described here are highly acceptable.

Now, Review What You Have Learned About Photographic Methods to Prepare Transparencies:

1. What film is used in this process? Is the same film used for making the transparency, whether of a high-contrast or continuous-tone subject?
2. Can you differentiate between a high-contrast and a continuous-tone or halftone subject for a transparency?
3. What is meant by *opaquing* the negative?
4. In what ways does the enlarging process differ from that of making the negative?
5. In what ways does the preparation of a continuous-tone transparency differ from the preparation of a high-contrast one?
6. How can you use the photographic process to make a transparency involving overlays?

Note: Answers to review questions can be found at the end of the chapter.

Summary of Methods for Preparing Transparencies

TABLE 22-1

	METHOD	EQUIPMENT	COST OF MATERIALS (APPROXIMATE)	TIME FOR PREPARATION	EVALUATION
Directly on acetate	1. With felt pens (page 202)	none	$0.05–$0.10	short to moderate	Suitable for quick preparation and temporary use; lack professional appearance
	2. With tapes and letters (page 203)	none	$0.15–$0.30	short to moderate	Limited applications but useful for charts and graphs
As reproductions of prepared diagrams	1. With spirit duplicator (page 203)	duplicator	$0.25	moderate	Good way to make simple transparencies in color; requires both care and practice when passing acetate through machine and when spraying; also easy to make paper copies for distribution
	2. On diazo film (page 204)	diazo printer and developer	$0.30	moderate	Excellent method for preparing color transparencies; requires translucent originals; a variety of applications of the process are possible
As reproductions of illustrations— with no size change	1. On heat-sensitive film (page 208)	thermo-fax machine; infrared-light copy machine	$0.25–$0.40	very brief	Good method for rapid preparation of one-color transparencies from single sheets
	2. On electro-static film (page 210)	electro-static copy machine	$0.30	brief	Requires an expensive machine, not always available, and a special film; quality not as good as other methods
	3. As picture transfer on pressure-sealing acetate (page 210)	none or cold roller laminator	$0.15	short	Converts any magazine picture printed on clay-coated paper to a transparency; a simple process to apply; results are very effective if suitable original pictures are available
	4. As picture transfer on heat-sealing acetate (page 212)	dry-mount press or heated roller laminator	$0.30	moderate	Similar to above process, but takes a few minutes longer; equipment often available in school or graphic production center

	METHOD	EQUIPMENT	COST OF MATE-RIALS (AP-PROXI-MATE)	TIME FOR PREP-ARATION	EVALUATION
As repro-ductions of illustra-tions— with size change	1. On high-con-trast film (high-con-trast copy) (page 215)	camera and darkroom	$0.40	long	Most complex process in terms of skills, equipment, facilities, and time; but essential when original materials must be changed in size; results in high-quality transparencies
	2. On high-con-trast film (continuous-tone copy) (page 216)	camera and darkroom	$0.40	long	Similar to above process; extends the use of high-contrast materials to preparing trans-parencies from color and gray tone subjects

Completing and Filing Transparencies

MOUNTING

Mounting adds durability and ease to the handling of a transparency, but it is not always necessary to mount transparencies in cardboard frames. Transparencies to be used only once can be left unmounted since the cost of frames and the time to attach them may not be justified. Some people prefer to keep transparencies unmounted for ease of filing in notebooks, but the standard-size cardboard or plastic frame easily fits into letter-size filing cabinets. If overlays are to be used, mounting is essential.

Tape a single-sheet transparency to the *underside* of the frame. Use masking or plastic tape rather than cellophane tape for binding.

If the transparency consists of a base and overlays, tape the base to the underside of the mount as usual, and the overlays to the face. Be sure the overlays register with the base and with each other (page 201). Then fasten each overlay with a tape or plastic hinge along one edge of the cardboard frame.

Overlays for successive or cumulative use can be mounted on the left or right sides of the cardboard frame, also if necessary on the bottom and

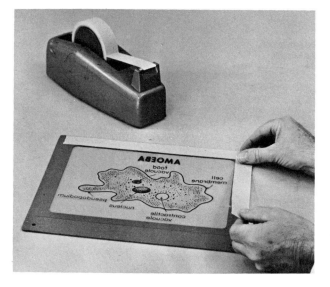

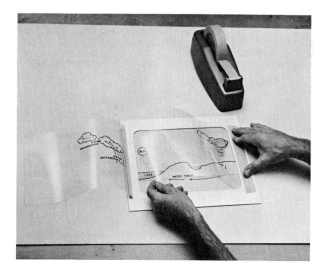

top (the top edge should be the last one used). Trim any excess acetate from the edges of overlays so opposite or adjacent ones fit easily into place.

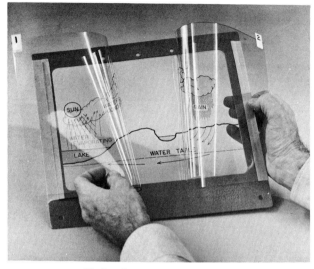

Transparency with Overlays

After mounting overlays, fold and attach small tabs of masking tape or adhesive-back labels on the loose upper corner of each overlay. Number them to indicate the order of use. These tabs are easy to grasp when overlays are to be set in place over the base transparency.

MASKING

To control a presentation and focus attention on specific elements of a transparency, use a paper or cardboard mask, as was mentioned on page 197. The mask may be a separate unit, mounted to move vertically or horizontally, or a hinged opaque overlay.

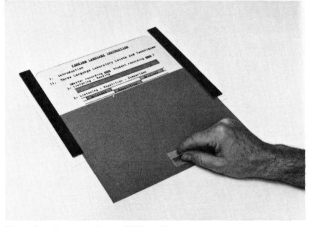

Exposing Areas under a Sliding Cover

Exposing Areas under Hinged Masks

ADDING NOTES

Write brief notes along the margin of the cardboard mount for reference during projection.

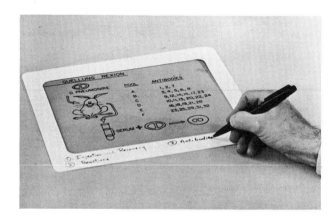

FILING

If your transparencies are in mounts 10×12 inches or smaller, they will fit in the drawer of a standard filing cabinet. File them under appropriate subject, unit, or topic headings.

Now, Review What You Have Learned About Completing and Filing Transparencies:

1. Do you correctly mount a single-sheet transparency on the underside or the face of the cardboard frame?
2. How is a transparency with overlays mounted?
3. What are two ways of masking transparencies?
4. What filing system for transparencies might you use?

Preparing to Use Your Transparencies

Remember that the success of your transparencies will depend not only on their content and quality, but also on the manner in which you use them before an audience. Follow the suggestions on page 73 as you prepare to use your transparencies.

Answers to Review Questions

PLANNING TRANSPARENCIES (PAGE 200)

1. Reader's activity, page 197.
2. Horizontal, because in low-ceiling rooms the lower portions of a vertical transparency cannot easily be seen by all members of an audience.
3. $7\frac{1}{2} \times 9\frac{1}{2}$ inches.
4. Reader's activity, page 198.
5. Vertical format rather than horizontal, quantity of information included, size of lettering, need for copyright clearance.
6. Clarify elements, give emphasis, increase interest.
7. $\frac{1}{8}$–$\frac{1}{4}$ inch (page 120).
8. Most suitable would be Wricoprint, Leroy, Koh-i-noor, and dry-transfer.
9. Register each overlay drawings with the master drawing by use of guide marks in two corners.

DIRECT PREPARATION ON ACETATE (PAGE 203)

1. Yes.
2. Use a solvent, like lighter fluid.
3. No.
4. Cover with a sheet of acetate.
5. They project in color, and there is no wax deposit around the letters.
6. Avoid making cut marks on the acetate, they may project as dark lines.

REPRODUCTIONS OF DIAGRAMS (PAGE 208)

1. Yes.
2. Frosted or matte side.
3. Push the acetate by hand into the machine, up against the drum.
4. To protect the image and make the transparency more transparent to light, thus a brighter image on the screen.
5. Reader's activity, page 204.
6. Translucent tracing paper.
7. Cover the area on the tracing paper with opaque paper.
8. Light source—master drawing—diazo film.
9. Ultraviolet exposure.
10. Overexposure. A shorter time.

REPRODUCTIONS OF PRINTED ILLUSTRATIONS (PAGE 214)

1. The material used to make the image on the paper had a carbon-base.
2. No.
3. Underexposed. Slow down the machine.
4. With felt pen or colored adhesive.
5. Electrostatic process.
6. Check the picture for clay coating.
7. First with a roller; second with dry-mount press.
8. Any remaining clay will appear as dark areas on the final transparency as the clay is opaque to light.
9. The temperature is set at 270°, extra pressure in the press is necessary, and metal plates and felt are needed.

PHOTOGRAPHIC METHODS (PAGE 217)

1. High contrast. Yes.
2. High-contrast subject: line drawings consisting of black ink on white paper.
   Halftone subject: Shades of gray from black to white comprise the illustration.
3. Brushing on a water-soluble carbon material to cover spots and areas so no light will pass during enlarging.
4. The enlarger is used instead of the camera. A larger sheet of film is used. Washing time should be longer.
5. The developer is a diluted paper developer, and development time may vary.
6. Shoot a number of negatives of the subject according to the number of overlays needed. Opaque out all but the necessary area for the overlay on each negative. Print each negative.

COMPLETING AND FILING (PAGE 220)

1. On the underside
2. Base on underside; overlays on separate sides, top of mount
3. Sliding mask and hinged section masks
4. Reader's activity, page 220.

23

MOTION PICTURES

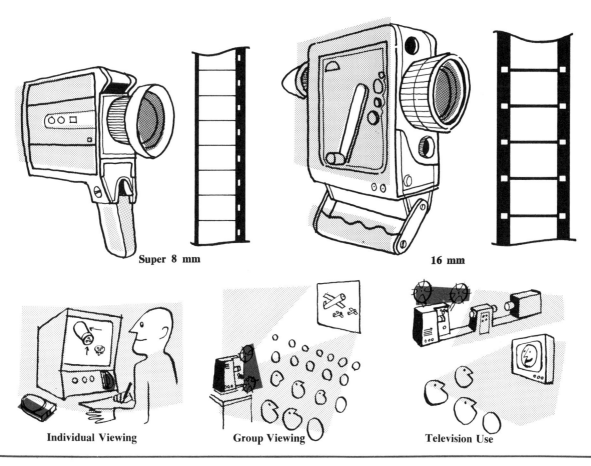

Super 8 mm

16 mm

Individual Viewing

Group Viewing

Television Use

Motion pictures for instructional use can be prepared as 8-mm or 16-mm films and with subtitles or with sound.

A motion picture may present information that involves motion, describes processes, and shows relationships in order to convey knowledge, teach **223** a skill, or affect an attitude through individual study, through group viewing, or by means of television.

For many purposes motion pictures continue to be the most effective and efficient medium of communications of all audiovisual materials. This advantage holds not only for treating subjects that require motion, but also for ease of presenting sequences of still pictures (known as *filmographs*), with or without narration, or even combinations of still and motion, as required by the treatment. For some individuals these latter uses may seem to violate the basic premise that *subject motion is required in a motion picture*. But, as will be explained later in this chapter, this premise is not necessarily true.

With the development of cartridge- and cassette-load projectors (silent and sound), the potential uses of motion pictures, especially for independent or self-instructional learning, are greatly enhanced. No longer need motion pictures be thought of as 10–30-minute complete treatments of total topics. Now fresh approaches to motion-picture planning and production can be made. For many purposes brief films, or *film clips*, often called *concept* films, can be prepared to illustrate a discrete skill or to present information on a limited aspect of a topic. Such films, generally in the 8-mm size, may be from a few seconds to a few minutes in duration—just long enough to serve the objective and without formal introduction or summary. Also, directions for viewer participation can be incorporated in such films—as in programmed instruction requiring responses to questions or actual performance.

Furthermore, in producing these brief films liberties can be taken with many of the formal "rules" of motion-picture photography without loss of communication effectiveness. But you should become aware of the standard procedures first. See page 251 for further discussion of some of the factors to be considered when making 8-mm single-concept films.

So today, film-making should be viewed in a broader perspective than solely as the traditional *motion* picture that rapidly presents an explanation and illustrations on a total topic. This broader approach requires consideration of these factors and techniques:

☐ Visualizing static subjects and using still as well as moving subjects on motion-picture film
☐ Flexibility in film length; sufficient length ranging from a few seconds to many minutes, to serve the objectives and to treat the subject
☐ Incorporating programming techniques in the film that require the viewer to participate through response or performance

☐ Using simple filming techniques that take liberties with traditional film-making procedures
☐ Relating the film to other materials as part of a package for instruction

But before you can consider departing from the rules you must be acquainted with the rules. This chapter presents the most important accepted techniques of film production for treating educational or instructional subjects. You should also review the evidence summarized from research on design elements in motion pictures. Much of the information presented in Chapter 3 bears directly on film production.

A growing use of the motion-picture medium in education is to permit or encourage students to plan and produce their own films as experiences in visual expression and for developing visual literacy. See the discussion on page 9, which provides a base for student activities in this area. All the explanatory information that follows is as appropriate for students who are planning their own films as it is for someone planning an instructional film.

Before any filming, planning is necessary—whether a brief single-concept film or a full-length production is to be made. The success of any film depends in great part on the care in planning. Consider this planning checklist:

☐ Have you expressed your *ideas* clearly and limited the topic (page 31)?
☐ Have you stated the *objectives* to be served by your motion picture (page 31)?
☐ Have you considered the *audience* that will use the film and its characteristics (page 33)?
☐ Have you prepared a *content outline* (page 38)?
☐ Have you considered whether a motion picture is an appropriate medium for accomplishing the objectives and handling the content (page 47)?
☐ Will your film be a *complete production* or will it be brief and treat a *single concept*?
☐ Have you written a *film treatment* to help organize the story (page 52)?
☐ Have you sketched a *storyboard* to assist with your visualization of the content (page 52)?
☐ Have you prepared a *scene-by-scene script* as a guide for your filming (page 54)?
☐ Have you considered the *specifications* necessary for your motion picture (page 57)?
☐ Have you, if necessary, selected other people to assist with the preparation of your film (page 36)?

Following careful planning, the preparation of

a motion picture involves a number of production steps:

1. Filming scenes, utilizing a variety of techniques
2. Preparing titles
3. Having film processed
4. Editing
5. Adding sound (if appropriate)
6. Duplicating the film (if appropriate)
7. Developing correlated materials
8. Preparing to use the film

The information in Part 3, Chapters 15 and 16, on photography and on graphic techniques is basic to the successful preparation of a motion picture. As necessary, refer to the page references indicated with the following topics.

Background Information

8-mm AND 16-mm FORMATS

Until 1965 most motion-picture production for education was done on 16-mm film. This was true for all commercially made educational films, and the majority of teachers who made their own instructional films did so in 16 mm. Eight mm was for the maker of "home movies." In comparison to 16-mm film quality, 8 mm was grainy and suffered a loss of image sharpness when projected, and duplicate prints made from an 8-mm film were of even poorer quality than the original. Also, 8-mm projectors had many deficiencies, which further restricted the film's use to the amateur level.

In 1965 Eastman Kodak Company introduced a new 8-mm film format called *super-8*. The terms *regular-* and *standard-8* were applied to the old format to differentiate it from the new super-8.

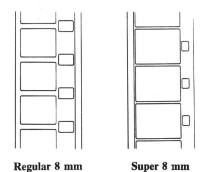

Regular 8 mm   **Super 8 mm**

As compared to regular-8, super-8 film has certain advantages—an exact 16-mm aspect ratio (4 to 3) which makes reduction from 16 mm to 8 mm accurate for covering the entire picture area, which regular-8 does not permit; an adequate area for a sound track alongside the picture area; and about a 50 percent larger picture area. The latter is permitted by a reduction in the size of the sprocket holes, their placement closer to the film edge, and a reduction in the width of the frame line. The sprocket holes are also spaced slightly farther apart, thus increasing the height of the picture area. In comparison to regular-8, super-8 film is 10 percent longer for the same running time.

Because of the larger picture area, the increase in quality of present-day projection lenses, and the increased light output of projection lamps for super-8 projectors, the projected image from super-8 film is appreciably sharper and brighter than the image from comparable regular-8 films. The projected-image quality of super-8 film approaches that from 16-mm films (about the same as 16-mm projected images approach those of 35 mm). This means that super-8 can be used satisfactorily for individual study or group viewing (up to 100 people).

Today 8-mm filming and projection are almost entirely done in the super-8 format. The regular-8 film, cameras, and projectors are infrequently used and are increasingly difficult to obtain. The following discussion will treat super-8 only.

But are there advantages in using 8 mm in preference to 16 mm, or in using 16 mm in preference to 8 mm? Table 23-1 compares typical features relating to each format that may be important to educators. (See page 226.)

Table 23-1 shows that super-8 film and cameras are suitable for producing motion pictures of average subjects, requiring only limited special effects. Laboratory services for 8 mm are restricted to film processing and making fair-quality duplicates from the original film. Super-8 projectors are suitable for use by both individuals and small groups. Table 23-1 also reveals that filming in 16 mm provides greater flexibility than 8 mm in terms of camera and film. While 16-mm film is more expensive than 8 mm as a camera film, when multiple 8-mm copies are required, a 16-mm original is preferred according to price and quality of resulting 8-mm prints.

YOUR MOTION-PICTURE CAMERA

In general, super-8 cameras are simpler to operate than 16-mm cameras. There are fewer features to which you must give attention. But some pro-

TABLE 23-1   Comparison of Super-8-mm and 16-mm Formats

FEATURE	SUPER-8 MM	16 MM
Film		
1. Length	72 frames per foot 50 feet common length	40 frames per foot 100 feet common length
2. Running time	3 feet 20 inches @ 18 fps[a] (50 feet) 2 feet 30 inches @ 24 fps[a] (50 feet)	3 feet 42 inches @ 18 fps[a] (100 feet) 2 feet 47 inches @ 24 fps[a] (100 feet)
3. Container	Closed cartridge, easy to insert in camera and remove at any time	Open reel, requires threading and run through camera before removal
4. Types	Black-and-white and color reversal, $3.00 per color roll and $2.75 processing	Black-and-white negative, black-and-white and color reversal, $9.00 per roll and $6.75 processing
Camera		
1. Threading	None	Required
2. Film movement	Battery-operated motor drive in common use, permits long film run	Spring-driven with limited run or requires attachment of separate motor
3. Exposure control	Automatic-setting or built-in meter shows reading for setting	Manual setting from separate exposure determination
4. Lens	Zoom-type on camera common, some focus to 2 feet or closer	Variety of lenses, including zoom-type can be interchanged
5. Viewfinder	Most often reflex, through-the-lens	May be reflex or separate viewing, depending on camera
6. Single-frame control	Sometimes	Most often
7. Double exposure (film windback)	Infrequently	Usually
8. Adjustable shutter (for fades)	Infrequently	Often
9. Synchronous sound recording	Only on few models	Costly on few models, additional equipment commonly used
10. Price	$100–$400+	$300–$600+

fessional-level super-8 cameras are comparable to 16-mm models in number of settings and adjustments.

Get to know your camera. Doing this takes time. Sit down for an evening with your unloaded camera. Study the instructional booklet and try

FEATURE	SUPER-8 MM	16 MM
Editing		
1. Viewers	Poor to good quality	Good to excellent quality
2. Splicers	Moderate to good quality	Moderate to excellent quality
3. Film handling	May be difficult	Easy
Laboratory Services	Film developing and direct duplication by some labs; duplicates fair to poor quality; $0.15 per foot for duplication	Complete range of film developing, printing, duplication, and reduction to super-8 at most labs; duplicates good quality; $0.12 per foot for duplication and reduction printing to super-8; 100 feet of 16-mm reduces to 50 feet of super-8
Projectors		
1. Use	Individual and small group viewing	Groups of all sizes
2. Threading	Self-threading common from cassette or cartridge	Manual or self-threading models
3. Cost	$150–$300 (silent) $300–$500 (sound)	$600–$800 (sound)

[a] fps—frames per second; 18 fps—silent speed; 24 fps—sound speed.

all the controls. Such experimentation is very useful.

Make certain that you can locate these external parts on your camera: lens, viewfinder, speed selector, footage counter, winding handle or battery housing, release button. In its operation, each one serves an important purpose.

☐ The *lens* (the single most important and often most expensive part of the camera) focuses light rays on the film.

☐ The *viewfinder* lets you see what will be included in the scene—either directly through the lens as *a reflex viewfinder* to give the same picture as that transmitted by the lens, or through its own window, resulting in a picture slightly different from that transmitted by the lens. This difference may be important when filming subjects at extremely close range. For a discussion of close-up techniques and the problem of parallax, see page 99. See following page for viewfinder illustrations.

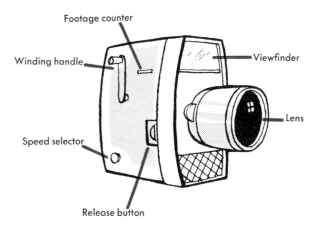

☐ The *speed selector* indicates the speed with which the film will move through the camera, expressed as *frames or pictures, per second* (fps). Silent-film speed is 18 fps, and sound speed is 24 fps. Some other settings found on cameras are 8, 12, 32, 48, and 64 fps.

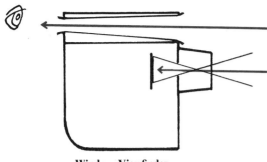

Window Viewfinder

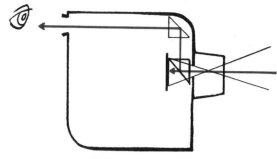

Reflex Viewfinder

☐ The *footage counter* indicates either the amount of film exposed or that still remaining unexposed in the camera (commonly a maximum of 50 feet for super-8 mm, and 100 feet for 16 mm).

☐ A *winding handle* on 16-mm cameras permits you to tighten the camera spring in order to run film through the camera. Most super-8 cameras operate on electric motors from batteries.

☐ The *release button* starts film through the camera and exposes the individual frames of film.

In addition to these standard parts, you may have some additional features on your camera that increase both the filming potential and the price of the camera.

☐ A *single-frame exposure-control* button, which permits taking one picture (one frame) at a time as opposed to continuous exposure of a number of frames per second. This feature is essential if special techniques like time-lapse or animation are to be used.

☐ A *rewind handle* to wind-back exposed film in order to expose it again. The ability to *double-expose* allows you to print titles over scenes or create the transition effect called a *dissolve* (page 244).

☐ An *adjustable shutter control*, which permits you to manually reduce the amount of light reaching the film by decreasing the open area between components of the shutter within the camera through which light must pass. With this feature you can fade out a scene (to unexposed black on the film) and fade another one in.

☐ A *frame counter*, either as part of the footage counter or as a separate dial. When winding film back, prior to over-printing a title, or keeping a record of single-frame exposures in animation, accurate frame counting is important.

The major difference between the inside features of super-8-mm and 16-mm cameras is the use of a light-tight film-holding cassette with most super-8 cameras, while film supply/take-up reels with sprocket wheel drive to direct film through the camera are common with 16-mm cameras. The principle of film movement in both kinds of cameras is the same and follows this sequence:

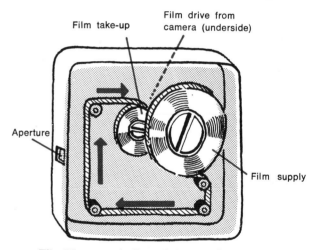

Film Movement in Super 8 Camera Cassette

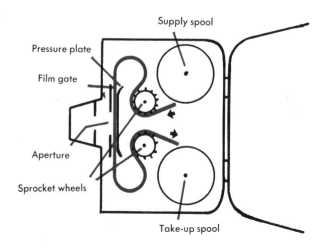

Film Threading in 16 mm Camera

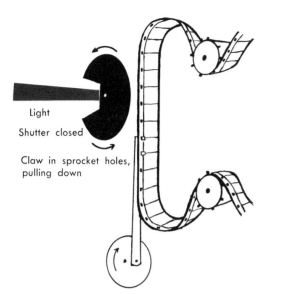

Light
Shutter closed
Claw in sprocket holes, pulling down

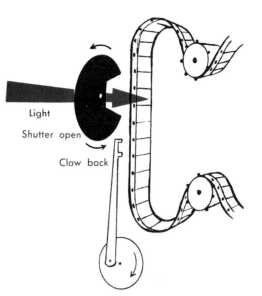

Light
Shutter open
Claw back

1. In super-8 cameras the cassette is inserted under a guide pin and pressed into place, ready for use. A pin from under the cassette engages it and advances film within the cassette, past the aperture, when the release button is pressed. In 16-mm cameras the supply reel is attached to a spindle; then film, drawn from it (as the supply reel turns clockwise), passes around one side of a toothed sprocket wheel and forms a loop before entering the film gate (film channel).

2. Within the gate the film passes behind the rectangular opening, the *aperture.* Alongside the aperture the *pull-down claw* (see below) engages film sprocket holes, advancing the film one frame at a time, then disengaging and moving upward to pull down the next picture area.

3. While the claw mechanism moves upward, the film is at rest behind the aperture, and light, passing into the camera through the lens and the open part of the shutter, reaches the film.

4. The movements of the pull-down claw and the shutter are carefully timed so that the opaque area of the shutter blade covers the aperture while the film is being advanced. Therefore light reaches the film only for a brief part of a second while the film is standing still and the shutter is open. For cameras operating at *sound speed* this cycle takes place 24 times a second, and the exposure time, as based on the movement of the open area of the shutter, is about 1/50 second; at *silent speed* the cycle takes place 18 times per second and the exposure is approximately 1/30 second.

5. After exposure, the film in a super-8 cassette forms its own second loop and is drawn into the take-up side of the cassette. With a 16-mm camera, after forming the lower loop, it passes

around one side of a *sprocket wheel* and onto the *take-up spool,* which also rotates in a clockwise direction.

Keep your camera clean and the inside free of dust, dirt, scraps of hair, chips of film, and other debris that might collect in the film channel. Such foreign matter can scratch film or appear as a distraction in a filmed scene. Use a soft camel's hair brush or a rubber blower syringe to clean the inside of the camera before each new roll or cassette is used. Keep your lens clean by removing dust and fingerprints with lens tissue.

Camera care for battery-operated units also requires a periodic check on the condition of the batteries. The camera has a battery-check feature (usually a glow-light). Use it to be certain you have power when ready to do your filming. Clean the battery terminals periodically, and remove batteries from the camera when it is not to be used for a period of time.

THE LENSES ON THE CAMERA

The dynamics of a motion picture often requires a variety of shots. These can be accomplished by changing the camera position in relation to the subject, or by using lenses of different focal lengths. The classification of lenses is according to their field of view (see page 82). For example the focal lengths of some common motion-picture lenses, listed according to the three common groupings, are:

	WIDE-ANGLE	NORMAL	TELEPHOTO
For 8-mm cameras	10 mm	13 mm	25 mm (or greater)
For 16-mm cameras	15 mm	25 mm	50 mm (or greater)

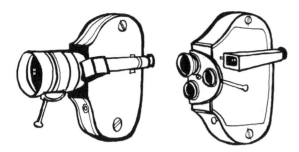

Camera with Zoom Lens and Camera with Three Separate Lenses on a Turret

Although your camera may be equipped with a single lens, additional lenses add to the versatility of your filming.

A single lens of the *zoom* type is capable of doing the work of several lenses of different fixed focal lengths. The focal length of a zoom lens can be varied from wide-angle to telephoto. The zoom lens on an 8-mm camera may vary in focal length from 10 mm to 40 mm (a 4 to 1 zoom ratio), while one for a 16-mm camera may be from 20 mm to 80 mm (also 4 to 1).

You choose your subject size by zooming in or out without moving the camera with respect to the subject. With this lens you can also continuously change the size of a subject by zooming while filming. However, there is a tendency to overuse the zooming feature, which can be distracting to the viewer. A slow zoom on occasion to center on action or to show relationships between elements of a scene can be effective as well as dramatic.

When using a zoom lens, always focus your subject with the lens set at the *longest* focal length (close-up view of the subject) and with the lens aperture at its *smallest* f/ number (largest opening). By following this instruction you will be sure to keep the subject in focus for all positions within the zoom operation.

As with still-camera lenses, motion-picture lenses (except for fixed-focus lenses) require *two* settings—f/ number and distance (shutter speed is determined by the fps setting). Understand what each of these settings means and how they are properly used (page 83). Also apply the *depth-of-field* principle to relations between f/ numbers and distance settings (page 86). This principle is particularly important in motion-picture photography when close-up scenes are filmed. With short camera-to-subject distances the depth of field is reduced greatly, especially for lenses of longer focal length. Notice the reduction in depth of field for the closer distances with the three common 16-mm lenses, and from one lens to the other at the same distances in Table 23-2.

Focusing scale (distance)

Lens opening (f/ number)

As an example, for a 25-mm lens set at f/2 and focused at 10 feet, the depth of field is 5 feet 8 inches, but when the same lens is focused at 4 feet the depth is only 10 inches. To increase the latter depth of field, bringing a whole scene into focus (which requires at least 1 foot of depth), it is necessary to increase the light level and film at a lens setting of f/4 (which permits a depth of field of 1 foot 7 inches at 4 feet). The other al-

Depth of Field for Lenses at Various Distance Settings

TABLE 23-2

LENS (FOCAL LENGTH)	DISTANCE SETTING (FEET)	FIELD AT SELECTED LENS SETTING		
		f/2	f/4	f/8
16 mm	4	3 feet 3 inches to 5 feet 2 inches	2 feet 10 inches to 6 feet 10 inches	2 feet 2 inches to 26 feet 2 inches
	10	6 feet 4 inches to 24 feet 0 inches	4 feet 10 inches to ∝	3 feet 2 inches to ∝
	25	10 feet 10 inches to ∝	7 feet 1 inch to ∝	4 feet 0 inches to ∝
25 mm	4	3 feet 7 inches to 4 feet 5 inches	3 feet 4 inches to 4 feet 11 inches	2 feet 11 inches to 6 feet 5 inches
	10	8 feet 0 inches to 13 feet 8 inches	6 feet 9 inches to 19 feet 6 inches	5 feet 1 inch to ∝
	25	16 feet 6 inches to 161 feet	12 feet 1 inch to ∝	7 feet 7 inches to ∝
75 mm	4	3 feet 11 inches to 4 feet 1 inch	3 feet 10 inches to 4 feet 2 inches	3 feet 9 inches to 4 feet 3 inches
	10	9 feet 9 inches to 10 feet 3 inches	9 feet 6 inches to 10 feet 7 inches	9 feet 0 inches to 11 feet 2 inches
	25	23 feet 5 inches to 26 feet 10 inches	22 feet 0 inches to 28 feet 10 inches	19 feet 8 inches to 35 feet 0 inches

ternative is to move the camera back and increase the distance to the subject, which, as Table 23-2 shows, also increases the depth of field.

Use the depth-of-field scale on your lens in the above way to select distances and $f/$ numbers insuring sufficient depth of field (or lesser depth if necessary) in your scenes. If your lens does not include such a scale, refer to a good motion-picture handbook, such as the one from which Table 23-2 was taken.[1]

In operation, motion-picture cameras are more complex than still cameras, since they require additional settings and special precautions. Develop the habit of checking all settings and adjustments before each scene is filmed. Possibly a reminder like the *SAFER* formula will help you.[2]

S peed of camera (18, 24, or other number of fps)
A perture of lens ($f/$ setting)
F ocus (distance setting)
E xpose the scene
R ewind the spring (unless battery-operated)

ACCESSORIES

As you prepare for filming you may find need for:

☐ A *pistol grip* for attachment to the camera so you can maintain a firm hold for steadiness. Slight camera movement may not be objectionable with normal and wide-angle lenses, but a scene with a telephoto lens magnifies any camera unsteadiness. A pistol grip, especially when used with an 8-mm camera, will insure more stability than by just holding the camera in your hands. When hand-holding a camera do not become too tense or strained, or too relaxed or loose. You may find it advantageous to hold your breath at the moment of shooting.

☐ A *tripod* to insure the best degree of camera stability. Select a tripod with strong legs and because you will want to pan and tilt the camera, it should have a smooth operating pan/tilt head with a long enough handle to insure a secure grip.

☐ A *photographic light meter* to determine exposure accurately, unless your camera is an automatic-setting type. Even then, if you can override the automatic feature, the meter may be helpful when deciding on the $f/$ number setting for close-ups, for copying, or other

special filming. See page 91 for further discussion on light meters.

☐ Three or more photoflood lights to illuminate indoor scenes (page 96).

FILM

Review the general characteristics of film on page 88.

Select a film balanced for the light conditions under which it will be used. For example:

LIGHT SOURCE	FILM	EXPOSURE INDEX (ASA)
Daylight	Ektachrome 160	160
Photoflood	Kodachrome II, Type A	40

For fluorescent lights, no example of film type can be suggested, since the many types of fluorescent tubes affect color film differently. For general purposes, unless true color is critical, assume that fluorescent light is similar to daylight, especially in rooms having windows that admit a great amount of daylight.

Some characteristics of various super-8 and 16-mm films are shown in Table 23-3. This table gives significant but not complete information, and lists representative films but not all films.[3]

The data about film in Table 23-3 are correct as of the time of writing, but changes and new developments can be anticipated. Carefully check the data sheet packaged with your film for the latest assigned exposure index and other details.

For 8-mm cameras, only color reversal films normally are available. Special orders may be required for black-and-white film.

For 16-mm cameras, the choice of film is somewhat broader. Your decision is made with reference to:

☐ Light conditions
☐ Black-and-white or color
☐ Reversal or negative
☐ Single or double perforations (sprocket holes)

Black-and-white or color? Consider whether color is an important feature of the subject or whether black-and-white film would be satisfactory. Recall the reports in Chapter 3 that color may not contribute significantly to learning over black-and-white unless color is an important feature of the subject. Color film is more expensive, and it requires higher light levels while filming.

1. Charles G. Clarke and Walter Strenge, (Hollywood, Calif.): American Cinematographer Manual, American Society of Cinematographers.

2. Adapted from *Better Movies in Minutes,* publication AD-4 (Rochester): Eastman Kodak Co.

3. For further information on all films, see the film information sheets packaged with each roll; for information on Kodak films see also *Selection and Use of Kodak and Eastman Motion Picture Films* (16 mm), publication H-1, and *Super-8 Films for Original Production,* pamphlet S-37.

TABLE 23-3   **Typical Super-8 and 16-mm Films**

FILM	S-8/16		TYPE	EXPOSURE INDEX (ASA)[a]		USE
				DAYLIGHT	PHOTOFLOOD	
Black-and-White						
Plus X		X	Negative	80	64	Exterior or interior scenes under good light
	X	X	Reversal	50	40	
Tri X	X	X	Reversal	200	160	Subjects under low light
4-X		X	Negative	500	400	Subjects under very low light
	X	X	Reversal	400	320	
Color Reversal						
Kodachrome II		X	Daylight	25	12 (80B)	Subjects under good light; intended for projection, not reproduction
	X	X	Type A	25 (85)	40	
Ektachrome EF		X	Daylight	160	40 (80)	Subjects under low light; intended for projection
	X	X	Tungsten	80 (85B)	125	
Ektachrome MS		X	Daylight	64	—	Subjects under moderate light
Ektachrome Commercial		X	Tungsten (3200°K)	16 (85)	25	Subjects under good light; low-contrast film intended for reproduction, not projection
GAF Color	X		Tungsten	25 (85)	40	Subjects under good light; intended for projection, not duplication

[a] Numbers in parentheses are filters recommended for converting film to use with other than recommended light sources. Note how the exposure index drops.

Reversal film or negative film? Reversal films, both black-and-white and color, are used commonly when one or only a few copies of the final film are required. During processing the image is reversed from a negative, resulting in positive pictures (page 106). Negative films have advantages when being exposed, but require positive prints before they are useful. Their use should be considered when many copies of the final film are to be made, although some film laboratories recommend that reversal film be used at all times.

Single or double perforations (sprocket holes)? The perforations or sprocket holes in 16-mm film may run along one side or both sides. Film with one row of sprocket holes should be used whenever it is anticipated that magnetic striping for sound may be added to the original reversal film.

For best results, motion-picture film should be processed by a professional film laboratory. For a list of processing laboratories see page 308. If you plan to do extensive filming, contact two or three laboratories in your area and check their services and prices.

Motion pictures from videotape? All television facilities include videotape recorders. Subjects for motion pictures, as well as for television programs, can be recorded on videotape and immediately viewed to determine whether a scene will be suitable. Many film producers use this videotape technique as a "dry run" prior to actual motion-picture filming.

But there is increasing use of videotape as the

filming medium, using two or more television cameras. The television director literally "edits the film as it is shot" by calling for a *long shot* with one television camera, then a *close-up* with a second camera, matching the action between the two scenes exactly. A poorly performed scene can be erased and repeated without waste of tape. Also, electronic editing equipment for videotape production can be used. Synchronous sound or narration is recorded on the tape along with the picture.

Certain film laboratories (page 308) can then convert the electronic images of sound and picture from the videotape to 16-mm film. From a good-quality videotape recording, the resulting film quality is very acceptable, although some loss in definition must be expected. This procedure can take place in either black-and-white or color. Some time and cost for materials can be saved when using videotape to produce a motion picture.

EXPOSURE

Exposure for motion pictures is determined by methods similar to those used in still photography (page 91). But realize that the still photographer has the advantage of being able to have partial corrections for wrong exposure made when printing. Some correction can be made with motion pictures when duplicates are made from the original footage. But when filming, if you are not sure of exposure, film a scene more than once, varying the lens setting.

LIGHTING

As in still photography, fast black-and-white and color films often require no supplementary lighting. But when lights are necessary, apply the basic photoflood lighting pattern—key, fill, back, and accent lights, explained on page 96. Then balance the lights and determine the exposure carefully.

Now, Apply What You Have Learned About Motion-Picture Formats, Cameras, Lenses, and Film:

1. Differentiate between a regular 16-mm instructional film and an 8-mm *concept* film.
2. What are advantages of the super-8 format over the former regular-8 format?
3. If many copies of a film in super-8 will be needed, should original filming be in 16 mm or 8 mm and with what film?
4. What are the common external features on motion-picture cameras?
5. Does your camera include any additional features? Specify.
6. Does your camera have a reflex or window viewfinder? Which one is preferred and why?
7. What is the threading path for loading film in your camera or does it use a cassette?
8. Explain why *still* pictures are taken even though film *moves* through the camera?
9. What is/are the focal length(s) of your camera lenses?
10. What are some advantages of having lenses of different focal lengths, as against a zoom lens that covers a range of focal lengths?
11. Do you have *more* or *less* depth of field, at the same distance setting, with your lens set at $f/8$ as compared to $f/4$?
12. If you use a 75-mm lens set at 10 feet and you wish to have a depth of field of at least 2 feet, what $f/$ number must be used? Does this require *more* or *less* light on the subject than if only 1-foot depth of field is required?
13. How might videotape be used in motion-picure production?

Note: Answers to review questions can be found at the end of the chapter.

Techniques of Motion-Picture Photography

Planning a motion picture is similar to planning other audiovisual materials. But a major difference becomes apparent when you load your camera and start filming. This difference lies in the word *motion.* Movement is basic to successful motion pictures, whether it is in the subject, caused by camera movement when filming still subjects, or created by editing. Motion gives a film its interest, its pacing, and its strongest feature— its sense of continuity or logical progression.

The mere fact that someone or something moves in a scene is not enough to supply this motion. The *ideas* of the film must move along their planned development, make progress. The audience must be given the sense of this kind of motion, even when the projector is throwing such stationary things as a mountain or a building on the screen.

Motion in film can be accomplished by action within a scene, by change of camera angles, by camera movement, by varying the length of scenes, by movement created as you edit and arrange scenes, or by combinations of these elements.

In addition to the concept of motion, you should keep in mind the element of *time,* which is related closely to motion in film production. A photographic print can be studied as long as the viewer wishes to "read" from it the information desired. Slides and filmstrip frames can also be held for any length of time for prolonged examination. But a motion-picture scene is displayed only as long as it takes for it to pass the projector aperture.

Therefore, you must control the period of time the viewer can see a scene. You do this by the length of time the scene is filmed and then projected. You must develop a *feel* for how much screen time is required for the viewer to (1) *recognize* the subject being visualized, and (2) *comprehend* the message or the impression desired.

To shoot and then edit scenes that are of proper length—not too long or too short—requires experience and practice. Some of this can be gained by viewing and studying other educational and entertainment films. Also watch documentary-type television programs for subject treatment and scene length.

In handling this matter of time, the motion-picture medium is unique because it permits you to condense real time by eliminating unnecessary action or extraneous details while the topic being treated remains logical and understandable to the viewer. A subsequent section on Transitions explains how this can be done.

If you want to express your ideas imaginatively with a motion-picture camera, you are encouraged to use the camera creatively, but be cautioned that too many unusual effects, like a continually moving camera, out-of-focus shots, double-exposed scenes, and the like, can result in a distracting and boring film. Steady, unobtrusive camera-work is often the best policy.

The same techniques as will be described for motion-picture filming apply to the visualization of a subject through the television medium.

SHOTS, SCENES, TAKES, AND SEQUENCES

A motion picture is made up of many scenes, filmed from different camera angles and put together into sequences to carry the message of the film.

The terms *shot* and *scene* will be used in this section interchangeably. Each time you start film moving past your camera lens and then stop it, you have recorded a scene or a shot. You can film a scene from the script two or more times, calling each one a separate *take* of the particular scene. A *sequence* is a series of related scenes depicting one idea. It corresponds to a paragraph in writing.

When filming, start the camera just before the action begins (the proper directions are, "Camera start" . . . "Action start") and keep shooting for a few seconds after the action ends unless you are filming so as to "edit-in-the-camera" (page 246). In this way you not only make sure of getting the complete action, but have some additional footage for overlap and splicing. Also, because of the "time" factor it may be better to have a scene that is too long than one that is too short and may have to be reshot. Remember that it may take the viewer somewhat longer to identify and comprehend the subject than it does you, because you are very familiar with the subject.

A scene may run from 2 seconds to as long as 30 seconds; average scene length is 7 seconds. There is no set rule on scene length; the required action and necessary narration must determine effective length. A scene with much detail and activity may require a longer viewing time than a static scene of only general interest. So keep scenes long enough to convey your ideas and present the necessary information, but not so long as to drag and become monotonous.

The manner in which you visually treat the action within scenes, and then relate the scenes, will determine the coherence and effective reality of your film.

Types of Camera Shots

The appearance of a motion-picture scene can be judged only when viewed through the camera lens. How the camera sees the subject is important, not how the scene appears to the director, to a person in the scene, or to others. Keep this in mind as you apply the following principles.

BASIC SHOTS

Three types of scenes make up the fundamental sequence in motion-picture photography:

☐ The *long shot* (LS)—a general view of the setting and the subject. It provides an orientation for the viewer, by establishing all elements in the scene, and if important, shows size proportions relating to the subject.

☐ The *medium shot* (MS)—a closer view of the subject, eliminating unnecessary background and other details.

☐ The *close-up* (CU)—a concentration on the subject, or on a part of it, excluding everything else from view.

When the subject is the same, three successive shots assume a relation to each other.

LS, MS, and CU do not mean any specific distances. A long shot of a building may be taken from a distance of hundreds of yards, whereas a long shot of a small child may be taken from only a few yards distance. You may be close-up to a building when you are across the street, but you may need to get within a few feet of the small child to take a close-up.

Although the subject does limit the kinds of shots that are called for in the script, two cameramen covering the same subject may film the three scenes differently, each imparting his own interpretation and emphasis. To say that one version is right and the other wrong would most likely depend on personal preference (see page 236).

At the two ends of the LS–MS–CU sequence you can introduce *extremes* if they are important to your story—*extreme* long shot (ELS) and *extreme* close-up (ECU).

Although LS–MS–CU is a fundamental sequence, it is not to be rigidly followed in successive sequences, and there is no set rule for the use of these three basic shots. The visual effect desired should determine the sequence. Because of the inability of 8-mm film to handle very fine detail, long shots should be used only rarely. Thus the 8-mm sequence might become MS–CU–ECU.

Sequences need variety; without variations,

Long Shot

Medium Shot

Close-up

Long Shot

Medium Shot

Close-up

LS, Cameraman A

LS, Cameraman B

MS, Cameraman A

MS, Cameraman B

CU, Cameraman A

CU, Cameraman B

Extreme Long Shot (ELS)

Extreme Close-up (ECU)

your film may become monotonous and lose its pacing, its motion. For straightforward explanation the LS–MS–CU sequence may be satisfactory. For a slower pace, gradually increasing interest, LS–MS–MCU–CU may be used. For suspense or drama, consider CU–CU–CU–LS.

Note the differences in two four-shot sequences (see page 237).

ANGLE AND POSITION SHOTS

Variety, emphasis, and dramatic effect can be accomplished through the use of *camera angles.* The normal or neutral camera position is at about eye level for a person standing. A camera in a higher position, looking down on the subject, makes a *high-angle shot* that gives the illusion

LS   **MS**   **MCU**   **CU**

MS   **CU**   **LS**   **MS**

of placing the subject in an inferior position, reducing its size and slowing its motion. A camera in a lower than normal position, looking up at a subject, makes a *low-angle shot* that seems to give the subject a dominant position, exaggerating its height and speeding up movement. High- and low-angle shots can be used to eliminate undesirable background or foreground details.

In most filming the camera is in the position of the eyes of an observer, that is, of the audience; this is *objective camera position.* But often the camera is put in the position of the subject's eyes and sees the performance of an operation or the behavior of an object as the subject sees it; this is *subjective camera position.* In the latter, in most instances, the cameraman shoots over the subject's shoulder, with the camera at a high angle.

MOVING-CAMERA SHOTS

Camera movement itself, during filming, adds to the variety of possible shots. These possibilities include:

☐ *Panning*—a horizontal movement of the camera
☐ *Tilting*—a vertical movement of the camera
☐ *Dollying*—a movement of the camera away from or toward the subject (Dollying the camera *parallel* to the subject is called *trucking.*)
☐ *Zooming*—a continuous change of the camera-lens focal length during a scene that simulates the effect of camera movement toward or away from the subject (page 229)

High-Angle Shot

Low-Angle Shot

Objective Scene

Subjective Scene

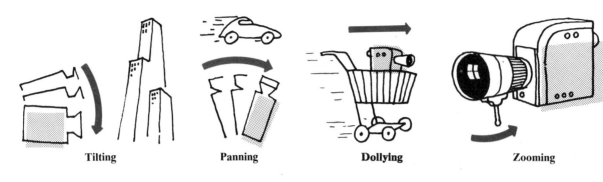

Tilting　　　　**Panning**　　　　**Dollying**　　　　**Zooming**

These techniques are generally too much used, are often unnecessary, and are frequently poorly done. If a subject in a scene moves, the camera might logically follow him. This is a good use of camera movement. Or, if a scene is too broad to be caught by the motionless camera, a *pan* (panorama) may show its size and scope. Or you may pan or tilt if it is important to connect two subjects by relating them visually. But do not pan across nonmoving subjects which can be handled satisfactorily by a longer still shot or by two separate scenes.

Closely related to pans and tilts is the use of a zoom lens—*zooming* (a smooth change of field within the LS–MS–CU relationship during a single scene, page 229). Here the same cautions apply about overuse. A series of straight cuts (MS to CU) is often more effective. Save the zoom shot until you feel a real need and one that makes an important contribution to the continuity of your film.

The dolly shot is the most difficult of the moving-camera shots to perform smoothly and effectively. A scene shot as the camera is held in a moving car is one example of a dolly shot. Or the camera, on a tripod, can be attached to some device with wheels—a wagon, an office chair, a grocery cart, or a motorized factory truck—and slowly pushed or pulled in relation to the subject.

When panning, tilting, dollying, or zooming, apply these practices:

☐ Attach your camera to a tripod, and adjust the head for smooth movement (a long handle on the tripod is desirable for good control).
☐ Always start a moving shot with the camera held still for a few seconds and end the shot in the same way.
☐ When shooting a moving subject, try to "lead" the subject in the frame slightly (page 97).
☐ Always rehearse the shot a few times before exposing film.

MS (Establishing)

CU

CU

CU

LS (Re-establishing)

CAUTIONS AS YOU PLAN YOUR SHOTS

When a sequence becomes long and you include a number of related close-ups, frequently *re-establish* the general subject for the viewer with an LS or MS so he does not lose his orientation to the subject. An establishing shot (LS or MS) is also important when moving to a new activity before close-up detail is shown.

If the viewer has to figure for himself where the camera has suddenly shifted or why an unexplained change has occurred in the action, then you have done something wrong. Always plan your scenes to keep the viewer oriented.

When you treat one subject in a number of related scenes (as in the LS–MS–CU sequence), change the angle between the camera and the subject for adjacent scenes (but not over 180°), or change the vertical camera position. If you do not, as you move directly in or back, you create the effect known as *pumping-in,* or *pumping-out,* which is quite jarring to the viewer. The differing impacts of good and faulty techniques in this respect can be appreciated fully only if the scenes are viewed in motion; but note the changes of angle in previous sequences and in the brief sequence of wire-welding scenes.

MS, Subject Directly before the Camera

MS, Subject Directly before the Camera

CU, Camera Moved Straight in

CU, Camera Moved in and 45° to Left

In summary, there is a variety of filming shots at your disposal:

☐ Basic shots—long shot, medium shot, close-up
☐ Extremes—extreme long shot, extreme close-up
☐ High-angle and low-angle shots
☐ Objective and subjective camera positions
☐ Pan, tilt, dolly, and zoom shots

And, remember to:

☐ Use a variety of shots purposefully; they contribute to good motion-picture technique.
☐ Use establishing and re-establishing shots to keep your audience oriented to the subject.
☐ Change angle between shots of the same subject; the change is important to smooth flow of action.
☐ Keep in mind both concepts necessary for viewing—movement and time—so that your film will communicate most satisfactorily.
☐ Shoot scenes slightly longer than actually needed; the extra frames will be helpful when editing.

For each scene, the camera angle and the selected basic shot (LS, MS, or CU) determine the *viewpoint* and the *area* to be covered. Thus, as you choose camera position and lens you must answer two questions: What is the best viewpoint for effectively showing the action? How much area should be included in the scene?

To help in visualizing the content of key scenes and the placement of the camera with respect to the subject, consider making simple sketches to show the subject position and the area to be covered by the camera. Two examples are shown. These sketches will aid other people (including members of the production crew) to understand what you have in mind. These sketches do not serve the same purposes as the general pictures made for the storyboard during planning (page 52), they apply more specifically to the actual scene being shot.

Scene 10 MS Child Reading

Scene 22 CU (High Angle) Inserting Drill

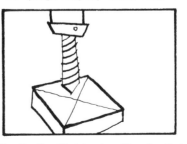

Visualization Sketches in a Shooting Script

Now, Apply What You Have Learned About Types of Camera Shots:

1. What are the two concepts that differentiate a motion picture from other forms of audiovisual materials?
2. Differentiate the terms *scene, shot, take, sequence.*
3. Relate the shots—high-angle, low-angle, objective, subjective—to the following situations:
   a. Exaggerate subject height
   b. Slowing subject movement
   c. Over-the-shoulder filming
   d. Filming from an audience viewpoint
4. Relate the use of these techniques—pan, tilt, dolly, zoom—to the following situations:
   a. Follow a person climbing stairs
   b. Smooth change from a MS to a CU
   c. Relate an object on a table to other nearby objects
   d. Filming a spread-out farm scene
   e. Filming as the camera passes by a number of buildings
5. What is a *re-establishing* scene?
6. What is meant by the term *pumping-in?*
7. Label the types of camera shots illustrated by each scene in the sequence that follows. In what order would you arrange these scenes to make a meaningful sequence?

a   b   c   d

e   f   g   h

Note: Answers to review questions can be found at the end of the chapter.

Providing Continuity

Selecting the best camera positions, the proper lens, and the correct exposure under the best light conditions may result in good scenes, but these do not guarantee a good motion picture. Only when one scene leads logically and easily to the next one do you have the binding ingredient of smooth *continuity.* Continuity is based on thorough planning and an awareness of a number of factors that must be taken care of during filming.

MATCHING ACTION

As you film scenes within the same sequence, the subject normally moves. Shoot adjacent and related scenes in such a way that a continuation of the movement is evident from one scene to the next. Such continuation *matches the action* between scenes.

In order to insure a smooth flow from the MS

to the CU, match the action at the end of the first scene to the beginning of the second one. Accomplish this matching by having some of the action at the end of the MS repeated at the beginning of the CU.

Medium Shot

Close-up

Scene 1

Splice

Scene 2

Scene 1	**Scene 2**	**Edited Sequence**

Then, when editing, from this overlap of action select appropriate frames at which the two scenes should be joined. This transition is most easily accepted by the viewer if the scenes are joined at a point of change—in direction of movement, when something is picked up or shifted, or similar change—rather than in the middle of a smooth movement where the natural flow of action may be disturbed.

In this way "action is matched" and a smooth flow results. As you plan matching shots remember to:

☐ Change angle slightly between adjacent shots (recall the improper practice of pumping-in, or pumping-out, page 239).

☐ Match the tempo of movement from an MS to a CU. Since action in a CU should be somewhat slower than normal or it will appear highly accelerated and disturbing to the viewer, the movement in the previous MS should be slowed down.

☐ Notice where parts of the subject or objects within the first scene are placed, which hand is used and its position, or how the action moves. Be sure they are the same for the second and any closely following scenes. Be particularly observant if scenes are filmed out of script order.

It is not always essential to match action unless details in adjacent scenes are easily recognizable to the viewer. An LS of general activity (for example, a playground scene) does not have to match an MS of a group at play, but when the camera turns from this group to an individual the action should be matched.

For some purposes action can best be matched by using more than one camera, one taking longer shots and the other taking close-ups, the two shooting scenes simultaneously while the action is continuous.

Shooting Close-up   **Shooting Long Shot**

This *multicamera technique* speeds up filming and insures accurate matching of action, even though it may require the use of more film than when shooting with only one camera. Waste can be minimized by starting the second camera on signal just before the first one stops in order to provide the overlap. Multicamera filming is particularly useful when documenting events like athletic meets, meetings, carnivals, demonstrations, and news events. Assign camera teams to work together and coordinate their filming to cover related activities at the same time from positions that will *cut* (edit) smoothly together.

SCREEN DIRECTION

Another kind of matching action is required when a subject moves across the frame. If he moves from left to right, make sure the action is the same in the next scene.

When action leaves the frame on one side, it must enter the next scene from the *opposite* side of the frame for proper continuity.

If directions must change between two scenes, try to show the change in the first scene by having the subject make a turn. If a turn is not possible, include a brief in-between scene of the action coming straight toward the camera. Then a new direction in the following scene seems plausible to the viewer.

Be careful when filming parades, races, and similar activities with more than one camera unless someone is assigned to show the action changing direction (going round turns, or moving directly toward or away from the camera). If you do not do this and cameras are located on opposite sides of the activity one will show action from left to right and another from right to left. The audience will be confused and receive the impression that the moving subject has turned

around and is returning to the starting point—and no one will ever get to the finish line!

If screen direction is to be reversed intentionally, include one or more scenes inserted between the two directions that show how the action reversed.

PROTECTION SHOTS

Careful though you may be, there are times when things go wrong with your planning or filming. Possibly you did not quite match the action between scenes; the left hand instead of the right one was used in the CU, the screen direction between two scenes changes, or you create a *jump* by momentarily stopping the camera during a scene and then starting it again while the action is continuing. Often such situations are not discovered until the editing, and then you may be in trouble. Therefore, by all means protect yourself from possible embarrassment and poor practice.

Protection is afforded by shooting *cut-in* and *cut-away* shots, even though these shots are not indicated in the script. A cut-in is a CU (or ECU) of some part of the scene being filmed. It also is called an *insert*. Examples of common cut-ins are faces, hands, feet, parts of objects, and other items known to be in the scene (see page 243).

A cut-away is opposite to a cut-in in that it is a shot of another subject or separate action taking place at the same time as is the main action. This other subject or action is not in the scene (hence *away*) but is related in some way to the main action. Examples of cut-aways are people or objects that complement the main action; faces of people watching or reacting to the main action are commonly used (see page 243).

Both cut-ins and cut-aways serve to distract the viewer's attention momentarily and thus permit acceptance of the next scene even though the action may not match the preceding one accurately. By using cut-ins and cut-aways in this way, two scenes can be given continuity even though they would be illogical in direct succession.

Keep these points in mind as you shoot cut-ins and cut-aways:

Cut-in Shot

**Cut-away Shot
(Reaction Shot)**

☐ Always shoot a number of them, as you may not know until editing whether you will need one or more. Complete the unused ends of film rolls with such brief scenes.

☐ Make them long enough: a minimum of 5 or 6 seconds, although you may only use 2 or 3 seconds.

☐ Make them logical, in keeping with the appropriate sequences (watch expressions and backgrounds so they will be consistent with the main action).

TRANSITIONS

One of the strengths of motion-picture photography is being able to take viewers from one place to another or to show action taking place at different times—all this presented in adjacent scenes within a very short period of actual screen time, and accepted quite realistically by the audience. How is this acceptance accomplished? It is achieved through the use of *transitional devices,* which bridge space and time.

The simplest method for achieving smooth pictorial transitions is by use of printed titles or directions placed between scenes (see page 244).

Also, cut-ins, and cut-aways can give the impression of time passing and may reduce a long scene to its essentials without the audience realizing that time has been compressed. An example of this may be showing the start of an activity, then a cut-in, then the completion of activity, with the insert scene 2–3 seconds in length (see page 244).

Exiting from a scene and subsequent entrance at another location creates an acceptable transition in time as well as in space. (Always film the scene for a few seconds after the subject has left the scene to insure an acceptable period of time for the subject to appear in the next scene at a different location.)

A *montage* is a series of short scenes connected by cuts, dissolves, or possibly wipes (see below), used to quickly condense time or distance or to show a series of related activities and places. The audience accepts this rapid series of scenes as if the complete operation or various places had been seen in their entirety.

Transition Scene (Title)   **Transition Scene (Cut-in)**   **Transition Scene (Exit/Entrance)**

Optical transitions are common ways of expressing time and space changes. But research evidence in Chapter 3 does not indicate that optical effects significantly contribute to learning. Opticals are sometimes created in the camera, but more commonly are added by a film laboratory when copies are made from the original film.

A *fade-out* and *fade-in* serve to separate major sequences in a film. They consist of the gradual darkening of a scene to complete blackness (fade-out) followed by the gradual lightening (fade-in) of the first scene of the next sequence. Fades are also used at the beginning of a film (fade-in) and at the end (fade-out). Use fades sparingly, as too many may produce a disturbing effect which disrupts the flow of the film.

A *dissolve* commonly indicates lapse in time or a change in location between adjacent scenes. It blends one scene into another by showing the fade-out of the first scene and the *superimposed* fade-in of the next scene. A dissolves is some-times used to soften the change from one scene to another that would otherwise be abrupt or jarring, due possibly to poor planning or incorrect selection of camera angles in adjacent scenes. The *jump-cut* discussed previously is an example of a mismatch in adjacent scenes, like sudden change in body position resulting in a jerk or sudden jump between scenes.

A *wipe* is an optical effect in which a new scene seems to push the previous scene off the screen. The wiping motion may be vertical, horizontal, or angular. This effect is infrequently used but may be important for situations that are closely related, like the start of an experiment followed immediately by the result. A group of scenes connected by wipes may give the impression of looking across a row or a series of objects.

Fades and dissolves can be created in many cameras. If yours has a variable shutter, move it smoothly from its open to its fully closed position (taking about 2 seconds) for a fade-out. Re-

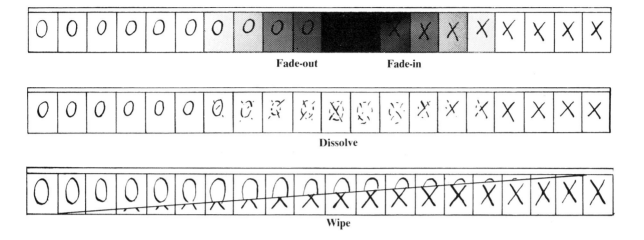

verse the procedure for a fade-in. To dissolve, make a fade-out, then wind the film back (with the lens covered) 48 frames and make a two-second fade-in.

Here are other ways to make a fade, or a simulation of one:

☐ Close down the lens diaphragm to the smallest opening (fade-out) and then open it to the proper setting (fade-in) as the next scene starts. The results of this technique are better with a manual-setting rather than with an automatic-setting camera. The latter camera tends to correct exposure continually, thus it may be difficult to reach a complete fade-out.

☐ Bring a black card down directly in front of the lens, covering it so the light is blocked out. Hold the card there for 2 seconds before stopping the camera. At the start of the next scene, start the camera with the lens covered and slowly raise the black card. The impression is that of a curtain dropping and then raising, as on a theatre stage.

☐ As a scene ends, turn the focusing ring on the lens slowly to throw the subject completely out of focus. Start the next scene with the lens still out of focus and adjust it slowly into focus.

If optical effects for your film are to be made at a film laboratory, be sure to provide sufficient footage for the fades and dissolves. Most laboratories require at least 48 frames of film at the ends of scenes for fade or dissolve overlap. Most major laboratories have instructions on preparing films for printing. Contact one or more of the film laboratories listed on page 308 for their requirements and services.

Now, Apply What You Have Learned About Providing Continuity in Motion Pictures:

1. What is "matching action"?

2. Why should a constant screen direction be maintained in a sequence?

3. How can you provide for acceptable change in screen direction?

4. What protection shot might you use in filming a sequence showing a woman sewing a lengthy seam?

5. What transition device would you use in each of these situations:
   a. A board being painted and then used after it has dried
   b. A man leaving home and arriving at his office
   c. A scoreboard showing the score after the first inning and then at the end of the game

6. What purposes are served by optical effects?

7. How might you make a fade-out and fade-in with your camera? Can you also make a dissolve?

Note: Answers to review questions can be found at the end of the chapter.

Special Filming Techniques

In this section we will examine a number of methods that require special explanations. Some are applications of basic motion-picture techniques, while others are unique procedures that can very effectively attract attention, hold interest, and convey information when used for specific purposes.

DOCUMENTARY FILMING

As explained on page 60, there may be times when a topic is filmed without first doing detailed planning. This approach can apply to the production of a slide series as well as to a motion picture or television program. Your understanding and application of all the forementioned production techniques relating to camera shots and continuity are essential in documentary filming.

To end up with scenes that can be edited together and result in a coherent product, you must keep in mind what you have shot as well as try to anticipate what may be next. Because you cannot anticipate all the action, you may miss something of importance, or what you expect may not happen. Therefore, always shoot a number of cut-aways and cut-ins to be used as protection shots for insertion between scenes that may not go together naturally.

The editing stage for a documentary film becomes especially important. Depending on the footage you have, editing may be a straightforward task or require careful decisions that can lead to alternative treatment or interpretation of the subject. See page 255 for suggestions on how to proceed with the editing of a documentary film.

EDITING-IN-THE-CAMERA

You may want to prepare your film without having to remove or rearrange any of the scenes shot. When you shoot one scene after another in sequence, from the first title through the END title, the film is edited in the camera. As opposed to the documentary approach, this technique requires careful planning and following the script scene-by-scene. Obviously, when scene locations require shifts from one place to another and back again, shooting in sequence can be very costly in time. But if you are producing a how-to-do-it film, it is possible to film each scene in the right order, and by doing this you can conserve film.

If the original camera film is to be projected, the avoidance of splices is a justification for editing-in-the-camera. Splices can be visually distracting or may cause a malfunction in the projector. On the other hand, if copies are going to be made from the film, the problems with splices are eliminated and editing-in-the-camera may be unnecessary.

In order to edit in the camera, each of the following is important:

- [ ] You are certain of the sequence of scenes.
- [ ] You can control all action to be filmed and know how long each scene will be. Rehearsals are important.
- [ ] Titles and illustrations are prepared and ready for filming. You must have the titles set up so you can turn the camera to them for filming in proper order and then go back to the next action scene.
- [ ] Exposure, other camera settings, and camera movement will be correct for each scene.

COMPRESSING AND EXPANDING TIME

Because a motion-picture camera can be set to operate at various speeds, it is possible to slow-down or speed-up normal action. This permits certain subjects to be viewed and studied that otherwise might not be possible.

To record action that normally takes place *too rapidly* for ease of study, use a *slow-motion* technique. Set the camera speed to *exceed* the projection rate—a speed of 32, 48, or 64 fps instead of 18 or 24 fps. When the film is projected at normal speed, a slow-down effect results because the action on the screen takes a longer period of time than the action took before the camera. Saying this another way, the projected image moves more slowly than the original action. This allows for detailed analysis of gross or fine movements which in real time would be too rapid for the eye to follow.

Remember to increase the illumination on the subject if possible, and compensate for change in exposure on a manual-setting camera when using faster speeds. This becomes necessary because there is a reduction in the amount of light reaching the film, caused by shorter exposure time per frame. Refer to your camera instruction booklet or to a motion-picture handbook for guidance (such as *Mascelli's Cine Workbook*).[3]

To record action that normally takes place *too slowly* for ease of study, use a rapid-motion

technique. By setting camera speeds *slower* than the projection rate and then projecting the film at normal speed, action is visually compressed or speeded up. Recall how rapidly the people and cars move in "old-time" movies that were filmed at 8 or 16 fps and are now projected at 24 fps.

The slowest setting on most cameras is 8 fps, so you do not have a wide choice of slower than normal filming speeds for increasing action. But the 8 fps rate may be suitable for speeding up some types of action you wish to study or use for a special effect.

A variation of the rapid-motion technique for accelerating action is *time-lapse* photography. When individual frames are exposed one at a time, this procedure is called *single framing*. Your camera may be equipped with a special control that permits single framing. In this way you can record subjects having a very slow movement, like the opening of a flower bud, the formation and movement of clouds, and color changes or growths in laboratory experiments. Individual frames are exposed at a predetermined rate, for instance 1 per second or 1 per minute or 1 per hour. Find out how long the action to be filmed normally takes. Then decide how much film time you want to use and determine how often a picture should be taken. Here is a problem:

Purpose: To film a color reaction change in a test tube
Normal time for reaction to take place: 8 hours (480 minutes)
Film time to be used: 10 seconds at 24 fps (240 frames)

$$\frac{480 \text{ minutes}}{240 \text{ frames}} = 2 \text{ minutes per frame}$$

This means that for a period of 8 hours a frame should be exposed every 2 minutes.
Result: Eight-hour change is shown in **10** seconds

Motor-driven commercial equipment is available for such automatic-timed single framing. See the references on page 298 for further details and techniques on time-lapse photography.

FILMOGRAPHY

A technique that employs single-framing and relates closely to the next topic, animation, is the filming of still pictures directly onto motion-picture film. The result is called a *filmograph.* Magazine pictures, historical photographs, drawings, and any other flat, still pictures can be placed under the camera on a copystand and the neces-

---

3. Joseph V. Mascelli, *Mascelli's Cine Workbook* (Hollywood: Cine Graphics Publications, 1973).

sary number of frames exposed according to the narration or effect to be created.

In filmography, motion can be simulated by moving or zooming the camera in to a picture to film a close-up of part of the subject, or moving out from a detail to a broader view. The picture can also be moved across the lens to create the effect of panning or tilting. In either situation, the camera position, lens focal-length setting, or picture shift should only be changed slightly as each frame is exposed. When this sequence of separate movements is projected continuously, the illusion of motion in, back, or across results.

One tendency in making a film this way is to shoot the still pictures for too short a length of time—sometimes 2–3 frames per scene. This may be too brief for the viewer to grasp the meaning of the picture. You may have to experiment with filming various numbers of frames to realize both the understanding and effect you want to create.

ANIMATION

The single-framing procedure can be extended to filming things that normally cannot move to make them appear as if they are moving on the screen. This is *animation*. It resembles time-lapse in that single-framing is used to film sequences and the method to determine movement per frame is similar. But here the sequence consists of successive drawings, slight movement of three-dimensional figures and objects, or progressively developed parts of a diagram. Animation is a fascinating area of motion-picture production, but one that takes patience and attention to numerous details.

Animation requires careful planning, particular storyboarding (page 52). A storyboard helps you establish the movements and time required for each action. Because of the repetition of details (movement, expose, movement, expose, . . .), develop a check-list of steps to follow—action, frames to expose, completion, etc. Keep a careful record (log sheet, page 61) as you shoot animation. Any mistake made when filming may require that you start again from the beginning, so plan and prepare completely and carefully.

Some of the common animation techniques, with examples, are:

☐ *Pop-on*—Set the first letter of a title in place, shoot three or four frames, add the next letter, shoot frames, and so on as each letter is placed in proper position; draw a line, a segment at a time, shoot three or four frames, add the next portion, and so on; prepare a series of drawings on a process, each of which adds a small detail to the previous one, then

film each drawing sequentially, on a few frames.

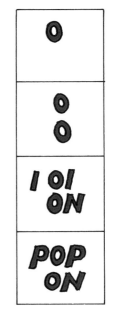

☐ *Cut-outs*—Figures and objects cut from colored paper or cardboard can be set under the camera, exposed, moved slightly, exposed, and so on; other figures can be constructed with hinged parts so that walking, throwing, and other humanlike motions can be animated.

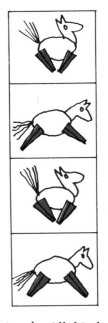

☐ *Three-dimensional*—All kinds of objects, including figures and shapes constructed from modeling clay, can be placed on a table and moved slightly between exposures, or altered in shape; or use people to simulate motion by single-framing such things as skating on grass, sliding down a hill, dancing with an object, and so on.

□ *Wipe-off,* or *scratch-off*—Prepare diagram or drawing on clear acetate with water-based inks or felt pens, small segments of the diagram are progressively removed as one or a few frames are exposed. In this procedure, when the film is turned end-for-end and projected, the diagram appears to develop from nothing and grow to completion. One limitation—it is only possible with 16-mm double-perforated film because of the need to turn the film and still have sprocket holes on the proper side for projection.

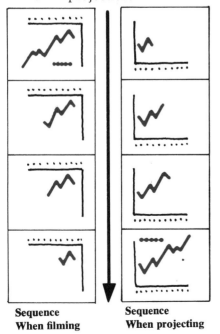

Sequence When filming   **Sequence When projecting**

□ *Cel*—A series of drawings made on clear acetate sheets (called "cels") with positions of figures or objects that can "move" by being altered slightly from one drawing to the next, are placed in careful *registration* under the camera and photographed with appropriate cel changes between frames.

Animated drawings

Filmed and Viewed Scenes

As you prepare to try one or more animation techniques, keep these suggestions in mind:

□ Necessary camera features for animation work include: through-the-lens viewing and focusing, close-up attachment if lens does not focus close enough, single-frame control, and preferable override on automatic-exposure setting (use a light meter).
□ Use a sturdy copystand or other frame to hold the camera immovable in a fixed position. Any slight camera movement will cause subjects to suddenly jump and usually require that you start filming the whole sequence again.
□ Prepare artwork and select objects large enough so you can handle them easily and

have a large enough field for shooting (minimum of 6×9 inch frame area), see page 122.

☐ Expose just a few frames per movement for smooth motion. One-frame exposure with very small increments of motion is preferred, but the time and care required become very demanding. Increments greater than four frames can result in erratic and sudden movements.

☐ Linear movements per exposure should be very slight (¼ inch or so for flat copy work). As with the number of frames to expose, if a segment of movement is too great, the subject will seem to move in a sudden and jerky rather than smooth and continuous manner.

☐ Determine length of time the animation sequence will be projected and then calculate the number of movements required. For example, if a twelve-letter title is to unscramble and move into position in 20 seconds, then: $20/12 = 1.7$ seconds of movement per letter at 18 fps—31 frames required for each letter; if 2 frames per movement—15 movements required per letter.

☐ Some actions normally accelerate and decelerate, like a moving ball. More rapid motion can be shown by having distance increments close together at the beginning and gradually increase their size as the subject slows down.

☐ Select a time for filming animation when you will not be disturbed or distracted. Keep careful records to check-off each movement, exposure, camera setting, and so on.

☐ Be sure the artwork or subject is placed right-side-up when you stand in a normal position for filming and sighting through the camera viewfinder.

There are many variations to the process of film animation and other problems you will need to solve if you become a serious film animator. For further discussion of animation, see the references on page 298.

STILL-MOTION COMBINATION

A new concept for using super-8 film as the medium for both still *and* motion pictures is being recognized and explored. Special projection equipment now allows the showing of still pictures with a single frame advance, continuous motion sequences, or any intermix combination of them. In addition, audio materials can be carried on an accompanying cassette and by means of a pulsing system, synchronized with the visuals.

This development offers many advantages for designing learning materials that can treat a topic with whatever combination of media is most appropriate, without requiring the learner to move from one piece of equipment to another as he studies still pictures or motion pictures. Ultimately, such a combination unit may replace both slide, filmstrip, and motion-picture projectors and tape recorders.

Those interested in this challenging new approach to audiovisual communication should explore its possibilities in local production as well as for commercial applications as a key element of multimedia packaged units. A partial list of projectors with the still-motion capability is included on page 305. Also, when you view the special films correlated with concepts in this book (see Appendix A) you will be using a simple viewer that applies the still-motion treatment.

If you plan to explore this new area, consider these matters:

☐ Your camera must have the single-frame feature.

☐ Carefully plan and storyboard the topic, deciding which items require motion, which can be satisfactorily treated with still pictures, where titles will be needed for cues or explanations, and what sound is required to accompany the visuals.

☐ Check the requirements of the projector you will be using and proceed with your production according to its requirements.

☐ Evaluate the results carefully because in a new approach such as this, experience may be the best teacher for improvement and widening your understandings.

Now, Apply What You Have Learned About Some Special Filming Techniques:

1. What two bits of information should you keep in mind when doing documentary filming?
2. How do you best insure continuity when documentary filming?
3. Why is editing in the camera difficult?
4. You wish to show the form of a diver by slowing down his action on the diving board. What camera settings would you change from the normal and what are possible new settings?

5. What attachment on a motion-picture camera is essential for *time-lapse* photography?
6. How often would a frame be exposed if you wished to show the changes in clouds across the sky from 10 A.M. to 4 P.M. and covering 20 seconds of film shot at silent speed (18 fps)?
7. What is a *filmograph*?
8. Name three animation techniques and give an application you could make for each one.

Note: Answers to review questions can be found at the end of the chapter.

Other Production Considerations

SUPER-8 CONCEPT FILMS

Much of the evidence gathered from research concerning the design and use of motion pictures can find more extensive applications in the 8-mm single-concept medium than in 16-mm-film production since the 8-mm approach narrows the variables (audience, objectives, content, and so forth), the practical situation may be closer to the conditions under which the experimental procedures took place. Review the research reports in Chapter 3 and determine how they can be applied in your 8-mm film-production activities in terms of the following suggestions:

☐ *Emphasis:* On simplicity of content treatment, action, composition, and detail.
☐ *Content:* Treating a single idea, concept, or limited topic concisely. This requires careful planning and a willingness to continually examine and evaluate development. The 8-mm films that correlate with this chapter, and with other chapters of this book, are examples of the single-concept treatment (see Appendix A).
☐ *Length:* Sufficient to do the job without including lengthy titles, credits, introduction, summary, and irrelevant material.
☐ *Filming techniques:* Often simplified, such as longer scenes of how-to-do-it activity filmed from one position; emphasis on close-up details; subjective camera angles from the learner's point of view. Other techniques, such as matching action, screen direction, accounting for passage of time, and so forth, should be considered, but can be dispensed with in some filming situations.
☐ *Pacing:* Owing to close-up filming, the action should be at a slightly slower pace than that found in other films, but not so slow as to drag and lose attention-holding power. It is recommended that a film be viewed more than once by the learner, if necessary for comprehension.

☐ *Scene content:* Limiting items in a scene to those that directly contribute to, or are required, by the action. All distracting background elements and movements should be eliminated.
☐ *Accompanying narration:* A minimum use of voice to cue and interpret action as shown. Sound must be related directly to visual activity.
☐ *Accompanying titles:* Topic headings and instructions, briefly worded, should be included in silent films (and probably in sound films for reinforcement) as separate scenes rather than as *overprints* on action scenes. The latter use tends to distract attention from the visual action. Overprint labels and arrows should be used as necessary.
☐ *Correlated materials:* Review outlines, details not covered in a film, related activities, participation questions, problems, and activities, should all be available in printed or other form to accompany the film. If a film is part of a programmed sequence, directions must be clear concerning the film's use at the proper place in the sequence along with lead-in and lead-out materials.

Silent-film production requires more careful attention to visual detail than is necessary in the production of a sound film. In the latter, directing attention and making explanations and interpretations can be the responsibility of the sound track. But in a silent film only the picture (and accompanying titles) can communicate. Therefore extreme care must be used to insure that a scene conveys its intent accurately and easily.

Making a silent film is a challenging form of production and can be very effective if it is done carefully. The required concentration of the viewer on a message carried through the single most perceptive sense—sight—can be a stimulating way of learning. Keep in mind the factors enumerated above and supplement them with others derived from studying available 8-mm silent films and from your own experiences.

If a motion picture is to be made directly on 8-mm film, certain cautions should be recognized:

☐ Too many splices can be troublesome if the film is to be used with many 8-mm projectors. Splices close together may catch on parts of the projector, stopping the film and resulting in damage. Therefore, when filming directly on 8-mm, try to edit the film in the camera as explained on page 246.

☐ One way of overcoming the problem of splices is to have a print made from the original film. This will be splice-free. The commonly used 8-mm film is Kodachrome II. This film is meant for projection and not for duplication. Duplicate prints from Kodachrome tend to be grainy and therefore not as sharp as the original; true colors are lost and the contrast between light and dark areas becomes greater (light-color areas become whiter and dark-color areas become blacker). Thus the appearance of a duplicate may be disappointing as compared with the original film.

☐ If prints must be made from original 8-mm film, the film should be handled and projected as little as possible. Scratches and embedded dirt will appear on prints as obvious dark lines and marks.

☐ If it can be anticipated that a number of super-8 prints of good quality may be needed, it is recommended that filming be done on 16-mm film and then reduced to super-8 (see procedure under Film Laboratory Services). The film to use is Ektachrome Commercial (page 232), which is a low-contrast film designed for duplication. It may not be available through regular dealers, but can be obtained from a store carrying professional or commercial film items.

COMPOSITION

As with still photography, composition is a matter of personal aesthetics. Note the general suggestions for good composition on page 97.[4]

The proportions of the motion-picture frame should always be kept in mind when selecting subjects and composing scenes. Since the frame has the proportions of 3 to 4 (page 113), preference should be given to subjects with horizontal rather than vertical configurations.

------

4. For detailed consideration of composition applied specifically for motion pictures, see Chapter 5 of *The Five C's of Cinematography* by Joseph Mascelli (Hollywood: 9 Cine Grafic Publications, 1965).

Special care must be taken in composing scenes involving motion. Always lead a moving subject with more area in the direction of motion, and carefully rehearse anticipated movement so that proper framing or camera motion can be planned.

When a person handles an object or performs an operation, the camera should be situated for the best view, although it may appear unnatural from the subject's viewpoint. Exaggeration and simplification are acceptable in information or in skill films in order to convey a correct understanding or impression.

SCHEDULING AND RECORD KEEPING

Follow the suggestions on page 59 for preparing a shooting schedule, making arrangements for filming, checking facilities, and keeping a record (a log sheet) of filming. To facilitate editing, identify each scene and its takes by *slating* just before the scene begins. To slate a scene, write the scene number and the take number boldly on a sheet of paper (a small blackboard is often used) and hold it in front of the camera at a readable distance. Film a few frames of it; then proceed with the actual scene.

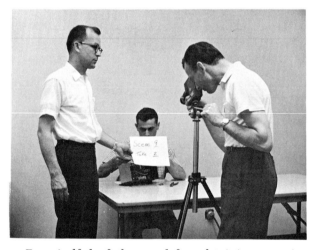

Be mindful of the need for obtaining permission from those appearing in scenes or from owners of copyrighted materials used. For a sample release form, see page 61.

TITLES AND ILLUSTRATIONS

Titles should serve the purposes noted on page 67. Often they are prepared as editing nears completion when the need for special subtitles, captions, or labels becomes evident. Preparing them at this time helps to insure their being properly placed and effectively worded.

The same techniques described for preparing

titles and illustrations for slides on page 174 can be used for making motion-picture titles. Review these procedures:

1. Word each title so it is brief but communicative.
2. Select materials or aids for appropriate lettering. As you select lettering sizes, be sure to consider the legibility standards for projected materials described on page 120.
3. Prepare the lettering and artwork (page 123), keeping in mind the correct 3 to 4 proportions of the film area, using simple design features (page 113), and selecting appropriate backgrounds (page 131). If your motion-picture camera is not equipped with reflex viewing (page 228), prepare titles and illustrations large enough to be filmed at a distance that will overcome the parallax problem (page 100).
4. Then attach each prepared title and illustration to a wall or easel and photograph it with your camera on a tripod (page 101), or use a copy or titling stand.

Special titles or captions can be *overlayed* on a prepared background. Black and colored lettering only can be superimposed over flat pictures (page 131). White letters, in addition to this, can also be *overprinted* on a filmed background (page 132). This latter method is often used for adding subtitles and captions to scenes. Film the background scene (slightly underexposed) and wind the film back to the start of the scene (with the lens capped). Then expose the white-lettered title (printed on black). This double-exposing prints the white title over the background scene. Most film laboratories can overprint titles for you if you supply them with footage of the background scene and footage of the titles prepared from black printing on white cardboard and photographed on 16-mm high-contrast positive film.

Film length for titles should be sufficient for you to read through the title twice. It may be shortened somewhat when editing, but film with this timing as a guide. A fade-in is commonly used with the main title and a fade-out at the end. Dissolves are appropriate between adjacent titles.

Film Laboratory Services

A list of commercial film laboratories is included in Appendix D on page 308. Contact one or more of them concerning their specific services, requirements, and prices.

As rolls of film are exposed you can send them to a film laboratory for processing. Seeing the footage shortly after it has been shot gives you a continual check on your exposure, on your filming techniques, and on the proper operation of your camera. On the other hand, some filmmakers hold all exposed film until shooting is completed so that it will all be processed at one time, thus eliminating inconsistencies that may arise from variations in developing.

Most commercial film laboratories offer a variety of services in addition to the processing of film. One of the most worthwhile is the preparation of a duplicate, or *workprint,* from the original 16-mm footage for use in editing. Handling the original film will blemish it with scratches and dirt; worse, a wrong cut or a tear during projection would be disastrous. The original film is irreplaceable. But if you have a black-and-white workprint made (at a cost of $0.05–$0.06 a foot) from the original, you need not handle it until the time comes to *conform* it to the edited workprint.

After the workprint is made, matching numbers, called *edge numbers,* are applied at each foot interval both to the original and to the workprint. These numbers make locating scenes easy when conforming the original film to the edited workprint. Certain films, like 16-mm Ektachrome Commercial, include edge numbers which print through to the workprint film, thus eliminating the need for additional number printing.

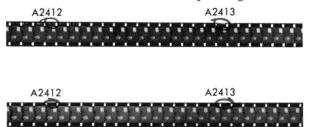

Then, if copies of the motion picture are to be ordered, it is customary for the film laboratory to prepare an *answer print* in which exposure corrections and optical effects (fades and dissolves) are included. Reduction printing of 16-mm film to 8-mm size may be done at this time also. Once an answer print is accepted, duplicate or release prints are made.

Film laboratories that prepare super-8 prints from 16-mm originals do this in one or both of the following ways:

☐ *Direct optical reduction of original 16-mm film to 8-mm print:* This method gives the sharpest

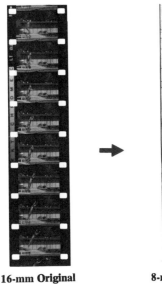

16-mm Original   **8-mm Print**

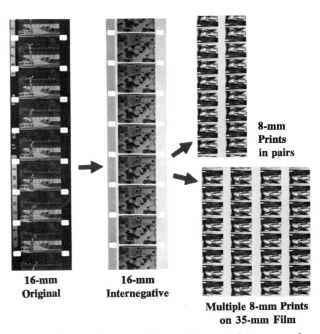

16-mm Original   **16-mm Internegative**

8-mm Prints in pairs

Multiple 8-mm Prints on 35-mm Film

print as nothing comes between the original and the final print. Costs are high, and the process is advisable only if a limited number of 8-mm prints is needed. There is always the possibility of damage to the original which is used to make every print.

☐ *Preparation of a 16-mm color internegative from the original 16-mm film and then optical reduction from internegative to 8-mm positive prints:* While this is a costly method for a few prints, the relative costs drop considerably as

numbers of prints above about eight are made. The quality is good, although there is some loss in sharpness as the final 8-mm print is now *two* generations (steps) away from the original. This method is commonly used for making super-8 prints, and in large-volume printing the internegative is optically reduced onto 35-mm positive film stock to make four side-by-side 8-mm prints.

Film Editing

The selection of visuals for the script, the choice of camera angles when filming, and finally the editing make up the main creative aspects of a motion-picture production. Film editing is the process of selecting, arranging, and shortening (cutting) scenes to remove superfluous footage so that the final result satisfies the objectives you established originally. Editing requires patience, some intuition, and talent. Also, it takes a lot of plain, hard work.

When all film has been returned from processing, editing starts. The script and the camera log sheet are essential guides for your editing. When editing you must do three things:

☐ Eliminate unusable film—bad exposures, blurred or out-of-focus shots, light flares, blank film, incomplete takes, poor action.
☐ Organize scenes in order of the script.
☐ Rearrange and cut scenes for the best continuity.

Tools and equipment for editing include:

A projector
A viewer
A pair of rewinds
Spare reels
A pair of scissors
A grease pencil
A scene-filing box

A splicer (tape or cement)
Film cement and a scraper, or tape splices
A pair of cotton gloves

Always do your editing on a clean table and keep the area neat. This requirement is especially important if you edit *original* film (the film from the camera). Be sure the film channel of the viewer and the film gate of the projector are kept clean. If possible, wear a pair of thin cotton gloves to help protect the film from collecting dirt.

The stages of editing, as described are:

1. String-out
2. Rough cut
3. Fine cut

FIRST EDITING STAGE—STRING-OUT

Using the viewer, cut all scenes apart. Roll each one separately, identifying it with a piece of masking tape marked with the scene (and take) number. A small reel, from which one side has been removed, makes scene-rolling easy.

During this process eliminate all unusable footage and slate marks. Splice all scenes (and multiple takes of scenes) together in proper order. The entire film should now be on one reel. In a *carefully cleaned* projector, view the footage, making notes which will help you to select the best takes and roughly indicating where to cut scenes for best action.

For studying details of scene content and specific movement, use a viewer; but for timing action and observing continuity, project the film at normal speed.

SECOND EDITING STAGE—ROUGH CUT

Return to the rewinds and the viewer. Eliminate all but the best take for each scene. Mark the points for cutting on the film base with a grease pencil. Then start removing unnecessary footage from the beginnings and ends of scenes. *Be careful not to shorten scenes too much as this stage.* Keep in mind all film techniques—LS–MS–CU relationships, establishing scenes, the use of cut-ins and cut-aways, screen direction, matching action, transitions, and the like.

As you accumulate *out-takes* (good footage, but not to be used in the film), roll and mark them with scene numbers just in case you have need for them later.

As the film takes definite form, review the script and particularly the narration. Revise it as necessary, keeping in mind the suggestions for writing narration on page 63. Then read narration as the film is projected at proper speed. You will find that about four words cover 1 foot of 16-mm film at sound speed. Observe the continuity. If scenes do not fit, rearrange them. If necessary, plan further filming to replace inappropriate scenes or to fill previously unrealized needs.

With the editing nearing completion, it may be advisable to show the film and to read the narration to other interested and qualified persons or to a potential audience group. See the suggestions on page 65 for developing a questionnaire to gather reactions that may help you to improve your film.

FINAL EDITING STAGE—FINE CUT

Working with both the film and the narration, gradually refine the two until they match and flow smoothly. This requires shortening scenes, splicing at matched-action frames between related scenes, and polishing the narration by eliminating words and by rephrasing. This final editing stage is a slow one that requires projection and reading, checking for pacing, marking the film places to cut, rechecking on the viewer, cutting and splicing, and then projecting again. But once completed, your efforts will result in a smoothly flowing film in which narration is closely correlated with the picture—a key element in successful sound motion-picture production.

EDITING UNSCRIPTED FILMS

Possibly all or part of your film was shot using a newsreel or documentary approach—with little preplanning or script preparation (see page 246 for a discussion of this method). If so, editing follows the same procedure outlined here, but requires a pre-editing step.

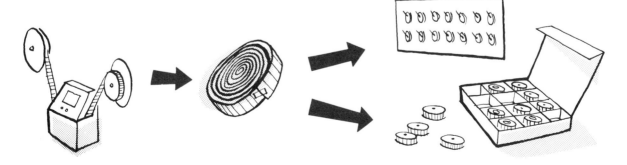

As you examine the footage for the first time (using a film viewer), write a brief description of each scene (type of shot, content, special remarks as to quality or action, and other information) on a separate, numbered 3×5 inch card. Then cut apart each scene, roll it, tape it, and give it the same number as the corresponding card. Now study the cards and rearrange them into a script. String together the scenes according to the order of the cards and proceed with the editing procedure as already explained.

SUGGESTIONS WHEN EDITING

- ☐ Avoid interruptions; try to complete a whole sequence during one work period.
- ☐ Keep your audience in mind, anticipating its lack of familiarity with the subject and the need for continuity of action, which you might overlook as a consequence of your own knowledge of the subject.
- ☐ Do not let your personal familiarity with a scene or action lead you to cut it too short.
- ☐ Avoid joining scenes where wide variations of exposure or color exist.

SPLICING FILM

You may have occasion to splice film at almost any time during the course of editing. While splicing is not a complicated procedure, attention to detail and care in handling your film are essential. Damage can result to film from incorrect or poorly made splices.

There are two methods for splicing motion-picture film: with transparent adhesive-backed tape, or with film cement. Either method produces satisfactory results. With the tape splice, the ends of the two pieces of film to be joined are *butted* together (hence, termed a butt splice) in a tape splicer. There are no lost frames. A cement splice requires the *overlap* of film and at least one frame is removed.

This is the procedure for tape splicing:

1. Align the cut ends of the film on the pins in the splicing unit.
2. Trim the ends so they match exactly. Use the cutter blade in the top of the splicer.
3. Place a piece of splicing tape over the pins and the joined ends of the film. Pull off the protective paper on one side.
4. Pull off the protective paper on the other side.
5. Rub the tape to insure good adherence.
6. Flip the film over and reset on the pins.
7. Repeat steps 3 and 4 with another piece of splicing tape.
8. Again rub the tape to insure good adherence.
9. Examine the finished splice.

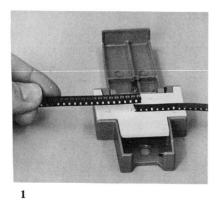

1

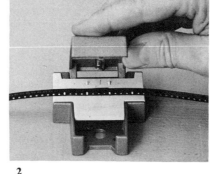

2

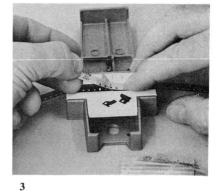

3

4

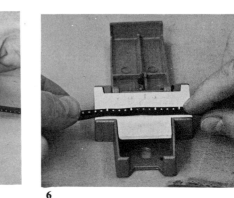

5

6

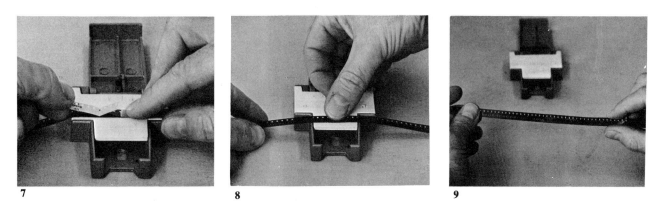

7   8   9

The second method for splicing motion-picture film uses film cement. The film cement is a fast drying solvent, capable of fusing the film base (cellulose acetate) of each end of film to the other. This is an *overlap* splice. To permit this, it is first necessary to remove the photographic emulsion that covers the base so the two pieces of film have base-to-base contact.

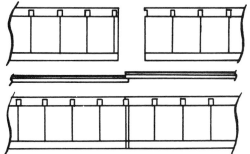

Cement Splicing. The Overlapping Area is One Frame Line

These items are necessary when splicing with cement—cotton gloves, a splicer, a scraper (here an emery board), a bottle of film cement.

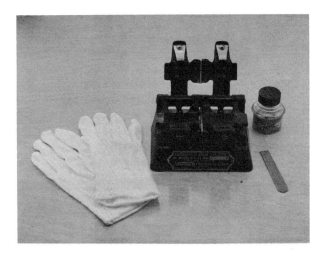

1. Set one piece of film on the sprocket pins at the right side of the splicer with the emulsion (dull) side up.
2. Lower the cutter bar and trim the film evenly. Then put the right section of the splicer up out of the way, with the film still in place.
3. Set the second piece of film, emulsion up, in the left side of the splicer.
4. Lower and secure the left upper section to hold the film in place.

5. Scrape the emulsion from the edge of the film exposed on the left. Work carefully but remove *all* the emulsion, down to the clear film base.
6. Remove any deposits from the scraped film.
7. Apply a small amount of film cement to the exposed film base.
8. Quickly lower the right upper section and secure the clamp.
9. After 20 seconds raise both upper sections and remove the spliced film carefully.

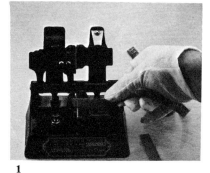
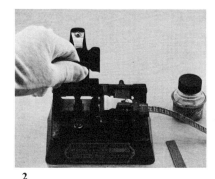
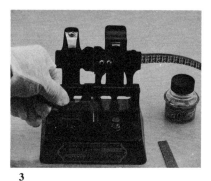

1   2   3

4   5   6

7   8   9

By following this procedure you should be able to make consistently good splices. If your splices do not hold, the reason may be one or more of several:

☐ Using old, thick film cement, probably caused because the cement bottle was left open and the solvent evaporated
☐ Not removing all the emulsion when scraping
☐ Excessive scraping that weakens the film base
☐ Getting oil from your hands on the film by excess handling (wear lint-free gloves)
☐ Delaying to bring the film ends together immediately after the cement is applied
☐ Removing spliced film from the splicer before the cement has set (minimum 15–20 seconds)
☐ Using a dirty splicer, caked with dried cement and scraps of film
☐ Poor adjustment of the splicer—faulty alignment of the sprocket pins or of the clamp, which puts pressure on the splice

PREPARING THE FILM FOR THE LABORATORY

If a workprint has been made from the original 16-mm footage for editing purposes, the original must be matched (conformed) to the workprint before laboratory services can be requested. To *conform* means to put in proper order the original footage that matches the footage in the workprint. This is accomplished by matching up the *edge numbers* printed on the original to the edge numbers of the workprint footage. Upon comple-

tion the original footage will exactly match the edited workprint.

Many times it is necessary to put the conformed original footage into *A and B rolls* for the laboratory. This is generally done when optical effects (fades or dissolves), overprint titles and labels, or other special laboratory services will be requested. This method is also used to avoid having any splice marks appear in the resulting prints. Alternate scenes are placed in the same roll. Thus scenes 1, 3, 5, 7, . . . become roll A, and scenes 2, 4, 6, 8, . . . are roll B. Adjacent scenes in the same roll are separated by lengths of black leader. The amount of leader used is determined by the length of the scene at the same place in the other roll. Only when scenes require double exposure (dissolves or overprint titles, for example) is black leader not used. The final A and B rolls will be of exactly the same length. The film laboratory will print each roll on the same film stock to make a negative or print.

The film laboratory prints each roll on the *same* length of film. First roll A and then roll B. Thus a *composite* print is made from the two rolls. All special effects—opticals, overprint titles, and so forth, appear in correct location on this composite print. It may then become a printing master for making further copies. A few film laboratories provide this service from super-8 original footage.

There are procedures to mark A and B rolls correctly for the laboratory. Check with the one that will serve you.

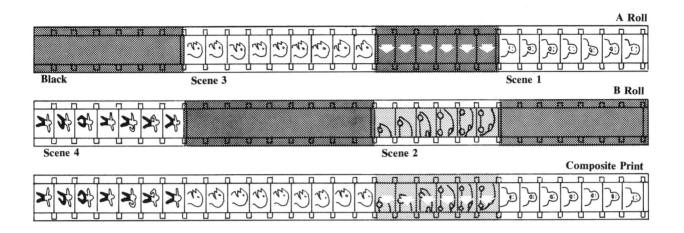

Adding Sound

When editing is completed, titles are in place, and the narration is in final form, you are ready to put sound on the film. There are various ways of correlating sound with picture. See Chapter 17 for recording procedures.

LIVE COMMENTARY

If proper equipment is not available for putting sound on the film, you can plan to read the narration as the film is projected. To be most effective, use a public-address system to give depth to your voice (talking into a microphone attached to the amplifier of the projector will feed your voice through the speaker). Sound effects and background music may be added on cue from disk recordings or from tape.

The shortcomings of this live-commentary method are obvious—the need for close coordination and timing by the narrator and by those operating the equipment; the involvement of a number of persons in addition to the projectionist; and the need to set up extra equipment every time the film is shown. But this method is suitable for limited uses of your film.

WITH A TAPE RECORDER

One of the simplest ways of adding sound to a film is to use a tape recorder. Record the narration as the edited film is projected, and add music to make it fit the narration. Thereafter, play the recording as the film is projected before audiences. Unfortunately, the sound may not stay in synchronization with the picture because of difficulty in starting both projector and recorder at the same instant, possible variations in the motor speed controlling the tape movement, or tape stretch.

Do not attempt to include lip synchronization or other sync-sound without having equipment designed for this purpose. Control units have been made which connect a recorder directly to the projector, thus guaranteeing their operation at the same speed and in fairly good synchronization.

MAGNETIC SOUND

It is better to use a magnetic sound projector, which includes a recorder. Using this equipment gives you the flexibility of synchronized sound recording (on a magnetic stripe that is on the film itself), immediate playback, erasing and re-recording as necessary. Models in both 8 mm and 16 mm are available.

Eastman Magnetic-Sound Recorder and Playback Projector

After editing is completed, send the film to a film laboratory for magnetic or *sound-striping* at $0.03–0.06 per foot. It will be returned ready for the addition of sound.

Record at the same speed as the film was taken (unless special effects were used). Normal sound speed, 24 fps, gives better sound quality than 18 fps. The latter is suitable if only voice is to be recorded. Refer to page 153 for suggestions

Magnetic Sound Track

concerning the selection and duties of recording personnel, recording facilities, the recording procedure, mixing music with sound, and so on.

On an original film that will be used with a magnetic sound projector, the splices should be made so that the *butt* is *toward* the tail of the film. In this way the magnetic head will drop off the splice, rather than run into it and cause a *click* sound.

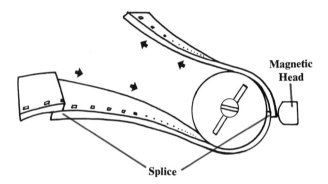

Magnetic Head

Splice

Splices may break at any time. Therefore, consider having at least one print made from the original film. A sound-striped print will insure a better-quality recording, and by having it you are protected since you can store the original film in a safe, dry, and cool place. If a number of prints are needed, the magnetic sound track can be converted to *optical sound* on additional prints and then used with a sound motion-picture projector.

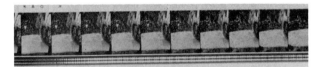

Optical Sound Track

SYNCHRONIZED SOUND

There may be times when it is desirable to record the speech of those appearing in the film (as during interviews, discussions, or dramatic sequences). To do this requires a *sound-on-film* motion-picture camera (which records the sound magnetically or optically on the film in the camera as it is being shot). Or, instead, separate mag-

netic recording equipment that can be synchronized with the camera can be used.

The term "lip-sync" is used when visible lip movements exactly coincide with the sound heard. Synchronous sound recording is complex and should only be attempted if suitable equipment is available.

For the super-8 format, equipment is available in both categories. At least one company (Eastman Kodak) has a sound-on-film camera (*single-system* sound) which uses magnetic-striped film for synchronous sound and picture recording. Because the sound is usually 18 frames ahead of its correlated picture, this film cannot be edited without removing sound for another picture area. Other manufacturers make combination units (*double-system* sound) in which a tape recorder attaches to the camera. Sound and picture are recorded at the same time on the separate units. The sound is played-back on the tape recorder, which is now plugged into a compatible super-8 projector. The tape recorder advances or slows down the projector's speed so as to maintain synchronization. Editing of these two separate pieces can be done, but care must be taken since it is easy to lose synchronization if the relation of film to tape is changed at any point.

In 16-mm production the procedure for recording lip synchronization is an ambitious undertaking, requiring specialized equipment. Also, editing becomes more complex because both sound and picture must be handled simultaneously, and additional, expensive editing equipment (like a *Moviola*) is required. A Moviola permits viewing and playing separate reels of picture and sound for editing purposes. For further information about preparing and editing films requiring lip synchronization, see the references on page 298.

Moviola for Editing Sound Film

Summary of Motion-Picture Production Steps

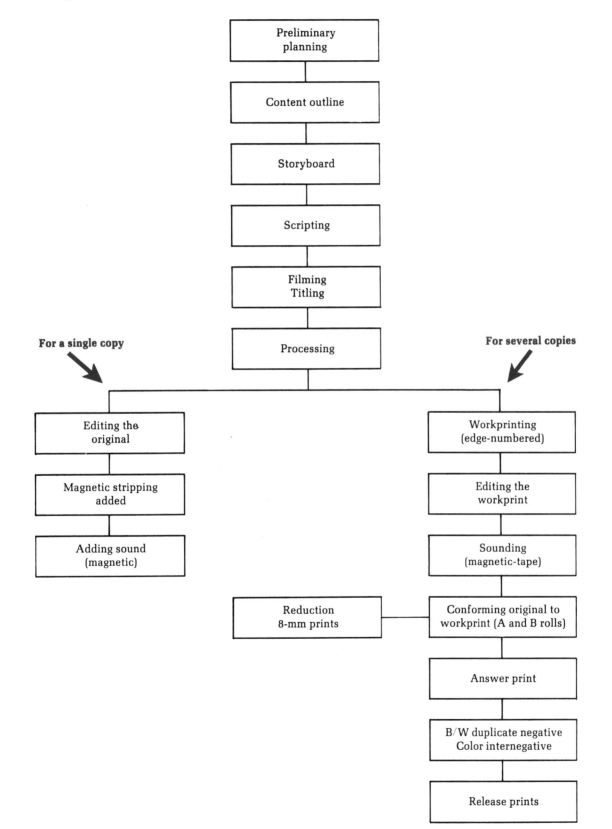

Now, Apply What You Have Learned About Other Production Considerations, Film Laboratory Services, Film Editing, and Adding Sound to Film:

1. What are some factors in film production to keep in mind as you plan and prepare an 8-mm silent film? Which of these directly relates to the findings of research?
2. What are advantages of slating scenes when filming?
3. What is the advantage of having a *workprint* made?
4. To which process is the term *edge number* related—printing, editing, conforming, splicing?
5. Which laboratory process for making 8-mm prints from 16-mm original footage results in the best quality? What are its drawbacks?
6. Which type of film splicing do you use or prefer to use? What are its advantages or disadvantages?
7. Explain these terms—*string-out, rough cut,* and *fine cut.*
8. How does the process of editing an *unscripted* film differ from that of editing a film *in the camera?*
9. What method of adding sound to film would you most likely use? What are its procedures?

Note: Answers to review questions can be found at the end of the chapter.

Preparing to Use Your Film

With the completion of the film and of your preparations for using it, consider the advisability of developing an instruction guide as described on page 70.

Selection of the projector for showing your film is an important element in successful use. Sixteen-mm sound projectors are standardized so that an optical sound film can be shown on any model. Magnetic-striped 16-mm films are generally shown with the same projector on which the sound was recorded.

In the super-8 format, the matter of projector selection is somewhat more complex. At present there are these types:

☐ Silent film, reel-to-reel (meaning that film moves through the projector from *feed reel* to take-up reel)
☐ Silent film, cartridge or cassette load
☐ Magnetic sound film, reel-to-reel or cassette load
☐ Optical sound film, cartridge load

Examine the various kinds of projectors available for your use. Then choose the one that will best serve your needs and those of the users. Take into consideration these factors:

☐ Requirements for film packaging (cassette—enclosed container with film movement from one roll to another, cartridge—enclosed container with endless loop of film, or reel-to-reel)
☐ Ease of operation by individual learners
☐ Simplicity of threading or placing the self-contained film package on the projector
☐ Features the viewer may find useful (stop-action, reverse, fast rewind controls)

Remember that the success of your motion picture will depend not only on its content and on the quality of your production, but also on the manner in which you introduce and project it for the audience. As you prepare for the first showing, follow the suggestions on page 73.

Answers to Review Questions

MOTION-PICTURE FORMATS, CAMERAS, LENSES, AND FILM (PAGE 233)

1. Regular 10–30-minute films treat many phases of a topic while the shorter concept films illustrate discrete, limited parts of topics; concept films may employ simpler filming techniques and be part of an instructional package.

2. Exact 16-mm format proportions, larger picture area, greater area for sound track, better-quality laboratory services, higher-quality projected images.

3. 16-mm, Ektachrome Commercial film.

4. Lens, viewfinders, speed selector, winding handle or batteries, release button.

5. Reader's activity, page 228.

6. Reader's activity, page 227.

7. Reader's activity, page 228.

8. See page 229.

9. Reader's activity, page 229.

10. Flexibility in selecting fields of view from various camera positions; different lenses give different perspective effects.

11. More.

12. Use f/8; more.

13. To view a scene before filming it; to produce the film already edited and ready for film laboratory services.

CAMERA SHOTS (PAGE 240)

1. Motion; time.

2. Terms *scene* and *shot* have same meaning, namely, the action represented by the exposure of a length of film; *take* refers to a number assigned each time the same scene is filmed; *sequence* is a series of scenes all related to the same idea or concept.

3. (a) Low angle, (b) high angle, (c) subjective, (d) objective.

4. (a) Tilt, (b) zoom, (c) pan, (d) pan, (e) dolly.

5. A scene that orients the viewer to the subject after a number of close-up scenes.

6. Jarring effect of shooting adjacent scenes when the camera is moved directly in or directly back from the subject; change camera-subject angle or vertical camera position at least slightly between adjacent scenes.

7. (a) MS, (b) XCU, (c) LS, (d) LS, (e) CU high angle, (f) CU, (g) MCU low angle, (h) MS low angle.
Sequence: c-a-g-b-h-e-f-d (your sequence may vary and still be acceptable to an audience).

PROVIDING CONTINUITY (PAGE 245)

1. Carefully relating the action at the end of one scene with that at the start of the next scene.

2. To keep the audience properly oriented.

3. Show direction of movement changing or a head-on shot directly toward the camera; cut-away to related action or an observer.

4. Close-up of her face; spool with thread coming off; or other scene you may think of.

5. (a) Hour hand of clock moving or title "Allow paint to dry"; (b) few seconds of closed house door, traffic on street; (c) fade-out/ fade-in.

6. As bridges for time and space.

7. Reader's activity, page 245.

SPECIAL FILMING TECHNIQUES (PAGE 250)

1. What you have just shot and what you anticipate to shoot next.

2. Shooting many cut-aways and cut-ins as protection to bridge scenes that may not match during editing.

3. To shoot scenes in exact order may take extra time and even travel; all action must be carefully rehearsed so it is correct the first time; all exposure and other technical matters also must be correct for onetime shooting.

4. Change fps to 32 or even 48; compensate for less light reaching the film by using a larger lens aperture opening (smaller f/ number).
5. Single-frame control.
6. 1 frame per minute for the six hours.
7. A film consisting of copy work from still pictures shot using the single-frame technique.
8. Reader's activity, page 248.

OTHER PRODUCTION CONSIDERATIONS, FILM LABORATORY SERVICES, FILM EDITING, AND EDITING SOUND (PAGE 263)

1. See page 251.
2. For ease of identifying scenes when editing.
3. Using the workprint protects the original film from handling, scratches, and dirt during editing.
4. Conforming.
5. *Direct reduction:* more costly and original film could be damaged since it is always used to make prints.
6. Reader's activity, page 256.
   Tape method: splice holds very well; some finger dexterity needed in splicing 8-mm film, splice can be troublesome in some projectors. *Cement method:* splice may come apart, splice line often visible when projected, splice can hang-up in some projectors; less costly to make.
7. *String-out:* putting all scenes filmed in proper order. *Rough cut:* shortening scenes to approximate length and eliminating multiple takes and unnecessary scenes. *Fine cut:* tightly editing the film into final form.
8. Unscripted film will have many more scenes than needed, some not usable; scene length will vary greatly, and many decisions about the character of the film will be determined during editing. Film edited in the camera will be very close to final form when filming is completed.
9. Reader's activity, page 259.

24
TELEVISION AND DISPLAY MATERIALS

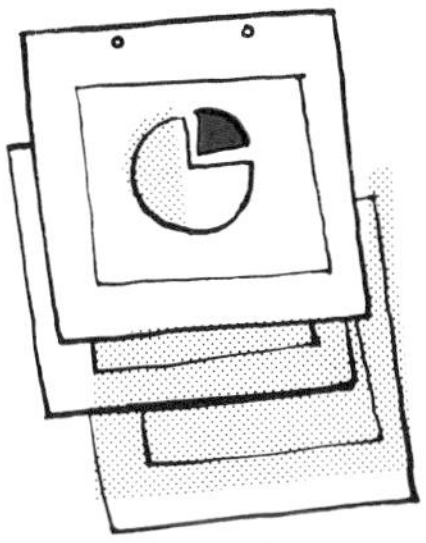

Graphics

Photographs

Transparencies

Slides

Motion Pictures

Displays

Visual materials for television and display may include graphics, photographs, slides, transparencies, motion pictures, and items on felt, hook-and-loop, and magnetic boards.

The use of numerous visuals does not in itself guarantee effective television programing. The principles of perception, learning, and communications theory, as well as research results, all discussed in Chapters 2 and 3, apply to the planning of television programs and videotaped segments for instruction. Review these matters as you plan for television and select materials for visualizations.

There is an increasing dependence on smaller, easy-to-operate television production and playback equipment, including cameras, videotape reel-to-reel and cassette recorders, and supplementary items for studio, classroom, or field uses. For many instructional needs via television, simple, quickly prepared visuals may be needed and are preferred to more elaborate commercial-type materials. The basic methods described in this book for making visual materials apply when preparing them for television use. In addition, keep in mind the special requirements of the television medium as you plan and prepare them.

Special Requirements for Television

FORMAT AND PROPORTIONS

The television format is 3 units high by 4 units wide. Therefore, whenever possible, arrange subjects with this orientation. Use proportions relating to this ratio (6 to 8, 9 to 12, . . .) when preparing graphic materials and plan photographic materials to fit the ratio closely.

Carefully consider content within the format size. Provide for loss of ⅙ the marginal area *on each side,* and keep important parts of the visual within the middle ⅔ portion. This restriction is necessary because of variations in the adjustment of television receivers.

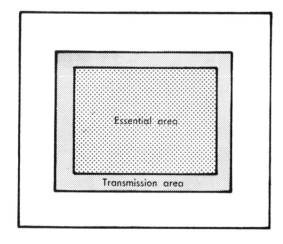

DETAIL AND SIZE

In general, it is preferable to use several diagrams, graphs, or charts rather than to put a great amount of information on a single visual. Graphic materials printed in books and other publications are designed for careful and lengthy study. Consequently they carry considerable amounts of information. As opposed to this, visuals used in television should never be kept on camera an

undue length of time. For this reason, as well as for legibility, each visual should be designed to convey a relatively limited amount of information. See page 199 for an example of how complex information can be handled for an overhead transparency. The same procedure applies to materials for television.

Another important feature of television is its use of the *close-up*—being able to center attention on the object or visual and bring it, greatly magnified, to the viewer. Therefore:

☐ Keep materials simple, bold, and free from unnecessary detail.
☐ Use suitable, clear-cut lettering.
☐ Adhere to recognized legibility stands for ease of reading—minimum letter size af 1/25 the height of the area (page 122).
☐ Limit outlines and other lists to four or five lines, each containing no more than three to five words.

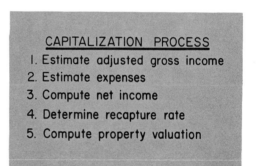

CONTRAST AND COLORS

Colored materials that are put before the television camera appear on the black-and-white television receiver screen as shades of gray. Thus a green line on a red background may disappear because the green and the red are equivalent to the same shade of gray, that is, have the same gray value.

The range of shades of gray reproduced by black-and-white television is limited. Only five or six shades can be clearly recognized. Avoid black symbols or drawings on white background or any materials with such extreme contrast (unless for special purposes). Lower contrast, as between shades of gray and black, is preferable.

Check the gray value of colors to be used for preparing visuals by holding *these* colors before the television camera. Only by this method can you make sure what effect they will exhibit in

BLACK					WHITE
brown	red		light blue	light gray	
dark green	medium blue		orange	tan	
dark blue	medium green			pastels	

use. The same color, on two different surfaces or under two different lighting conditions, may be picked up as different shades of gray; contrasting colors may match and fail to contrast when television has grayed them. For rough planning *only*, you may assume that colors will group themselves as shades of gray according to the lists shown in the diagram.

When producing for color television give special attention to the *color temperature* of light sources so that flesh tones and objects in a scene will appear with proper tonal gradations. Color temperature is measured in degrees Kelvin. A photoflood lamp rates 3400°K (toward red end of visible spectrum), while sunlight is about 6000°K (blue end of spectrum). Also, do not consider color relationships only for their importance in color transmission, but for their viewing on black-and-white receivers, as described above, as well.

Preparing Materials

Before making any visuals, always consider this planning checklist:

☐ Has careful planning for the program taken place (Chapters 4–14)?

☐ Have the visuals been developed as an integral part of the planning?

☐ Are the selected visuals the most suitable ones in terms of—

—The objectives of the program?

—The ideas to be communicated?

—The most effective visual medium to use?

—The time and expense for preparation?

The inevitable problem with television production work is *time*—generally not enough time for careful and detailed preparation of materials. Therefore, select and develop techniques that not only will help you to prepare your visuals rapidly, but also will result in attractive and effective instructional materials.

GRAPHIC MATERIALS

Charts, diagrams, outlines, summaries, and titles can be presented "on the set" (that is, displayed before the television camera directly) so that the television instructor himself, or an assistant, can indicate features of the visual and control the rate of use.

1. Prepare a rough pencil sketch of the visual and show layout and proportions for all elements (8½×11 inch paper will approximate the 3 to 4 ratio).

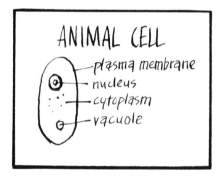

2. Select a convenient size of cardboard for working and for storage. Use fourteen-ply television illustration board or a dull-finish gray board ("middle gray"). Stay within a 9×12 inch working area on 14×17 inch cardboard, or 6×8 inch area on 11×14 inch board to insure plenty of bleed space.

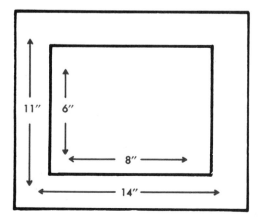

3. Select suitable lettering aids (page 123) and practice the necessary lettering. Note the suggestions for preparing lettering on page 120. Apply recommended legibility standards for lettered materials (page 122).

4. Sketch the visual on cardboard, using a simple illustrative technique (page 116). Then locate the areas for lettering.

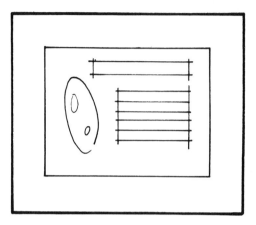

5. Do the lettering, then complete the diagram with pen and ink, felt pen, crayon, or gray pencils. Erase all guide lines. (Retouch colors that match cardboard colors, for correcting mistakes, are available from art-supply stores.)

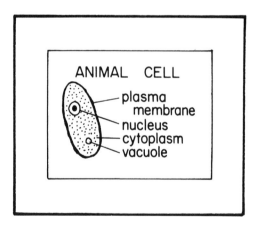

PHOTOGRAPHS

Enlargements from camera negatives have the same "on-the-set" uses as graphic materials.

1. Record activities on film (page 166) or photographically copy materials (page 99). If captions and labels on materials are too small, block them out if they are unnecessary, or re-letter them on slips of paper and lay the slips in place before photographing. *Remember,*

written permission is necessary for using copyrighted materials on television (see the release form on page 61). Then develop the film.

2. Print the negative, being sure that the important parts of the picture are kept within the selected working area (for the 9×12 inch area use 11×14 inch enlarging papers; for 6×8 inch use 8×10 inch paper). The printing paper should be of *matte type* (an "A" or "C" surface is acceptable) to avoid light reflections during use on the set. Maintain a low contrast level in photographs by avoiding deep shadow areas or brilliant white areas. When printing negatives that will produce large white areas, "flash" the paper before use to gray the white areas (exposure to the darkroom white light for 1–4 seconds is satisfactory).

3. Mount photographs on fourteen-ply gray cardboard backing using the dry mount method (page 135).

2×2 INCH SLIDES

Size 2×2 inch slides are inexpensive visuals for television. They are usually shown from a remotely controlled projector directly into a preset television camera, thus requiring no on-the-set handling. Slides can also be projected from behind and onto a translucent screen, as part of the set. This method permits the instructor to control the slide projector himself, and to indicate features directly on the projected image.

Make slides as records of activities, as copies of printed materials, and for titles. For slide-making techniques, see page 171.

Keep the following points in mind as you plan, prepare, and select slides for use on television:

☐ The projected area must conform to the

OVERHEAD TRANSPARENCIES

There are many worthwhile television uses for overhead transparencies. They can be placed over a light box to be viewed by an overhead television camera, or projected onto a rear screen for regular camera pick-up. (The rear-screen method for displaying visuals is described on page 272.) The feature of a large, bright image, of being able to write on the transparency as it is projected, and the techniques of progressive disclosure, adding overlays to a base transparency, and simulating motion, all merit consideration (page 197).

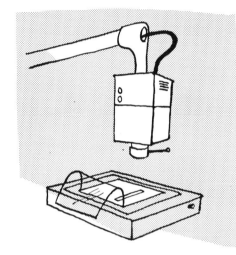

The preparation of transparencies outlined in Chapter 22 can be applied to materials for television. Photographic high-contrast transparencies (page 215) with clear white areas and sharp black lines and letters are most suitable. Continuous-tone black-and-white transparencies (page 216), when projected, serve as suitable backgrounds for studio sets as well as for illustrations of subject matter.

wider-than-high television format, 3 units high by 4 units wide.

☐ The slide image must provide for loss at the sides and top in consequence of two conditions: first, the difference in proportion between the television 3 to 4 format and the slide 2 to 3 format cuts off some of the image at the sides; second, ⅙ of the television camera's image may be lost at top, bottom, and each side of the receiver image, as was explained on page 266.

☐ Many slides will have been made in color. Remember the gray-scale limitations on televising color.

☐ A slightly overcast day for outdoor filming and a low contrast ratio for indoor filming are preferable.

☐ For fast preparation of black-and-white slides use Polaroid transparency film or direct-positive film (page 189).

☐ For superimposing titles use 35-mm high-contrast film to prepare negative title slides (page 174).

☐ For adding labels when copying printed materials, see suggestions on page 268.

☐ If desirable, when slides are completed, mount them between glass and then number them according to the program script (page 178).

☐ If comments are to accompany a series of slides, tape record the instructor's narration to insure consistency and pacing.

FILMSTRIPS

Only rarely are filmstrips prepared for television use. Projectors which handle filmstrips are not normally a part of television equipment. It is more common to prepare slides, or to cut frames from a filmstrip (page 177), and mount them as slides for handling in a remotely controlled projector.

MOTION PICTURES

Motion pictures are especially compatible with television. The mechanical equipment is adapted to handle the film, and the picture-story techniques of motion pictures and television are much alike. Complete films or short film subjects (*film clips*) may bring to the audience personalities otherwise unavailable and also activities, examples, and processes, either too varied, too complex, or too distant, to telecast from the studio.

Film projection, like slide projection, is remotely controlled, generally by the program director.

☐ Keep in mind the special requirements of television—low picture contrast, the ⅙ marginal loss of picture area when projected, and the value of close-up scenes.

☐ Keep long shots to a minimum because of the small size of the television screen as related to a motion-picture screen and the inability of television to resolve a great amount of detail.

☐ Use 16-mm film at normal sound speed of 24 fps. (Some educational television stations are adapting equipment for using super-8 mm film as part of the film chain.)

☐ Apply the basic production techniques that start on page 234.

☐ Consider using *multiple cameras* for speed in shooting film materials (page 241).

☐ Add sound to film through the use of magnetic striping (page 259), or more commonly, let the television instructor narrate the film as it is projected. Synchronous sound may be recorded when filming if proper equipment and experienced personnel are available.

Videotape Recording

In the last few years the cost and complexity of videotape recorders have been reduced appreciably. Such equipment is now within the price reach of all school television facilities. Therefore instructional modules, selected portions, or complete television presentations can be recorded on videotape and played back at any convenient time.

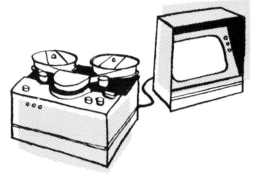

Electronic editing equipment permits flexibility in program development. As with motion pictures, materials on two or more videotapes can be combined or sections eliminated. Using this editing procedure, visuals can be recorded separately from the main action and then edited into the tape at a later time.

The usual requirements of television, as noted in this section, apply when materials are to be recorded on videotape. Also, a common practice is to convert the original videotape recording to 16-mm motion picture film for continual use and distribution. As indicated on page 232, in motion-picture production, a videotape recording may be used to preview the action before actual filming takes place. See the list on page 308 for laboratories that can convert videotape recordings to film.

Displaying Materials

The way in which visuals are used in a television program controls some aspect of their preparation. The controlling qualities involve answers to questions like these:

☐ Is it necessary for the instructor to handle the materials?

☐ How can the use of the visuals best be coordinated, paced, and given variety?

☐ Will it be best to develop an idea sequentially or can the whole visual be shown at one time?

These questions must be in mind as the planning and preparation of the visuals take place. To make the decisions, you need to become familiar with the methods commonly used for displaying materials.

For a long time teachers have used felt and flannel boards to display materials that present information and develop concepts. Recent developments, such as magnetic and other surfaces,

extend the effectiveness of such display boards by providing increased flexibility. Whether these display surfaces are to be used in a classroom or in a television studio, the following information is basic.

DISPLAY EASELS

A set of visuals may be placed on a table easel or floor stand, and their use controlled by the instructor or an assistant, in the studio or in the classroom.

FLANNEL (FELT) BOARDS

This display surface frequently is used to develop concepts or processes by the progressive addition of prepared parts. The board itself is made of plywood, masonite, or wallboard covered with high-grade flannel or felt. It is set on an easel for use. Pastel or light colors are advisable for the

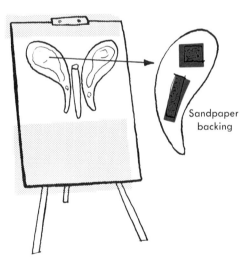

Sandpaper backing

cloth covering. Prepare lettered materials and diagrams in black ink on gray cardboard (unless different colors are important to register shades for separation). Back the cardboard with strips of felt or sandpaper. This textured or rough backing will adhere to the flannel or felt surface.

HOOK-AND-LOOP BOARDS

A new type of presentation board, the *hook-and-loop board,* safeguards against the possible slippage of flannel-covered surfaces. The surface material consists of a cloth containing countless tiny nylon loops, while display materials are backed with small strips of tape having numerous nylon hooks.

Commercial hook-and-loop boards are avail-

able from school supply companies and manufacturers of display materials. See sources on page 305. If you prefer to prepare your own hook-and-loop board, you can purchase the nylon loop material as yardage from major distributors of fabrics. The material should be adhered to plywood or other stiff backing with contact cement or white glue.

Also, use a strong adhesive, such as white glue or an epoxy cement, to attach the tape to the back of objects. In use, the nylon loops intertwine with the nylon hooks, joining the two surfaces securely. The strength of this union is sufficient to hold not only paper and cardboard objects, but also heavy three-dimensional items.

MAGNETIC CHALKBOARDS

The magnetic chalkboard is even more flexibly useful and permits more versatility than the flannel board or the hook-and-loop board, since the television instructor can draw or write on the board in addition to positioning prepared materials. The magnetized materials hold their position and can be moved at will. The painted writing surface does not interfere with magnetic attraction.

Magnets

The magnetic board consists of sheet steel or fine-mesh steel screen covered by a writing surface. Small magnets are cemented or taped to the backs of objects or graphic materials. Magnets may be of metal or of magnetized rubber strips with adhesive backing.

Portable magnetic chalkboards are available commercially. Flexible metallic-surfaced materials can be obtained and are easily framed for use. Also, a home-made magnetic chalkboard can be made from a galvanized-steel oil drip pan sold in auto supply stores. To give the drip pan a chalkboard surface, vinegar and chalkboard spray paint (carried by major paint suppliers) are needed. Follow these instructions to prepare the chalk surface over the galvanized metal:

1. Pour some vinegar on the pan and, with a cloth, spread it over the surface for 15 minutes. This will clean and "cure" the galvanized surface.
2. Rinse off the vinegar with water.
3. After the surface is dry spray it with chalkboard paint. At least two coats are recommended. Sand the first coat lightly with extra fine sandpaper before applying the second coat.
4. Before use, thoroughly chalk the surface by working it over with the side of a large piece of soft chalk. This will insure smooth writing and easy erasure of chalk marks.

FILM CHAIN

Slides and motion pictures generally are handled on what is called the *film chain* of the television system. Each projector is aimed (or the projection beam is reflected) into a special television camera. Projection is controlled by the program

Slide Projection for Television

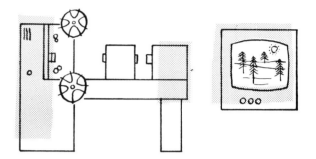

Motion-Picture Projection for Television

director or by his assistant according to the script, or by verbal instructions from the instructor.

REAR-SCREEN PROJECTION

Slides, transparencies for the overhead projector, and even filmstrips can be displayed from the rear onto a translucent screen. Such a screen is made from a sheet of high-quality tracing paper held between pieces of glass, or from commercial rear-screen material (source on page 306). Careful studio lighting is necessary in order to protect against reflections and dimming of the image on the screen. A television studio camera picks up the projected picture from the front side of the screen. Either of two methods may be used:

☐ Place the projector directly behind the screen (depending on the screen size and on the lens, a distance of 8–12 feet may be required). By using a remote-control accessory, the instructor himself may control slide changes, but an assistant must show overhead transparencies on cue. Slides and transparencies must either be projected backwards so they read correctly on the front of the screen; or the image must be reversed by attaching a 90° prism to the front of the projection lens, thus permitting the use of materials in their correct position.

In either case, the instructor stands beside the projected image, where the television camera can pick him up as he points to the projected picture or comments on it.

☐ Place the overhead projector beside the rear screen, where the television instructor can operate it, and project the image onto a mirror behind the screen and thus onto the rear of the screen. (For best reflection, a front-surface mirror should be used; a wide-angle projecting lens is necessary.) The instructor can point to features on the transparencies while facing the television camera. Slides can also be projected via a mirror in this fashion, but the instructor refers to the screen. The mirror method permits using a shallower studio.

Now, Apply What You Have Learned About Preparing Visual Materials for Television and Display:

1. What three categories of special requirements must be considered when planning materials for television?
2. On what bases do you decide whether materials should be used in the studio or via projection on the film or slide chain?
3. How might you adapt equipment in order to use overhead transparencies on television?
4. What are some advantages of hook-and-loop material over flannel or felt?
5. What is an advantage of the magnetic chalkboard over the other two display boards?
6. How might you proceed to prepare your own magnetic chalkboard?

Answers to Review Questions

1. Format and proportions; detail and size; and contrast and colors.
2. Does the instructor need to handle them? In what form may they be most available?
3. See page 269.
4. The ability to make materials adhere to the surface is more certain with hook-and-loop. Heavier materials can be displayed on hook-and-loop boards.
5. The chalkboard surface permits writing as well as displaying materials.
6. See page 272.

25
MULTI-IMAGE/MULTIMEDIA

Multi-image Presentation

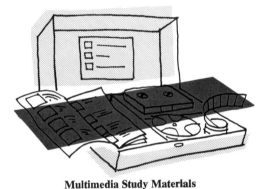

Multimedia Study Materials

The combined or coordinated use of audio-visual materials can take two forms. As used here, *multi-image* refers to the *simultaneous projection* of two or more pictures. Most often these are slides, but overhead transparencies or motion pictures may also be used in conjunction with slides. As used here, *multimedia* relates to the *sequential use* of a variety of instructional media, either for presentations to groups or for independent study by students. In planning and developing either multi-image or multimedia programs, attention should be given to a number of factors in addition to those you would normally consider when producing a single type of audio-visual material. These will be discussed under the two major headings that follow.

Multi-image Projection

In all conventionally projected visual forms—slide series, filmstrips, motion pictures, or television—the images are single and presented sequentially. The only exceptions are when split-screen or some other special technique is applied in order to present a simultaneous comparison or relationship. The sequential continuity of separate images conveys meanings to the viewer. When two or more images are viewed simultaneously, their immediate interaction can be more dynamic for the viewer, requiring him to grasp the meaning of the multiple images in one act of vision.

In a study of multi-image projection, Perrin concluded that "the immediacy of this kind of communication allows the viewer to process larger amounts of information in a very short time. Thus information density is effectively increased and certain kinds of information are more efficiently learned."[1]

Besides being a motivating, exciting experience for the viewer, this efficiency of communi-

1. Donald G. Perrin, "A Theory of Multi-Image Communication," *AV Communication Review* 17 (Winter 1969): 368–82.

cation should be a major reason for using the multi-image presentation technique. The variety inherent in such presentations can be designed for audiences of any size.

PURPOSES SERVED

There are many informational and instructional purposes that can be served by multi-image presentations. Among these are:

☐ Panoramic or wide view of a subject across two or more screens

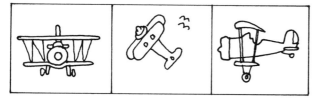

☐ Comparing or contrasting objects and events

☐ Showing a subject from different camera angles or distances

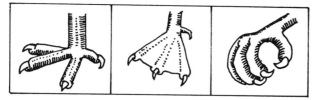

☐ Presenting sequential time segments relating to a single event

☐ Simulating motion of a still subject across multiple screens

☐ Giving meaning to an abstract idea with several supporting visuals

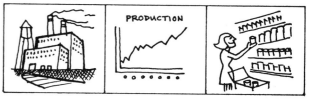

☐ Emphasizing a fact or concept by repeating identical images

☐ Illustrating relationships, such as parts to whole, form to function, model or diagram to actual object

☐ Developing concepts aesthetically, like growth, change, or interrelationships

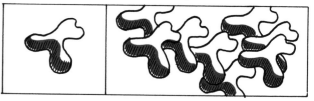

PLANNING

The same planning steps as for other audiovisual materials are not only important, but are essential for successful results when developing multi-image presentations.
Consider this checklist:

☐ Have you clearly expressed your *idea* and limited the topic (page 31)?
☐ Have you stated the *objectives* your multi-image presentation should serve (page 31)?
☐ Have you considered the *audience* which will see the presentation (page 33)?

☐ Have you prepared a *content outline* (page 38)?

☐ Have you written a *treatment* to help organize the content (page 52)?

☐ Have you decided that a multi-image presentation is a *valid method* for accomplishing the objectives (page 47)?

☐ Have you made a *storyboard* or prepared a *script* for the images on each screen, including accompanying sound (page 52)?

☐ Have you considered the *specifications* necessary for your presentation (page 57)?

☐ Have you, if necessary, selected *other people* to assist you with locating, preparing, and eventual use of materials and to help with other technical matters relating to multi-image presentation (page 36)?

Because of the complexity of using two or more screens and possibly multitrack sound, special attention should be given to preparing the storyboard or script. A form can be used that has separate columns for describing the images that will appear on each screen, columns for each sound element—narration, music, sound effects—and a column in which to specify the length of time for each component to be seen or heard. This form can also serve as a programming or cue sheet when readying the presentation for use.

VISUAL TECHNIQUES

A multi-image presentation is a complex production. Too often those planning such a program become fascinated with the gimmickry of using multiple screens, multiple-track sound, and sophistical control equipment. Visuals and sound may have little relationship or continuity. The message may be overpowered by the techniques and prove to be an uncoordinated collection of visual and audio misimpressions.

If this is your first experience with multi-images, start with only two screens. Apply many of the ideas presented in this chapter. Then with this background move to the three-screen level for suitable subjects.

The effectiveness of a multi-image presentation can better be assured by giving careful attention to these factors:

☐ Treat ideas and concepts one at a time. More than one message, either visually or verbally, divides the viewer's attention, and both messages may lose effectiveness.

☐ Use the screen purposefully to communicate your message by not projecting images on all screens at all times unless pertinent to the message.

Multi-image Script/Cue Sheet						
Visuals Number/Description			Time/Cueing (minutes/seconds)	Sound		
Left	Center	Right		Narration	Music	Effects

☐ Select relevant pictures that directly treat the subject being developed.

☐ Prepare or select pictures important to the subject without extraneous or distracting details.

☐ Think of pictures on two or more screens much like a multiple-page magazine layout consisting of a series of related images.

☐ Face people and objects on side screens inward toward the center screen if possible, unless a direction to simulate movement is necessary.

☐ Compose picture elements and organize picture relationships with greater care than for conventional presentations, taking into consideration that the center screen normally carries the major message and side screens show related pictures. Use this rule flexibly by purposefully changing the center of attention from one screen to another as the subject development may dictate or for reasons of variation.

☐ Juxtapose images at times in varying sizes and shapes; mixing different-format slides (horizontal and vertical) can provide visual variety.

☐ Allow a picture to remain on the screen long enough for the viewer to grasp its impression or comprehend it message, but not for so long as to bore him.

☐ Plan to vary the pace of image changes which can contribute to interest and hold the viewer's attention.

☐ Balance the appearance of simultaneously projected slides for aesthetic purposes by maintaining the same degree of brightness, contrast, and color intensity (unless a different contrast or other elements are part of the impression to be communicated).

☐ Prepare panoramic scenes across two or three screens by first securing the camera to a tripod, taking the two or three pictures of sections of the subject by turning the camera on the *axis of its lens,* and matching a vertical element along the edge of one shot with the same element in the adjacent slide.

☐ Use cut pieces of 2×2 inch cardboard as slides to block light to a screen when no image is to be projected from a projector; or for pleasant effect, use a solid color slide (for example, a piece of unexposed and fully developed color diazo film, as described on page 205, placed in a slide mount) instead of a cardboard blank.

☐ Select and arrange slides for a sequence by studying them while on a light box or light table (page 177), but ultimately judge their quality and relationships while being projected onto a screen.

☐ For the presentation, use sufficiently large screens, all of the same type (matte, lenticular, or beaded) so the images have visual impact for the audience and can contribute to physical and psychological factors relating to realism and personal involvement.

☐ Mark all slides with numbers and screen designations (L, C, R) according to the script or cue sheet. Then, when slides are placed in a tray, draw a felt pen line across the top edge, starting with slide number 1 and progressing diagonally to the last slide in a tray. If, at a later time, you notice a break in the line, one or more slides are either out of correct order, upside-down, or backwards.

☐ If the presentation extends beyond a single tray with any projector, plan to shift to the next tray when the screen is blank (an opaque slide being projected), or when the last slide in a full tray is in the projection position.

☐ When using slides, try to obtain similar model projectors and lenses so the brightness of images will be the same.

☐ Be sure to check yourself and any assistants on the operation of all equipment and rehearse the presentation before the first showing.

☐ Make certain to use good projection practice —set projectors 90° to the screen to avoid the keystone effect, align so images will be at the same height, and adjust images either as close as possible side-by-side without overlapping or with narrow well-defined space (like the black edge of the screens) between them.

☐ Consider combining slides with other visual forms, like overhead transparencies containing diagrams, or motion picture sequences, if effective for serving your objectives and communicating your message.

These are some of the many visual techniques that need consideration when planning a mutiimage presentation. During your own experiences while developing such programs, you will discover many more useful principles.

AUDIO TECHNIQUES

If the images are to be controlled manually by the projectionist during the presentation as he follows the script, then a monaural tape recorder or high-output cassette recorder can be used for recording the narration, music, and sound effects. See suggestions in Chapter 17 for recording techniques and how to mix the necessary sounds directly onto a single audio track.

A preferred method, which allows more flexibility when mixing sounds and is essential when

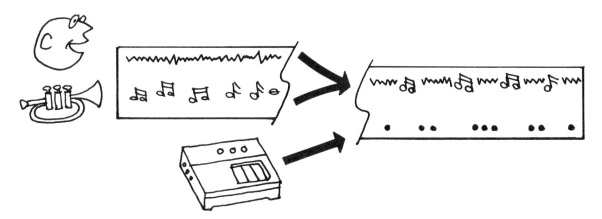

images are to be changed automatically, requires use of one or two *stereo* reel-to-reel or cassette tape recorders. Record the narration on the first track with one stereo recorder; then music and other sound effects, in proper relation to the narration, on the second track. If any errors are made while recording on the second.track the recording can be erased and a rerecording made without damage to the narration.

Then the two tracks can be mixed onto the first track of another stereo recorder by connecting the output of the playback stereo recorder to the input of the first track of the second recorder. The second track of the resulting tape remains blank for program cueing signals.

Be sure to select music, narration, and other sounds so they contribute to the coherence of the message and do not conflict with the visuals or communicate irrelevant information of their own. Refer to other suggestions regarding selecting a narrator and music in Chapter 17.

PROGRAMMING THE PRESENTATION

In a single-screen audiovisual presentation, verbal comments and audible or inaudible cue signals are used to pace the pictures correctly with the narration. Carefully programming all elements is of even greater importance in the complexities of a multi-image presentation.

The starting point for synchronizing pictures and sound is the storyboard or script sheet. Once it is finalized, it becomes the cue sheet for programming the presentation. There are several practical ways to do this. Here are some suggestions, from simple methods to those that require complex and costly equipment:

1. Control the image changes manually by pushing the control button for each projector according to the narration or music cues on the script.
2. While listening to the narration recorded on the first track of a stereo tape recorder, verbally record, at proper times, the slide changes onto the second track (call out "left . . . right . . . center . . . right . . . left . . ."). During the presentation the operator wears a headset, listening to the slide change cues on the second track and pushing the appropriate projector control button. The audience only hears the music and narration sound track.
3. Add a *programmer* in circuit with the stereo tape recorder and the projector. The programmer will accept inaudible signals at slide change points, previously put on the second track of the recorder, (by the operator pushing a button on the programmer which carries the signal to the tape recorder). This signal causes the programmer to trigger one or more slide

projectors, thus changing slides. Two common types of programmers are available. One group uses punched paper or mylar tape and the other magnetic tape.

Programmer

With punched tape units, the projectors are activated by impulses received through the holes in the punched tape. A signal from the tape recorder causes the tape in the programmer to move a short distance between a metal drum and electric contact brushes. When a hole is in position, the brushes can make contact with the metal drum, a circuit breaker is tripped, and a slide is directed to change on a certain projector. The number of columns for potential holes determines the number of separate projectors (slide or other media) that can be activated in any combination or timing.

The magnetic tape programmers are finding wider use than are the punched tape units. They utilize a series of different audio frequency tones, one for each channel or projector to be controlled. The tape within the programmer is recorded with sequences of selected audio-frequency tones. On playback, a signal from the cue track coding on the stereo recorder acts on one frequency on the programmer tape, by-passing all other frequencies, and the projector in circuit with that frequency signal is triggered to change slides, project motion picture film, or whatever is to be sequenced next.

4. Add dissolve units to function in conjunction with the programmer. A dissolve unit increases or decreases electrical resistance in the lamp circuits of two projectors, thus increasing the intensity of light in one projector while decreasing it in the other. The two projectors are carefully aimed at the same screen so their images coincide. The images superimpose and change on command from the programmer, with one image fading out and the next one on the screen fading in, thus creating an effec-

tive impression of gradual change and transformation as images blend one from another.

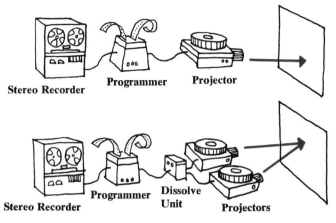

Stereo Recorder   **Programmer**   **Projector**

Stereo Recorder   **Programmer**   **Dissolve Unit**   **Projectors**

When dissolves are used, the screen is always illuminated during slide changes, which helps to hold audience attention. Employing this technique of dissolving from one slide to the next creates a smooth visual flow as compared with the usual single projector slide change procedure that causes a sudden black screen between adjacent slides.

If a three-screen multi-image presentation is to be made, then six slide projectors and three dissolve units are needed, all activated through a programmer with sufficient control capabilities.

As with any presentation involving audiovisual materials, attention to numerous details must be handled prior to the actual program use. Some of these are enumerated in Chapter 13. Because of the complex electronic equipment required for the multiple images and the sound, special attention should be given to these details and a thorough rehearsal of the presentation is required.

In spite of all precautions, problems may be encountered that disrupt carefully produced multi-image programs, especially when an automated programmer is used. Ambient sounds in an area, like radiation from fluorescent lights or other 60-cycle interference noise, might be recorded or picked up on the cueing tape, which can add unwanted signals during playback that trigger slides at wrong times. But newer developments can be anticipated to make programmers more reliable. They could even be directed to control other devices, which can provide *multisensory* dimensions of odors, taste, and sensations of heat, cold, movement, and vibrations in the viewing room to make multi-image presentations even more effective and exciting!

Now Review What You Have Read About Multi-image Presentations:

1. What is the difference between multi-image and multimedia?
2. What are two general reasons why a multi-image presentation might be selected for use with a group?
3. List four instructional purposes that such a presentation can serve.
4. Which of these statements are true according to information in this chapter?
   a. Project images on each one of three screens continuously during a presentation.
   b. In planning, relate a multi-image presentation to a multipage magazine layout.
   c. Each separate screen can be used to treat its own idea or concept.
   d. In composition, generally face people on side screens toward the center one.
   e. Major messages most often should be on the center screen.
5. If you have a stereo recorder available, what simple method could you use to synchronize a two-screen presentation?
6. Do you have a programmer available? If so, what material is used to carry the signal?
7. On what principle does a dissolve unit operate?

Note: Answers to review questions can be found at the end of the chapter.

Multimedia Applications

For presenting certain information or for achieving specific instructional objectives, one type of audiovisual material may be preferred or considered to be more effective than other forms. In this regard, see the discussion of Media Selection on page 47. For example, the explanation of a principle might be illustrated with graphics on 2×2 inch slides. Immediately following the slides, applications of the principle might be shown with a brief motion-picture sequence. The topic can then be summarized with one or more overhead transparencies. The sequential use of the three media—slides, motion picture, and overhead transparencies—is an illustration of a multimedia application for group instruction.

There are major differences between the customary uses of audiovisual materials and their applications within newer programs based on multimedia. The background information in Chapter 1 and the discussion of learning theory on page 15 should be studied if you are planning to employ multimedia.

While the planning methods and the production techniques for individual media are essentially the same as for regular uses, recognition should be given to factors that differentiate the conventional from the newer approaches. Table 25-1 compares the customary with the newer uses in multimedia programs.

The most important and most difficult decision when exploring multimedia use is to select appropriate media forms in terms of the needs or objectives to be served, whether for group presentation or independent study. As previously noted, some assistance with these decisions can be made by referring to the Media Selection diagrams and discussion on page 49.

GROUP USE

TABLE 25-1　Comparisons of Media for Conventional Use with Multimedia Uses

CONVENTIONAL USE	MULTIMEDIA USE
1. Treats a topic	1. Each medium treats a concept within a topic
2. Serves general purposes or broad objectives	2. Serves narrow, specific objectives leading to learning competencies
3. Most often for group presentation	3. May be for group use, but increasingly for individual student use
4. Relatively long in length (10–20 minutes, 40–60 frames, etc.)	4. Each medium of short length in keeping with concept treatment
5. Almost entirely expository with students passively receiving information	5. Active student participation through coordinated paperwork (completing exercises, self-check of learning, etc.) or other activities
6. Each medium used as a separate entity	6. Integration of media in structured sequence
7. All students view and hear same materials	7. Variety of materials available so students have choice for selected study
8. Materials usually used at instructor's presentation pace	8. Students work with materials at own pace and convenience

Multimedia presentations designed for use with groups may incorporate any projected audiovisual material—slides, filmstrip, overhead transparencies, motion picture, or television. In addition, tape recordings, either alone or in conjunction with visual forms, are suitable, although some presenters prefer to make their own comments with visuals as part of their presentation.

In developing multimedia presentations, refer to the planning steps described in Part 2. Give particular attention to:

☐ Establishing *objectives* for the program (page 31).
☐ Selecting *content* to serve the objectives (page 38).
☐ Designing a *storyboard* and/or *script* to insure a smooth flow from one medium use and idea to the next (page 52).
☐ Obtaining necessary assistance in planning and program preparation (page 36).

Setting up the required equipment and rehearsing the use of materials for a multimedia program, including their coordination and timing, are as important as the arrangements and details for a multi-image presentation.

Study the example of plans for the *Rotary Engine* multimedia presentation on page 283.

INDIVIDUAL USE

As indicated above, the major application of multimedia techniques is in individual learning programs. Many commercial kits and learning packages include a number of instructional resources. Students are either directed through a preset sequence of study, or, preferably, a variety of ma-

Example of Plan for
Presentation to Group
Using Multimedia

Topic: Rotary Combustion Engine

Student Group: High-school physics

Learning Objectives	Media
1. To identify the five main parts of the rotary engine	Overhead transparency of engine diagram, names on overlay
2. To explain the "eccentrical" motion of the rotor	16-mm film clip showing action of rotor
3. To describe the position and action of the three cavities in the housing during the four cycles	Overhead transparency with movable plastic rotor; overlays review position of rotor, action in each cavity with name of cycle
4. To discuss advantages of the rotary engine in comparison with the reciprocating engine	2 x 2 inch slides of engine parts, placement in car, drive action to wheels, smog emission, etc.

[and so on]

terials treat the topic objectives and permit students to make their own selection of study items. As an example, see the description of materials in the *English Composition* program on page 284.

In this example, students may select their own method and resources from the options available to accomplish the objectives. The instructor has not only prepared certain items, but has collected suitable commercial materials also. Thus, in planning individualized study units, attention should be given to readily available resources that can be supplemented with locally-prepared items.

When developing a self-learning multimedia package special questions like these need attention:

1. How many copies of the various items will be needed?
2. What are the costs (specifications, page 57) for developing the original materials and the duplicates?
3. What guides or direction sheets are needed to insure proper use of the materials?
4. Is equipment for individual use available in sufficient quantity?
5. Where will the use take place (classroom, learning center, or home)?
6. Should aides or other students be oriented to assist with the use of materials (check-out, directions for use, maintenance, etc.)?

In addition to these questions and other possible problems, there can be three major limitations to the use of any type of media for independent study—cost of the materials, cost of necessary equipment, and difficulty in operating the equipment. Try to select items for use which can provide positive answers that will overcome these limitations. Most of the time it is not necessary to use expensive, complex equipment for independent study. For example, a series of photographic color prints may be just as good instructionally as slides for projections, and, in terms of equipment, a great deal less costly.

In summary, see the Independent Study Media Selection diagram on page 49 for those media forms that are most applicable for individualized learning uses. Then, as you select the category that will best communicate the content of your objectives, refer to Table 7-2 on page 50 which can guide you in making a final choice of media within a specific category. This is one objective way to make media selection. Other writers have developed alternative approaches to media selection. Check the references on page 294.

We can expect to see more equipment that will *combine* media forms like still pictures and motion pictures, with or without sound, requiring a single device for viewing. Such a development can reduce the cost of equipment and materials and makes them easier to use. The viewer that accompanies the 8-mm films correlated with topics in this book is a move in this direction. See page 289 for further discussion of this concept.

Example of Independent
Study Program Using
Multimedia

Course: English Composition

Student Group: College freshmen

Unit Objectives

1. To eliminate run-on sentences and meaningless fragments
2. To eliminate improper use of pronouns, verbs, adjectives,
   and adverbs
3. To eliminate errors in punctuation and capitalization
4. To eliminate spelling errors
5. To eliminate problem sentence construction

[and so on]

Resources

For each unit the following resources are available for student
selection. One or more are to be used, results checked by
instructor or tutor before student self-check and instructor
evaluation of competency. Repeat study with other resources
if necessary.

1. Reading material and exercises in basic text
2. View minipresentation (10 minutes) by instructor on
   videotape and complete worksheet of correlated activities
3. Study appropriate module(s) in A Curse on Confusion
   (Westinghouse Learning publication)
4. Programmed minicourse on unit topic (booklet and audio
   tape) from Educulture Company
5. Audio tape and filmstrip review of unit (prepared by
   instructor)
6. Writing assignment
7. Self-check of competency

Now Review What You Have Read About the Multimedia Concept:

1. State five differences relating to media development and use in new-type independent-study programs as compared to conventional instruction.
2. Select a topic you might treat through a group presentation. State two or three objectives relating to the topic. Choose a variety of media to accomplish the objectives.
3. Select a topic for independent study. State two objectives. For each objective choose at least two kinds of media that would provide different learning experiences.
4. Which of the questions relating to multimedia-package development on page 283 do you feel are most important? Are there other questions you would add?

Answers to Review Questions

MULTI-IMAGES (PAGE 281)

1. Multi-image—simultaneous projection of two or more pictures. Multimedia—sequential use of a variety of media.
2. A motivational experience for the viewer; processing large amounts of information effectively in a short time.
3. See page 276.
4. (a) F, (b) T, (c) F, (d) T, (e) T.
5 Put narration on one track and slide-change cues by voice on second track.
6. Reader's activity, page 280.
7. By changing electrical resistance, projector-lamp intensity is reduced or increased, thus providing overlap fade-out and fade-in of images as slides are changed.

MULTIMEDIA (PAGE 284)

1. See page 282.
2. Reader's activity.
3. Reader's activity.

APPENDIXES

APPENDIX A
CORRELATED STILL/MOTION SUPER-8mm FILMS

Throughout this book there are references to *Still/Motion* films that correlate with the topics, processes, or techniques under discussion. Each of these films consists of either a series of still pictures as a filmstrip, a motion-picture sequence, or a combination of both still and motion, as required, to illustrate or demonstrate the topic or technique.

The visual format is continuous-loop super-8-mm color film in a sealed cartridge. The film is used with a newly designed, hand-operated portable or table viewer. According to his preference or learning needs, a person can view individual frames, can view action in slow or rapid motion, as he prefers, and can go back or skip ahead.

These *Still/Motion* films are designed for independent study to aid the reader in preparing to apply the concepts presented in this book. They can also be used for quick review at a later time.

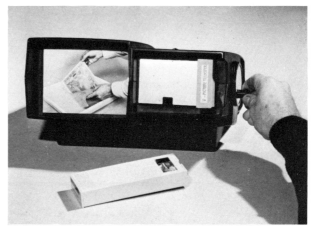

Following is a list of Still/Motion films in production at the time this book was published. For further information on the distribution source for these films and viewers, and an up-to-date list of the films currently available, contact the author:

Dr. Jerrold E. Kemp
Faculty and Instructional Development Office
San Jose State University
San Jose, California 95192

PLANNING

Constructing a Planning Board
Visual Ideas for Storyboards

PHOTOGRAPHY

Camera Types
Camera Lenses
Camera Settings
Picture Composition
Determining Exposure
Film Selection
Lighting Scenes
Close-up and Copywork
Making Titles
Developing Black-and-White Roll Film
Opaquing and Spotting Prints
Contact Printing Black-and-White Negatives
Enlargement Printing Black-and-White Negatives

GRAPHICS

Design Principles and Tools
Bulletin Boards and Displays
Coloring Techniques
Using Transfer Letters
Felt-Pen Lettering
Wrico Signmaker Lettering
Wricoprint Lettering
Leroy Lettering
Varigraph Lettering
Varitype Lettering
Rubber Cement Mounting
Using the Dry-Mount Press
Using a Hand Iron for Mounting
Mounting a Cut-Out Picture
Mounting a Two-Page Picture
Overcoming Dry-Mounting Problems
Mounting on Cloth (Roll)
Mounting on Cloth (Fold)
Laminating Flat Materials
Preparing Spirit Masters (Hand)
Preparing Spirit Masters (Thermal)
Operating the Spirit Duplicator

RECORDING

Operating the Tape Recorder
Operating the Record Player
Splicing Magnetic Tape

OVERHEAD TRANSPARENCIES

Features of Overhead Projection
Preparing Overlays
Adding Color to Transparencies
Making Transparencies with Felt Pens
Making Transparencies with Tapes and Transfer
    Letters
Making Transparencies with the Spirit Duplicator
Principle of the Diazo Process
Making Transparencies with the Diazo Process
Making Transparencies with the Thermofax
    Machine
Making Transparencies with the Masterfax
    Machine
Making a Picture Transfer Transparency (Seal
    Dry Mount)
Making a Picture Transfer Transparency (Contact
    Shelf Paper)
Making High-Contrast Film Transparencies
Mounting Transparencies
Masking Transparencies

MOTION PICTURES

Motion-Picture Shots
Using the Motion-Picture Camera
Building Motion-Picture Sequences
Developing Film Continuity
Making Transitions
Multicamera Uses
Animation Techniques
Time-Lapse Photography
Making Still/Motion Films
Editing Film
Splicing Film

MULTI-IMAGES

Techniques of Multi-image Projection

APPENDIX B
BOOKS, FILMS, PAMPHLETS, AND PERIODICALS

Audiovisual Communications

TRENDS IN EDUCATION AND TECHNOLOGY

Brown, James W. *Educational Media Yearbook.* New York: R. R. Bowker (annual publication).

Carnegie Commission on Higher Education. *The Fourth Revolution: Instructional Technology in Higher Education.* New York: McGraw-Hill, 1972.

Hack, Walter G. *Educational Futurism 1985.* Berkeley, Calif.: McCutchan, 1971.

Lessinger, Leon M., and Tyler, Ralph W., eds. *Accountability in Education.* Worthington, Ohio: Charles A Jones, 1971.

McBeath, Ronald J., ed. *Extending Education through Technology.* Washington, D.C.: Association for Educational Communications and Technology, 1972.

————. "Is Education Becoming?" *AV Communication Review,* Spring 1969, pp. 36–40.

Shane, Harold G. *The Educational Significance of the Future.* Bloomington, Ind.: Phi Delta Kappa, 1973.

Tickton, Sidney G., ed. *To Improve Learning: An Evaluation of Instructional Technology.* From a Report to the President and the Congress of the United States by the Commission on Instructional Technology. New York: R. R. Bowker, 1970.

AUDIOVISUAL MATERIALS IN INSTRUCTION AND TRAINING

Audio-Visual Communications. United Business Publications, Inc., 750 Third Avenue, New York 10017 (monthly journal).

Audiovisual Instruction. Association for Educational Communications and Technology, 1201 16th Street, N.W., Washington, D.C. 20036 (monthly journal).

AV Communication Review. Association for Educational Communications and Technology, 1201 16th Street, N.W., Washington, D.C., 20036

Brown, James W., et al. *AV Instruction: Technology, Media and Methods.* New York: McGraw-Hill, 1973.

Dale, Edgar. *Audiovisual Methods in Teaching.* New York: Holt, Rinehart & Winston, 1969.

Taylor, C. W., and Williams, Frank E. *Instructional Media and Creativity.* New York: John Wiley, 1966.

The Teacher and Technology. 16-mm motion picture, sound, black-and-white, 49 minutes (includes 11 subfilms). Columbus: Department of Photography, Ohio State University, 1966.

Training in Business and Industry. Gellert Publications Corp., 1 Park Ave., New York 10016 (monthly journal).

INDIVIDUALIZED LEARNING

The Audio-Tutorial System. 16-mm motion picture, sound, color. Lafayette, Ind.: Audio Visual Center, Purdue University, 1968.

Johnson, Stuart R., and Johnson, Rita B. *Developing Individualized Instructional Materials.* Palo Alto, Calif.: Westinghouse Learning Press, 1970.

Keller, Fred. "Goodbye, Teacher . . ." *Journal of Applied Behavior Analysis* 1 (1968): 79–89.

Langdon, Danny G. *Interactive Instructional Designs for Individualized Learning.* Englewood Cliffs, N.J.: Educational Technology Publications, 1973.

Postlethwait, S. N., et al. *The Audio-Tutorial Approach to Learning.* Minneapolis: Burgess Publishing Co., 1972.

Russell, James D. *Modular Instruction.* Minneapolis: Burgess Publishing Co., 1974.

Weisgerber, Robert A. *Developmental Efforts in Individualized Learning.* Itasca, Ill.: F. E. Peacock, 1971.

291

————. *Perspectives in Individualized Learning.* Itasca, Ill.: F. E. Peacock, 1971.

————. *Trends, Issues, and Activities in Individualized Learning.* Palo Alto, Calif.: ERIC Clearinghouse on Media and Technology, Stanford University, 1972.

INSTRUCTIONAL DEVELOPMENT AND DESIGN

Baker, Robert L., and Schutz, Richard E. *Instructional Product Development.* New York: Van Nostrand Reinhold, 1971.

Briggs, Leslie J. *Handbook of Procedures for the Design of Instruction.* Pittsburgh: American Institutes for Research, 1970.

Davies, Ivor K. *Competency Based Learning: Technology, Management and Design.* New York: McGraw-Hill, 1973.

Davis, Robert H., et al. *Learning Systems Design.* New York: McGraw-Hill, 1974.

Diamond, Robert M., et al. *Instructional Development for Individualized Learning in Higher Education.* Englewood Cliffs, N.J.: Educational Technology Press, 1975.

Filbeck, Robert. *Systems in Teaching and Learning.* Lincoln, Nebr.: Professional Educators Publications, 1974.

Gagné, Robert M., ed. *Psychological Principles in System Development.* New York: Holt, Rinehart & Winston, 1962.

Gerlach, Vernon, and Ely, Don. *Teaching and Media: A Systems Approach.* Englewood Cliffs, N.J.: Prentice-Hall, 1970.

Glaser, Robert. "Psychological Bases for Instructional Design." *AV Communication Review,* Winter 1966, pp. 433–49.

Gropper, George L. *Instructional Strategies.* Englewood Cliffs, N.J.: Educational Technology Press, 1974.

————. "Toward a Behavioral Science Base for Instructional Design." In *Teaching Machines and Programmed Learning II: Data and Directions.* Washington, D.C.: National Education Association, 1965.

Heinich, Robert. *Technology and the Management of Instruction.* Washington, D.C.: Association for Educational Communications and Technology, 1970.

Kemp, Jerrold E. *Instructional Design: A Plan for Unit and Course Development.* Belmont, Calif.: Fearon Lear/Siegler, 1971.

Mager, Robert F., and Beach, Kenneth M. *Developing Vocational Instruction.* Belmont, Calif.: Fearon Lear/Siegler, 1967.

Mager, Robert F., and Pipe, Peter. *Criterion-Referenced Instruction.* Los Altos Hills, Calif.: Mager Associates, 1974.

Merrill, M. David. *Instructional Design: Readings.* Englewood Cliffs, N.J.: Prentice-Hall, 1971.

Popham, W. James, and Baker, Eva L. *Systematic Instruction.* Englewood Cliffs, N.J.: Prentice-Hall, 1970.

Tosti, Donald T., and Ball, John R. "A Behavioral Approach to Instructional Design and Media Selection." *AV Communication Review,* Spring 1969, pp. 5–25.

Twelker, Paul A., et al. *The Systematic Development of Instruction: An Overview and Basic Guide to the Literature.* Palo Alto, Calif.: ERIC Clearinghouse on Media and Technology, Stanford University, 1972.

Wong, Martin R., and Raulerson, John D. *A Guide to Systematic Instructional Design.* Englewood Cliffs, N.J.: Educational Technology Press, 1974.

VISUAL LITERACY

Bendick, Jeanne, and Bendick, Robert. *Filming Works like This.* New York: McGraw-Hill, 1970.

Debes, John L. "Some Foundations for Visual Literacy." *Audiovisual Instruction* 13 (November 1968): 961–64.

Dondis, Donis A. *A Primer of Visual Literacy.* Cambridge: MIT Press, 1973.

Elements of Visual Literacy. Pamphlet T-25. Rochester: Eastman Kodak Co.

The Elephants of Visual Literacy. Pamphlet T-90-1-2. Rochester: Eastman Kodak Co.

Fabun, Don. *Communications, the Transfer of Meaning.* New York: Macmillan, 1968.

Fransecky, Roger B., and Debes, Jack L. *Visual Literacy: A Way to Learn—A Way to Teach.* Washington: Association for Educational Communications and Technology, 1972.

Let's Make a Film. 16-mm motion picture, sound, color, 13 minutes. New York: Van Nostrand Reinhold, 1971.

Lidstone, John, and McIntosh, Don. *Children as Film Makers.* New York: Van Nostrand Reinhold, 1970.

Rynew, Arden. *Filmmaking for Children.* Dayton: Pflaum/Standard, 1971.

Trojanski, John, and Rockwood, Louis. *Making It Move.* Dayton: Pflaum/Standard, 1973.

Visual Language of the Film. 16-mm motion picture, sound, color, 28 minutes. Los Angeles: Hour of St. Frances OFM Productions, 1966.

Visual Literacy Materials (includes films, still picture sets and references). Washington, D.C.: Association for Educational Communications and Technology.

Williams, Clarence, and Debes, John. *Visual Literacy.* New York: Pitman, 1970.

Perception, Communications, and Learning Theory

Ball, John, and Byrnes, Francis C. *Research, Principles, and Practices in Visual Communication.* Washington, D.C.: Association for Educational Communications and Technology, 1960.

Bruner, Jerome, ed. *Learning about Learning.* Washington: Government Printing Office, 1966.

———. *The Process of Education.* Cambridge: Harvard University Press, 1960.

———. *A Theory of Instruction.* Cambridge: Harvard University Press, 1966.

Bugelski, B. R. *The Psychology of Learning Applied to Teaching.* Indianapolis: Bobbs-Merrill, 1971.

Carpenter, C. R. "Psychological Concepts and Audio-Visual Instruction." *AV Communication Review,* Winter 1957, pp. 361–69.

A Communications Primer. 16-mm motion picture, sound, color, 20 minutes. Los Angeles: Classroom Films Distributors, 1952.

Dale, Edgar. "Principles of Learning." *News Letter* 29, no. 4 (January 1964). Columbus: Bureau of Educational Research and Service, Ohio State University.

Fabun, Don. *Communications: The Transfer of Meaning.* New York: Macmillan, 1968.

Fleming, Malcolm I. *Perception Principles for the Design of Instructional Materials. Bulletin of the School of Education* (Indiana University, Bloomington) 46, no. 4 (July 1970): 69–200.

Gagné, Robert M. *The Conditions of Learning.* New York: Holt, Rinehart & Winston, 1970.

———. "Instruction and the Conditions of Learning." In *Instruction: Some Contemporary Viewpoints,* ed. Laurence Siegel. Scranton: Chandler, 1967.

Hilgard, Ernest R., and Bower, Gordon H. *Theories of Learning.* New York: Appleton-Century-Crofts, 1966.

McLuhan, Marshall. *Understanding Media: The Extension of Man.* New York: McGraw-Hill, 1964.

Meierhenry, Wesley, ed. "Learning Theory and AV Utilization." *AV Communication Review,* September–October 1961.

Norberg, Kenneth, ed. "Perception Theory and AV Education." *AV Communication Review,* September–October 1962.

Perception and Communication. 16-mm motion picture, sound, black-and-white, 32 minutes (includes 6 subfilms). Columbus: Department of Photography, Ohio State University, 1966.

The Process of Communication. 16-mm motion picture, sound, black-and-white, 45 minutes (includes 8 subfilms). Columbus: Ohio State University, Department of Photography, 1966.

Smith, Karl U., and Smith, Margaret F. *Cybernetic Principles of Learning and Educational Design.* New York: Holt, Rinehart & Winston, 1966.

Research in Design of Audiovisual Materials

Allen, William H. *Intellectual Abilities and Instructional Media Design.* Stanford, Calif.: ERIC Clearinghouse on Information Resources, Stanford University, 1974.

———. "Research on Educational Media." In *Educational Media Yearbook 1973,* ed. James W. Brown. New York: R. R. Bowker.

Conway, Jerome. "Multiple Sensory Modality Communications and the Problem of Sign Types." *AV Communication Review,* Winter 1967, pp. 371–83.

Gropper, George L. "Learning from Visuals: Some Behavioral Considerations." *AV Communication Review,* Spring 1966, pp. 37–70.

Hartman, Frank R. "Single and Multiple Channel Communication: A Review of Research and a Proposed Model." *AV Communication Review,* November–December 1961, pp. 235–62.

Hoban, Charles F., Jr., and van Ormer, Edward B. *Instructional Film Research 1918–1950.* Technical Report No. SDC 269-7-19. Port Washington, N.Y.: Special Devices Center, U.S. Navy, 1950.

Levie, W. Howard, and Dickie, Kenneth E. "The Analysis and Application of Media." In *Second Handbook of Research on Teaching,* ed. Robert M. W. Travers. Chicago: Rand McNally, 1973.

Lumsdaine, A. A. "Controlled Variations of Specific Factors in Design and Use of Instructional Media." In *Handbook of Research on Teaching.* ed. N. L. Gage. Chicago: Rand McNally, 1963.

May, Mark A. *Enhancements and Simplifications of Motivational and Stimulus Variables in Audiovisual Instructional Materials.* Washington: U.S. Office of Education Contract No. OE-5-16-006, 1965.

———. *The Role of Student Response in Learning from the New Educational Media.* Washington: U.S. Office of Education Contract No. OE-5016-006, 1966.

———. *Word-Picture Relationships in Audio-Visual Presentations.* Washington: U.S. Office of Education Contract OE-5-16-006, 1965.

May, Mark A., and Lumsdaine, A. A. *Learning from Films.* New Haven: Yale University Press, 1958.

Saul, Ezra V., et al. *A Review of the Literature Pertinent to the Design and Use of Effective Graphic Training Aids.* Technical Report SPECDEVCEN 494-08-1. Port Washington, N.Y.: U.S. Naval Training Devices Center, 1954.

Travers, Robert M. W. *Research and Theory Related to Audio-Visual Information Transmission.* Kalamazoo: Western Michigan University, 1967.

Planning Audiovisual Materials

OBJECTIVES

Bloom, Benjamin S., et al. *A Taxonomy of Educational Objectives: Handbook I, the Cognitive Domain.* New York: Longmans, Green, 1956.

Canfield, Albert A. "A Rationale for Performance Objectives." *Audiovisual Instruction,* February 1968, pp. 127–29.

Contributions of Behavioral Sciences to Instructional Technology: Affective Domain. Washington, D.C.: Communications Service Corp., 1970.

Contributions of Behavioral Sciences to Instructional Technology: Cognitive Domain. Washington, D.C.: Communications Service Corp., 1970.

Contributions of Behavioral Sciences to Instructional Technology: Psychomotor Domain. Washington, D.C.: Communications Service Corp., 1970.

Geis, George L. *Behavioral Objectives: A Selected Bibliography and Brief Review.* Palo Alto, Calif.: ERIC Clearinghouse on Media and Technology, Stanford University, 1972.

Gronlund, Norman E. *Stating Behavioral Objectives for Classroom Instruction.* New York: Macmillan, 1970.

Hernandez, David E. *Writing Behavioral Objectives.* New York: Barnes & Noble, 1971.

Kibler, Robert J., et al. *Behavioral Objectives and Instruction.* Boston: Allyn & Bacon, 1970.

Krathwohl, David R., et al. *A Taxonomy of Educational Objectives: Handbook II, the Affective Domain.* New York: David McKay, 1964.

Kryspin, William J., and Feldhusin, John F. *Writing Behavioral Objectives.* Minneapolis: Burgess Publishing Co., 1974.

Mager, Robert F. *Preparing Instructional Objectives.* Belmont, Calif.: Fearon Lear/Siegler, 1962.

———. *Goal Analysis.* Belmont, Calif.: Fearon Lear/Siegler, 1971.

Plowman, Paul D. *Behavioral Objectives.* Chicago: Science Research Associates, 1971.

Smith, Robert G. *Controlling the Quality of Training.* Alexandria, Va.: Human Resources Research Office, George Washington University, 1965.

———. *The Development of Training Objectives.* Alexandria, Va.: Human Resources Research Office, George Washington University, 1964.

STORYBOARDS AND SCRIPTING

Audiovisual Planning Equipment. Pamphlet S-11. Rochester: Eastman Kodak Co.

Beveridge, James A. *Script Writing for Short Films.* New York: Unesco Publishing Center USA, 1969.

MacLinker, Jerry. *Designing Instructional Visuals: Theory, Composition, and Implementation.* Austin: Instructional Media Center, University of Texas, 1968.

Parker, Norton S. *Audiovisual Script Writing.* New Brunswick, N.J.: Rutgers University Press, 1968.

Planning and Producing Visual Aids. Pamphlet S-13. Rochester: Eastman Kodak Co.

Rowe, Mack R., et al. *The Message Is You: Guidelines for Preparing Presentations.* Washington, D.C.: Association for Educational Communications and Technology, 1971.

SELECTING MEDIA

Bretz, Rudy. *The Selection of Appropriate Communications Media for Instruction.* Publication R-601, PR. Santa Monica, Calif.: Rand Corp., 1971.

Briggs, Leslie J., et al. *Instructional Media: A Procedure for the Design of Multi-media Instruction.* Pittsburgh: American Institutes for Research, 1967.

Kemp, Jerrold E. "Which Medium?" *Audiovisual Instruction* 16 (December 1971): 32–36.

Tosti, Donald, and Ball, John. "A Behavioral Approach to Instructional Design and Media Selection." *AV Communication Review,* Spring 1969, pp. 5–25.

USING MEDIA

Audiovisual Projection. Publication S-3. Rochester: Eastman Kodak Co.

PROGRAM EVALUATION

Block, James H., ed. *Mastery Learning.* New York: Holt, Rinehart & Winston, 1971.

Bloom, Benjamin S., et al. *Handbook on Formative and Summative Evaluation of Student Learning.* New York: McGraw-Hill, 1971.

Gronlund, Norman E. *Preparing Criterion-Referenced Tests for Classroom Instruction.* New York: Macmillan, 1973.

Mager, Robert F. *Measuring Instructional Intent.* Belmont, Calif.: Fearon Lear/Siegler, 1973.

Nagel, Thomas S., and Richman, Paul T. *Competency-Based Instruction.* Columbus: Charles E. Merrill, 1972.

Popham, W. James. *Criterion-Referenced Instruction.* Belmont, Calif.: Fearon Lear/Siegler, 1973.

General Photography

(Many references in the following sections are available from Eastman Kodak Co., 343 State Street, Rochester, N.Y., 14650, or from a local photographic supply dealer. Following each of these titles is the Eastman publication code number without any other source indication.)

PICTURE TAKING

Advanced Camera Techniques for 126 and 35mm cameras, AC-56.

Adventures in Existing Light Photography, AC-44.

Color Photography Outdoors, E-75.

Composition, AC-11.

Exposure. 16-mm motion picture, 1959, sound, color, 12 minutes. Indiana University, Bloomington 47401.

Exposure Meter—Theory and Use. 1959, 16-mm motion picture, sound, color, 10 minutes. Bloomington: Indiana University.

How to Make and Use a Cartridge Pinhole Camera, T-23.

How to Set Your Adjustable Camera, AC-27.

Movies and Slides without a Camera, S-47.

Photography of Television Images, AC-10.

FILMS

Data: Kodak Black-and-White Films—Roll, 135, and 126, AF-16.

Filter Data for Kodak Color Films, E-23.

Kodak Color Films for Still Cameras—Roll, 135, and 126, AE-41.

Selection and Use of Kodak and Eastman Motion Picture Films, H-1.

LIGHTING

Controlled Photographic Lighting. 16-mm motion picture, sound, color, 9 minutes. Bloomington: Indiana University, 1959.

Millerson, Gerald, *The Technique of Lighting for Television and Motion Pictures.* New York: Hastings House, 1972.

Motion Picture Production—Basic Lighting. 16-mm motion picture, sound, color, 5 minutes. Eastman Kodak Co., 1971.

Studio Lighting for Product Photography, O-16.

CLOSE-UP AND COPYING

Basic Copying, AM-2.

Basic Titling and Animation, S-21.

Close-up Photography, N-12A.

Close-up Pictures with 35-mm Cameras, AB-10.

Copying, M-1.

Principles of Close-up Photography and Copying. Series of five 35-mm color, sound filmstrips. Santa Monica, Calif.: BFA Educational Media.

Simple Copying Techniques with a Kodak Ektagraphic Visual-maker, S-40.

A Simple Wooden Copy Stand for Making Title Slides and Filmstrips, T-43.

FILM PROCESSING AND PRINTING

Basic Developing, Printing and Enlarging, AJ-2.

Benedict, Joel A. ed. *Creative Photography: Darkroom and Camera Manual.* Tempe: Audiovisual Services, Arizona State University, 1974.

Enlarging in Black-and-White and Color, AG-16.

Photographic Darkroom Procedures, 35-mm black-and-white filmstrips, six filmstrips in set 1 (developing and printing), six filmstrips in set 2 (advanced techniques). New York: McGraw-Hill.

Photolab Design, K-13.

Stabilization with Kodak Ektamatic Products, G-25.

HANDBOOKS AND JOURNALS

Carroll, John S. *Photo-lab Index,* Hastings-on-Hudson, N.Y.: Morgan & Morgan (quarterly supplements).

The Focal Encyclopedia of Photography, New York: McGraw-Hill, 1969.

Index to Kodak Information, L-5 (annual reference).

Industrial Photography. 750 Third Avenue, New York 10017 (monthly journal).

Neblette, C. B. *Photography: It's Materials and Processes.* New York: Van Nostrand Reinhold, 1962.

Photo Methods for Industry. 33 West 60th Street, New York 10023 (monthly journal).

Photographic Applications in Science and Technology. 257 Park Avenue South, New York 10010.

Graphic Arts

GENERAL

East, Marjorie. *Display for Learning,* New York: Holt, Rinehart & Winston, 1952.

Frye, Roy. *Graphic Tools for Teachers.* Mapleville, R.I.: Roy Frye Publisher, 1975.

Garland, Ken. *Graphics Handbook,* New York: Van Nostrand Reinhold, 1966.

Minor, Ed, and Frye, Harvey R. *Techniques for Producing Visual Instructional Media,* New York: McGraw-Hill, 1970.

Morlan, John E. *Preparation of Inexpensive Teaching Materials.* New York: Intext, 1973.

MOUNTING

Dry Mounting Instructional Materials. Series of 16-mm motion pictures, sound, color, each 5 minutes in length. Iowa City: University of Iowa.

Seal Instruction Booklet. Bulletin 421. Derby, Conn.: Seal, Inc.

LETTERING

Lettering Instructional Materials. 16-mm motion picture, sound, color, 20 minutes. Bloomington: Indiana University, 1955.

Meeks, Martha F. *Lettering Techniques,* Austin: Visual Instruction Bureau, University of Texas, 1960.

STANDARDS

Legibility—Artwork to Screen. Pamphlet S-24. Rochester: Eastman Kodak Co.

McVey, Gerald F. *Educational Facilities: Man, Media and the Learning Environment,* Boston: Dept. of Media & Technology, Boston University, 1974.

Space for Audio-Visual Large Group Instruction. Madison: Universities Facilities Research Center, University of Wisconsin, 1964.

ILLUSTRATING

Creating Cartoons. 16-mm motion picture, sound, black-and-white, 10 minutes. Santa Monica, Calif.: BFA, 1956.

Halas, John. *Film and TV Graphics.* New York: Hastings House, 1968.

Horn, George F. *Cartooning.* Worcester, Mass.: Davis Publications.

How to Do Cartoons. 16-mm motion picture, sound, black-and-white, 20 minutes. Trenton, N.J.: Samuel Lawrence Schulman Productions, 1957.

Linker, Jerry Mac. *Designing Instructional Visuals: Theory, Composition, Implementation.* Austin: Instructional Media Center, University of Texas, 1968.

GRAPHS AND STATISTICS

Meyers, Cecil H. *Handbook of Basic Graphs: A Modern Approach.* Encino, Calif.: Dickenson, 1970.

Modley, Rudolf, and Lowenstein, Dyno. *Pictographs and Graphs.* New York: Harper & Bros., 1952.

Spear, Mary E. *Practical Charting Techniques.* New York: McGraw-Hill, 1969.

DUPLICATING PROCESSES

Pett, Dennis W. *Copying and Duplicating Processes.* Booklet and six sound, color filmstrips. Bloomington: Audio-Visual Center, Indiana University, 1973.

Sound Recording

Basic Magnetic Sound Recording for Motion Pictures. Publication S-27. Rochester: Eastman Kodak Co.

Nisbett, Alex. *The Technique of the Sound Studio.* New York: Hastings House, 1972.

Sloan, Robert, Jr. *The Tape Recorder.* Austin: Visual Instruction Bureau, University of Texas, 1972.

Tall, Joel. *Tape Editing.* Scottsdale, Ariz.: ELPA Marketing Industries, 1972.

Tape Recording for Instruction. 16-mm motion picture, sound, black-and-white, 15 minutes. Bloomington: Indiana University, 1956.

Turnbull, Robert B. *Radio and Television Sound Effects.* New York: Holt, Rinehart & Winston, 1951.

Photographic Print Series

Bergin, David P. *Photojournalism Manual: How to Plan Shoot Edit Sell.* Hastings-on-Hudson, N.Y.: Morgan & Morgan, 1967.

Fox, Rodney, and Kerns, Robert. *Creative News Pho-*

tography. Ames: Iowa State University Press, 1961.

Morgan, Willard, and Lester, Henry. *Graphic Graflex Photography.* Hastings-on-Hudson, N.Y.: Morgan & Morgan, 1971.

Slide Series and Filmstrips

(Many of the following references are available from Eastman Kodak Co., 343 State Street, Rochester, N.Y., 14650 or from a local photographic supply dealer. Following each of these titles is the Eastman publication code number without any other source indication.)

Adventures in Indoor Color Slides, AE-7.

Adventures in Outdoor Color Slides, AE-9

Black-and-White Transparencies with Kodak Panatomic-X Film, F-19.

Coltharp, Joe. *Production of 2″ x 2″ Slides for School Use.* Austin: Visual Instruction Bureau, University of Texas, 1958.

Effective Lecture Slides, S-22.

Facts You Should Know About Filmstrips. San Fernando, Calif.: Frank Holmes, Laboratories, 1965.

Lord, John, and Larson, Robert. *Handbook for Production of Filmstrips and Records.* St. Charles, Ill.: DuKane Corp., 1971.

Photographic Slides for Instruction. 16-mm motion picture, sound, color, 11 minutes. Bloomington: Indiana University, 1956.

Reverse-Text Slides from Black on White Line Artwork, S-26.

Slides with a Purpose for Business and Education, VI-15.

Transparencies for Overhead Projection

Adams, Sarah, et al. "Readable Letter Size and Visibility for Overhead Projection Transparencies." *AV Communications Review,* Winter 1965, pp. 412–417.

Harsell, Horace, and Veenendaal, Wilfred. *Overhead Projection.* Buffalo: American Optical Co., 1960.

High Contrast Photography for Instruction. 16-mm motion picture, sound, color, 14 minutes. Bloomington: Indiana University, 1956.

How to Make Transparencies with a Xerox Copier Using Zelar Films. Chamblee, Ga.: Sepsco Films, 1968.

Kelley, Galen B., and Sleeman, Phillip J. *A Guide to Overhead Projection and the Practical Preparation of Transparencies.* Leeds, Mass.: Chart-Pak Rotex. 1967.

Making Black-and-White and Color Transparencies for Overhead Projection. Pamphlet S-7. Rochester: Eastman Kodak Co.

Projecting Ideas on the Overhead Projector. Series of three 16-mm motion pictures, sound, color. Iowa City: University of Iowa.

Ring, Arthur, and Shelley, William J. *Learning with the Overhead Projector.* New York: Intext, 1969.

Smith, Richard E. *The Overhead System: Production, Implementation and Utilization.* Austin: Visual Instruction Bureau, University of Texas.

Snowberg, Richard C. "Bases for the Selection of Background Colors for Transparencies." *AV Communication Review,* Summer 1973, pp. 191–207.

VU-Graphics: A Manual on Vu-Graph Projection. East Orange, N.J.: Charles Beseler Co., 1952.

Motion Pictures

(Many references in the following sections are available from Eastman Kodak Co., 343 State Street, Rochester, N.Y., 14650, or from a local photographic supply dealer. Following each of these titles is the Eastman publication code number without any other source indication.)

TECHNIQUES

Baddeley, W. Hugh. *The Technique of Documentary Film Production.* New York: Hastings House, 1963.

Basic Production Techniques for Motion Pictures, P-18.

Broadbeck, Emil E. *Handbook of Basic Motion Picture Techniques.* New York: Hastings House, 1966.

Buchanan, Andrew. *Film Making from Script to Screen.* New York: Macmillan, 1951.

Coltharp, Joe. *Filming Athletic Events with 16mm Camera.* Austin: Visual Instruction Bureau, University of Texas.

Fielding, Raymond. *The Techniques of Special Effects Cinematography.* New York: Hastings House, 1965.

A Film About Filmmaking. 16-mm motion picture, sound, color, 17 minutes. Chicago: International Film Bureau, 1972.

Film Problems. 16-mm motion picture, sound, black-and-white, 8 minutes. Bloomington: Indiana University.

Filmmaking Fundamentals. 16-mm motion picture, sound, color. Wilmette, Ill.: Films, Inc., 1972.

The Filmograph. 16-mm sound, black-and-white, 5 minutes. Los Angeles: University of Southern California, 1958.

Gaskill, Arthur, and Englander, David. *How to Shoot*

a Movie Story. Hastings-on-Hudson, N.Y.: Morgan & Morgan, 1969.

Gordon, Jay E. *Motion Picture Production for Industry.* New York: Macmillan, 1961.

Livingston, Don. *Film and the Director,* New York: Putnam, 1970.

Mascelli, Joseph V. *The Five C's of Cinematography.* Hollywood, Calif.: Cine/Grafic Publications, 1965.

Mercer, John. *An Introduction to Cinematography.* Champaign, Ill.: Stipes Publishing Co., 1967.

Motion Picture Production—Basic Lighting. 16-mm motion picture, sound, color, 5 minutes. Rochester: Eastman Kodak Co., 1971.

Motion Picture Production—Continuity. (2 parts). 16-mm sound color. Rochester: Eastman Kodak Co., 1972.

Offenhauser, William H. *16-mm Sound Motion Pictures: A Manual for the Professional and Amateur,* New York: Interscience Publishers, 1958.

Pincus, Edward. *Guide to Filmmaking.* New York: Signet Books, New American Library, 1969.

Selection and Use of Kodak and Eastman Motion Picture films, H-1.

Spottiswood, Raymond. *Film and Its Techniques.* Berkeley: University of California Press, 1951.

EDITING

Editing Synchronous Sound. 16-mm motion picture, sound, color, 10 minutes. Bloomington: Indiana University, 1957.

Film Editing: Interpretation and Values. 16-mm motion picture, sound, black-and-white, 25 minutes. Hollywood, Calif.: American Cinema Editors, 1958.

Film Problems. 16-mm sound, black-and-white, 8 minutes. Bloomington: Indiana University, 1970.

Reiz, Karl, and Miller, Gavin. *The Technique of Film Editing.* New York: Hastings House, 1968.

SOUND

Basic Magnetic Sound Recording for Motion Pictures, S-27.

Kodak Sonatrack-Coating Service, D-27.

Manvell, Roger, and Huntley, John. *The Technique of Film Music.* New York: Hastings House, 1969.

Sound Recording for Motion Pictures. 16-mm motion picture, sound, color, 9 minutes. Bloomington: Indiana University, 1970.

SPECIAL APPLICATIONS

Anderson, Yvonne. *Make Your Own Animated Movies.* Boston: Little, Brown, 1970.

Animation Goes to School. 16-mm sound, color, 15 minutes. Bronx, N.Y.: Horace Mann School, 1965.

Animation: Its History, Techniques and Applications. New York: Associated Educational Services, 1967.

Basic Titling and Animation, S-21.

Fielding, Raymond. *The Technique of Special Effects Cinematography.* New York: Hastings House, 1965.

The Filmograph. 16-mm, sound, black-and-white, 6 minutes. Los Angeles: University of Southern California, 1958.

Halas, John, and Manvell, Roger. *The Technique of Film Animation.* New York: Hastings House, 1968.

Halas, John, and Privett, Bob. *How to Cartoon for Amateur Films.* London: Focal Press, 1958.

Levitan, Eli L. *Animation Techniques and Commercial Film Production.* New York: Holt Rinehart & Winston, 1962.

Madsen, Roy. *Animated Films: Concepts, Methods, Uses.* New York: Interland Publishing Co., 1969.

Ott, John. *My Ivory Cellar.* Old Greenwich, Conn.: Devin-Adair, 1958.

Photography—Stop Motion Miracles. 16-mm sound, black-and-white, 12 minutes. New York: Hearst Metronome News.

Time Lapse Photography. 16-mm sound, color, 10 minutes. Chicago: International Film Bureau, 1961.

8 MM

Glenn, George D., and Scholz, Charles B. *Super 8 Handbook.* Indianapolis: Howard W. Sams, 1974.

Movies with a Purpose, VI-13.

Super 8 Films for Original Productions, S-37.

Yulsman, Jerry. *The Complete Book of 8 mm Movie Making.* New York: Coward, McCann & Geoghejan, 1974.

HANDBOOKS AND JOURNALS

American Cinematographer. Hollywood, Calif.: American Society of Cinematographers.

The Aperture. Kansas City, Mo.: Calvin Communications.

Journal of the University Film Association. Columbus: Ohio State University, Dept. of Photography, Motion Picture Division.

Mascelli, Joseph V. *Mascelli's Cine Workbook.* Hollywood, Calif.: Cine/Grafic Publications, 1973.

MPL Recorder. Memphis: Motion Picture Laboratories.

Rewind. Hollywood, Calif.: DeLuxe General Film Laboratories.

SMPTE Journal. New York: Society of Motion Picture and Television Engineers. 9 East 41st Street, New York 10017.

Super 8 Filmaker. 145 East 49th Street, New York 10017.

Television Materials

Battison, John H. *Movies for TV.* New York: Macmillan, 1956.

Mattingly, Grayson, and Smith, Welby. *Introducing the Single-Camera VTR System: A Layman's Guide to Video-Recording.* New York: Scribners, 1973.

Millerson, Gerald. *The Technique of Television Pro-*duction. Hastings-on-Hudson, N.Y.: Morgan & Morgan, 1968.

Spear, John. *Creating Visuals for Television.* Washington: National Education Association, 1962.

Zettl, Herbert. *Television Production Workbook.* Belmont, Calif.: Wadsworth Publishing Co., 1968.

Multi-image

Benedict, Joel A., and Crane, Douglas A. *Producing Multi-Image Presentations.* Tempe: Audiovisual Services, Arizona State University, 1973.

Goldstein, E. Bruce. "The Perception of Multiple Images." *Audio-Visual Communication Review* 23 (Spring 1975): 34–68.

Perrin, Donald G. "A Theory of Multi-image Com-munication." *AV Communication Review,* Winter 1969, pp. 368–82.

Roberts, Alvin B., and Crawford, Don L. "Multiscreen Presentations: Promise for Instructional Improvement." *Audiovisual Instruction,* October 1966, pp. 528–30.

Wide-Screen and Multiple-Screen Presentations, S-28. Rochester: Eastman Kodak Co.

APPENDIX C
SOURCES FOR EQUIPMENT AND MATERIALS

Many of the common items needed for the preparation of your audiovisual materials can be purchased from local art, stationery, photography, and engineering-supply stores. Other equipment and specialized materials are listed here. Although the headquarters or main-office address is given, you will find local offices or local dealers distributing most products. If you do not, write to the address given for further information.

The following sources are organized under headings that approximate the order in which topics are presented in this book.

Planning Boards and Strips

Chicago Box Company, 732 North Morgan Street, Chicago, Ill., 60622

Medro Educational Products, P.O. Box 8463, Rochester, N.Y., 14618

General Art Supplies

Dick Blick, P.O. Box 1267, Galesburg, Ill., 61401

Arthur Brown and Bros., 2 West 46th Street, New York, N.Y., 10036

Flax's Artist Materials, 250 Sutter Street, San Francisco, Calif., 94108

Lewis Art Supply Co., 6408 Woodward Avenue, Detroit, Mich., 48202

Illustrations

A. A. Archibold Publishers, P.O. Box 57985, Los Angeles, Calif., 90057

Artype Inc., ModulArt, 345 Terra Cotta Avenue, Crystal Lake, Ill., 60014

Redi-Art Inc., 30 East 10th Street, New York, N.Y., 10003

Harry Volk Art Studio, Pleasantville, N.J., 08232

Photo Modifiers

Arthur Brown and Bros., 2 West 46th Street, New York, N.Y., 10036

Lacey-Luci Products, 2679 Route 70, Manasquan, N.Y., 08736

Scott Graphics, Holyoke, Mass., 01040

Coloring and Shading Materials

B. Aronstein and Co., 41-02A 162nd Street, Flushing, N.Y., 11358 (Synchromatic Transparent Watercolors)

Bourges Color Corp., 80 Fifth Avenue, New York, N.Y., 10011 (Cutocolor)

Cell-tak Manufacturing, 35 Alabama Avenue, Island Park, Long Island, N.Y., 11558

Chart-Pak Rotex, 1 River Road, Leeds, Mass., 01053 (Contak)

Craftint Manufacturing Co., 18501 Euclid Avenue, Cleveland, Ohio, 44112 (Craf-tone)

Mico-Tape, 7005 Tujunga Avenue, North Hollywood, Calif., 91605

Para-tone, P.O. Box 136, La Grange, Ill., 60525 (Zip-a-tone)

Peerless Color Laboratories, 11 Diamond Place, Rochester, N.Y., 14609 (transparent water colors)

Thayer & Chandler, 215 West Ohio Street, Chicago, Ill., 60610 (transparent water colors and air brush)

Webster Brothers, Laboratories, R.R. 3, Box 41, Lake Villa, Ill., 60046 (photo colors)

Lettering Equipment and Materials

PAPER CUT-OUTS

Demco, Box 1488, Madison, Wis., 53701

Mutual Education Aids, 1946 Hillhurst Avenue, Los Angeles, Calif., 90027

Stik-a-Letter Co., Route 2, Box 1400, Escondido, Calif., 92025

DRY-TRANSFER LETTERS

Artype Inc., 345 East Terra Cotta Avenue, Crystal Lake, Ill., 60014

Chart-Pak Rotex, 4 River Road, Leeds, Mass., 01053 (Deca-dry)

Graphic Products Corp., 3810 Industrial Avenue, Rolling Meadows, Ill., 60008 (Formatt)

Letraset Inc., 2379 Charleston Road, Mt. View, Calif., 94040

Para-tone Inc., 150 Fencl Lane, Hillside, Ill., 60162

Prestype Corp., 194 Veterans Boulevard, Carlstadt, N.J., 07072

GUMMED-BACK PAPER CUT-OUTS

Demco, Box 1488, Madison, Wis., 53701

Dennison Manufacturing Co., Framingham, Mass., 01702

W. W. Holes Manufacturing Co., St. Cloud, Minn., 56301

Stik-a-Letter Co., Route 2, Box 1400, Escondido, Calif., 90027

The Ticket and Tablet Co., 1021 East Adams Street, Chicago, Ill., 60607

THREE-DIMENSIONAL CUT-OUTS

Beckley-Cardy Co., 1900 North Narragansett, Chicago, Ill., 60639

Craft Industries, P.O. Box 11341A, Palo Alto, Calif., 94306

Gaylord Brothers, Inc., P.O. Drawer 61, Syracuse, N.Y., 13201

Hernard Manufacturing Co., 375 Executive Boulevard, Elmsford, N.Y., 10523

Mitten Designer Letters, 39 West 60th Street, New York, N.Y., 10023

Redikut Letter Co., 12617 South Prairie Avenue, Hawthorne, Calif., 90250

Scott Plastics Co., 423 10th Avenue, Palmetto, Fla., 33561

STENCIL GUIDES

The C-Thru Ruler Co., 6 Britton Drive, Bloomfield, Conn., 06002

Koh-i-noor Rapidograph, Inc., 100 North Street, Bloomsburg, N.J., 08804

Wood-Regan Instrument Co., 184 Franklin Avenue, Nutley, N.J., 07110 (Wrico)

TEMPLATE LETTERING GUIDES

Keuffel & Esser Co., 15 Park Row, New York, N.Y., 10038 (Leroy)

Letterguide Co., P.O. Box 4863, Lincoln, Nebr., 68509

Varigraph Co., 1480 Martin Street, Madison, Wis., 53701

PHOTOCOMPOSING UNITS

Filmotype Corp., 7500 McCormick Boulevard, Skokie, Ill., 60075

Fototype Inc., 1414 West Roscoe, Chicago, Ill., 60657

Pierce Corp., Kroy Industries, 6238 Oasis Avenue, North, Stillwater, Minn., 55082 (Varifont)

Strip-Printer, 21 Northwest 41st Street, Oklahoma City, Okla., 73118

VariTyper Corp., 720 Frelinghuysen Ave., Newark, N.J., 07114 (Headliner)

HOT PRESSES

Kensol-Olsenmark Corp., 40 Melville Park Road, Melville, N.Y., 11749

S.O.S. Photo-Cine-Optics, 387 Park Avenue South, New York, N.Y., 10016

Mounting Equipment and Materials

RUBBER CEMENT

Craftint Manufacturing Co., 18501 Euclid Avenue, Cleveland, Ohio, 44112 (Kleen-Stik)

Union Rubber and Asbestos Co., P.O. Box 1040, Trenton, N.J., 08606 (Best-Test)

DRY MOUNT

Bogan Photo Corp., 100 South Van Brunt Street, Englewood, N.J., 07631

Ditto, Inc., 6800 McCormick Road, Chicago, Ill., 60645 (Masterfax)

Eastman Kodak Co., 343 State Street, Rochester, N.Y., 14650

Seal, Inc., 251 Roosevelt Drive, Derby, Conn., 06418

Southwest Plastic Binding Co., 123 Weldon Parkway, Maryland Heights, Mo., 63043

LAMINATORS

General Binding Corp., 1101 Skokie Boulevard, Northbrook, Ill., 60062

Laminex, Inc., Matthews, N.C., 28105

Nationwide Adhesive Products, Inc., 19600 St. Clair Avenue, Cleveland, Ohio, 44117 (Transeal)

Southwest Plastic Binding Co., 123 Weldon Parkway, Maryland Heights, Mo., 63043

WAX COATERS

Addressograph-Multigraph Corp., 1200 Babbitt Road, Cleveland, Ohio, 44117

Daige Products, 160 Denton Avenue, New Hyde Park, N.Y., 11040 (Speedcote)

Letro-Stik Co., 3721 Broadway, Chicago, Ill., 60613

M. P. Goodkin Co., 112 Arlington Street, Newark, N.J., 07102

Photo-Stabilization Equipment

Agfa-Gevaert, 275 North Street, Teterboro, N.J., 07608

Eastman Kodak Co., 343 State Street, Rochester, N.Y., 14650

Ilford, Inc., West 70 Century Road, Box 288, Paramus, N.J., 07652

Binding and Displaying Materials

CLOTH TAPE

Demco Library Supplies, Box 1488, Madison, Wis., 53701

Dennison Manufacturing Co., Framingham, Mass., 01702

Minnesota Mining and Manufacturing Co., St. Paul, Minn., 55101

Mystic Adhesive Products, 2635 North Kildare Avenue, Chicago, Ill., 60625

PLASTIC RINGS

General Binding Corp., 1101 Skokie Boulevard, North-Brook, Ill., 60062

Tauber Plastics, 200 Hudson Street, New York, N.Y., 10039

DISPLAY ADHESIVE

Brooks Manufacturing Co., P.O. Box 41195G, Cincinnati, Ohio, 45241 (Plasti-tak)

Delkote, Box 1335, Wilmington, Del., 19899

School Service Co., 647 South La Brea Avenue, Los Angeles, Calif., 90036

Projectors

See the *Audio-Visual Equipment Directory* (annual publication), National Audio-Visual Association, 3150 Spring Street, Fairfax, Va., 22030, for manufacturers and sources of the following:

  2 × 2 inch slide projectors
  Tape and cassette recorders
  2 × 2 inch slide projector and tape recorder combination units
  35-mm filmstrip projector and record-player combination units
  Individual slide and filmstrip viewers
  Individual slide or filmstrip viewers—synchronized tape recorders

8-mm and 16-mm motion-picture projectors
Television equipment

TAPE-SLIDE SYNCHRONIZERS

Audiscan Products Corp., P.O. Box 1456, Bellevue, Wash., 98009

Eastman Kodak Co., 343 State Street, Rochester, N.Y., 14650

North American Phillips Corp., 35 Abbett Avenue, Morristown, N.J., 07960

Optisonics Division of Elco., 1758 West Grant Avenue, Tucson, Ariz., 85705

Slide Mounts

Eastman Kodak Co., 343 State Street, Rochester, N.Y., 14656

Karl Heitz, 979 Third Avenue, New York, N.Y., 10022

Pako Corp., 6300 Olson Memorial Hiway, Minneapolis, Minn., 55440

Phototechniques, 2321 Fourth Street, Northeast, Washington, D.C., 20002

Seary Manufacturing Corp., 19 Nebraska Avenue, Endicott, N.Y., 13760

Wess Plastics, 50 Schmitt Boulevard, Farmingdale, N.Y., 11735

Plastic Sheet Slide Holders

Joshua Meier Division of W. R. Grace Co., North Bergen, N.J., 07847

Plastic Sealing Corp., 1507 North Gardner Street, Los Angeles, Calif., 90046

Plastican Corp., 33 Laurel Street, Butler, N.J., 07405

Reliance Folding Carton Corp., 108-180 Queens Boulevard, Forest Hills, N.Y., 11375

20th Century Plastics, 415 East Washington Boulevard, Los Angeles, Calif., 90015

35-mm Filmstrip Aids

FILMSTRIP CANS

Film Kare Products Co., 446 West 43rd Street, New York, N.Y., 10036

Richard Manufacturing Co., 5914 Noble Avenue, Van Nuys, Calif., 91404

PACKAGING FILMSTRIPS AND CASSETTE RECORDINGS

Coast Book Cover Co., 2930 South Vail Avenue, Los Angeles, Calif., 90040

Reliance Plastics and Packaging Co., 108-18 Queens Boulevard, Forest Hills, N.Y., 11375

PRINTERS AND SLIDE COPIERS

Bogen Photo Corp., 100 South Van Brunt Street, Englewood, N.J., 07631 (Illumitran)

Forox Corp., 511 Center Avenue, Mamaroneck, N.Y., 10543

Honeywell Photographic Products, 5501 South Broadway, Denver, Colo., 80120 (Repronar)

Sickles Inc., P.O. Box 3396, Scottsdale, Ariz., 85257

Overhead Transparency Projection Materials

TRANSPARENCY SUPPLIES

Audio Visual Communications, Inc., 159 Verdi Street, Farmingdale, N.Y., 11735

Charles Beseler Co., 219 South 18th Street, East Orange, N.J., 07018

Johnson Plastics Inc., 526 Pine Street, Elizabeth, N.J., 07206

Scott Reprographs Division, Holyoke, Mass., 01040

Valiant Industries, 172 Walker Lane, Englewood, N.J., 07631

MOUNTS

Creative Visuals, Box 310, Big Springs, Tex., 79720

The Holson Co., Belden Avenue, Norwalk, Conn., 06897

Sherburn Graphic Products Inc., P.O. Box 7503, Ft. Worth, Tex., 76111

POLARIZING MATERIALS

Keuffel & Esser Co., 20 Whippany Road, Morristown, N.J., 07960

Metro Supply Co., 1420 47th Avenue, Sacramento, Ca., 95822

Projection Optics, 217 11th Avenue, East Orange, N.J., 07018

Scott Graphics, Holyoke, Mass., 01040

Technamation, 30 Sagamore Hill Drive, Port Washington, N.Y., 11505

TAPES

ACS Tapes, 217 California Street, Newton, Mass., 02158

Applied Graphics Corp., 58 Shore Road, Glenwood Landing, N.Y., 11547

Chart-Pak Rotex, 1 River Road, Leeds, Mass., 01053

Craftint Manufacturing Co., 18501 Euclid Avenue, Cleveland, Ohio, 44112

Labelon Tape Co., 10 Chapin Street, Canandaigua, N.Y., 14424

Mico-Tape, 7005 Tujuanga Avenue, North Hollywood, Calif., 91605

Para-Tone, P.O. Box 136, La Grange, Ill., 60525

DIAZO EQUIPMENT AND MATERIALS

Blue-Ray Inc., 345 Westbrook Road, Essex, Conn., 06426

Charles Bruning Co., 1800 West Central Road, Mt. Pleasant, Ill., 60056

General Aniline and Film Corp., 140 West 51st Street, New York, N.Y., 10020

Keuffel & Esser Co., 29 Whippany Road, Morristown, N.J., 07920

Scott Educational Division, Scott Graphics, Holyoke, Mass., 01040

VariTyper Corp., 720 Frelinghuysen Street, Newark, N.J., 07114

HEAT-PROCESS EQUIPMENT AND MATERIALS

A. B. Dick Co., 5700 West Touhy Avenue, Chicago, Ill., 60648

Columbia Ribbon & Carbon Manufacturing Co., Glen Cove, N.Y., 11542

Ditto, Inc., 6800 McCormick Road, Chicago, Ill., 60645

Labelon Corp., 10 Chapin Street, Canandaigua, N.Y., 14424

Old Town Corp., 750 Pacific Street, Brooklyn, N.Y., 11238

Speciality Coatings, Inc., 15169 Northville Road, Plymouth, Mich, 48170

3M Company, Visual Products Division, 2501 Hudson Road, St. Paul, Minn., 55101

Valiant Industries, 172 Walker Lane, Englewood, N.J., 07631

XEROGRAPHY FILM

Arkwright, Main Street, Fiskeville, R.I., 02823

Gladwin Industries, Box 370A, Route 1, Oakwood, Ga., 30566 (Zelar)

PICTURE-TRANSFER FILM AND EQUIPMENT

General Binding Corp, 1101 Skokie Boulevard, Northbrook, Ill., 60062

Laminex Inc. Matthews, N.C., 28105

Nationwide Adhesive Products Inc., 19600 St. Clair Avenue, Cleveland, Ohio, 44117

Seal Inc., 251 Roosevelt Drive, Derby, Conn., 06418

HIGH-CONTRAST FILM

Anken Chemical & Film Corp., Newton, N.J., 07860

Agfa-Gevaert, 275 North Street, Teterboro, N.J., 07608

Eastman Kodak Co., 343 State Street, Rochester, N.Y., 14650

Ilford Inc., West 70 Century Road, Box 288, Paramus, N.J., 07652

Motion-Picture Equipment

GENERAL

Calvin Communications, 215 West Pershing Road, Kansas City, Mo., 64108

SOS Photo-Cine-Optics, 315 West 43rd Street, New York, N.Y., 10036

LIGHTING

Berkey Colortran, 1015 Chestnut Street, Burbank, Calif., 91502

Mole-Richardson Co., 937 North Sycamore Avenue, Hollywood, Calif., 90038

Smith-Victor Corp., Griffith, Ind., 46319

BACKGROUND AND LIGHT SUPPORTS

The B D Co., P. O. Box 3057, Erie, Pa., 16512

Brewster Corp., 50 River Street, Old Saybrook, Conn., 06475 (Polecat)

STILL/MOTION PROJECTORS

Audiscan, P.O. Box 1456, Bellevue, Wash., 98009.

Charles Beseler Co., 8 Fernwood Road, Florham Park, N.J., 07932 (Cue-See)

Eastman Kodak Co., 343 State Street, Rochester, N.Y., 14650 (MFS-8)

North American Phillips Corp., 35 Abbett Avenue, Morristown, N.J., 07960 (Norelco PIP)

Technicolor Audiovisual Systems, 299 Kalmus Drive, Costa Mesa, Ca., 92626 (Single Loop System).

Television Display Supplies

EASELS AND DISPLAY BOARDS

Advance Products Co., P.O. Box 2178, Wichita, Kans., 67201

Arlington Aluminum Co., 19303 West Davison Avenue, Detroit, Mich., 48223

Chart-Pak Rotex, 1 River Road, Leeds, Mass., 01053

Oravisual Co., Box 11150, St. Petersburg, Fla., 33733

FLANNEL BOARDS AND MATERIALS

Ideal School Supply Co., 11000 Lavergne Avenue, Oak Lawn, Ill., 60453

The Instructo Corp., Paoli, Pa., 19301

The Judy Co., 310 North Second Street, Minneapolis, Minn., 55401

The Ohio Flock-Cote Co., 13229 Shaw Avenue, East Cleveland, Ohio, 44112

School Service Co., 647 South La Brea Avenue, Los Angeles, Calif., 90036

HOOK-AND-LOOP BOARDS AND MATERIALS

Charles Mayer Studios, 140 East Market Street, Akron, Ohio, 44308

The Ohio Flock-Cote Co., 13229 Shaw Avenue, East Cleveland, Ohio, 44112

MAGNETIC BOARDS

Creative Playthings, Princeton, N.J., 08540

Madison A-V Co., 62 Grand Street, New York, N.Y., 10013

Magna Magnetics, 777 Sunset Boulevard, Los Angeles, Calif., 90046

Weber-Costello Co., 1900 Narragansett Avenue, Chicago, Ill., 60639

MAGNETS

Edmund Scientific Co., Barrington, N.J., 08007

Ronald Eyrich, 1091 North 48th Street, Milwaukee, Wis., 53208

Madison A-V Co., 62 Grand Avenue, New York, N.Y., 10013

Magnet Sales Co., 3955 South Vermont Avenue, Los Angeles, Calif., 90037

Miami Magnet Co., 7846 West 2nd Court, Hialeah, Fla., 33014

REAR-SCREEN MATERIAL

Commercial Picture Equipment Co., 5725 North Broadway Avenue, Chicago, Ill., 60660

Polacoat Inc., 9750 Conklin Road, Cincinnati, Ohio, 45242

Trans-Lux Corp., 625 Madison Avenue, New York, N.Y., 10022

Multi-image Programmers

PUNCHED TAPE

Audio Visual Systems, 830 Linden Avenue, Rochester, N.Y., 14625

Behavioral Controls, 1506 Pierce Street, West, Milwaukee, Wis., 53246

Dukane Corp., St. Charles, Ill., 60174

Hoppmann Corp., 5410 Port Royal Road, Springfield, Va., 22151

Montage Productions, 9 Industrial Drive, Rutherford, N.J., 07070

Spindler & Sauppe, 13034 Saticoy Street, North Hollywood, Calif., 91605

United Audio Visual Corp., 6410 Ventnor Avenue, Ventnor, N.J., 08406

MAGNETIC TAPE

Arion Corp., 825 Boone Avenue North, Minneapolis, Minn., 55427

Electrosonic Systems, 4575 West 77th Street, Minneapolis, Minn., 55435

Honeywell Audio Visual., Box 22083, Denver, Colo., 80222

North American Phillips Corp., 35 Abbett Avenue, Morristown, N.J., 07960

Optisonics, Division of Elco, 1758 West Grant Avenue, Tucson, Ariz., 85705

Wollensak 3M Co., St. Paul, Minn., 55101

Compressed Speech Recorders

Discerned Sound, P.O. Box 217, Palm Desert, Calif., 92260

Hitachi Sales Corp. of America, 48–50 34th Street, Long Island City, N.Y. 11101

Lexicon, Inc., 60 Turner Street, Waltham, Mass., 02154

Magnetic Video Corp., 2343 Industrial Park Court, Farmington, Mich. 48024 (Copycorder)

PKM Corp. 1935 West County Road B-2, St. Paul, Minn., 55113

APPENDIX D
SERVICES

Various services are available to assist you in the preparation of your audiovisual materials. For a complete listing of laboratories and services, see the annual directory issue of PHOTO METHODS FOR INDUSTRY, PMI Directory, 33 West 60th Street, New York, N.Y., 10023, and the INDUSTRIAL PHOTOGRAPHY GOLD BOOK TECHNICAL DATA DIRECTORY, 200 Madison Avenue, New York, N.Y., 10016. Samplings of laboratories from various sections of the country are listed. Those selected offer a wide range of services under each of the following categories.

Color Print, Slide, and Filmstrip Services

Includes processing color films, making color prints, producing slides from art work and color negatives, duplicating slides, and complete filmstrip preparation.

NORTHEAST

Admaster, Inc., 425 Park Avenue, New York, N.Y., 10016

Audio Slide Corp., P.O. Box 88, Rome, N.Y., 13440

Bebell, Inc., 416 West 45th Street, New York, N.Y., 10036

Berkey K & L Custom Service, 222 East 44th Street, New York, N.Y., 10017

The Color Studio, P.O. Box 1, New Haven, Conn., 06501

World-in-Color Productions, P.O. Box 392, Elmira, N.Y., 14902

MIDWEST

Calvin Communications, Inc., 215 West Pershing Road, Kansas City, Mo., 64108

Gamma Photo Labs, Inc., 319 East Erie Street, Chicago, Ill., 60610

K & S Photo Labs, 180 North Wabash Avenue, Chicago, Ill., 60601

Multimedia Group, 502 Wayne Avenue, Dayton, Ohio, 45410

SOUTH/SOUTHWEST

A-V Corp., 2518 North Boulevard, Houston, Tex., 77006

Byron Motion Pictures, 65 K Street, N.E., Washington, D.C., 20002

Dixie Films, 1314 Madison Avenue, Memphis, Tenn., 38104

Jamieson Film Co., 3825 Bryant Street, Dallas, Tex., 75204

Meisel Photochrome Corp. Box 6067, Dallas, Tex, 75222

PSI Film Laboratory, 3011 Diamond Park Drive, Dallas, Texas, 75247

WEST

Consolidated Film Industries, 959 Seward St., Hollywood, Calif., 90038

Drewry Photocolor Corp., 211 South Lake Street, Burbank, Calif., 91502

Frank Holmes Laboratories, 1947 First Street, San Fernando, Calif., 91340

Transfer Videotape-Film and Film-Videotape Service

Byron Motion Pictures, 65 K Street, N.E., Washington, D.C., 20002

Consolidated Film Industries, 959 Seward Street, Hollywood, Calif., 90038

National Video Center, 730 Fifth Avenue New York, N.Y., 10019

W. A. Palmer Films, 611 Howard Street, San Francisco, Calif., 94105

Reeves Cinetel, Inc., 304 East 44th Street, New York, N.Y., 10017

Scientificom, Division LaRue Films, 708 North Dearborn Street Chicago, Ill., 60610

Video Dynamics, 10722 Trask Avenue, Garden Grove, Calif., 92643

Videosonics, 216 East 49th Street, New York, N.Y., 10017

Vidtronics Co., 855 North Cahuenga Boulevard, Hollywood, Calif., 90038

Music Libraries and Recording Services

Includes recorded title and background music, sound effects, transfer of tape recordings to disk, and multiple duplication services.

EAST

Audio Master Corp., 17 East 45th Street, New York, N.Y., 10017

Boosey & Hawkes, 30 West 57th Street, New York, N.Y., 10019

Cinemusic Inc., 30 West 60th Street, New York, N.Y., 10023.

Corelli-Jacobs Film Music, 723 Seventh Avenue, New York, N.Y., 10019

Charles Michelson, 45 West 45th Street New York, N.Y., 10036

Thomas J. Valentine, 151 West 46th Street, New York, N.Y., 10036

MIDWEST/SOUTH

Columbia Scientific Industries, 3625 Bluestein Boulevard, Austin, Tex., 78762 (Musi-Que)

Speed-Q Sound Effects, P.O. Box 141, Richmond, Ind., 47374

Standard Record Transcription Services, 360 North Michigan Avenue, Chicago, Ill., 60601

WEST

Capital HQ Library Services, Hollywood and Vine, Hollywood, Calif., 90028

MP-TV Services, 7000 Santa Monica Boulevard, Hollywood, Calif., 90038

Motion Picture Services—16-mm

Includes film-planning services, processing black-and-white and color films, preparing workprints, printing and special effects, and sound services.

NORTHEAST

Capital Film Laboratories, 470 E Street, S.E., Washington, D.C., 20024

Cine Magnetics Film Labs., 650 Halstead Avenue, Mamaroneck, N.Y., 10543

Filmaker's Labs., 3515 South Pennsylvania Avenue, Lansing, Mich., 48910

Movielab Film Laboratories, 619 West 54th Street, New York, N.Y., 10019

Reela Sight and Sound, 209 West 40th Street, New York, N.Y., 10018

WRS, Inc., 210 Semple Street, Pittsburgh, Pa., 15213

SOUTHEAST

Byron Motion Pictures, Inc., 65 K Street, N.E., Washington, D.C., 20002

Motion Picture Labs, 781 South Main Street, Memphis, Tenn., 38101

Reela Films, 65 N.W. 3rd Street, Miami, Fla., 33128

MIDWEST

Calvin Communications, 215 West Pershing Road, Kansas City, Mo., 64108

George W. Colburn Laboratories, 164 North Wacker Drive, Chicago, Ill., 60606

Film Associates, Inc., 4600 South Dixie Highway, Dayton, Ohio, 45439

Lakeside Laboratories, Box 2408, Gary, Ind., 46403

SOUTHWEST

Jamieson Film Co., 3825 Bryant Street, Dallas, Tex., 75204

Southwest Film Labs, 3024 Ft. Worth Avenue, Dallas, Tex., 75211

WEST

Cine-Chrome Labs, 4075 Transport Street, Palo Alto, Calif., 94303

Consolidated Film Industries, 959 Seward Street, Hollywood, Calif., 90038

DeLuxe General, 1546 North Argyle Avenue, Hollywood, Calif., 90028

Dymat Motion Picture Labs, 2704 West Olive Avenue, Burbank, Calif., 91505

W. A. Palmer Films, 611 Howard Street, San Francisco, Calif., 94105

Technicolor Corporation, 6311 Romaine Street, Hollywood, Calif., 90038

Western Ciné Services, 312 South Pearl Street, Denver, Colo., 80209

Motion Picture Services—8-mm

The following laboratories are noted for their services relative to 8-mm film work:

Byron Motion Pictures, 65 K Street, N.E., Washington, D.C., 20002

Calvin Communications, 215 West Pershing Road, Kansas City, Mo., 64108

Capital Film Labs, 470 E Street, S.E., Washington, D.C., 20024

Cine-Chrome Labs, Inc., 4075 Transport Street, Palo Alto, Calif., 94303

Dymat Motion Picture Labs., 2704 West Olive Avenue, Burbank, Calif., 91505

Motion Picture Labs, Inc., 781 South Main Street, Memphis, Tenn., 38101

Technicolor Corporation, Motion Picture Division, 6311 Romaine Street, Hollywood, Calif., 90038

APPENDIX E
GLOSSARY

accent light a spotlight that accentuates and highlights an object in a scene.

acetate (clear) a plastic sheet permitting a high degree of light transmission, resulting in a transparent appearance.

acetate (coated or treated) a clear-appearing plastic sheet, to each side of which a special coating has been applied; the coating will accept ordinary drawing inks.

acetate (matte or frosted) a plastic sheet with one side etched or roughed so as to take regular inks and colored-pencil markings easily.

affective domain category of instructional objectives relating to attitudes, values, and appreciations within human behavior.

animation a filming technique that brings inanimate objects or drawings to apparent life and movement.

answer print the first duplicate copy of an audiovisual material (slides, filmstrip, or motion picture) made from the original, with exposure corrections and special effects included.

background light the illumination thrown on the background to lighten it, giving the scene depth and separating the subject from the background.

captions the printed explanations to accompany the visuals of an audiovisual material.

cassette (see *film cassette* or *tape cassette*)

clearance form (see *release form*)

clip books printed booklets containing a variety of of commercially prepared black-and-white line drawings on various subjects.

close-up a concentration of the camera on the subject, or on a part of it, excluding everything else from view.

cognitive domain category of instructional objectives relating to knowledge, information, and other intellectual skills within human behavior.

colored adhesive a translucent or transparent color printed on a thin acetate sheet having adhesive backing for adherence to cardboard, paper, acetate, or film.

communications specialist a person having broad knowledge of audiovisual media and capable of organizing the content of audiovisual materials to be produced so that the stated purposes will best be served.

conforming the process of matching original motion-picture footage to the edited workprint.

contact print a photographic print the same size as the negative, prepared by exposing to light the negative and positive films (or paper), placed together.

continuity the logical relationship of one scene leading to the next one and the smooth flow of action and narration within the total audiovisual material.

continuous-tone subjects illustrations consisting of shades of gray, varying from black to white.

copy stand a vertical or horizontal stand for accurately positioning a camera when photographing flat subjects very close to the lens.

credit title a listing of those who participated in or cooperated with the audiovisual project.

cut-away shot a motion-picture scene of a subject or action taking place at the same time as the main action, but separate from it, and placed between two related scenes which have a discontinuity of action.

cut-in shot a close-up feature of a subject being filmed as a motion picture and usually placed between two scenes having a discontinuity of action.

depth of field the distance within a scene from the point closest to the camera in focus to the farthest in focus.

developer a solution in which the chemicals set the image by acting on silver salts on exposed film that have been affected by light during picture-taking.

diazo process a method for preparing overhead transparencies requiring film containing one of a possible number of dye colors, which is exposed, in contact with an opaque original prepared on translucent or transparent paper or film, to ultra-violet light, and then developed in ammonia vapor.

dissolve an optical effect in motion pictures involving two superimposed scenes in which the second one gradually appears as the first one gradually disappears.

documentary approach a method of taking pictures without preplanning or detailed script preparation.

dolly shot a motion-picture scene filmed as the camera is moved away from, toward, or across the subject.

double-frame filmstrip a series of pictures aligned lengthwise along 35-mm film, each double frame being 24×36 mm.

dubbing the transfer of recorded sound from one unit to another; commonly record-to-tape, tape-to-tape, tape-to-film.

edge number a series of matching numbers printed at 1-foot intervals along the edge of original motion-picture footage and also along the workprint edge so that after the editing the workprint and original can be easily matched together.

editing the selection and organization of visuals after filming and the refinement of narration or captions.

editing-in-the-camera filming motion-picture scenes in sequence according to their listing on the script.

educational media all audiovisual and printed materials used for instructional purposes.

electronic mixer a control mechanism through which a number of sound-producing units can be fed in order to combine voice, music, or sound effects at desired recording levels onto a single tape or film sound track.

electrostatic duplication use of coated, electrically charged, light-sensitive paper or film to reproduce original and printed pages.

establishing shot a medium or long shot that establishes the whereabouts of a scene and serves as orientation to action photographed at close range.

exposure index a number assigned to a film by the manufacturer which indicates the relative emulsion speed of the film for determining camera settings (f/ number and shutter speed).

exposure meter (*see photographic light meter*)

exposure-value system (*EV*) a series of numbers for setting exposures by a single number, which represents combinations of f/ number and shutter speed, and will vary depending on the exposure index of each film.

f/ number (f/ stop) the lens setting selected from a series of numbers consisting partially of . . . 2, 2.8, 4, 5.6, 8, 11, 16, 32, . . .

fade-in an optical effect in motion pictures in which a scene gradually appears out of blackness.

fade-out an optical effect in motion pictures in which a scene gradually disappears into blackness.

fill light the secondary light source illuminating a scene, which brightens dark shadow portions created by the key light.

film cassette container holding a 50-foot length of super-8mm film, which, when placed into the camera, will advance from one side of the container to the other as exposure is made, without any threading or other handling.

film chain the part of a television system that includes the slide and motion-picture projectors connected optically to a television camera.

film clip a brief, filmed sequence used generally on television without having titles or special effects.

filmograph a sequence of still pictures on a motion-picture film.

fine cut the final step in editing a motion picture, on completion of which the scenes are of proper length and action between adjacent scenes is matched.

fixer a solution in which the chemicals harden the developed film image and change all undeveloped silver salts so they can be removed by washing.

flannel (felt) board a presentation board consisting of a flannel or felt surface to which objects backed with flannel, felt, or sandpaper will adhere.

focal frame a camera attachment that overcomes the parallax problem and permits accurate framing and focusing of objects very close to the lens.

focal length a classification of lenses, being the distance from the center of a lens to the film plane within the camera when the lens is focused at infinity.

frame an individual picture in a filmstrip or motion picture.

guide number or exposure guide number a number assigned to a film for the purpose of calculating exposure when flashbulbs or electronic flash units are used; it is based upon the film speed, the type of flash bulb or electronic unit, and the shutter speed.

halftone subjects printed illustrations consisting of uniformly spaced dots of varying size, which blend together and convey shades of gray.

high-angle shot a scene photographed with the camera placed high, looking down at the subject.

high-contrast subject an illustration consisting solely of black lines or marks on white paper.

hook-and-loop board a presentation board consisting

of a cloth surface textured with minute nylon loops to which display materials backed with strips of tape having nylon hooks will intermesh and hold firmly.

incident-light method the measurement of light falling on a scene by the use of an incident-light meter held in the scene and aimed at the camera.

instructional design plan procedure for instructional planning that involves application of a number of interrelated steps relating to objectives, instructional strategies, and evaluation of learning.

instructional development process of designing an instructional program employing an objective, systematic procedure, like an instructional-design plan.

instruction guide suggestions for good utilization of an audiovisual material; it normally includes a description of content and preparatory, participating, and follow-up questions and activities.

instructional system a coordination of all aspects of a problem toward answering a specific objective and following a logical series of steps to reach a solution.

instructional technology includes two components: (1) the equipment and media resources for instruction, and (2) the process of systematic instructional planning termed instructional development.

jump action a discontinuity in the smooth action within a motion-picture scene, caused by momentary stopping and then starting the camera motor or by incorrectly removing a section of film within a scene during editing.

jumper cord (see *patch cord*)

key light the brightest light source on a scene, forming a large portion of the total illumination.

lamination applying a thin adhesive-backed clear acetate coating over a picture or other graphic material.

lens diaphragm the opening through which light enters a camera; its size is controlled by an adjustable diaphragm.

lighting ratio the relationship between the intensity of the key light and the intensity of the fill light as measured with a light meter.

lip synchronization (lip sync) a recording of the speech of a person appearing in a motion picture so that the sound is heard at the same time his corresponding lip movements are observed.

log sheet a written record of all pictures taken, including scene numbers, takes, camera settings, and special remarks.

long shot a general view of a subject and its setting.

low-angle shot a scene photographed with the camera placed low, looking up at the subject.

magnetic chalkboard a presentation board consisting of a metal sheet, covered with chalkboard paint, to which magnetic-backed objects will adhere and on which chalk marks can be made.

magnetic-striped film 8-mm or 16-mm motion-picture film to which a narrow stripe of magnetizable material is added which will accept sound impulses in the form of magnetic variations.

main title the name of the production, shown at the start of an audiovisual material.

matched action the smooth continuation of action between two adjacent, related motion-picture scenes.

media attributes the capability of a medium to show motion, color, simultaneous picture and sound, and other features pertinent to the medium.

medium shot a view of a subject that eliminates unnecessary background and other details.

monobath a combination developer-fixer solution for one-step black-and-white film processing.

montage a series of short scenes in a motion picture used to condense time or distance or to show a series of related activities or places.

multicamera filming recordings of the same action with two or more cameras operated at the same time and located at different position in relation to the subject.

multi-image simultaneous projection of two or more pictures on adjacent screens for group viewing.

multimedia sequential use of a variety of instructional materials for presentation or for self-study programs.

narration the verbal comments made to accompany the visuals.

negative opaque a water-soluble carbon material brushed on high-contrast negatives to eliminate marks, spots, and areas.

objective scene a scene recorded with the camera aimed toward the subject, from a theater-audience point of view.

opaque projector a projector that can enlarge information from paper, pages from a book, or other nontranslucent or nontransparent materials.

optical sound track a narrow band of light and dark areas or lines along one side of a motion-picture film which through the action of light is converted into the film's sound.

overhead projector a projector that accepts transparent and translucent film or other plastic and projects the information prepared on them into a screen.

overlay one or more additional transparent sheets with lettering or other matter that can be placed over a base transparency or an opaque background.

overprint the superimposition of one scene over another; generally titles, captions, or labels over a background scene or a specially prepared background.

out-takes usable motion picture footage that has been removed during the editing process.

pan (panorama) the movement of a motion-picture camera, while filming, in a horizontal plane (sideways).

pantograph a linked-lever device for enlarging or reducing diagrams by tracing the original under one point and duplicating it at the other point in suitable proportion.

parallax the difference between the vertical position of an object in a filmed scene as viewed through a viewfinder and as recorded on film through the camera lens.

paste-up the combination of illustrations and lettering, each unit of which is rubber-cemented in position on paper or cardboard by a temporary method.

patch cord an electrical wire used to connect together two pieces of sound equipment (such as tape recorders and record players) so that electrical impulses can be transferred between the units in order to make a recording.

permanent mounting the application of rubber cement to the back of a flat material to be mounted and also to the mount surface, then permitting the two surfaces to dry before adhering them together; or the use of dry-mount tissue placed between the material and the mount surface, with heat and pressure being applied to seal the layers together.

photographic light meter a device for measuring light levels, either incident upon or reflected from a scene.

photo modifier a large-size camera used to enlarge or reduce art work.

photo stabilization a two-step rapid processing method for photographic paper.

picture transfer—the transfer of printing ink from a magazine picture to a special acetate sheet after the two are sealed together with heat and/or pressure and then submerged in water to remove the paper.

pinboard (see *register board*)

planning board a 3×4½ foot board with strips of acetate channels, designed at Eastman Kodak Company, for holding storyboard cards.

programmer a control unit to activate one or more projectors to change images on screens according to scripted sequencing.

progressive disclosure exposing a series of items on a transparency or slide by moving an opaque mask during use or preparation.

pumping in (pumping out) the change of camera position from one motion-picture scene to the next without change of camera angle with relation to the same subject.

rangefinder a camera attachment that, upon proper setting, indicates the distance from camera to subject or sets the lens in focus at that range.

rear-screen projection projecting on the back side of a translucent screen, the projector being behind the screen or off to one side projecting on a mirror.

reflected-light method the measurement of light reflected from a scene by the use of a reflected light meter held near the camera and aimed at the subject.

register board a surface with two or more small vertical posts for holding paper, cardboard, or film materials all correctly aligned when more than one layer must be assembled for filming.

release form the form used to obtain written permission for use of pictures taken of persons or of their copyrighted materials.

release print a duplicate print of an original audiovisual material prepared for general use.

reversal film film which, after exposure, is processed to produce a positive image on the same film.

rough cut the second step in editing a motion picture, on completion of which the length of scenes has been shortened somewhat but not necessarily to final length, and action between adjacent scenes is not yet exactly matched.

scene (shot) the basic element that makes up the visuals of an audiovisual material; each separate picture or amount of motion-picture footage exposed when the release button is pushed and then released.

script the specific directions for picture-taking or art work in the form of a listing of scenes with accompanying narration or captions.

sequence a section of an audiovisual material, more or less complete in itself, and made up of a series of related scenes.

shading film textures and patterns printed on acetate sheets having adhesive backing for adhering to cardboard, paper, acetate, or film.

shot (see *scene*)

shutter speed the interval between opening and closing of the shutter of a camera, measured in fractions of a second.

single concept a discrete skill or limited aspect of a topic.

single-frame filmstrip a series of pictures oriented horizontally across the width of 35-mm film and of such a size that two adjacent pictures (or frames) combined are 18×24 mm.

single-framing exposing one frame at a time on motion-picture film, as opposed to continuous exposure (8 fps or faster).

single-lens reflex camera a compact camera employing a mirror or prism for accurate viewing directly through the camera lens.

slating putting on film a few frames of printed information prior to the regular filming of a motion-picture scene in order to identify the scene and take number.

sound striping (see *magnetic-striped film*)

specifications the framework and limits within which audiovisual materials are produced; may include such factors as length, materials, special techniques, assistance required, completion date, and budget.

squaring method the method for enlarging or reducing a diagram by placing a grid over the original and copying relative positions of lines on a grid of another size (smaller or larger scale, or proportioned).

stop bath a solution in which the chemicals stop the action of a developer on exposed film.

storyboard a series of sketches or pictures which visualize each topic or sequence in an audiovisual material to be produced; generally prepared after the treatment and before the script.

string out the first step in editing a motion picture, on completion of which all scenes are of original camera length and have been spliced together in proper sequence.

subject specialist a person having broad knowledge of the subject content for an audiovisual material to be produced.

subjective scene a scene recorded with the camera placed in the subject's position and aimed at action he is performing.

subtitles words, phrases, or sentences that appear over a visual to explain, emphasize, or clarify a point.

take (of a scene) one exposure among two or more for the same scene; successive takes of the same scene are numbered from 1 upward.

tape cassette enclosed feed and take-up reels of ⅛ inch magnetic tape; used with cassette tape recorders.

technical staff a person or persons responsible for the photography, graphic-art work, and sound-recording in producing audiovisual materials.

telephoto lens a camera lens that permits a closer view of a subject than would be obtained by a normal lens from the same position.

temporary mounting the application of rubber cement to the back of an illustration or lettering and immediate placement on a mount surface while the cement is still wet.

thumbspot a visible mark placed in the lower left corner of a slide to indicate the proper position for correctly viewing the slide.

tilt the movement of a motion-picture camera in a vertical plane.

time-compressed speech method of increasing the word rate of recorded speech without distortion in vocal pitch.

time-lapse photography the exposing of individual motion-picture frames at a much slower rate than normal, for projection at normal speed; the method accelerates action that normally takes place too slowly for motion to be perceived.

toner a black powder used in the electrostatic duplicating process to deposit on the charged paper or film and provide the visible, opaque image.

transitional devices the use of such techniques as fade-out–fade-in and dissolves to bridge space and time in motion pictures.

treatment a descriptive synopsis of how the content of an audio-visual material can be organized and presented.

visual literacy skills an individual develops in interpreting, judging, responding to, and using visual representations of reality.

wide-angle lens a camera lens that permits a wider view of a subject and its surroundings than would be obtained by a normal lens from the same position.

wipe an optical effect in motion pictures in which a new scene seems to push the previous scene off the screen.

workprint an inexpensive copy of original motion-picture footage used during editing, and to which the original film is matched before duplicate copies are made.

zoom lens a camera lens of variable magnification that permits a smooth change of subject coverage between distance and close-up without changing the camera position.

INDEX

97751

7½″

The area enclosed in the black line gives the outline of a mask opening for a transparency to be used with an overhead projector.

371.33
K32
c.1

97751

9½″